CREATING A NATION

PATRICIA GRIMSHAW is Professor in History at The University of Melbourne, where she teaches women's history, American history and feminist theory. She is currently writing a study of colonial representations of indigenous women in the Polynesian Pacific and Australia.

MARILYN LAKE is Professor in History at La Trobe University, where she was Founding Director of Women's Studies between 1988 and 1994. She is the author of numerous publications on gender relations in Australian society and is currently working on studies of citizenship, the history of feminism and women's political thought. As well as teaching and writing, she is also well known as a media commentator on men, women and Australian history.

ANN McGRATH is Associate Professor in History at The University of New South Wales, where she teaches Australian history and is the Director of the Centre for Community History. She has published on colonial gender relations, outback mythologies and representations of Aboriginal women. As well as leading the History Project for the Royal Commission into Aboriginal Deaths in Custody she has worked on numerous land claims.

MARIAN QUARTLY is Dean of the Arts Faculty at Monash University. Her historical interests focus on Australia in the nineteenth and twentieth centuries. Her publications include the co-authored *Australians 1838* (1987). Her next book will be about gendered citizenship and the shape of the Australian state around 1900.

Other books by the authors of *Creating A Nation*:

PATRICIA GRIMSHAW
Women's Suffrage in New Zealand
Paths of Duty
Australian Women (co-edited)
The Half Open Door (co-edited)
Families in Colonial Australia (co-edited)
Studies in Gender (co-edited)

MARILYN LAKE
A Divided Society
The Limits of Hope
Double Time (co-edited)
Australians at Work (co-edited)
Freedom Bound II (co-edited)
Gender and War (co-edited)

ANN McGRATH
Born in the Cattle
Contested Ground
Aboriginal Workers (co-edited)

MARIAN QUARTLY
Australians 1838 (co-edited)
Stepping out of History (co-edited)

For Sylvia – great to meet in Australia, hope to meet again in your part of the planet. (ANN)

CREATING A NATION

PATRICIA GRIMSHAW

MARILYN LAKE

ANN MCGRATH

MARIAN QUARTLY

Marilyn Lake
Patricia Grimshaw

PENGUIN BOOKS

What the critics have said about *Creating A Nation*:

'A new, distinctive and highly successful history of Australia by four of our leading historians.'
Stuart Macintyre, Ernest Scott Professor of History

'This is not just another feminist challenge to yesterday's orthodoxy, but an effective move to displace it ... *Creating A Nation* is a power-taking, centralizing exercise in mainstream national history – one shaped by white feminist priorities, but designed for general use. This is a splendid achievement'
Meaghan Morris, *Meanjin*

'This is a significant book, signalling a shift from "women's history" to a general Australian history foregrounding the relations between men and women ... *Creating A Nation* ... has made Australian history much richer, more complex and more interesting'
Ann Curthoys, *Age*

'For general audiences the book succeeds very well. This is a major text which clearly sets Aborigines, women, workers, and the poor at the centre of the Australian story ... complex issues and historical processes are synthesised and distilled with remarkable clarity and presented in lucid sharp prose'
Stephen Garton, *Labour History*

'The careful, controlled, fair-minded fulfilment of their arduous course is breathtaking. But they are an outstanding team'
Noel McLachlan, *Australian*

To our children

David, Kathy, Sarah, Andrew
Katherine, Jessica
Venetia, Naomi
Ben, Chris, Sara

Penguin Books Australia Ltd
487 Maroondah Highway, PO Box 257
Ringwood, Victoria 3134, Australia
Penguin Books Ltd
Harmondsworth, Middlesex, England
Viking Penguin, A Division of Penguin Books USA Inc.
375 Hudson Street, New York, New York 10014, USA
Penguin Books Canada Limited
10 Alcorn Avenue, Toronto, Ontario, Canada M4V 3B2
Penguin Books (NZ) Ltd
182–190 Wairau Road, Auckland 10, New Zealand

First published by McPhee Gribble 1994
This edition published by Penguin Books Australia Ltd 1996

10 9 8 7 6 5 4 3 2 1

Copyright © Patricia Grimshaw, Marilyn Lake, Ann McGrath, Marian Quartly, 1994

All rights reserved. Without limiting the rights under copyright reserved above, no part of this publication may be reproduced, stored in or introduced into a retrieval system, or transmitted, in any form or by any means (electronic, mechanical, photocopying, recording or otherwise), without the prior written permission of both the copyright owner and the above publisher of this book.

Typeset in 11/12½ pt Garamond Euro by Midland Typesetters
Printed and bound in Australia by McPhersons Printing Group

National Library of Australia
Cataloguing-in-Publication data:
Creating a nation.
Bibliography.
Includes index.
ISBN 014 025905.8.
[1]. Aborigines, Australian – History. 2. Australia – History.
I. Grimshaw, Patricia, 1938–
994

Photographic sources (clockwise from top right): Aboriginal woman, La Trobe collection; Balmain collier, private collection; ex-convict Mary Nye, Queen Victoria Art Gallery & Museum; Chinese-Australian child, La Trobe collection; John Curtin (1917), Argus collection; WAAF woman, Argus collection; swagman from 'A rest on the road', National Library of Australia; young woman (centre), courtesy Ponch Hawkes, photographer.

Contents

Introduction	1
1 Birthplaces	7
2 Conceiving A Colony	27
3 Transplanting Patriarchy	55
4 Making Male and Female Worlds	79
5 Man's Space, Woman's Place	107
6 Sex, Violence and Theft: 1830–1910	131
7 Contested Domains	151
8 Gendered Settlements	177
9 Giving Birth to the New Nation	205
10 Depression Dreaming	231
11 Freedom, Fear and the Family	255
12 The State as Father: 1910–60	279
13 Affirmations of Difference	297
Endnotes	315
Bibliography	339
Index	349

Introduction

The creation of nations has traditionally been seen as men's business. In the fomenting of revolutions, the forging of new political orders and the fashioning of national identities, men have positioned themselves as the main players. We wish to challenge this view of history, by asserting the agency and creativity of women in the process of national generation. Whether in giving birth to babies, or in refusing to do so, in sustaining families and multicultural communities, creating wealth, shaping a maternalist welfare state or in inscribing the meanings of our experience in culture, women have clearly been major actors in the colonial and national dramas. This book explores the myriad ways in which both women and men, Aboriginal and non-Aboriginal, have contributed to the economic, political and cultural life of the separate colonies and then the nation.*

In agency there is also responsibility. As the beneficiaries of the dispossession of Aboriginal peoples, European women, along with men, were complicit in an imperialist, civilising project that saw the near-destruction of Australia's indigenous peoples and their languages and culture. Aboriginal women's memories of white brutality focus on the domestic violence and confinement perpetrated by the mistress in the home, as well as the exploitation and sexual violence that so often characterised their encounters with white men on the frontier. Aboriginal people's memories also focus with pride on their survival as a people against extreme odds. For despite

---

* 'Aborigines' or 'Aboriginal people' are used in this book as comprehensive terms for the indigenous people of Australia. In southern and eastern Australia 'Koorie' and 'Murrie' have become more acceptable terms, while in other parts of Australia, a variety of clan or language names are used as specific identifications.

the systematic attempts of Australian governments to destroy their family and community life through segregation and the removal of children to private and institutional white homes, Aboriginal people continued to nurture each other and strenuously resisted separation, individual oppression and the erasure of their culture. New European skills, knowledge and resources were often turned to political advantage in the continuing battle for survival.

The process of creating a nation, we wish to suggest, always involves conflict in the encounter between diversity and the incitement to national uniformity. In this country, the pursuit of the goal of White Australia, the founding principle of our nationality, meant the prolonged exclusion of Aborigines and other non-whites from citizenship. The 1902 Franchise Act that gave white women the vote simultaneously excluded Aborigines and other non-whites from the same political rights. Similarly, Aborigines were denied pensions and the maternity allowance. A nation state was welded, with more or less force, into a unity, composed of people of different sexes, sexualities, races, ethnicities, class interests, experiences and desires. National needs, as defined by dominant interests, have often been at variance with the needs and priorities of the different groups that comprise the nation. Thus, for example, the command to populate or perish increasingly came into conflict with women's desire for self-realisation.

Nationalist mythologies have always been gendered: in Australia the self-conscious elaboration of the national identity has involved the celebration of a particular style of white masculinity embodied in the Australian bushman and updated in such films as *The Man from Snowy River* and *Crocodile Dundee* – a style that was often explicitly defined in opposition to a feminine domesticity and forms of masculine behaviour that were similarly stigmatised and stereotyped. Furthermore, to the extent that nationalism involved an assertion of the rights of man against a demeaning imperial domination, it could come into conflict with a feminist interest in the rights of woman. Australian national stereotypes and mythologising have more recently come to be seen as inappropriate to the variety of cultural traditions and identities deriving from Europe, South America and Asia, which have become influential in Australia, largely since World War II. The tension between the recognition and assertion of sexual, racial and cultural differences, on the one hand, and the assimilationist drive of the nation state with its enshrining of one law and one way of life, on the other, is a major theme of our history. We document the many ways in which racial, ethnic and sexual differences have been turned into conditions of subordination. Subjugated groups have in turn oscillated between making claims in terms of their similarity to the dominant group – stressing the attributes they share – and asserting their different priorities and interests. Thus feminists alternated between demanding equal political and civil rights, equal pay and opportunities on the one hand and campaigning for the special rewards and recognition due to women as mothers and carers on the other. Women were thereby forced into an impossible choice between the two in a state whose practices were designed to meet the interests of the ideal autonomous white man.

Women's history is now seen to be a more complex and contradictory saga than was evident in the heady days of the early 1970s. A nation that was comparatively progressive in its provisions for white women (the vote, the maternity allowance, old age and invalid pensions, women's hospitals, free infant welfare clinics) was explicitly discriminatory against non-white women. It was not just a matter of a double oppression, although it was also that. Postcolonial scholarship has begun to illuminate the ways in which the feminist espousal of the advancement of women has itself rested on the construction of categories of 'backward' women – most often non-white, non-western, non-independent women. Such women have been expected, often enough, to embrace a western model of emancipation. Feminism contains a missionary impulse, but in its bid to forge alliances across racial, ethnic and class barriers feminism also, importantly, opens up the possibility of solidarity between women in common struggles for freedom from men's personal and military violence and the other diverse effects of masculine power.

While writing women into a history of Australia then, we wish also to acknowledge the complexity of discussing the category 'women'. There are none who live only or purely as women. Rather, women experience the world as lesbian women and as white women, as Italo-Australian women and as working-class women, as mothers and as Aboriginal women – and as much else besides. As Jill Matthews has written, femininity is at once an empty and an overflowing category. The meaning of femininity is never fixed and always contested. It has changed historically in conjunction with changes in other domains such as the organisation of work and sexuality. We resist, however, the more radical post-structuralist conclusions that there are no real women or that their reality cannot be known or is of little interest. On the contrary, our historical project pays tribute to and is crucially dependent on the past labours and insights of countless real women who have in numerous ways made this work possible.

Just as the meaning of womanhood has been constantly in flux, so, too, has the meaning of manhood. It was the women's movement that pointed out that the woman problem was also a man problem. Feminist scholarship has drawn attention to the sexual specificity of men, who have for so long been able to disguise themselves in history books as sexless, neutral, historical subjects – as squatters, convicts, workers, politicians, Australians. As a result of feminist scholarship, the construction of various forms of masculinity has now become an important topic of historical research. Recognition of the interdependence of femininity and masculinity and of the way in which they shape and are shaped by all social relationships and processes has led to the indentification of gender as a central category of historical analysis.

This book starts from the premise that gender is integral to the processes that comprise the history of Australia – that political and economic as well as social and cultural history are constituted in gendered terms. It explores the relationship that was forged between the domestic government exercised by the male head of the household and the government of the state that has also institutionalised male political rule. It explores the appropriation of women's procreative powers by men in their assertion that they gave birth to the nation. It explores the challenge to a national political economy organised around the wage system by feminists intent on establishing an income for the work of mothering. It also considers the difficulty encountered by women who attempted to carve a place for non-party women's interests in a political system organised around the conflict between capital and labour, between employers and workers.

Our book aims to reconceptualise familiar themes in the national story and to introduce new ones. Its methods are diverse and draw

INTRODUCTION

on a range of new sources as well as a rereading of old ones. The earlier parts of the history, dealing with small-scale societies, present more detailed ethnographic accounts of individuals engaged in social interaction; the latter parts, tracing the emergence and consolidation of a more populous, integrated but complex nation state, highlight participation in national political and economic processes, identifying general patterns and dynamics rather than local events. In a bid to give sufficient attention to their very distinctive history, we have chosen to devote three separate chapters to the Aboriginal experience of British colonisation and Australian nation building. Where appropriate, however, we have also integrated accounts of racial interaction and the constitution of racial identities throughout the remaining chapters. Ann McGrath wrote chapters 1, 6 and 12 on the Aboriginal experience, Marian Quartly wrote chapters 2, 3 and 4 on the colonies up to 1860, Patricia Grimshaw continued the story through federation until 1912 in chapters 5, 7 and 8, and Marilyn Lake wrote the introduction and chapters 9, 10, 11 and 13 on the twentieth century. Our writing was also a collective enterprise, however, the product of continual discussion, comment and rewriting.

Many colleagues and friends have encouraged us in this project and we thank them for their support. We particularly wish to acknowledge the help of Stuart Macintyre, who read and commented on the manuscript, and of Penny Russell, Kate Gray, Glenda Sluga, Melanie Raymond, Katie Holmes, Judy Smart, Alison Holland, Heather Gunn and Esther Faye, whose research and other assistance made the writing possible. The employment of research assistance was made possible by grants from the Australian Research Council, La Trobe University and the universities of New South Wales and Melbourne. We thank them for this.

1 Birthplaces

We do not know the date on the Christian calendar, but some time after the beginning of 1791 Warreweer, a woman of the Wangal clan and Eora people, went into labour at the township of Sydney Cove. For Warreweer, such chronology was irrelevant, and she probably saw it as some winters after her brother Bennelong was kidnapped from his clan. This had occurred during a November 1789 meeting when his people befriended and danced with some of the British visitors. The Wangal clan owned and occupied the area around the present Balmain and its surrounds – the inner-west of today's real estate advertisements.

Some time before Warreweer's labour her clan had agreed to camp near the newcomers; Bennelong's hut was located inland from the present Sydney Opera House site. Warreweer had befriended some of the British women and she agreed to their presence at the birth. Their observations, mediated through Lieutenant David Collins's journal, led to the first written record of an Aboriginal woman giving birth.

At least two women, probably her close relations, attended Warreweer during the delivery. Boorong poured cold water from time to time on her abdomen to soothe and comfort her. For pain relief, a transference method was used whereby a woman tied one end of a small line around Warreweer's neck, and rubbed her own lips with the other end until they bled. Birthing songs, some relating to the baby's totemic identity and country, were also performed during the labour; they offered encouragement, distracting the woman from her pain. Although men, boys and young girls were barred, Warreweer's husband could sing at a distance to expedite her progress.

During Warreweer's labour, the Aboriginal attendants, her close relations, 'lived through' the birth with her, giving moral support and physical comfort, and ensuring she never felt alone. They prepared and kept a fire going close by to keep the mother (and eventually the baby) warm, and for heating, preparing tools and ritual purposes. But they avoided any interference with the biological process, and did not touch her genitals or the baby's head. Warreweer was upright, probably squatting. Her baby was not caught, but let drop in a hole prepared with a soft bed of bark and leaves over which Warreweer had positioned herself. Collins was surprised that the child came 'into the world by the sole efforts of nature'. In addition to nature and supportive midwives, Warreweer also deserved some acknowledgment for her efforts.

Yet perhaps the baby was reward enough. Sighs of relief, wonder, excitement, joy were breathed as the healthy newborn baby fell softly onto its ti-tree bark mattress. (Like all newborn Aboriginal babies, its skin was light-coloured but would darken in the days to follow.) The midwives were pleased that their special massages of goanna fat and ash ointment in the later stages of Warreweer's pregnancy had ensured that her reproductive organs functioned properly and the baby was born easily. The first thing noticed was the baby's sex; a little later they looked for marks or characteristics of its dreaming animal.

The British guests did not remain mere onlookers, for they quickly cut the umbilical cord. While sharp scissors and knives would have been welcomed, their rapid action probably seemed cruel to the Aboriginal women, who also believed cutting the cord too short could kill the baby. The cord was viewed as having special powers by some groups, and the mother carried it for several months to ensure the baby's good health.

After the birth, Warreweer squatted over a small hole, which had been prepared in advance, and waited for the placenta. Its burial near the birth site linked mother, child and land. Meanwhile the British women decided to wash the child. The Aboriginal midwives objected, as their babies were not washed until some days after delivery. Although Warreweer reportedly agreed to the baby's bath, it is doubtful whether she had the energy left for an argument. Her body had just withstood what is for most women the ultimate physical exertion. Initially distracted by the baby's cries, the midwives did not notice Warreweer about to fall across the fire. But they acted quickly, and she was not injured. The new mother was then ceremonially 'smoked' with medicinal herbs on different parts of her body to stop bleeding, to encourage a good milk supply, and for cleansing and strength.

This encounter between two sets of women reveals some of the ways in which British technological superiority and cultural arrogance were to determine future relations between the two groups.

The case of Barangaroo tells us a little more about Aboriginal 'borning' or the process and cultural significance of giving birth, as well as introducing the colony's leading public figure, Governor Phillip. For a variety of social and political reasons Barangaroo, a Cammeray woman, wanted to have her baby at Government House. In anticipation, she dyed the twine and wove the soft dillybag for the baby's things, which she then wore from her neck or slung around her head. She selected and carefully folded some soft, silky ti-tree bark for the baby's bed and blanket. Close relatives ensured she had the special cutting and heating tools required for the birth. When Arthur Phillip, Governor of the British settlement of New South Wales, saw the newly made bag, he wanted it as a specimen artifact, and Barangaroo agreed. The following day Phillip engaged a British woman to crochet an English net, and Barangaroo, interested in the weaving technique and unusual materials, was reportedly pleased with the exchange. Bennelong, Barangaroo's young husband, asked Phillip for a blanket, which he also supplied. Bennelong prepared a special kangaroo bone and hemp anaesthetising tool for the final severance of the protruding umbilical cord. Concentrating on things material, Phillip concluded that Aboriginal women made little preparation before giving birth. Indeed, the British layette for a well-off baby consisted of at least sixty-eight items, including headbands to keep the head straight, swaddling cloth to bind the baby tight, and up to twelve ordinary pins per outfit. Even poorer women had to find over forty-five 'essentials'.

Barangaroo had been the first Aboriginal woman to be invited to dine at Governor Phillip's house. Refusing several times, she eventually accepted, and came to be on familiar terms with Phillip. She and Bennelong had taken over the rearing of a number of children whose parents had died; she and the children enjoyed eating Phillip's bread and other foods.

Barangaroo attracted much attention from British observers.

Lieutenant Hunter commented that she was 'very strait and exceedingly well made'. She wore a bone or stick through her nose for an ornament, but otherwise went entirely naked. Captain Watkin Tench was deeply impressed by her 'feminine innocence, softness and modesty'. Her relations with the governor and Bennelong show her to be proud and assertive. Barangaroo held ritual authority within her group, the Cammeragal, from the north shore of Port Jackson, one of the most powerful in the region. She was estimated to be in her forties at the time of this pregnancy.

Towards its later stages, Bennelong announced to Governor Phillip that his wife 'intended doing him the honour' of giving birth in his house. The two men were close; they relied on each other. Her husband also shared the title 'governor' and Barangaroo knew of secluded rooms and gardens where men could be avoided. Phillip refused, however, insisting that she would be 'better accommodated' at the hospital. A serious misunderstanding had occurred, for Barangaroo was not seeking more comfortable accommodation or medical assistance. A hospital birth among a crowd of sick strangers and a male surgeon was repulsive. Worse still, the hospital was contaminated by spirits of the recently deceased and it was her people's tradition to burn down such residences.

But why did Barangaroo decide upon the governor's house for the birth of her baby? Birthplace was important in Aboriginal society, for it allowed the child special association with a site. For Barangaroo, Government House (on the present intersection of Phillip and Bridge streets, Sydney) was not part of her or Bennelong's traditional country. It belonged to the Cadigal, a band whose numbers had been reduced by the 1789 smallpox epidemic from about fifty to only three. The Cadigal were a Daruk-speaking people like the Wangal, and they would have met regularly for religious and political business. In moving into Cadigal clan territory, Bennelong's clan was forging new land associations, and a prime way of deepening and perpetuating them was through the birthplaces of their children. Cadigal survivors needed new custodians to manage the land, though the task was problematic amid the overbearing force of British occupation.

The only way to manage it was through incorporating the British newcomers into their own kin networks. Bennelong had already slotted in Phillip, whom he called Beenena or Beanga, meaning father. Bennelong called himself Doorow or son. Their age difference made this appropriate, and as well as offering an explanation for Bennelong's abduction, it fitted Phillip's generous provision of food and reliance on him for assistance. (It is no wonder Bennelong felt torn by conflicting obligations when Phillip was speared in September 1790.) Government House had become much frequented by Aboriginal 'guests', being used both as a resource centre and a place of protection from British and Aboriginal aggressors. On several occasions, Aboriginal women used Government House and its well-guarded grounds as a refuge from attacks by their men, a function which the British upper class were pleased to perform in the name of chivalry.

Barangaroo also wanted to give her child a future in a world where so many Aboriginal clans had been destroyed by the smallpox epidemic, and where the British, who had some sort of power over this illness, now dominated. About half of the Aborigines in the Sydney region had died as a result of the outbreak; traditional burials had ceased as there were so few left to bury the bodies. Aborigines in the Port Jackson region knew Phillip held chief authority over the newcomers, and around his dwelling important British ceremonies and rituals were conducted, including flag-raising, military parades, and so on. Before the erection of the first government house, this protected high land may also have been a prime Aboriginal camp site.

By giving birth at Government House, Barangaroo would have provided her child with special rights to a very important piece of land, with its significance both as a traditional dreaming site and its transformation as an 'increase site' for seemingly boundless British resources. Barangaroo's gesture may thus be seen as a politically significant attempt to incorporate the introduced world into an Aboriginal one.

While we do not know where Barangaroo eventually gave birth, it was close enough to the main settlement for Lieutenant David Collins to see her soon afterwards. A few hours after the delivery Barangaroo was walking about alone, picking up sticks to attend to her fire and ensure the baby's warmth. The reddish coloured newborn lay not on Phillip's blanket but on a piece of soft bark on the ground. Barangaroo was heating the special tool made by her husband to anaesthetise the protruding three inches of cord. Once deadened, she cut it with a shell.

Collins looked on, fascinated that a woman who had just given birth would actually walk, let alone so busily and carefully do things for herself and the baby. The British viewed babies and post-partum mothers as frail, even fleeting things, as it was not uncommon for baby or mother to die after the birth. English middle-class women were expected to 'lie in' or remain in bed days or even weeks before and after delivery.

Other accounts refer to Aboriginal women who undertook lengthy treks from Botany Bay to Port Jackson with their newborn babies, but this was reportedly frowned upon by the Aboriginal men. Aboriginal women's independence and apparent physical stamina amazed Europeans of the late eighteenth century. Their work and travel made them fitter than middle-class European women, as they were used to walking, throwing out lines, fishing, gathering and carrying. They were also not restricted by tight bodices and other clothing that was particularly dangerous during pregnancy. They were, however, subject to prenatal food restrictions and were barred from eating some highly prized meats, so, depending on the availability of other food sources, they might at times have been undernourished.

In Aboriginal Australia, the birth site was closely related to the place where women did their productive work. Aboriginal women's working lives were spent harvesting the land and hunting its animals, often in all-female parties; the site on or near where the baby was born related to a plant or animal that was part of their subsistence economy, and also part of their religious belief-system. Aboriginal women selected a place of special significance to them and the imminent baby, whose identity as part of their group was already established. The baby's birthplace thus further entrenched its niche in the social and physical world.

Aboriginal knowledge of physiological paternity has been hotly debated. It seems most likely that Aborigines understood the logistics of reproduction, but that the male role was rarely discussed because it was taken for granted. Aborigines had a spiritual and land-related explanation for conception, placing little emphasis on sexual intercourse except in creating a path by which the baby spirit could enter a woman's body.

Within four or six weeks the baby received a totemic name, though there was no formal name-giving ceremony like a christening. The baby born to Barangaroo and Bennelong was called Dilboong, after a small bird. Other babies were named after fish, such as Ballooderry (leatherjacket), or Patyegarang after the large grey kangaroo. Everyone had a number of names, used at different ages and times and in different contexts; some were secret and for exclusive ritual use. Each person also had a kinship classification or 'skin', which came from the parents, and defined them in particular relationships to both close relations and strangers.

The dreaming or totemic identity was usually passed on through the father and related to his country. But sacred stories and associated land ownership and custodianship could also be passed on through the mother. Additionally, a baby had a conception dreaming that was established a long time before birth, with the baby's first kicks or turns. The baby's social father often had a dream that revealed the baby's identity. But the mother might also be the first to recognise the baby spirit. The foetus signalled its totem animal by making the mother ill when she ate it, or when she walked past a land feature, such as a hill or rockpool representing its dreaming, or saw some other meaningful sign. Some women 'caught' babies from actual baby spirit trees or places. In these special locations, baby spirits waited for a beautiful mother to jump into. The spirit thus chose its own mother and family. Young girls were warned to avoid these baby places. Dramatic natural forces, like whirlwinds and collusions of superhuman powers, were usually necessary to cause incarnations of babies. Dreamings, conception sites and birthplaces all contributed special rights to land.

Ethnologist Kate Langloh Parker described the beliefs of northern New South Wales Aborigines:

The bronze mistletoe branches with their orange-red flowers are said to be the disappointed babies whose wailing in vain for mothers has wearied the spirits who transform them into these bunches, the red flowers being formed from their baby blood. The spirits of babies and children who die young are reincarnated, and should their first mother have pleased them they choose her again and are called millanboo – the same again.

Analysts like Ashley Montagu have argued that babies were not thought of as the mother's flesh so she was merely a vehicle for their entry into the world. The process can also be viewed another way: that birth is a privilege bestowed by a mother to a spirit baby – one that she can voluntarily avoid. Newborn babies were sometimes killed if they were deformed or when their mother was unable to care for them. It was believed that these babies could await another chance to be born.

Like northern New South Wales Aborigines, the Eora people from the coastal area around Sydney may have believed that babies were freshly manufactured by the spirits, and that only babies who died young were reincarnated. Eora babies were held a great deal, fondled by everyone in the camp, and suckled by their mothers whenever possible. The mothers didn't have to worry about embarrassment or indecency as it was not customary to cover or disguise breasts. Nor did they have to worry about milk leaking onto their clothing. They knew how to encourage milk supply and how to keep lactating when away from their babies for prolonged periods. Babies were generously breastfed until three or four years old, depending on whether a brother or sister had been born in the meantime. One early painting shows a woman breastfeeding a small baby in a sitting position on the ground: she is simultaneously grilling fish on an adjacent fire. Babies were given baths when convenient, washed when dirty.

In the first days of life, the Eora baby or nabungaywuidalliez, the name for a very young baby at the breast, was carried everywhere in the soft paperbark carrier or coolamon. When strong enough, although only weeks old, the baby was sat up on its mother's shoulder with its legs across her neck, and taught to cling on tightly to her matted hair. The baby at this stage of travelling was called malgun or wongara juggame. The increasingly mobile eight-month-old child was called boregooroo.

Eora mothers decorated their babies with bush ornaments. Their hair was adorned with pieces of bone, teeth or parrot feathers stuck with yellow gum from the grass tree (*Xanthorrhoea resin*), and with white clay. Hair was decorated with a fascinating variety of objects: the front teeth of kangaroo; jawbones of large fish; human teeth; pieces of wood; feathers; the tail of a dog; and shark, whale and fish bones. Red or white ochre was also worn in the hair. Children's skin was covered with fatty fish or meat oil to ward off wind and sunburn, and protect against mosquitoes and stinging flies.

Young Aboriginal children were much loved and indulged. They were frequently nursed and fondled by a variety of male and female relatives, and expected to be given food whenever they wanted it. Rather than being taught the importance of private property, they were taught not to hoard but to share everything with other children. Male care of babies and children was commended by Tench and Hunter. Colbee treated his three-day-old with 'great tenderness' and Bennelong was devoted to his young child. It was observed that a man who slept with his little boy in his arms took great care in shifting the child first, and protectively turning round to him.

Children were allowed to join in most adult activities, for this was their means of education. Rather than being encouraged to ask questions, they were taught to observe carefully and mimic activities so that they learnt how to carry them out independently. As they grew older, boys were encouraged to spend more time with their father and other male relatives, participating in male hunting and ceremonial activities. Girls continued on with the women and, like boys, were taught there were places that each sex had to avoid.

Children played games that improved their dexterity and, later, their hunting and food-gathering skills. Around the Sydney region they enjoyed several ball games. One consisted of throwing a ball up high, then ducking and catching it. In another, a ball or other round object was rolled along in front of a row of children who tried to strike it with a stick as it passed. This was their favourite, and they excelled at it. Boys and girls also played with reeds, imitating spear-throwing, and soon becoming highly skilled. They also played at kidnapping the girls, a practice thought by British observers to be customary.

One of the most important things that Aboriginal children learnt about was their kinship system: who their relations were and the appropriate behaviour towards them. Complex reciprocal kin relationships bound the child to and distanced them from particular people. By making every known or unknown person a relative in some capacity, this kin system created a familiar world where everyone knew where they stood in relation to everyone else. Favours and obligations were constantly being bestowed or expected but they always had to be repaid. 'Avoidance' rules had to be followed. A boy could not look at or talk freely with his sister past a certain age. Girls could be freer with a man who belonged to the kin classification of 'husband', though she might be coy with the man promised as her actual husband. Mothers, fathers and grandparents were owed special gifts and kindness, but they also had all sorts of responsibilities. A mother's sister or a father's brother was also called mother or father, and all their children were sisters and brothers. Children were thus well protected from orphan status, with a good collection of mothers and fathers to choose from. But more distant relations could also be brother or sister due to kinship classifications. The reciprocal obligations of the kinship system determined the distribution of food and implements, so they were of integral economic as well as social significance.

Status and responsibility were also demarcated by age and gender. Little girls wore possum hair (or barrin) around their waists until puberty, when special ceremonies introduced them to their new responsibilities. Eventually they were married to their promised husband. Girls' ceremonies occurred when they first menstruated; older women then gave them an intensive education program that they did not reveal to the male journal writers. Two joints of the little finger of the left hand were removed by ligature, or malgin. The transformed finger was prestigious and said to be good for fishing. Girls also had special ceremonies around puberty to symbolise their adult status and prepare them for new roles, but these ceremonies were kept secret, and a shortage of female inquirers combined with drastic social disruptions means that the details have been lost.

More obvious fuss was made about the boys' ceremonies, with adults of both sexes participating in large numbers. The men of the British settlement were fascinated. Collins described the seizure of boys of sixteen or seventeen for special initiation into manhood. One stage of the initiation demanded that the boys remain in the same position all night, without eating, drinking or looking up. Dances and ceremonies represented dreaming stories of kangaroos, dingoes and other animals. Some aspects, such as boys passing over bodies writhing like snakes on the ground, were dramatic and frightening. Despite the curiosity of white observers, and the detailed descriptions, little information on the meaning of these ceremonies was given to the uninitiated. Collins was frustrated that his many inquiries did not elicit satisfying explanations for he could only ascertain 'that it was very good; that the boys would now become brave men; that they would see well, and fight well'. Since young men did not undergo the ordeal of parturition, this form of social rebirth was an artificially created trial by ordeal. The initiation climaxed in the removal of a tooth, so this became a symbol of true manhood. Phillip, with his missing front tooth, was therefore privy to more information than other British observers. Older women played important roles in key parts of the ritual, but had to absent themselves from some sequences.

Although these were men's rituals, the women knew what was going on. They had to feign ignorance during sections where women were barred, but generally they had some role in making arrangements. Daringha, Colbee's wife, procured three of the boys' teeth, one from Nanbarray, Colbee's relation. They were given in secrecy, and the women reportedly dreaded being observed; perhaps they also took some delight in conniving to procure these forbidden objects.

Women also played an important healing role, curing sick children, men's headaches, and other women, but the greatest healing power belonged to the feared and esteemed men of medicine, the caradyee. Ceremonial activity was closely tied up with production, especially through 'increase' rituals which were performed to encourage reproduction of plant and animal foods. These were performed by men and women separately at the sites for which they were responsible. For example, women performed rites on the yam dreaming sites, and men on the kangaroo dreaming sites. A girl or boy who was 'kangaroo', however, would not be able to eat their totemic animal.

Women were valued as reproducers of people and producers of food. It is, however, extremely difficult to judge the exercise of power in Aboriginal society, since whatever criterion is chosen contains culturally based value judgments. In addition the power balance in Aboriginal societies differed throughout Australia. In the case of the Eora, the scant surviving evidence was left predominantly by late eighteenth-century British men who were keen to perpetuate a belief in the superiority of their behaviour towards white women, whom, despite this, they themselves kept in an inferior position.

As in most known societies, Aboriginal men's rituals were considered more prestigious than women's, though women may have been privately sceptical of this. Ritual activity was an important means of defining social status. Gender, age and land associations determined status in this relatively egalitarian society. Status increased with age and proper behaviour towards land and kin, so an older woman often held authoritative roles in her clan. Certain male elders seem to have held ultimate authority, and older men were entitled to more than one wife. Where interests clashed, these elders secured their authority through the threat of force.

Aboriginal men's behaviour towards Aboriginal women was often condemned by early British observers. They saw Aboriginal women as the men's chattels because they carried food and children, and were often observed fishing in canoes. According to British middle-class ideals, women performed the domestic labour and child rearing and men were the breadwinners. Elizabeth Macarthur added that the men were not gallant because they did not escort their ladies, as was popular in the tradition of knightly chivalry. What these observers overlooked were the advantages the women enjoyed as a result of their relative economic and spiritual independence. They did not have to ensure their men were around to provide for them. Women as a group had a great deal of autonomy, owning and being responsible for certain land areas, associated ceremonies and resources. They often left on all-female expeditions while men fended for themselves. As well as deriving company, support and political strength from female kin, they had a network of protectors among their male relatives to ensure that their husbands performed their duties and did not maltreat them.

Nonetheless, violence between men and women certainly occurred, and women often came off worst with bad head-scarring and broken limbs. Women were skilled fighters, however, using waddies for assaulting offenders. Bennelong suffered a permanently divided lip as punishment for taking a woman without permission, and received permanent scars on the back of his hand from a woman evading his sexual advances. Yet he was also seen beating Barangaroo on the day she gave birth to Dilboong.

Women's political power should not be underestimated, however, with roles in organising marriages and rituals, and spiritual control over 'love magic', a powerful force in shaping social arrangements. In Eora or Daruk society, a girl was usually promised in marriage to a particular man from another clan group, and was allowed to join him when she reached puberty. The young woman had to live in her husband's country; other female relations who had married into the clan provided familiar faces, and common meetings between clans enabled her to travel regularly to visit her kin. While both husband and wife knew a common language, dialects varied from region to region. A first marriage was often to an older man, while an older woman could marry a young man. Laws relating to marriage were very strict, and only people in a particular kinship relationship (that is, distant blood relations) could marry. Transgression resulted in severe punishment, social ostracism or death. Those who eloped illegally, however, were sometimes forgiven once children were born.

Lieutenant David Collins's description of Aboriginal family life affords a graphic illustration of the convergence of childrearing or reproductive activities and the productive labour of the hunting and gathering economy. A party of British men, including Collins, observed Warreweer and her family a short while after the birth of her baby.

One of Bennelong's wives, Gooroobarrooboollo, and one of his sisters were returning from a fishing trip, and sang with 'good humour and harmony' as they kept time with their paddles. When Goroobarrooboollo got out of the canoe, she casually urinated. Bennelong, who had been minding his sister's child, met them on the shore with the child on his shoulders. The women cooked and ate on board, bringing some remaining fish for Bennelong who had to clean and cook them. As Collins narrated:

On the same rock [as Bennelong] lay his pretty sister Warreweer asleep in the sun, with a new born infant in her arms; and at some little distance were seated, rather below him, his other sister and his wife, the wife opening and eating some rock-oysters, and the sister suckling her child Kahdier-rang, whom she had taken from Bennelong.

Although contemporary writers argued that Aboriginal women were chattels, this picture of Bennelong looking after the young child and cooking his own food, and the two women fishing while another rested with her young baby, indicates a more complex picture.

Both women and men played crucial roles in food production, and as with other clans/groups throughout Australia, Daruk women collected the most reliable supply of sustenance, while the men procured the larger and more valued game. Labour was organised according to gender, age and family responsibilities, with pregnant women and recent mothers not expected to procure as much food. Older people had much of their food collected for them.

Fishing in canoes was generally women's work. Eora women used shiny turban-shell hooks, which also served as lures, or bone hooks and lines made by twisting long strands of the inner bark of trees such as the acacia and kurrajong. Chewed shellfish was often used as bait. Although they fished in small groups, bays and estuaries were sometimes full of women's canoes dotted at a practical distance from each other. The women kept fires burning in a small amount of earth on the bottom of their canoes; these were used for cooking the fish as soon as they were caught. Canoeists had remarkable balance, managing to keep afloat in the relatively unstable boats, sitting on their haunches, knees pressed strongly into the side of the boat. From this position they tended children, kept the fire going, paddled the boat, baited their lines with mussels or periwinkles, caught and grilled fish. Mothers did not jump to their babies' first cries; if the children continued, the women stopped fishing and fed them. Babies were held securely in between a woman's legs as she sat in the canoe. Children had the chance to listen to and join in the dreaming songs about certain species of fish, about birds that flew by, about ancestors, about related sites in the landscape. As they passed particular inlets, hillocks, rows of trees, rocks, the children heard about the significance of these places. As well as forming links in a wider story, each site had some personal relevance to their close relations or other people they knew.

Women also collected mussels and oysters, and caught crabs, turtles, worms and grubs. Away from the coast, they collected the yams that flourished near river banks, wood-grubs, xanthorrhoea, palmhearts, fern roots and other vegetable foods. Native figs, lilly pilly trees, lily orchids, tubers, native grapes, apple-berries, native currants and the nectar of banksias and grevilleas were also collected. They hunted smaller animals too, such as possums, goannas, lizards and birds, often in all-female groups, but sometimes alone or with their husbands and family.

Most goods were manufactured by the owner from handy materials or were gifts from kin. Some goods were exchanged over long distances. The women manufactured their own clubs, digging sticks, grinding and cutting implements, water and food carrying containers. The men collected bark and made the canoes.

The men also fished, but with fish-gigs or multipronged spears, and although they sometimes used canoes to catch fish in season, they usually operated near beaches, off rocks or river banks. Shellfish bait was thrown into the water to attract fish. Men tended to hunt alone, although they also cooperated with other men. Their techniques demanded eyes that were attuned to the smallest movement or changes, and extremely fast reactions. In the cooler winter months, when fish were scarce, the men fished at night with the aid of bark torches. Men were also responsible for hunting wallabies, kangaroos, possums, birds and other game. Inland people climbed trees and used snares and fish traps as aids to hunting. Burning was widely employed to flush out animals, to encourage fresh growth to attract kangaroos, and to keep country passable and usable for hunting. Fire-making was a time-consuming process based on friction, so travelling parties carried bark torches. The men also sang as they worked at fishing, tool manufacture and other duties. These songs related to the local environment and its mythology; new tunes heard from the British and French were also adopted and sung note perfect.

The Daruk usually went entirely naked, although they tended to wear a variety of ornaments. Inland groups used possum and kangaroo fur for coats. In the Sydney area, men's and women's bodies were decorated with white clay, with circles drawn around the eyes and with wavy lines down the arms and legs and over the ribs. Special body painting was usually performed for ceremonies, and was accompanied by the same sense of excitement and consciousness of a novel appearance as someone wearing a new outfit. Different shapes and patterns signified totemic associations and the purpose of dances or corroborees. Although chest and arm scarring was valued for ornamental reasons, it was also closely associated with initiation ceremonies for both women and men. Scars on breast, arms, and the back were cut with a sharp shell, and a raised effect was achieved by rubbing ashes into the open cuts. Men's scars usually differed from women's.

Both men and women liked to wear a bone or reed ornament or fish hook through their noses. The operation in which the hole was bored was called gnah-noong. Adults wore additional ornamentation for special occasions, and one favoured hairstyle was achieved by shaping the hair into moppy locks with gum. Although often worn matted and curly-looking, the people of the Sydney region generally had straight or wavy hair.

Men and women also wore necklaces, headbands decorated with shell and other decorations and woven bands designed for glare protection. While men's and women's ornamentation differed, there was obviously no need for clothing to demarcate sexual identity. Nonetheless, modest postures prevented uninvited eyes viewing women's genitals.

The British were eager to let Aborigines know which practices they abhorred. These included nudity generally, nasal decoration, and the removal of the joints of the girls' little fingers. Aborigines thus became self-conscious in the presence of white disapproval. Collins reveals their sensitivity, describing them as 'extremely reserved and delicate' in his presence. They often wore clothes in deference to British sensitivities, discarding them away from settlements.

Dress, body paint, scarring and ornamentation did not differentiate classes in the western sense, but they did signify differences between people, especially relating to status as initiates, affiliation with dreamings, and clans. The symbols used in ornamentation referred to sacred matters, actual land, people, and the activities and rituals of distinct (though not entirely separate) gender traditions.

First encounters between whites and Aborigines were peaceful; as William Bradley wrote in his journal, 'our People & the Natives were mixed together, the Boats Crews amused themselves with dressing the Natives ... [with] paper & other whimsical things to entertain them, with which they were pleas'd for the moment'.

But Aborigines were soon deeply concerned by disturbance to the land. Lieutenant Bradley referred to Aboriginal reactions to a party of men sent to clear the ground to channel water on the south side of the bay. 'The natives were well pleas'd with our People until they began clearing the Ground at which they were displeased & wanted them to be gone.' When convicts began to cut down trees, George Worgan noted that some Aborigines loudly expressed their rage.

From the first days of settlement, all sorts of clearing, ploughing and building works were underway. Trees were chopped down for building and firewood, shrubs and grasses cleared, and a number of temporary shelters and buildings erected. Midshipman Daniel Southwell depicted the flurry of activity in July 1788 in a letter to his mother in England. Barracks had been erected for soldiers, and brick manufacture and other building work ensued – 'Add to this gardening, farming, and a thousand other things ... carrying on with all possible expedition'.

The resources of the Sydney area were heavily exploited from January 1788 as the fleet could bring only limited supplies. Fresh water was not plentiful, so available resources were exploited and rapidly polluted. Huge seines or nets were used to haul in shoals of fish. When a group of Aboriginal men tried to reclaim their fish, the governor ordered that large catches be shared with them. Even by 1790, introduced vegetables, such as cabbages, were not growing well, nor was wheat; and there was a meat shortage: 'fish being served out as pork, only a larger proportion, by way of making the provis's hold out'. Kangaroos and other animals were intensively hunted for meat by convicts; by 1790 hunters were specially appointed to supplement the supply. Convicts also raided the local environs for sarsaparilla plants for making tea, and wild greens for vegetables.

Aboriginal production had been dramatically disturbed and impeded by the British presence. The arrival of a thousand hungry mouths, followed by hundreds more, put unprecedented pressure on local food resources.

So what would the Daruk people have thought of all this? To them such large-scale destruction of sacred places and strange, violent behaviour towards their land were inexplicable. The newcomers seemed to knock down trees without any reason, for they were not making canoes, gathering bush honey or catching animals. Stones were moved and stacked together, clay dug up, shaped and cooked, holes were made in the ground, large unwieldy structures built. At first they may have equated the clearing with the creation of a sacred ceremonial ground, or bora ring. Such a large gathering of people was unprecedented, and perhaps they thought a huge ritual gathering was to be held, dangerous business from which they should steer well clear. There is no doubt the Daruks subsequently avoided the settlement, for the only way to bring them back was by an official kidnapping.

Aborigines may have originally thought that the newcomers were ancestors, and greeted them accordingly. The large groups of strangers who had suddenly come into their world were perhaps there because the sky had fallen down, letting in all the deceased from past generations, and overpopulating their world.

A contemporary map of the settlement of Sydney in April 1788 reveals the importance of sex and rank divisions in the newly transplanted world. The governor's mansion, signifying the ultimate authority, was the most prominent structure. Most of the buildings were temporary, consisting of tents and marquees. The marines had a special barracks, with quarters for the officers, captain, the judge advocate and the Reverend Johnson and his wife. The convicts were divided into separate men's and women's camps, one for each sex on either side of the cove. Some convict women lived as servants and mistresses in the quarters of the upper-ranking officials. Other new features reflected British economic and cultural priorities: gardens and farms, a bakery, kitchen, a blacksmith's quarters, a storehouse and a large stone quarry. Sydney Cove was also dotted with large sailing boats which were visible from some distance.

Interactions between the ranks were generally hierarchical. Floggings and other punishments frequently awaited convicts, and brawling and drunkenness were rife. The majority of arrivals had been shipped to Botany Bay against their will, transported as social outcasts, to be punished for disobeying British laws and to serve as cheap labour for New South Wales. Men and women had been forcibly separated from children, partners, mothers and fathers. They had also been severed from their homes and homeland.

Twelve years after the first ships arrived in Botany Bay, the ecological impact was dramatic; the colony consisted of 5200 non-Aboriginal people. Some cattle and animals had gone wild. In captivity there were 830 cattle, 3090 goats, 2390 hogs and 5700 sheep. Much land was also taken up by agriculture. Besides domestic plots and market gardens, there were 4665 acres of wheat and 2930 acres of corn. At Parramatta stood large brick barracks and other buildings, a windmill tower, mills, and a double-logged gaol. Trees were constantly being cut down for building, ship repairs, farm machinery, wheels, gun carriages and fuel. By 1802 settlers had started logging cedar for private sale. While the British associated such activities with a lively industriousness, the Aborigines perceived most of it as crazy destruction.

To the Europeans, Aborigines who set fires were arsonists. Although Aborigines may have sometimes used fire as a guerilla strategy, it was more commonly used in carrying out traditional land management techniques. Fire was regularly employed to clear land for hunting and to prevent more devastating blazes. Regular firing was a prime means of 'looking after the country'. It is also known as fire-stick farming because larger game, such as wallabies, was attracted by the vegetation that grew after burn-off.

The Aboriginal economy could be changed more rapidly than their social system or minds. With their own food resources badly depleted, the apparent availability of British foods seemed attractive, even seductive. Aborigines were prepared to secure these goods through kinship affiliations and through the casual exchange of services, but they were not so interested in permanent participation in the cash economy, or in growing and harvesting foods themselves. Some started to need European foods and had to wear European clothing in order to obtain it. Others became dependent on the alcohol and pipe tobacco that governors and leading members of the elite had earlier been so keen to introduce them to. For fleeting moments the Aboriginal adoption of European clothing, drugs and alcohol created the illusion that Aborigines actually belonged to the newly established society in their midst.

Sexual interactions between military men, convicts and Aboriginal women became increasingly common. Introduced venereal diseases seriously curbed fertility among Aborigines who, as a group had already been devastated by smallpox; the effect of both on Aboriginal numbers was compounded by the deaths of many women of childbearing age. Some white settlers employed and had longer term sexual relations with Aboriginal women. As a result Aboriginal men had difficulty finding wives. Children of mixed descent were born, initially posing a confusing problem for Aboriginal communities. Their skin was the wrong colour; should they be allowed to live? Extreme disruption to the land meant that men were unable to or prohibited from hunting game using traditional methods, while women could, to some extent, continue their nurturing role as reproducers and also procure sustenance through prostitution. Sometimes Aboriginal women exploited the newcomers' romantic interests, securing food for their community by moving into settlers' huts.

Many tragedies were endured by Aboriginal women and men. Although Barangaroo had not been able to give birth to her baby at Government House, there were not the same objections to her being cremated nearby less than a year later. Along with Barangaroo's Aboriginal kin, Lieutenant Collins, Surgeon White, and Governor Phillip were invited to attend the funeral ceremony. Although severely depressed, Bennelong focussed his attentions on the survival of the infant Dilboong, whose care he wanted to entrust partly to Phillip. Bennelong, who had formed a close relationship with Phillip, hoped he could procure a white woman to suckle Dilboong, and these plans raised his spirits. It was not long, however, before he was maintaining a sad nightly vigil near the Government House garden where he had buried his infant daughter. In later years Bennelong was unsympathetically portrayed as a simple drunkard and was virtually unknown by the time of his death.

After the coming of the Europeans, the land upon which Eora life had been conducted was dramatically disturbed and reshaped. So were the sites that bound together humans, birthplace, hunting and ritual. Relations between Aboriginal men, women and children were impinged upon in many ways by the demands of the white intruders. By 1798 the people who walked on top of this earth were predominantly white-skinned and of British origin. The majority of the babies being born were white too, their first moments experienced not on the land but in the confines of a bedroom or the government hospital. From where had their spirits come?

2 Conceiving A Colony

In 1783 James Matra had suggested that the British Government should establish a colony in New South Wales. Matra had been a midshipman with Captain Cook on the *Endeavour*, and was now looking for government employment. He proposed a colony at Botany Bay as a refuge for Americans like himself who had fought on Britain's side in the American War of Independence.

Matra imagined a colony in which men would rule over women, and Europeans would rule over people of other races. He had in mind a society on the American model, based on plantation-owning white families employing coloured labour. Its public life would be ruled by himself, as governor, its private life by male heads of families, men who 'shall adventure there ... to repair their broken fortunes, and again enjoy their domestic felicity'. Matra assumed that the Aboriginal inhabitants were so few, so uncivilised and so unwarlike that their land was available for the taking – that it was in law *terra nullius*, a land unoccupied and without a sovereign. Labourers, he believed, could be brought from China, and that a ship could be sent to 'New Caledonia, Otahito, and the neighbouring islands to procure a few families there, and as many women as may serve for the men left behind'. He expected no difficulty in recruiting the island women, believing them to prefer European sexual partners to men of their own race.

The Home Secretary, Lord Sydney, interviewed Matra about his plans in 1784. Sydney was interested in only one possible use for New South Wales – its potential 'for the reception of criminals condemned to transportation'.

The revolt of the American colonies had created a crisis in Britain's gaols. Each year before 1775, about 1000 convicts sentenced to transportation, a quarter of them women, were sold – or more precisely seven years of their labour were sold – in the tobacco growing colonies of America. Male labourers brought about 10 pounds each, skilled men 15 to 25 pounds, and women about 8 pounds. The American war put a stop to this trade, but it did not halt the numbers sentenced to transportation. The sentence was integral to the British system of justice. England in the late eighteenth century was a country of great riches and great poverty, in which people without property often thought little of stealing, and there was no organised police force to prevent them. To protect property the legislators relied on cruel punishments, hoping to terrify those they could not catch.

Death and transportation disposed of those committed for all but the most trivial of crimes. Simple larceny merited transportation for seven years. Compound larceny – stealing goods worth more than a shilling, stealing with violence, stealing from a dwelling or on a highway – merited death by hanging. The list of capital offences grew every year, as new kinds of property like steam mills and canal machinery were thought to need protection. In practice judges and juries tended to commute death sentences to transportation, swelling the numbers sent across the Atlantic.

Imprisonment as such was a sentence rarely passed in the eighteenth century. The common gaol was a place of detention, where the accused awaited trial and the judged awaited punishment. The long-term residents were those who could not pay their fines, or their debts. The gaoler ran the gaol as a business; prisoners had to pay him for food. Inmates huddled together indiscriminately, men and women, young and old, hardened and innocent, lying in rags, vermin, and their own filth. They came into court rotting with ulcers, and sometimes dying of highly contagious 'gaol fevers'; twice during the century the stinking breath of prisoners carried fevers into the dock that infected judges and spectators alike. This was another kind of justice.

These prisons could not hold the numbers of convicts waiting to be transported, especially in London, where several score were sentenced to exile every session. In 1776 the government of the day brought in a bill to allow offenders liable to transportation to be punished by hard labour instead. Women and infirm men were to labour in houses of correction, able-bodied men on the rivers and harbours of England, working from hulks moored midstream.

In 1779 parliament authorised the erection of two large penitentiaries, where prisoners might be reformed by religious instruction and regular labour. But Treasury baulked at the expense, and the first British penitentiary was not built for a further forty years.

The young men transferred to the hulks found them as bad as the gaols; there was no clothing, no bedding, no hospital, mouldy rations, and 'a most disagreeable smell'. In June and September 1778 convicts on the hulks rose up and attacked their keepers. To the citizens of London, the stench of the hulks carried across the water the threat of gaol fever and bloody revolt.

Governments searched for other places that would take convicts. A committee considered India, the West Indies and Africa, but nothing was done. In 1783 and 1784 a London merchant made several attempts to carry convicts for sale in America as before, but some of his cargoes mutinied and the Americans refused to take the rest.

The second of these mutinies involved many convicts later sent to Botany Bay. In April 1784, at about the same time as Matra's interview with Lord Sydney, 179 convicts were gathered on the *Mercury*, twenty-two of them women. On the eighth day out they overpowered the crew and put the officers into 'darbies' (handcuffs). For six days they 'held possession of the ship as commanders', then as many as could took to the ship's boats and rowed towards the Devonshire coast. Most of them were captured before reaching shore. About eighty of these men and women were later retransported.

The *Mercury* mutineers were typical of the men and women sentenced to transportation. Most were petty thieves, stealing from people not much richer than themselves. Women usually stole from the person, or from dwellings. Elizabeth Dudgens and Susannah Garth were sentenced together for taking 9 guineas from a man's pocket. Men more often stole in the streets, with some show of violence. John Leary and five other young men were sentenced to hanging for assaulting a carrier and stealing 12 yards of muslin.

The recaptured mutineers were placed in a hulk off Plymouth. Matra added a note to his plan, proposing Botany Bay as the site of a convict settlement. Rather than forcing the convicts to labour in the interests of other people, he proposed giving them 'a few acres of land as soon as they arrive in New South Wales'. Then 'they must work or starve', and most likely would become 'moral subjects of society'. A parliamentarian echoed his sentiments in a debate on the transportation question: give every convict man a woman, and let them settle New Zealand.

The government found New South Wales and New Zealand too distant, and looked to Africa. Matra and other men who knew the Pacific continued to put the case for New South Wales. They stressed the potential of the flax plant and the easy availability of wives from Tahiti. In 1785 a committee recommended that the government establish a convict colony that would also bring commercial and political benefits to Britain. Their first choice was Das Voltas Bay, on the south-west coast of Africa, but a survey vessel reported the site to be unfit for a settlement.

In March 1786 the convicts on the Plymouth hulk rose against their keepers, and were not subdued until eight were dead and thirty-six wounded. The Pitt government did its sums; it reckoned that transportation to New South Wales would be initially more expensive than keeping the convicts on the hulks, but cheaper over time. In August 1786 cabinet approved the Home Office's proposal to transport about 750 convicts to New South Wales.

Accepting that convicts could not be left to rule themselves, the government appointed a governor and civil officers to superintend the settlement, and three companies of marines to preserve 'a proper degree of subordination and regularity'. To the same end they adopted Matra's idea of fetching women from Tahiti, as 'without a sufficient proportion of that sex it is well known that it would be impossible to preserve the settlement from gross irregularities and disorders'. Rations enough for 200 island women were ordered alongside those needed for 750 convicts and about 200 marines and officers.

The plan met a mixed reception in press and parliament. Critics scoffed at the idea of a convict colony contributing to the growth of empire, and argued that convicts could be better reformed in penitentiaries in Britain. Supporters welcomed the prospect of a trading and naval base in the Pacific. One writer ('R.H.') looked forward to the reform of the convicts through marriage with the island women, 'the most beautifully formed Women that the Sun beholds'. He hoped that from 'the sober gravity of the Males' and 'the airy Lightness of the Females ... a generation of social

Benevolent Beings might arise, and in time become a flourishing nation'.

It was left to the capain-general and governor-in-chief of the new colony to consider how the convicts might be employed and the next generation raised. Captain Arthur Phillip was a retired naval officer, nearly fifty years old. He was appointed Governor of New South Wales in October 1786.

Arthur Phillip first imagined two societies in New South Wales. He wished to keep convict society separate from that of 'the garrison and other settlers that may come from Europe' – 'as I would not wish Convicts to lay the foundations of an Empire'. Like most gentlemen of his day, Phillip believed that the convicts lived by rules and needs different from his own; that convict women 'possessed neither Virtue nor Honesty', and that the lusts of the men were so urgent that time should be allowed for the most abandoned women to receive the men and service their imperative needs. But he hoped that by allowing men and women to keep company 'when not at work' that they would be encouraged to marry. He thought that in time the Aboriginal men would 'permit their Women to Marry and Live' with the convicts, while the Tahitian women might choose husbands from the garrison. His imaginary societies were ordered by both race and gender.

The dream of a separate 'free' settlement receded. By April 1787 Phillip's official instructions authorised him to establish a settlement that was neither gaol nor free, but something of both. New South Wales was under British law, and even convicts under sentence retained their civil rights. But the governor's powers were effectively absolute, 'under the rules and discipline of war'. His instructions were concerned first with survival, with shaping all the convicts, men and women both, into a self-supporting workforce. Those sections that looked to the future assumed a gender order, a society based like Matra's on landowning families ruled by men. In the case of well-behaved convicts, 'To every male shall be granted 30 acres of land, and in case he shall be married, 20 acres more; and for every child who may be with them ... a further quantity of 10 acres'.

Historians who have thought about the kind of state that Phillip planned have generally condemned it. They point to the irony of a state based on 'the authority of brute force' being created in an antipodean backwater just when the people of France were declaring the brotherhood of man – and briefly of woman. Feminists have described the transported women as 'sexual commodities' and the British Government as an 'imperial whoremaster'. Perhaps this better describes intentions than outcomes.

Phillip's immediate concern in 1787 was to keep the convicts and marines alive on the long voyage to New South Wales. The departure of the First Fleet – six transports, three storeships, and two naval vessels – was delayed several times as Phillip insisted on better medicines, rations and clothing. During their long wait he saw to it that the convicts on the transports received fresh meat and vegetables, a great improvement on their diet in the hulks.

The mutineers from the *Mercury* were among the first to be transferred to the transports, 'all secured in irons, except the women'. Many of these prisoners had been confined for three years or more. In the last months of 1786 they had been joined on the hulk by women who had been confined almost as long in county gaols. These had been gathered in a vain attempt to balance the numbers of men and women sent to New South Wales. Of the men, only the young and fit were sent in the First Fleet; for women the net was cast wider.

Elizabeth Pulley and Susannah Holmes were brought by their turnkey, John Simpson, from Norwich gaol in September 1786. Both were sentenced for stealing from a dwelling; Pulley stole large quantities of food and Holmes Irish linen and clothes. Neither claimed any trade or occupation. Holmes was younger, nineteen in 1787 compared with Pulley's twenty-six, and Pulley had been held in Norwich a year longer than Holmes. None of this explains why Holmes inspired sympathy among gentlemen of the ruling class, and Pulley inspired loathing.

Susannah Holmes took with her from Norwich her seven-month-old son Henry, conceived and born in the gaol. His father was Henry Kable, sentenced to transportation for burglary. John Simpson described young Henry to the readers of the *Scots Magazine* as a 'very fine baby' much loved by his parents. Susannah's way of nursing him at the breast was 'peculiarly tender'. Kable begged in vain to accompany them to New South Wales.

When John Simpson and his party arrived at the Plymouth hulk, the captain refused to take the baby on board. Simpson set off for London with the baby on his knee to ask Lord Sydney to reunite mother and child. As in all moral tales Sydney proved difficult but not quite impossible to see, he gave the necessary orders to reunite mother and child and to send the father to Botany Bay as well. Simpson was rewarded by their joy: 'the tears which flowed from their eyes, with the innocent smiles of the babe, on the sight of the mother, who had saved her milk for it, drew tears likewise from my eyes'.

Elizabeth Pulley inspired no such emotion. While the fleet lay off the Isle of Wight the crew broke through the heavy bulkheads of the *Friendship* into the women's quarters, and four women – one of them Pulley – were found in bed with four of the seamen. Lieutenant Ralph Clark of the marines was appalled at these 'abandoned women' – 'they are ten thousand times worse than the men'.

On board the fleet were 586 male convicts, 192 female convicts, and thirteen children. They were accompanied by 40 officers, 160 marines, and 30 women and 12 children, the families of the marines. Some soldiers' wives could accompany their husbands at the crown's expense; their presence was preferred to that of local prostitutes. Officers' wives were discouraged from taking on such hardship. There were at least six births on the eight-month voyage, mostly to the soldiers' wives. That the newly born were likely to die before journey's end was seen as an unfortunate fact of nature.

Some saw the numbers of conceptions on board as just inevitable. Phillip separated men and women convicts, and tried to keep the seamen from the women. But some captains turned a blind eye. On the *Lady Penrhyn* most of the crew found bedmates for the voyage. An officer reported sourly that at every port along the way the sailors spent their wages buying clothes and presents for the women.

Chastity meant little to the classes from which the convicts, seamen and soldiers were drawn. Young couples without property did not bother about marriage until a child was born, and often not then. Promiscuity was more acceptable in a man than a woman. But a woman might live with a series of men, and a child from an earlier liaison was no barrier to finding a new partner. Gentlemanly views of chastity were more complicated. Ladies had to be chaste; how else could property be safely inherited? But many gentlemen did not feel themselves bound to chastity, at least with women from the lower classes. Polite society cheerfully accepted that gentlemen kept mistresses as well as wives.

It was unfortunate for Elizabeth Pulley and her fellows on the *Friendship* that Lieutenant Clark of the marines was a new husband, much in love, sentimental about chaste women and fearful and angry towards the sexually aggressive. After a few weeks at sea the crew broke through the bulkhead again, and the women were reunited with their lovers. Next morning the men were flogged and the women were ordered into irons. Pulley spent the next three months in and out of various kinds of irons and handcuffs.

Of the twenty-one women on the *Friendship*, nine were punished on the voyage, seven of them frequently. These women appalled their keepers as much by what they said as what they did. One of the *Mercury* women was Elizabeth Barber, a skilled bookstitcher by trade. Barber took no part in the bulkhead breakouts. But in the tropical heat off Rio de Janeiro she got roaring drunk and accused the ship's surgeon of wanting 'to fuck her'. When the captain ordered her into irons she abused him, saying that 'she was no more a whore than his wife was'. The captain had her gagged, but not before she told him 'that she would see us all thrown overboard before we got to Botany Bay'. It was a threat that the officers took seriously.

Lieutenant Bowes on the *Lady Penrhyn* found his charges 'totally abandoned and callous'd to all sense of shame', 'barely rational or even human beings'. His specific complaint was of 'the oaths and imprecations they daily make use of in their common conversation', of their 'little disputes with each other', and of their petty thieving. The women's continual insubordination pushed their keepers to extreme measures: thumbscrews, iron fetters, head shaving and finally flogging. And none of it stopped the women from answering back.

The fleet reached New South Wales in January 1788. Phillip had carried nearly 1500 souls across more than 15 000 miles of ocean, with the loss of less than twenty lives. Merely keeping the vessels together was an extraordinary achievement.

The transports dropped anchor in Sydney Cove on 26 January, and began landing the male convicts the next day. They were set to work unloading cargo and stock, clearing the ground, felling trees, pitching tents, hauling nets for fish, and digging the ground to plant vegetables. Most of the women were not landed until 6 February. Bowes described them leaving the *Lady Penrhyn* in new clothes issued for the occasion: 'dressed in general very clean, and some few amongst them might be said to be well dressed'. He added that 'the men convicts got to them very soon after they landed, and it is beyond my abilities to give a just description of the scene of debauchery and riot that ensued during the night'. The orgy has been a favourite subject in history books, but accounts are probably exaggerated. 'A just description' eluded Bowes because he spent that night not on shore, but with the drunken sailors on board the *Lady Penrhyn*.

The next day, 7 February, all the settlers gathered to hear the official reading of the governor's commissions, the legal basis of the colony, its government, and its judicial system. The occasion was as solemn and splendid as parading redcoats, flying colours, and drums and fifes could make it. The formal reading of the commissions concluded with three volleys from the marines, with the first bars of 'God Save the King' played between each volley.

If the Aboriginal inhabitants of what came to be known as Sydney Cove observed these celebrations, their presence was not recorded. In the previous weeks small parties of white men had several times met much larger groups of black men, and occasionally women. The invaders were surprised at the numbers of Aborigines living around the harbour; Phillip estimated that the whole of the continent must support close to a million Aborigines. Mostly the meetings had been cordial, with an exchange of gifts and of cultural information. But the Aborigines had protested at the clearing of the land, and had demanded a share of the large catches of fish netted in the harbour. Phillip was instructed to conciliate the 'natives', to live peacefully with them without interrupting the pattern of their daily lives. But the powers he assumed on 7 February would inevitably bring him and his administration into conflict with the owners of the land.

After the reading of the commissions, Phillip spoke severely to the assembled convicts. He spoke of the two things that were to dominate their lives in the coming years – their duties as workers, and their relations with the opposite sex. All had to contribute to the settlement, and those who did not work would starve. Promiscuity was as dangerous as idleness, and men taking their sexual pleasure where they found it would be punished. He concluded by recommending marriage as a source of happiness and comfort.

The work proved harsh – for men much harsher than for women. Respectable women in England rarely laboured in public, in the fields, or on roads or building sites, and Phillip seems to have assumed that it would be inappropriate – or useless – for convict women to do such work in New South Wales. So women were put to light work, such as gathering shells to make lime for mortar. The men laboured to clear the bush, cut timber, dig gardens and build against the rainy weather – first a timber-framed hospital, then barracks for the troops and a storehouse. A dozen convicts could spend five days grubbing out the soil around the roots of a tall tree, only to find that the trunk was rotten. It was bitter work for men who had chosen theft ahead of 'honest labour'.

Temporary cabbage-tree huts built by convicts and troops in their own time went up much faster, but often fell in under the driving rain. By May the barracks and the hospital were still unfinished, and the gardens failed. Scores of patients with scorbutic ulcers – scurvy – joined those suffering from respiratory diseases in the makeshift hospital tents. Governor Phillip was also ill; he suffered continual pain in his side, first contracted sleeping in the open while exploring to the north.

Samuel Barsby accosted fellow convict Catherine Prior and her new baby at the hospital, calling her an 'infernal fury', and said that 'if he had a knife he would cut her bloody life out'. Historians have tended to see the women convicts as victims of male violence. Certainly women were threatened with rape and worse. But a kind of order was maintained. The convicts' camps were their own territory, and sailors and marines caught in the women's camp were liable to be beaten, or drummed out dressed in petticoats. Prior was rescued by fellow convicts, and Barsby got fifty lashes from the court.

In mid-1788 Phillip proposed two policy changes. He asked the home government to authorise the use of convict labour by the officers, to raise meat and grain to augment the public stock. And he rejected the experiment of breeding a new race in the Pacific, 'because to send for women from the Islands, in our present situation, would answer no other purpose than that of bringing them to pine away in misery'. Instead he asked the home government to send more convict women, presumably for their usefulness as wives rather than as public workers.

Phillip's recommendation to the convicts to marry had drawn a better response than his command to work. Five couples married on the first available Sunday, 10 February 1788: William Parr and Mary MacCormack, Simon Burn and Francis Anderson, Henry Kable and Susannah Holmes, William Haynes and Hannah Green, and William Bryant and Mary Brand.

Historians have observed that women were obliged to marry for protection. But couples married for reasons other than the pressure of governors and violent men. Some of these seem to have been marrying old friends. Kable and Holmes we already know. Green and Haynes may have been as long, if not as closely acquainted; they were tried together at the same session of the Old Bailey, and sailed together on both the *Mercury* and the *Friendship*. Parr and MacCormack both came from Liverpool, where he was a 'noted swindler', and she a receiver of stolen goods. Anderson and Burn were Irish Catholics long resident in London.

Three of Clark's 'great whores' were married by May. Elizabeth Barber, the bookstitcher who had told the captain of the *Friendship* she was no more a whore than his wife was, married Thomas Brown on 17 February. Just forty weeks later she produced a son. Elizabeth Dudgens, flogged for insolence on the *Friendship*, married George Clayton in April 1788.

Elizabeth Pulley from Norwich hesitated the longest. She did not decide to marry Anthony Rope until mid-May, by which time she knew that she was carrying his child. Rope was a labourer, transported from Essex for the same crime as Pulley, housebreaking. He was one of the convicts detailed to live and work at the brickfields outside the settlement. Elizabeth and Anthony Rope celebrated their wedding in a style that wrote it into the colony's court records. A party in the Ropes's newly built hut were served 'a very hearty Supper' consisting of a sea pie made of salt beef, salt pork, and some highly prized fresh meat, topped with a steamed piecrust. The usual way of cooking meat and flour was in a sort of pudding, tied up in a piece of cloth and boiled in a communal copper. Rope and his workmate James Price told the party that the fresh meat was kangaroo, but it was goat, from the carcass of a beast belonging to an officer. When charged, Price persuaded the court that the animal had been killed by a dingo.

Some fifty couples had married by the end of 1788, almost one in three of the women. Only another six married before the coming of the second fleet, when the pattern began again. Many of the women who did not marry moved into men's huts as housekeepers and bedmates, apparently by choice.

Mary Marshall and Robert Sideway seem to have chosen not to marry. Marshall was a London servant girl transported for theft. During the first year at Sydney Cove she was in trouble for stealing shirts from soldiers, and was flogged for bad language. In 1789 she began living with Sideway. He was a flashy dresser when he could afford it. His original crime had been the theft of a complete set of clothing, shoes and all, and he soon gathered extra shirts and waistcoats in the colony. Clothes were almost the only property held by the poor, at once a form of currency and of conspicuous consumption. Sideway was an educated man who had been a watchcase maker in London. In the colony he became the government baker, working the oven that replaced the government copper.

Phillip's vision extended above and beyond the huddle of tents and huts on the foreshore. At the head of the cove he had a gang mark out the principal street of a township, with a site for Government House commanding a fine view of the harbour. And to convert Sydney's clay into something more durable, he established brickfields about a mile from the settlement. Gangs moved out from the government farms around the cove to the brick kilns and to quarrying and construction sites. When better land was discovered at Parramatta and beyond, government farms and working convicts were relocated there, despite Aboriginal protests.

Phillip attempted to include the Aboriginal people within his vision, welcoming them into the settlements and punishing white men who injured them. But the white invaders took too many kangaroos from the land and too many fish from the sea. White men were speared and black men were shot in the competition for food. In the areas closest to the white settlement Aboriginal women and children were found to be starving in the winter of 1788.

Then in April 1789 the Europeans discovered that they – or some other visitors – had brought upon the Aborigines a far greater injury. Every day dead and dying Aborigines were found on the shores of the harbour, suffering from smallpox. 'The number that was swept off' was, a white observer wrote, 'incredible'. Beaches where hundreds had lived were deserted; 'the excavations in the rocks were filled with the putrid bones of those who had fallen victims to the disorder'. For years one could not walk in the bush without finding skeletons. The disease spread far beyond Sydney, probably down the south-eastern river systems to what was to be South Australia and Victoria. Around Sydney it killed one in two of the Aboriginal population, most commonly the young adults. Historians have estimated that the numbers of Aborigines in New South Wales fell from 250 000 in 1788 to some 145 000 in 1800, mostly as a result of smallpox.

With the arrival of the second and third fleets in 1790 and 1791, the white population of New South Wales increased to about 4000 men and 600 women. Grain and vegetables grew more readily on Norfolk Island than on the mainland, and the governor sent on to Norfolk many of the new arrivals, especially the women, who were put to light field work. At Parramatta they were required to sew clothing for the men. Some were detailed to work as 'washer-women' for the officers – providing all the services of wives – or as hutkeepers and cooks for working gangs of convicts. Either way they worked to task, unsupervised. Skilled men – blacksmiths, carpenters, boatbuilders – also worked to task, and found opportunities to do their own work, in and out of government hours. Some men learnt skills as they laboured. James Bloodsworth, convict architect and builder, earned his emancipation 'by the pains he had taken to teach others the business of a bricklayer'. Anthony Rope called himself a bricklayer by the end of his sentence.

Work was much harsher in the gangs. Hours of labour during the week were set from sun-up to 11 a.m., and from 2 p.m. to sundown. In 1790 convicts on the government farms had to hoe one-tenth of an acre a day, or about twice that attempted by men working in their own time. Rations of salt meat and flour were adequate when supplemented with fresh fish and vegetables. But in winter government stores ran low and rations were reduced, just when the gardens died. In the lean months of 1790, 1791 and

1792 people were so sick with hunger that the hours of work had to be cut. In summer men straight from England were expected to labour in century degree heat and winds like a blast furnace. Refusal to work was likely to lead to a flogging and a sentence to work in chains.

In November 1791 about twenty new arrivals – all apparently Irish – took to the bush with newly issued clothes and provisions. The jeers of more seasoned settlers could not dissuade them from the belief that far to the north across a wide river lay 'the back part of China', where lived 'a copper coloured people, who would receive and treat them kindly'. Some of the bolters died of fatigue and hunger, or were killed by Aborigines; others wandered back to the settlement, or were brought in by search parties – but reluctantly, saying they wanted 'nothing more than to live free from labour'.

Some First Fleet convicts tried to escape by a different route. Several told the judge advocate that their sentences had expired and that in future they expected to receive rations without working. Their faith in the law was misplaced. Their leader, John Calleghan, was sentenced to 600 lashes and six months hard labour in irons. The severity of the sentence reflected the government's embarrassment. Phillip did not know the expiry dates of many of the convicts' sentences, and feared a mass refusal to work.

Phillip saw no point in restoring expirees to the rights and privileges of free people while they remained dependent on the public store. Ideally he hoped that ex-convicts would support themselves on their own land. In 1790 James Ruse, who described himself as a 'husbandman' from Cornwall, was given land and convict labour to clear it. When the convicts were withdrawn, he chose a wife, Elizabeth Perry: by Ruse's account 'an industrious woman'. By Christmas 1791 the farm was supporting Ruse, Perry and their daughter. After this success Phillip granted land to a number of other small settlers at Norfolk Island and around Parramatta.

Among the first convict smallholders were William and Mary Parr and Simon and Fanny Burn, married on the same day in 1788 and now settling on the same day in 1791 on adjoining land. Neither woman had baptised children in the colony. William Parr was flogged for stealing a pumpkin in the hungry days of 1790. Simon Burn was demoted from overseer for assaulting two soldiers, and lost an eye splitting timber in a sawyers gang. Late in 1791 a government visitor to the farms found Parr and Burn to be 'men of great industry', with 'good houses, which they have hired people to build for them'. Both were cultivating about 3 acres of the 50 allowed them and their wives, and Parr claimed to have spent 13 guineas hiring labour. The nearby settlement at 'the Ponds' was less impressive: the houses were mostly 'wretched hovels' and the corn was blasted by caterpillars. Here Anthony and Elizabeth Rope were cultivating 1 acre of the 70 granted to them. Rope was still under sentence, and worked as a bricklayer during the week, but Elizabeth apparently lived on the grant with Robert, aged three, and Mary, aged about six months.

Phillip was generous to the settlers. Those who continued to cultivate for five years were promised full ownership of their land. They continued 'on the stores', getting the same food, clothes and medicines as the working convicts, for eighteen months after taking up their land. Every landholder received a hatchet, a tomahawk, two hoes, and a spade and shovel. Seed grain was supplied the first year, and sow pigs were promised.

Working alone, or man and woman together, the settlers felled the larger timber, burnt off what they could, dug in the ashes, then laboriously hoed the ground, broke up the clods and dug in the weeds before finally sowing the seed. First yields were good. A visitor in mid-1792 found the farmers 'very comfortably lodged', with enough vegetables and maize to feed themselves and a couple of pigs, and an acre or two in wheat. But within a few years crops began to fail. The problem had been identified by James Ruse as early as 1790. The soil on his farm, he said, was 'middling, neither good nor bad'. He could 'make it do' with the aid of manure, 'but without cattle it will fail'. Stock-keeping on any scale was beyond the financial resources of the small settlers.

Governor Phillip saw another difficulty. He feared that the settlers would grow 'tired of a life so different to that in which they have been brought up', a life that cut them off 'from the gratifications in which most of them have always placed their happiness'. Feasting with friends and displaying fine clothes had made life bearable in Sydney Cove. The rewards of independence and family could not always make up for the loneliness of life on the farms.

Loneliness, and also fear. Phillip's generosity included the stationing of soldiers at each settlement to protect the settlers from hostile Aborigines. In the second half of 1790 a sort of peace was made with the survivors of those Aboriginal groups who were the first to come into contact with the invaders. The survivors seem to have chosen to accept the governor's invitation to live among the white settlers and to share some of their scarce resources – too often the scraps. But groups further out, towards Parramatta and later on the Hawkesbury, remained actively hostile to the rape of their lands.

Phillip returned to England in December 1792. He left a colony whose existence was still fragile. Around Parramatta 1500 acres were under cultivation, and at Norfolk Island 100 acres. The farms produced food enough in good times, but in bad seasons people went hungry. Family life was barely established. Men outnumbered women by five to one in New South Wales, and two to one on Norfolk. In a total population of about 4250 settlers and convicts there were some 700 women, about 250 of them married, and 250 children.

Botany Bay was early rumoured to make the barren fertile. In July 1790 people gathered to marvel at 'an old female convict, her hair quite grey with age, her face wrinkled, who was suckling a child she had born in the colony'. But it was the sudden appearance of children in an almost childless community that gave the illusion of fecundity. The baptism registers kept by the Reverend Johnson may not be a wholly reliable guide to patterns of birth in the colony, especially among women who did not bother to marry legally – though Johnson noted with surprise that even bastards were generally brought to be christened. For what they are worth, the chaplain's records suggest that to May 1790, married convict women baptised on average almost one baby to every three potential mothers, and unmarried convict women only slightly less. The wives of the marines were much more prolific, producing about two children to every three potential mothers.

The evidence suggests that convict women, even married ones, were less fertile than might be expected. Perhaps they had some means of contraception. Leather condoms were known in the brothels of Europe, but it seems unlikely that they had been brought to Botany Bay. Abortion seems more likely, or infanticide. Syphilis may have left women infertile, and depleted rations may have delayed ovulation. Whatever the cause, childless women like Mary Parr and Mary Marshall were typical of their generation.

After Phillip's departure imaginings about the colony's future became more implicit, more trapped in the present.

For three years the governor was not replaced, and the commandants of the New South Wales Corps ruled in the interests of the civil and military officers of the colony. In something like the manner that Matra imagined for his American loyalists, the officer–entrepreneurs repaired their fortunes and enjoyed a domestic felicity based upon the labour of male convicts assigned to their fields, and of female convicts assigned to their homes. Public farming was cut back and convicts redirected to work for the officers, producing grain for the commissariat. The state paid twice for grain supplied by the officers, once in buying it and once in giving it back as rations.

The officers took their profits from the commissariat in spirits, for use in barter with the convicts. Alcohol had always been available for those eager enough to sleep or steal for it. But now it came to rival grain as a means of exchange in a colony with no stable currency. Trading in spirits and other goods produced profits of up to 600 per cent. The officers clubbed together to buy whole cargoes from incoming traders. The goods were retailed by the officers' convict 'washerwomen' – often the mothers of their children – or by enterprising emancipist men with some capital to invest.

The officers quickly grew rich – and none more quickly than John Macarthur. Macarthur had come to the colony with the newly formed New South Wales Corps in 1790, intent on making enough money to become a gentleman. Ideally, gentility depended not on money but on birth, connections and manners, but in practice money had always been able to buy all but the first of these. Macarthur's family were shopkeepers, but education and a commission in a third class regiment had given him a foothold in the world of the gentry. His wife, Elizabeth, was the daughter of a yeoman farmer, educated to be a lady. She was attracted by his 'proud and haughty' ambition, as she described it later; it offered an escape from her 'humble fortune and expectations'.

It was a risky escape route. When they married, with Elizabeth more than three months pregnant, Macarthur's military future was doubtful. Their first child was jostled prematurely into the world by a hurried coach journey across England in an attempt to avoid garrison duty at Gibraltar. Macarthur took up a position with the New South Wales Corps as the only possible alternative to service in the Mediterranean.

At the beginning of their voyage to New South Wales John Macarthur put his life in danger by challenging the captain of their transport to a duel. Towards its end he lay raving and incapable with rheumatic fever, baby Edward wasted almost to death, and Elizabeth gave birth to a baby girl who lived only an hour. For all that, their sufferings were slight in comparison with those of the convicts of the second fleet. Fever and bad food killed almost one in four during the voyage. The Macarthurs feared the convicts' fevers and shrank from their noise and smell. They could not pity creatures so utterly different from themselves.

Once achieved, Sydney seemed worth the perils. Elizabeth Macarthur found her company in demand for dinners and rural excursions. The officers were hungry for intelligent female conversation. Under their tutelage she came to appreciate the peculiar beauties of the bush. She met some of the Port Jackson Aborigines, finding them gentle and interesting.

While Elizabeth Macarthur worked to build up the family's social capital, John Macarthur sought more tangible assets. Government posts gave him access to personal power: as regimental paymaster he had use of the regimental funds, and as inspector of public works he controlled the public grain stores and the labour of convicts on public farms at Parramatta. The lieutenant governor granted him a hundred acres of the best land yet discovered near Parramatta, and ten convicts to work it, plus 'a very fine cow in calf'. Now with two small children, Elizabeth Macarthur found the cow 'a gift beyond any value that can be placed upon it'. By 1798 his Parramatta farm had grown to nearly 500 acres, largely under wheat. His livestock included 50 head of cattle, 12 horses, 1000 sheep, and hundreds of pigs and goats. The government bricklayers had built an excellent brick house for the family, with fine gardens and orchards.

Life was more difficult on the small farms. In autumn 1798 the seventeen families still farming at the Ponds had only 80 bushels of wheat between them for winter food and next season's sowing. By this time most of the colony's farmers tilled the banks of the Hawkesbury River, where frequent flooding kept the soil fertile. Ex-convicts often held tiny plots of land, living on the potatoes and corn that grew easily in the rich black soil, and washed away in the floods. Anthony and Elizabeth Rope did better than most. They increased their holding at the Ponds to 30 acres, and moved later to the upper Hawkesbury, buying 40 acres there in 1806 to employ themselves and their seven children.

Governor Hunter arrived in 1796 with orders to expand public farming at the expense of private. By 1798 he was being asked to rescue the private farmers. The 'sober, industrious men' of the Hawkesbury blamed their distress on excessive wages and prices, the traditional objects of public protest among English tenants and labourers. The villains they identified were also familiar ones – middlemen who were inflating prices at the expense of honest consumers and producers. Two years later a new set of villains was emerging. A petition from the Hawkesbury accused the officer farmers of monopolising government stock and labour, sales to the commissariat, and importation of goods, all to the detriment of ordinary settlers. Hunter dismissed this version of the colony's political economy as a slur upon his administration.

The Burn family did not make the move to the Hawkesbury. In mid-1794 the Reverend Samuel Marsden was outraged by something Simon Burn said to him 'in a most daring manner' as he finished a sermon at Parramatta. The subject was undoubtedly the relative virtues of the Church of England and the Catholic Church. Marsden claimed that Burn was drunk. He was outraged again when Captain John Macarthur, the local magistrate, dismissed his complaint as 'vexatious'. Simon Burn's first protest had been more polite. In November 1792 he and four others had petitioned for the appointment of a Catholic 'pastor'. They told Phillip that they were loyal citizens of New South Wales, and 'that nothing else could induce us ever to depart from his Majesty's colony here unless the idea of going into eternity without the assistance of a Catholic priest'.

Burn and Frances Anderson had been married by a Church of England minister in the first weeks of settlement; presumably his faith grew more exclusive as more Irish men and women joined him in New South Wales. The first convicts sentenced in Ireland arrived in 1791, some convicted of overtly political crimes, and many of the others for crimes of violence that carried an element of protest against British rule.

In the event Simon Burn went into eternity without clerical 'assistance'. Only a few weeks after his argument with Marsden, Burn was stabbed to death when he tried to stop a husband from beating a wife. Six years earlier Fanny Burn had protected a mother and child from a drunken convict. She buried Simon Burn 'in a corner of his own farm', with an all-night wake. Settlers from miles around ate and drank to his memory. An official dismissed the Burns as an 'unfortunate' couple, too fond of 'spiritous liquors' to succeed on their farm. Their neighbours knew them better.

In 1800 and 1801 many hundreds of Irish prisoners arrived, pushing the percentage of Irish to more than one-third of those under sentence, and one-quarter of the white population. Governor King nervously estimated that more than half of the recent arrivals were Catholic 'Defenders', summarily transported for their part in the massive Irish rebellion of 1798. The governor set up Loyal Associations in Sydney and Parramatta, on the model of Protestant Ireland. The volunteers were given rations, armed, officered and drilled on military lines. Elizabeth Paterson, wife of officer William Paterson, reported that the military and the Loyal Associations 'would not be sorry' for an excuse to put down the Irish; her private 'terror' was of 'assassins, breaking into our houses at dead of night'.

In March 1804 several Defenders at the farming settlement of Castle Hill persuaded and bullied more than 300 men – many of them Protestants – to take up rifles, swords and improvised pikes, and to march upon Parramatta. Their battle cry was 'death or liberty'; their aim the capture of vessels in Sydney Cove to take them home. The rebels hesitated outside Parramatta – defended only by its Loyal Association – but turned and straggled towards the Hawkesbury. After a forced march from Sydney, Lieutenant George Johnston overtook them with a handful of men: twenty-eight soldiers and a score of armed volunteers. He pretended to parley, captured the leaders and mowed down the followers in a bloody crossfire. Johnston commended the bravery of his troops, only regretting their 'being too fond of Blood' in their eagerness to slaughter survivors.

Castle Hill should be remembered as the largest revolt in Australian history, and perhaps as the most dangerous to authority. Historians have tried to read the uprising as evidence of a united convict response to their servitude. They point to the presence of English convicts among the rebel leaders, to Governor King's belief that the rebels' numbers would double once they reached the Hawkesbury, and to Johnston's furious efforts to halt them short of the river flats. But beyond the fears of the authorities, evidence of convict and emancipist solidarity is hard to find. Far from welcoming the rebels, the ex-convict population of Parramatta signed up as loyal volunteers to defend the town. The Hawkesbury reaction in 1804 is beyond knowing – but three years later a petition supporting the suppression of yet another Irish plot was signed by almost 500 settlers of the region, mostly ex-convicts and their children.

British politicians still thought of Botany Bay as a gaol, when they thought of it at all. But on the numbers it already belonged to the ex-convicts and their children, and many were already comfortably settled. By 1805 the 5000 adults in New South Wales included more ex-convicts – about 2200 – than convicts under sentence. In the struggling new settlements in Van Diemen's Land the few hundred white inhabitants were mostly convicts or soldiers, but they would soon be joined by scores of emancipist families resettled from Norfolk Island. Botany Bay was a gaol whose inmates worked independently for their living, or for that of their families.

A majority of the freed men – and many of the serving convicts – worked for wages. Demand for labour far exceeded the supply, and men could ask for high wages by British standards. Governors Hunter and King tried several times to fix the task rates for agricultural work by proclamation, settlers having complained that 'the wages demanded by the free labouring people' ate up all their profits. But the rates that were regularly paid exceeded the set rates by as much as 500 per cent. And yet high wages did not guarantee prosperity. Prices were also higher than in Britain. Workers received part of their wages in kind, often in spirits, which did nothing to encourage thrift. Families on wages would normally have needed additional income to survive, and in years of bad harvests everyone must have been in want.

Some ex-convicts grew rich. Of the dozen men holding more

than 300 acres of farming land in 1806, four were emancipists. But landowning on this scale was not the result of wage labour. All the large landowners in the colony – ex-convicts, officers and free immigrants – bought most of their acres from the profits of more varied enterprises: trading, retailing, renting, shipbuilding, sealing and whaling, manufacturing, and government employment.

Henry Kable, the young burglar from Norwich, was by 1806 a wealthy trader and shipbuilder in Sydney. His career shows the kinds of money-making activities available to the enterprising – and lucky – ex-convict. The basis of the Kables's fortune was a gift of books and clothes donated in 1788 by the sentimental readers of *Scots Magazine*. The goods were plundered in transit, but the colony's first civil action awarded 15 pounds damages to the Kables, and established that convicts under sentence in New South Wales could still enjoy the legal rights of freeborn Englishmen.

Their next benefactor was the colonial government. Henry Kable held a series of minor appointments under the crown: overseer, constable, member of the night watch, keeper of the gaol and chief constable. As gaoler he was thought by some to be too friendly with his richer prisoners, and he was dismissed as chief constable in 1803 for breaking port regulations. The government favoured him with grants of farming land in 1794 and 1795, which he consolidated by buying the land of four of his neighbours within a week of their grants being signed. What the officers achieved on a grand scale, Kable and his fellow emancipists wrought a little more humbly.

Profits from these activities were invested firstly in trade within the colony, and then from 1800 in harvesting the produce of the Pacific Ocean. In company with another ex-convict, James Underwood, Kable took up boatbuilding, sending out crews to slaughter seals and whales as they calved in the bays on the southern coast. Underwood's skill lay in turning and shaping wood, Kable's in keeping accounts and juggling figures as 'ship's husband' – a role he later filled in a profitable partnership with Underwood and an even more 'opulent' emancipist, Simeon Lord.

Lord's vision spanned the Pacific. He was endlessly inventive in what economic historians have called the search for a 'staple' – sealskins, seal and whale oil, trepang, sandlewood – any article that could be profitably traded in India, China or Britain in exchange for the goods the colony needed to import. Lord was second only to John Macarthur in setting up contacts with British and American traders to circumvent the East India Company's monopoly in the Pacific. By the end of the decade more than a dozen emancipists were making profits matching those of the officer traders.

What were women doing as convicts and workers and traders? The sentence of transportation fell differently on men and women. In 1800 women made up about a quarter of those still under sentence, but about half of those freed. The imbalance reflected both the better survival rate of women during the famine years, when men were worked more cruelly, and the inability of women to escape the colony by working their passage back to England. Transportation treated men as workers, and women as reproducers – lovers and mothers. The system was easier on women, and trapped them more securely.

Governor King devised a novel form of 'public labour' for those women who remained 'on the government' – mostly, he said, the 'incorrigible' women. The governor still cherished the hope that had sent him to Norfolk Island in 1788, the hope of supplying naval stores for Britain's fleets in the Pacific. King wrote confidently to Sir Joseph Banks that hemp and flax grew in the colony 'with the utmost luxuriance'. He anticipated that all unassigned convicts might be used to raise flax, 'which with the ship-timber and the sail cloth that might be exported from hence, would well entitle this colony to the attention of England'.

So in 1804 King made the first floor of the new gaol at Parramatta a 'manufactory' for weaving cloth from flax and wool grown in New South Wales. Nine looms produced linen, duck, blanketing, flannel, sacking and sailcloth. Sixty women were employed in 1804, and ninety-six a year later. The Female Factory, as it came to be known, supplied most of the convicts' needs for clothing, and some of the boatmakers' needs for sailcloth. It also served as a very crowded 'asylum' for women newly arrived in the colony, and a sleeping place for those women working the looms who did not choose to find beds and bedmates in Parramatta.

A convict woman who chose to marry exchanged the authority of the government for that of a husband, and laboured in his house. Many were prepared to take the gamble; more than two-thirds of the women still under sentence in 1804 seem to have been working only as wives, legal or otherwise. Governor King reported that some were 'very useful not only in domestic concerns and rearing stock, but also in agriculture'. He admitted that 'Although ... they do no public labour, yet their domestic concerns and providing for their families is an advantage to the society they are placed in.'

Margaret Catchpole chose not to marry. Her crime was dressing as a man in order to steal a thoroughbred stallion to help her lover, a smuggler. She was transported in 1801 and assigned as a cook. Catchpole wrote home that she and her women friends did 'very well'. They did not have to slave like the men convicts: 'we are free of all hard work'. When her sentence was completed Catchpole rented a small farm on the Hawkesbury, and by hiring labour and working 'a great deal myself' she raised enough corn and stock to live alone and independently. She reassured her English family that her two dogs took care of her, and that 'I have a good many friends that I go to see when I think proper, such as I have nursed when they lay in [in childbirth] cannot do without me, I am looked upon very well thank God'.

Catchpole was an exceptional woman, and chose an exceptional way of life. Most convict women could see no alternative to some form of marriage. The 1806 muster lists less than sixty self-employed women among more than 800 ex-convict women in the colony, and another score with some trade or occupation – 10 per cent in all. A few women became successful small traders, often in partnership with an officer. Sara Bird, transported in 1794, managed 'a little trade' at ports along the way, and arrived at Sydney with 'a number of small articles, such as sugar, tea, tobacco, thread, snuff, needles, and every thing I could get anything by'. She also sold her clothes – her petticoats at 2 guineas each, and her black silk cloak at 10 guineas. With the profits she opened a public house under the sign of the 'Three Jolly Settlers'. She wrote to her father that she lived by herself, and enjoyed 'a tolerable success in the public line'. But Sara Bird lost her independence in 1804 when she was attacked and crippled by a man she had rejected.

Mary Reiby, another horse stealer, traded successfully in the Pacific after her husband's death. Some historians have seen this as proof a woman could succeed on her own. Others have claimed that the success belonged to her husband. Perhaps one should ask whether a man could succeed on his own. Most of the Sydney traders carried on their businesses from houses located close to the wharves, and while they were away at sea or on the Hawkesbury their wives seem to have handled their affairs. Mary Hyde bore Simeon Lord's children and managed the mansion in Bridge Street where he entertained visiting sea captains; the upper rooms were at the disposal of men dealing with Lord while they were in port. Lord's warehouses and later his manufactories were located next to his house, and after his death Mary Hyde carried on his manufacturing activities.

Some men acknowledged their debt during their lifetime. While under sentence Sam Terry lived and worked with Mary Shipley, who was charged at the same Lancaster quarter sessions and arrived on the same convict transport as Terry in 1801. When Sam Terry married another businesswoman in 1809 he made a settlement on his old partner, Mary Shipley, 'in consideration of her faithful services'. It included the house they had shared in Pitt Street, a cow and a heifer, and a chaise and driving horse whose opulence had annoyed their neighbours. Shipley turned the Pitt Street house into a public house, and took herself a husband before the end of the year.

In 1806 the Reverend Samuel Marsden gathered evidence of the sinfulness of the women of New South Wales. He hoped to persuade the bureaucrats of the Colonial Office to increase the numbers of moral missionaries – priests and schoolmasters – they supported in the colony. He drew up a 'Female Register', a list of all the women in the colony, noting in each case whether or not the woman was legally married, and the number and legal status of her children. The sum of his findings was that of the 1430 women in the colony, almost two-thirds were what he called 'concubines'.

Marsden's 'evidence' damned the reputation of the women of Botany Bay, but it was patently false. His 'concubine' category included native-born girls of twelve and widows of seventy. Margaret Catchpole, living alone, was entered as 'C' for concubine. So were a number of Irish women married by Catholic rites in the colony. Beyond this, the judgment implied in the term 'concubine' was unjustified. Governor King wrote of Marsden's 'unmarried and concubine' category that there were 'very few of the unmarried but who cohabit openly with one man', in other words in long-term stable relationships unsanctified by the Church of England.

King had lived with a convict woman, Ann Innett, on Norfolk Island, and cared for their two children as members of his family. He rejected any proposal 'to lock all the females up until they are so fortunate as to obtain husbands'. He argued 'against compelling the women and men to marry beyond their own inclinations', and believed that marriage would be brought into disrepute, as 'a mere act of convenience'. But his arguments carried less weight with the Colonial Office than Marsden's tales of corruption.

The governors who followed King were sent out with instructions to promote marriage. In a rare moment of generosity, the Colonial Office told Governor William Bligh to abandon the policy of disposing of convict women 'to improper Persons' merely to get them off the stores; rather he should 'endeavour to make the Reformation of the Female Convict and her regular settlement by marriage a Consideration superior to the saving, for any short period, the expense of maintaining her'.

Bligh was a sailor, a ship's boy become captain in His Majesty's navy. He was a short-tempered, foul-mouthed man who hated to be crossed; his belief in rigid discipline in small things had already caused one mutiny against him. He despised the traders, believing them to be dishonest, litigious and disrespectful. He had Kable, Lord and Underwood fined and imprisoned for a month for writing to him in improper terms. He shouted at visiting merchants for minor breaches of port regulations. And he harangued John Macarthur – a man even more fiery tempered than himself – for seeking to have more land and flocks in New South Wales than any other man had had before.

Bligh's sympathies were with the small settlers attempting to make a living from the soil. He feared that they were 'not honest, have no prudence, and little industry', but he attempted to help them. Acting on one of Marsden's suggestions, Bligh banned the exchange of liquor 'for grain, animal food, labour, wearing apparel, or any commodity whatever'. He intended an economic as well as a moral effect, to bring 'labour to a due value and support the farming interest'.

The prohibition ran directly against the interests of the importers, officers and emancipists alike, uniting them against the governor. And to ban the barter of spirits without introducing another form of currency gave little relief to small employers and consumers. The exchange of goods for spirits went on. Rumour had it that even Bligh's daughter bought eggs for his breakfast with a glass of rum.

Direct assistance to the settlers was more useful. Bligh allowed them more convict labour, and supplied government cattle at half the market price, encouraging them 'not only to plough, but to manure and fence in their grounds'. He believed that by fallowing, by manuring, and by growing only as much grain as 'the Farmer can keep clean and secure ... his family wants in the year should be provided, his excess should be capable of being turned into good payments to procure his other necessities, and the independence which every good man looks forward to, and blessed hope tells him to expect'. Here already is the belief, so influential in Australian history, that honest agricultural toil by a man and his family is a sure basis for economic and moral independence.

Many of the smallholders responded to Bligh by signing one or another of a series of formal addresses to the governor – signing, or marking their name with a cross. The addresses thanked Bligh for his measures on behalf of 'proprietors of landed property', and asked for further legal and economic reforms. One complained that John Macarthur had signed an address 'For the Inhabitants' without the settlers' authority. On 1 January 1808, a month before Macarthur engineered a military coup to depose Bligh, 833 signatories thanked the governor for his 'Arduous, Just, Determined and Salutary Government over us'. These addresses were among the papers that Bligh hurried to gather up when the rebels invaded Government House, bayonets fixed and flags flying, on 26 January 1806.

When the soldiers found Governor Bligh he was considering escape through a side window (and not hiding under a bed, as his detractors later claimed). He told the British court investigating the rebellion that his goal was the Hawkesbury, 'where I was sure that the people would flock to my standard, and give all their aid in defending me'. There has been much debate about what the Hawkesbury settlers thought of Bligh. Sceptics have argued that the addresses do not speak for ordinary farmers. Certainly it was large landowners, emancipist and free, who were busy getting up the addresses. Some small farmers had no part in it; Anthony Rope and his grown sons signed none of them. But more than half the landholders on the Hawkesbury signed at least one address, including many of the poorest. Bligh may well have had more chance of calling the Hawkesbury settlers to his standard than the Irish rebels would have. Years later an old emancipist looked back to Bligh's golden years: 'Them were the days for the poor settler, he had only to tell the Governor what he wanted and he was able to get it from the store'.

Women signed the addresses too, but only when no man was present on the property. Signing was a political act, proper only for the head of the household – a token, perhaps, of the manly independence that Bligh promised.

3 Transplanting Patriarchy

In 1810 Mary Marshall was some forty years of age. She had lived more than twenty years with the well-dressed baker Robert Sideway, working with him in various business ventures, including the colony's first theatre. The couple were childless, and a young girl whom they adopted in the early 1790s died in 1806 after Mary had nursed her through paralysis and insanity. They had never married, perhaps because of a radical dislike of church and state. Sideway died in 1809, leaving to his partner their jointly earned property and a library large by colonial standards.

Early in 1810 Marshall wrote to the new governor, Lachlan Macquarie, asking him to confirm her in possession of some 'Leased Ground and Premises' held by Sideway. Macquarie refused her the lease. In February he issued a proclamation condemning 'the scandalous and pernicious custom generally and shamelessly adopted throughout the territory of persons of different sexes cohabiting or living together, unsanctionned by the legalities of marriage', and promising to withdraw his 'favour and patronage' from all people living in illegal unions. Whether careless or principled, Marshall's neglect of marriage could not go unnoticed.

Like previous governors, Macquarie was instructed to abate what the British authorities saw as the flagrant immorality of the colony. He took up the challenge gladly. The son of a poor Scottish crofter, Macquarie had been educated and placed in a British army post by the patronage of wealthy clansmen, and risked his career to bring his young cousins and nephews after him into a more civilised imperial world. He approached the squalid settlements of New South Wales like 'an improving landlord intent on developing a personal estate'. In the words of his latest biographer, office as governor gave Macquarie 'the means of translating his private values into a public sphere'.

In his personal life Macquarie was ruled by restraint and self-discipline, and he hoped to remake his citizens in the same mould. He tried to order public morals by prohibiting nude bathing, profanation of the Sabbath, and 'riotous assemblies' in pubs and brothels. But the problem lay deeper, in 'the sanction given to Fornication'. Like Marsden he hoped that matrimony would restore domestic order, between men and women and between parents and children. 'Without matrimony no Instruction given by the Schoolmasters, no labors of the Clergy, no Power of the executive Authority can render any moral and religious advantage to the rising Generation.'

The godly people of Sydney were delighted. The evangelical *Sydney Gazette* published the cautionary tale of a convict beauty, Clorinda, who neglected to marry the father of her five 'blooming babes', thus denying them their patrimony on their father's untimely death. Could such 'ill-fated orphans', asked the *Gazette*, ever forgive the mother 'whose preference to immoral habits hath intailed calamity upon you?'

Numbers of cohabiting women felt the lash of the new morality. Some lost land, like Mary Marshall. Sarah Wood lost her freedom. Sarah Wood had been nineteen years old when she was sentenced in 1801 to transportation for life. Her occupation, farm housekeeper, and her crime, theft of two 10 shilling bills, both suggest responsibilities beyond her years. In New South Wales she worked as an assigned servant for three years before leaving the government service to live with a 'husband'. By 1806 she was renting a farm at Georges River to support herself and two small children. In 1809 her old employer asked and received a free pardon for her from Colonel Paterson. In 1810 Macquarie revoked her pardon, facing her with a return to assignment and the loss of her surviving child to the government orphanage.

The early years of Macquarie's rule saw the marriages of most of the ex-officers and wealthy emancipists who still lived 'unsanctionned'. Sam Terry put aside Mary Shipley and married Rosetta Marsh in March 1810. Thomas Arndell, surgeon on the *Friendship* – the object of Elizabeth Barber's accusations – married Elizabeth Dalton, mother of his eight children, in the same year. George

Johnston married Esther Abrahams in 1814, after fifteen years and seven children. The marriage of Mary Hyde to Simeon Lord took place in 1814 also.

More humble couples made the same strategic decision. Sarah Wood escaped the government in 1810 by taking up residence with a young ex-convict farmer, Thomas Galvin. By 1814 they had four children – one from Sarah's previous partnership, and three from this. They did not marry immediately; Sarah may have been reluctant to accept a husband's authority, and Thomas was a committed Roman Catholic, suspicious of the Church of England. But in October 1815 the Galvins travelled in to Parramatta to be married by the Reverend Samuel Marsden, taking with them their two youngest children to be baptised. Earlier the same year Sarah received a conditional pardon from Macquarie – conditional upon good behaviour and residence in the colony.

Historians have seen Macquarie's proclamation as establishing legal marriage as the norm in New South Wales, at least for couples 'who aspired to the protection of government'. But it is not clear how far his writ ran. Magistrates and clergymen reported large increases in the numbers marrying during his governorship, but these may reflect no more than the increasing numbers of convict women arriving in the colony and native-born women coming of age.

In 1819 a government clerk made a list of the seventy-five convicts working for the government in Sydney – overseers and skilled artisans in charge of other men – who were permitted to draw rations for women and children living with them. It is some test of Macquarie's power to compel matrimony (and of his need for skilled men) that fully one-third of these favoured couples remained unmarried.

The circumstances of these couples reveal something of the uses of cohabitation to ordinary women and men in New South Wales. The men were mostly convicts still under sentence and as such were lucky to enjoy domesticity; from June 1819 almost all the 2000 government men working round Sydney had to live in barracks or camps. Overseers often carried on their trades alongside their work for the government, and for this a partner was invaluable; the chief engineer reported to Commissioner Bigge that 'their wives attend to the business in the Shop' – or workshop, in the language of the time. So when Margaret Birgin married the tailoring overseer Martin Quinn in 1819 she would have been expected to supervise the work of his assigned servant, a shoemaker, and probably to sell the goods they made.

For the men, domestic life was a privilege and a benefit. For women it was almost a necessity. For those women still under sentence, almost half the number of men, public commitment to one man was an escape from government control and a necessary refuge, the old Female Factory being hopelessly overcrowded and the new one unfinished. 'Free' women had little more choice. A handful of the sample were wives who had 'come free' to the colony, choosing to follow a convicted husband. A few more were native born, daughters of convicts. Most were 'free by servitude', in theory able to return to their old lives in Britain, in practice constrained by the lack of paid work to much the same range of choice as their sisters under sentence.

One decision still open to these couples, despite Macquarie's blustering, was whether or not to marry – and here the free women clearly preferred to keep their options open. Little more than half of them were legally married to their partners, compared to almost three-quarters of those still under sentence. The governor's word lay heavier on the latter. Children were another constraint; women with children were more often married than those without, and married women had three times as many children as their less committed sisters. When Harriet Blake, a thirty-five year old widow, married George Johnson, in 1819, her three surviving children were aged four, eight and eleven. A husband was useful to a woman with small children.

The governor's word lay still heavier in the years that followed. Governors Brisbane and Darling were instructed to make the system of assignment both cheaper and more efficient in reforming the convicts. Both men believed that female virtue (and male obligation) were best nourished in the home, and Darling hoped to extend the joys and duties of matrimony throughout the community. In 1826 he wrote into the regulations the privileges long informally allowed to men and women still under sentence – assignment of bond wives to free husbands (and occasionally vice versa), residence outside the barracks and Female Factory, a common master where both partners were still under sentence – but limited these privileges to those legally married.

Darling also looked more closely at convicts' applications to marry, requiring applicants to prove themselves to be of good character and unmarried. In practice the first requirement was often ignored, the second rigidly enforced. Male convicts arriving in the colony rarely admitted to being married. Women often did, apparently having heard that matrimony was useful in New South Wales. They were cruelly mistaken; as a historian has written recently, 'it was the availability to marry which mattered', for it was the act of marriage that released convicts from government service. Government records from the 1830s carry a rich lode of petitions, affidavits, recommendations and letters from back home telling of the sad death of spouses, the last regularly forged: all good evidence of the urgent desire of convicted men and women to escape the government — by the 1830s, necessarily by legal marriage.

The marriage applications offer practical reasons for matrimony; potential husbands and wives are presented as sober, industrious and well conducted. This was what the authorities wanted to hear. But the convicts themselves seem to have undertaken marriage in a calculating way, without much sentiment. Women often applied to marry several men within a few weeks, choosing the best prospect when all the bids were in. Thus early in 1831 Margaret Allen wavered between David Reghan, an emancipist, and Joseph Woodcock, ticket of leave, finally choosing the older and better established Woodcock.

The experience of the seventy-five couples listed in 1819 suggests that convicts could look for little permanence in sexual relationships. Of the forty couples whose lives could be traced, only fifteen were still living together in 1828. Legally married couples where the wife was free and had no need to marry seem to have been the most inclined to stay together. The presence of children, on the other hand, made little difference to a couple's chances. In cases where the circumstances are known, couples were commonly separated by death or desertion, or the action of government. The tailor Martin Quinn was undergoing secondary punishment in a road gang in 1828, forcing his wife, Margaret, to put the eldest of their three children into the Orphan School. The case of Thomas Messling, a carpenter, may illustrate the fate of many untraceable relationships. Messling told Commissioner Bigge that having received an absolute pardon, he intended returning to England, leaving his 'wife' his tools to sell to support her and her child.

Relationships between cohabiting couples – by the 1830s between husbands and wives – were premised on male authority and too often enforced by male violence. But passion could draw men and women into settled relationships, and affection could grow in arrangements based on calculation and convenience. Samuel Marsden told Commissioner Bigge of a convict couple he married at Parramatta. They 'seemed to be very happy' until news came of the arrival of the wife's first husband, a sailor whom she had thought dead. 'She was so Distressed she did not know what to do.' The two husbands and the wife came to Marsden, 'all Three greatly affected'. 'She said that her second husband had been a kind and good husband to her, and he said that she had been a good wife and lived happily together', but when Marsden asked her to choose, the woman preferred her first husband. Marsden believed the law concurred, and the woman left with her sailor. 'The second husband', said Marsden, 'has been unhappy ever since'.

The tearful interview with Marsden shows how the government's marriage policy put the personal decisions of convict women and men into the hands of magistrates and clergymen and ultimately governors. By the 1820s critics of government would characterise such intervention as tyranny. But ordinary couples got so used to a public ordering of their private lives that ex-convicts and even the native born asked the governor's permission to marry. As late as 1836 the colonial secretary needed to inform a clergyman that 'His Excellency does not interfere with the marriage of free persons'.

Macquarie also set about ordering the lives of those Aborigines who had survived the European invasion of their lands. Convict bolters, and disease endangered Aboriginal life and culture far beyond the boundaries of white settlement on the plains north and west of Sydney Town. But the groups whose lands lay within those boundaries suffered most acutely. Where corn grew and cattle grazed, settlers and armed soldiers prevented the Aborigines from hunting and gathering food. Bands of warriors resisted, sometimes driving settlers temporarily back to Sydney; spears were more deadly than muzzle-loaded guns in a brief encounter. But sustained warfare was foreign to Aboriginal culture, and the bands were weakened by hunger and disease; they could not stand against armed troops. The survivors had two choices: to move beyond white settlement, onto the lands of often hostile Aboriginal neighbours, or to become beggars, dependent on white charity.

The new governor respected Aborigines as individuals. He believed that their acts of hostility against settlers were the result of 'Provocation or Aggression', and that 'Kindness, Encouragement and Social Intercourses' with European society would bring the Aborigines rapidly and easily into 'Civilization'. To that end he attempted two experiments. In 1814 he established a 'Native Institution' to educate some of the Aboriginal children, and he offered land in Port Jackson to 'a few of the Adult Natives, Who have promised to Settle there and Cultivate the Ground'. Convicts cleared the land, built huts, and turned up the ground for vegetable patches. Rations and clothes were supplied to the Aborigines, and a fishing boat. A European was detailed to live on the site and assist the Aboriginal settlers.

In 1816 clashes between black and white on the Hawkesbury again became too violent to be ignored. Macquarie's solution reveals a community at war. A proclamation forbad Aborigines to carry weapons; any six or more men gathering near an isolated settlement could be regarded as enemies and fired upon. On the other hand 'passports' would be issued to all Aborigines agreeing to act in a 'peaceful, inoffensive and honest Manner'. Those laying down their spears would be protected by the British Government and given land and every assistance to cultivate it, and to 'relinquish their wandering idle predatory Habits of Life'.

In December 1816 Macquarie instituted what he hoped would become an annual 'Congress' of Aborigines at Parramatta. More than 700 men, women and children attended, some coming from as far away as the Blue Mountains, first crossed by Europeans in the previous year. They feasted on beef, bread, potatoes, lemonade and rum, and doubtless took advantage of the occasion to negotiate trade and marriages with distant kin.

The event initiated the visitors into the ways of British patriarchy. Aboriginal society had no individual leaders whose words were always to be obeyed; men and women both acted as leaders of different activities. Macquarie identified a prominent man within each language group, seated him upon a chair above the rest, and presented him with an engraved breastplate declaring him to be the chief of his tribe. Then the dozen Aboriginal children living and studying at the Native Institution arrived 'in a neat procession' with Mrs Macquarie and their teacher, Elizabeth Shelley. The boys were wearing tailored suits and caps, the girls linen bonnets and crisp white dresses. In the school the boys were taught gardening and the girls dressmaking. The Aboriginal women cried when they saw their children. The male chiefs were brought forward to 'examine' the children's skills in 'the civilized habits of life', in this case their ability to recite the Christian catechism and to read aloud. One Aboriginal man reportedly exclaimed that his 'pickaninny' would make 'a good settler'.

But none of Macquarie's experiments succeeded. On the Hawkesbury the passport system soon degenerated into an excuse for armed white settlers to harass and sometimes murder unarmed groups of Aborigines. The Native Institution taught dozens of Aboriginal children to read and write, some to high levels of literacy; when the colony's schoolchildren were examined in 1819 an Aboriginal girl won the chief prize. But after their schooling almost all the Aboriginal children chose to return to their families, putting away white culture, and within a few years the institution closed for want of pupils. The Aboriginal settlers at Port Jackson found little value in continually tilling the soil. Some sold their land; others went in search of traditional food, and the huts and gardens were destroyed in their absence. The conduct of the annual congress at Parramatta charted the decline of Aboriginal population and culture across the 1820s; by the end of the decade only a few score attended to receive the blankets that had replaced their possum-skin cloaks.

Macquarie's vision included a physical as well as a moral reshaping of New South Wales. Civilisation as he understood it would flourish in a cultivated landscape, in villages well served with roads and bridges, and townships graced with wide straight streets and elegant public buildings.

To construct all this the governor transformed the scruffy government work gangs into an industrial workforce. By late 1819 the man in charge of public works, the government engineer, Major George Druitt, controlled more than 1900 male convicts in the Sydney area. Most were labourers in unskilled work gangs, cutting grass, building roads, gathering shells for lime, working the government farms. Perhaps 800 were skilled men, working in the dockyard, the lumberyard, the brick kilns, and various building sites around Sydney as cooks, bakers, tailors, shoemakers, weavers, carpenters, sawyers, brickmakers, wheelwrights, blacksmiths and whitesmiths, founders, painters, plasterers, bricklayers, saddlers, masons and boatbuilders. Within these trades were specialisations unheard of today – shingle splitters, hammerers, cutters, nailers. Most of these were trades that the convicts had followed in Britain before their conviction.

Historians have often described the convicts as habitual criminals, living by their wits and their light fingers. To argue this is to disregard the occupations that many men and women claimed on their arrival. A recent study of the convicts suggests that rather than 'a criminal class' they represented a fair selection of the working people of Britain. Flash young women and men who probably preferred prostitution and theft to wage labour made up a significant minority. But most were domestic servants of various kinds, farmworkers, and young artisans, newly trained in their crafts and wandering in search of work. As such they were probably distinguished from more stay-at-home fellows mainly by a sense of adventure, a carelessness about property, and bad luck.

The convicts' mobility in Britain marked them not as criminals, but as members of a class of workers almost as worrying to British employers – the class of 'free labour'. Such women and men were not tied to employers by bonds of locality, or status, or long-term indenture; they were wage labourers employed by the task or the day, and they were always ready to argue, to strike, or to move on in search of better money. In the colony, convicts still under sentence had won certain rights from both government and private employers, rights to money wages in addition to their rations, to a limited working day, to payment by the task, and the right to work 'on their own hands' in the afternoon. Even with these incentives – and the threat of the lash, or of retransportation to Van Diemen's Land – convicts failed to come to work, or failed to work when they came. In his search for efficiency, for industrial discipline, Macquarie had again to change the pattern of the convicts' lives.

That 'handsome brick structure', the men's barracks, was intended to be both the symbol and the means of that remaking. It is strange to recall that before the barracks were opened in June

1819, government convicts were supervised only while they were at work. Where and how they ate, slept, and (within limits) enjoyed their leisure time was their own affair. Macquarie told a reluctant home government that a common barracks was necessary 'to enable the executive Authority to keep a due control' over the convicts, and 'by that Means to lay the Foundation for their more Speedy Reformation'. Inmates rose, slept and ate by the bell. They worked longer hours, were marched to and from work, and could not earn money after hours – at least in theory. In practice the men won back many of their privileges in the years that followed, refusing to work without them.

Macquarie's workforce was criticised by colonial landowners and businessmen hungry for the skilled labour that he devoted to roads and public buildings. Governing New South Wales was a thankless task in these decades. Every governor found himself and his policies aground between changing tides of government in Britain and gales of criticism in the colony. The difficulty lay in steering a course between public and private interest in the colony, and between changing definitions of those interests.

Macquarie's understanding was close to Phillip's. He took the public interest to include the penal concerns of the home government – the punishment and reform of the convicts – and equally the creation of a new civil society for ex-convicts and their children. Private interests he came to see as selfish; he unrepentantly told the commission of inquiry into his conduct of the colony that he would 'continue to prefer the interests of the Crown to the unreasonable and impertinent applications of many who ... have already received more favour and indulgence' than they deserved.

The bitterest opposition to Macquarie centred on his attempts to open public life in New South Wales to men of the emancipist class. Public life – defined as the polite and powerful world of officers and gentlemen, not the roistering life of the streets and the pubs – revolved around the governor and his chosen circle. Power lay in access to land and labour, to government employment and to the magistracy, the central sign and means of gentility. But Macquarie's elevation of emancipists like Simeon Lord to the magistracy created nothing like the outrage caused when he opened his table at Government House to ex-convict men and the more respectable of their wives. The governor's private life was to this extent public, and his wife was implicated in his attempt to redraw the limits of 'society'. Elizabeth Macquarie gladly supported her husband and went beyond him in plain speaking about social justice and pretension. Samuel Marsden called her Herodias, the tyrannous wife of a tyrant, misusing power for public ends.

Those wishing to exclude the emancipists objected also to Macquarie's refusal to favour them in the allocation of land and convict labour, and to his preference for small farming. The British Government was more worried about the expense of his public building program, and the very success of his hope of making 'this country ... the home and a happy home to every emancipated convict who deserves it'. Believing that exile to New South Wales was no longer a sentence fearful enough to deter the desperate from theft and violence, the government sent J. T. Bigge to discover how – if at all – transportation could be made at once more terrifying and less expensive.

Commissioner Bigge solved the problem by recommending that most convicts be set to work for private employers, at the employers' expense, and that those who would not work be punished with penalties severe enough to damn the names of the convict colonies in Britain. He was persuaded by John Macarthur and others that rural assignment would at once reform urban criminals and support the growth of a colonial wool industry profitable to British manufacturers. Bigge believed that the growth of civilisation in the colonies required a 'moral ascendancy' of freeman over emancipist and of landowner over labourer. By restricting the access of ex-convicts to land, labour and public office he left them no alternative but wage labour. Phillip's dream of a contented peasantry had always been doomed by economics; now it was killed by bureaucracy.

Assignment during the 1820s and 1830s was thus directed to the profit of landowners, ideally gentlemen, and to the reform of convicts, reform being understood as transformation into a docile labour force. In principle the landowners and their families became the agents of reform; convicts had to be fed, clothed and housed at a level arguably better than that enjoyed by rural labourers in Britain, and were to be removed if treated too harshly or too much like family. In practice their working lives were shaped by their usefulness as workers, and the skilled fared much better than the unskilled.

Convicts fought for what they saw as their rights. Individuals like James Mclaughlin protested: 'I shall not work a bloody stroke ... until I get a jacket'. Groups often chose passive resistance, like the six men assigned to George Innes who agreed among themselves not to leave their huts and start work because, they said, 'they had not got their beefs'. Innes's men succeeded in getting a bullock killed for their breakfast. Employers were usually ready to try the carrot before the stick to get men to work, sweetening their leisure hours with 'indulgences' like tea, sugar, tobacco, and rum, and yielding them some control of their working life in terms of hours, allocation of tasks and even wages. A New South Wales landowner reported that 'kindness was more effective than severity', for 'the belly was more vulnerable and sensitive than the back'.

But for all that, the back was often lacerated by the scourger. In Van Diemen's Land during the 1830s about one man in eight of the convict population outside the penal settlements was flogged every year; in New South Wales the ratio was nearer one in four. Employers unable to exert their authority by other means referred their servants to the local magistrates, charged with 'colonial offences' such as insolence, negligence and disobedience – offences against work discipline that might have merited a fine for a labourer in England. In the convict colonies they earned fifty or a hundred lashes for first offenders, and a term in a work gang or worse for men who consistently refused to obey.

Women were almost always assigned as domestic servants. Their work was usually less arduous than the men's, but more oppressive, and more solitary. Women servants in Britain had almost no privacy, being at their mistresses' call for most of their waking hours. Assigned servants in the colonies suffered worse tyrannies, exacerbated by their inability to give notice. Catherine Neale declared 'she would never cut any more bread and butter for the children' of her employer after they swore at her and kicked her. There were usually more women needing positions than families to take them, so their services were little valued, and they were prone to be brought before the law to be disciplined for the pettiest offences. One woman was sentenced to the punishment class of the Female Factory for three months for insisting on wearing her fine lace collar and cuffs on Sunday.

On the other hand women could not be flogged after 1817, and were rarely worked in chains. The punishments available for women – imprisonment on bread and water or in solitary confinement, return to the factory – rarely seem to have persuaded them to submit gracefully to their employers' authority. A fellow servant reported of Caroline Thomas that 'after sundown yesterday I hear some high sounds took place in the kitchen and I saw my mistress and the prisoner pushing each other'. Ann Walker was charged with dipping her master's head in a bucket of water and marching off, singing, 'If I had a bean for a soldier, who'd go, Do you think I'd refuse him, O' no, no, no'. Studies of court records suggest that once a mistress sent a servant before the magistrates for punishment, the servant's resistance usually escalated, pushing up the level of domestic discord until the situation was unbearable.

Women gathered together in places of secondary punishment – the factories or the penal settlements – were as ready as men to join in protest at the injustice of their situation. Perhaps they were readier. Protests ranged from the famous moment in the Cascades Factory, Hobart, when a roomful of women simultaneously turned and slapped their bare bottoms at a sermonising minister, to concerted showers of missiles hurled in court at a bloody-minded magistrate, to riots that took over the Parramatta Factory. In 1827 and 1831 women broke out of the factory en masse, enraged at cuts in their rations and threats to shave their heads. In 1833 Samuel Marsden set off a ferocious riot when he tried to keep the women 'under the hand of power' by cutting their hair – 'they one and all determined not to submit to this operation'. No wonder the authorities preferred where possible to hand over their female charges to the rule of husbands.

Marsden's attempts at head shaving were part of a general increase in the severity of colonial punishments. Governors were urged to stronger and stronger measures by a British Government anxious to make transportation fearful to its subjects. Banishment to rural work gangs and distant penal settlements, labour in chains and under the lash, starvation rations and minimal shelter, solitary confinement in total darkness – these became the fate of those who would not work. At the same time punishment became less bloody; the new science of penology recommended action on the mind rather than the body as the best means of reform.

Reform also became a more conscious object of assignment,

though not necessarily an effect. During the 1830s the assignment of convicts was made less 'arbitrary' – less open to pressure from powerful men and women – by a set of rules tying the number of servants to the number of acres held. The new rules did not exclude small farmers, allowing one man for every 20 acres under cultivation, but magistrates had to certify that smallholders, mostly ex-convicts, were fit and proper people to undertake the reformation of men and women still under sentence.

Overall the rules favoured large landowners, especially pastoralists. The demands of the British wool market triggered a huge increase in the colony's sheep flocks, and a corresponding demand for land and labour. By the end of the decade almost three-quarters of convicts assigned were employed at some distance from Sydney and the closely settled districts. It seemed that John Macarthur's words to John Bigge had come true: rural New South Wales offered the mother country a field both for investment and penal reform. 'The labors which are connected with the tillage of the earth, and the rearing and care of Sheep and Cattle, are but calculated to lead to the Correction of vicious habits – When Men are engaged in rural occupations their days are chiefly spent in solitude – they have much time for reflection and self examination.'

But the country could teach vicious habits too. Observers unsympathetic to transportation described the farm workers on large estates as 'a peasantry unlike any other in the world', 'a peasantry without domestic feeling and relations, without wives, children, or homes; one more strange and less attached to the soil they till, than the negro slaves of a planter'. Such men spent their days in hard labour and their nights 'gratifying their appetites for liquor, gaming, and every species of debauchery'. The picture is overdrawn, but the detail is confirmed by court records; men had little else to do with their lives.

On pastoral holdings further out, the shepherds – rudely called 'crawlers' by the men on horseback – endured days and weeks of solitude, broken only by sometimes terrifying visits from Aborigines hostile at the invasion of their land. The result was as often madness as 'self examination'. More capable men were recruited as mounted stockmen and long-distance drovers. Such men often achieved a kind of reform, though not the internal kind Macarthur had envisaged. Rather they learnt useful skills and acquired some cattle and sheep of their own, good preparation for a life as small proprietors when their sentence was up.

But it was these men on horseback – aristocrats among the bush workers – who learnt the most vicious habits towards the Aborigines. Shepherds learnt to live with local groups, sometimes sharing food and sexual favours. Stockmen were encouraged by their employers to see themselves as shock troops in a battle for the land. Massacre and rape were a normal part of the expansion of British flocks and herds into the inland plains. When eleven men, convicts and ex-convicts, were tried for the murder of some tens of Aboriginal women, children, and old men in 1838, the defendants were amazed that their deed was seen as a crime. They had just been doing their job. As a local poet observed in *The Colonist*, 'Felonry' on the frontier acted to 'embrute and poison'.

By 1828 there were some 36 000 white inhabitants of New South Wales, and perhaps 90 000 Aborigines. Of the whites, 9000 had been born in the colony, about a quarter of the population, though less than two in five of these were over twelve. Colonists born in New South Wales had long called themselves 'currency' – the term used for the ragtail collection of dumps and dollars and promissary notes that served as a means of exchange in the colony. 'Currency' gave the white Australian born an identity distinct both from their convict parents and from those who 'came free' to the colony – 'sterling', whose credentials were like British coinage, acceptable outside New South Wales.

Observers often presented the currency lasses and lads as proof that something good could come from the evil of Botany Bay. Bigge found them 'a remarkable exception to the moral and physical character of their parents' – more sober and honest, and also taller and fairer. Bigge was interested in them as workers. He found them 'capable of undergoing more fatigue, and less exhausted by labour than native Europeans'; active, but also clumsy, and 'quick and irascible, but not vindictive' in temper.

Colonial authorities were less sanguine. Governors and clergymen regularly reported to the Colonial Office that the native born were growing up either abandoned or overindulged by their undisciplined parents. Either way the solution was more clergymen and schoolmasters, to teach children to read their bibles and to reject their parents' feckless ways. By Macquarie's time government support gave colonial children a better schooling than their English cousins. By the standards of the day an ability to sign one's name was a fair test of literacy, as children were taught basic reading skills before writing ones. In the early 1820s more than 80 per cent of native-born men marrying in Sydney and Parramatta signed the marriage register, and more than 75 per cent of native-born women, much higher percentages than those among British-born brides and grooms.

In the more distant parts of the colony schools were less common, and children less schooled. At the church in Windsor, at the Hawkesbury, barely half of the currency could sign the register. In 1822 Thomas Galvin wrote from Minto on the Nepean to the Anglican authorities who distributed government funds for teaching, asking them to support a schoolmaster. He wrote as a man among men, confidently addressing the Reverend Thomas Hassall on behalf of 'fathers of families' of Minto. He had as he said 'the largest family in this settlement', Sarah Galvin having presented him with six children in ten years – but mothers were invisible here, having no part in dealings with authority.

Thomas and Sarah's family was the largest in the settlement and also the most well-to-do, a common pattern in the colony. They were farming 80 acres, all cleared, three-quarters sown with cereal, plus a kitchen garden and orchard and pasturage for horses, cattle, oxen and pigs. The three eldest girls at twelve, ten and eight years of age were old enough to help on the farm; the oldest boy at six was probably too young. Galvin's first concern was their schooling; for the previous fifteen months he alone had supported a schoolmaster for the locality as 'the majority of the people cannot afford to pay for their children'. Galvin was a man certain of his own worth and that of his neighbours. He reminded Marsden that the reverend had publicly pledged himself 'to support our schoolmaster' some ten months before; 'we consider it has slipt his memory'.

Less worthy parents were equally ungrateful. The Orphan Schools were intended to house and educate 'all orphans, and other children whose parents are not proper for such a charge'. The children were to be 'entirely secluded from the other people – and brought up in habits of religion and industry'. Over several decades the schools sheltered some thousands of children, mostly placed there by a single parent unable to care for them because of pressures of work. At twelve or fourteen the children were to serve a seven-year 'apprenticeship' with respectable employers, but few did so; more often their 'improper' parents came to claim them. Babette Smith's recent study of a group of convict mothers and children discovered that all the women who gave up children to the orphanage made some effort to retrieve them as soon as employment or another marriage allowed it.

The Orphan Schools were large, crowded buildings with barred windows and guards at the gates. They taught children to submit to a brutal discipline, but did little to convert them to a morality different from their parents'. In 1826 Eliza Darling, Governor Darling's wife, founded the Female School of Industry to save young girls 'from the twin evils of destitution and immorality'. The school was a pleasant building in an elegant garden, housing about thirty-five girls, both destitute 'foundation scholars' and 'boarders' paying 10 pounds a year. Parents signed bonds of 100 pounds giving the school complete authority over their daughters until they reached the age of eighteen. Costs were covered by the government and by wealthy subscribers, who were promised first pick of the school's graduates as domestic servants.

The school was run by an all-female committee, principally the wives and daughters of government officials, women mostly committed to an aggressive Christianity. Committee members took an active interest in every detail of the students' lives, setting lessons and testing academic progress, hearing their prayers, and overseeing the monthly visits permitted to parents. Parents were a threat, interrupting walks to church with presents of fruit that made the girls 'noisy and disorderly'. Within the school an invariable daily routine taught 'regularity, industry and cleanliness'. Discipline was kept not by physical force but moral example. When twelve girls refused their oatmeal porridge at breakfast 'the eldest of the refractory party' was punished with twelve hours of solitary confinement. The aim was to teach the girls to discipline themselves. Ideally they learnt self-restraint through a sense of their unworthiness – a moral state that the committee women sought just as earnestly for themselves and their families.

From this perspective the perfect graduate of the school was Margaret Gold, whose exemplary life and death were described in a pamphlet published by the committee. A sermon had converted Margaret to a deep sense of her own sinfulness and an anxious desire to be 'holy in thought, word, and deed'; in her own words:

> What is there, Lord, a child can do
> That feels with guilt oppress'd?
> There's evil which I never knew
> Before within my breast

The school produced very few servants, to the annoyance of subscribers. The typical graduate left with a glory box filled with clothes and household linen, mostly of her own making, to marry a husband of her own or her parents' choice. She had learnt to read the bible, perhaps to write and do simple accounts, and basic sewing and cooking. Ideally she knew that humility brought peace on earth and riches in heaven.

Marriage was the almost invariable lot of the currency lasses, but their reproductive lives were often less orderly than the good ladies of Sydney might hope. Elizabeth Rope's eldest daughter, Mary, bore three illegitimate children in seven years to the son of well-to-do neighbours. Then at twenty-seven years of age, she married John Ryan, a convict assigned to her father, and gave him six children in the next sixteen years – interrupted by two daughters fathered by another convict. Elizabeth's second daughter, Sarah, married a convict constable at seventeen, bore her first child exactly nine months later, and produced ten children in twenty-eight years of faithful marriage. The third surviving daughter, Elizabeth Anne, had a fatherless child at sixteen, then married yet another convict two years later and bore him seven children.

These women were typical of their generation: in their early marriages, in their fecundity, and in their choice of partners. The Rope daughters and sons all married people living and working close to their home farm at Evan on the Nepean. Studies have shown that the native born were largely content to follow in the patterns of their parents' lives. Grown children lived at home and worked on family farms or in workshops, and when they married they chose the sons and daughters of men in the same line of work as their fathers. Often they lived in the same part of the country, especially farming families. When William Rope's wife died he moved back to his parents' farm with his three young children. Educated observers who saw the native born as rejecting their parents' way of life were mistaken.

Parents worked hard to educate sons and daughters – though they cared more for practical literacy and numeracy than for the moral education admired by employers. And they struggled to place their sons in work that might make them independent of wage labour – in apprenticeships to skilled artisans, or as farmers on their own land. Where family connections could not find a boy an apprenticeship, parents wrote to the governor seeking a place in the government workshops or shipyards, and Macquarie delighted in such paternal patronage. The granting of land to the native born was also in the gift of the governor. Macquarie was generous, making land grants to some 265 native-born applicants, with loans of stock from the government herds to get them started. By 1828 the commonest occupation claimed by currency lads was that of landholder, followed at a distance by carpenter, blacksmith and other skilled tradesmen.

But the pattern was changing. By 1828 numbers of native-born youths were returning themselves as 'of no occupation', or 'labourer', usually on their parents' farms. Until 1825 'lads' able to present themselves as being 'of industrious habits' readily received small grants of land. In his application William Rope relied on his father's accomplishments: that he 'had arrived in the First Fleet' and 'since arrival his character has been honest and upright and his demeanour such as to merit the approbation of his superiors'. But Governor Darling came with instructions to tie land grants not to moral worth but to capital invested in the colony, and 'he was not authorised to issue small plots to any settler'.

Like Macquarie, Darling was to be caught in a struggle to redefine the public interest, the public arena and politics itself. The right of native-born sons to the land became central to that debate. William Charles Wentworth, Cambridge educated, native-born son of a convict mother, chose this issue to open an attack on the governor's dictatorial powers. Wentworth liked to present himself and his newspaper, the *Australian*, as 'the people's voice'. He revived Macquarie's idea that the public interest was identical with that of the emancipists and especially their sons, asserting that every white man born in New South Wales had a right to 'his own farm' 'as soon as he arrives at his years of maturity'. He pictured the currency as true Australians robbed of their inheritance, 'brooding in the distant hills'.

Darling's critics called also for trial by jury and newspapers free from censorship; in effect they were demanding a place for public opinion in New South Wales politics. That Wentworth should do this in the name of the native-born sons tells us nothing about *their* political opinions. But from this time the currency were expected to take a discontented, radical stance in politics, alongside their emancipist fathers; to this extent Wentworth's claim created its own reality. And note its limits: the presumption that only sons have political opinions.

The currency had another public spokesperson, perhaps a voice more authentic than Wentworth. 'Betsey Bandicoot' wrote to the *Sydney Gazette* in defence not of the political but of the cultural rights of the native born. Betsey's true identity and gender are unknown, but her language suggests a close acquaintance with local values. There is irony in her praise of currency cooking – 'a panful of pork, swimming in fat', and of currency relaxation – 'he lounges like any swell, with a nice short pipe, and smoaks and whiffs, and whiffs and smoaks, all afternoon'. But her picture of Bill, the currency lad, is true to the type; he 'can play the flute, hunt the wild cattle, and shoot and swim with the best in the Colony'. And when Betsey presents her own qualities irony turns to admiration; she can gallop bareback and shoeless, swim with her clothes on her head 'without wetting so much as my comb', make pounds and pounds of butter, talk better than Bill and write better than her father.

Sport was the passion of the currency lads, the arena where they could flaunt their manly superiority – and win a bet or two on the side. Promoters working out of public houses organised illegal contests between champions of sterling and currency. Foot-racing and bare knuckle boxing attracted thousands of spectators. Jack Kable, ninth of the eleven children born to Henry and Susannah Kable, declared 'he would fight anything alive for a purse of five hundred guineas' and proceeded to defeat nearly all comers. His brother Edgar was more concerned with promoting matches and bookmaking.

Sport and gambling kept the currency in trouble with the law. Jack, Edgar and their brother Charles were variously charged with assaulting two soldiers 'so that their Lives were greatly despaired of', with failing to assist a constable to break up a 'riotous assembly', and with assaulting a chief constable in the execution of his office. In this last case Edgar Kable, riding a fine gelding, had cleared a ring for a fight in the thick of the crowd at the Windsor races. The chief constable, mounted on an 'old, Greasy' stallion, rode into the ring and broke up the fight. Kable assaulted him with a riding whip, berating him for daring to ride 'an Entire Horse' onto the race course – though his steed was clearly no threat to anyone's mare. The mounted confrontation roused the crowd against the constable, and he was lucky to escape. The Kables were not political actors in the sense aspired to by William Wentworth, but their arrogance provided a focus for a very public and masculine rejection of authority.

Anthony Rope and his son William provide a more private example of the same impulse. By 1825 Anthony Rope was approaching seventy years of age, many times a grandfather, settled on his land at Evan with his sons and daughters around him. Respectable referees agreed that 'since arrival ... his demeanour such as to merit the approbation of his superiors'. But there was fire in the man yet. A runaway convict was 'dogged' by his overseer to the hut behind Rope's farm. When the overseer attempted to seize the runaway, Rope and his son intervened. At first they pretended to suspect the overseer was a bushranger, then Rope admitted that he knew him 'perfectly well ... he was Mr. Hayes' butcher', or scourger. They took the runaway into the house and in the morning he was gone.

In 1830 the well-reported death of a bushranger, John Donohoe, moved a young currency lad to write a play concerned among other things with the problem of individual will and authority. Bushrangers were already the most popular colonial subjects in Sydney newspapers, along with sport and the undue severity of the penal system, and the first and last of these were being linked – and used to berate governors – by editors claiming that convicts were driven to the bush by authority abused. Edward Hall of the *Monitor* wrote at the time of Donohoe's death that bushrangers were made by harsh punishments: 'it is fit and proper, that cruelty should be visited on the nation which practises it'.

Charles Harpur was the son of convicts, his mother transported at fourteen and his father 'a kind of highwayman' who became a public schoolmaster in New South Wales. His Donohoe is no hero: a betrayer of trust, a would-be rapist and a murderer. Harpur has two explanations for this evil. Donohoe is 'the slave of passion'; 'shame, fear, respect, gratitude' struggle unsuccessfully in him with 'a thousand rash desires'. The committee of the Female School of Industry would approve the struggle, if not the outcome. But Donohoe is also driven to crime by 'scorn and oppression'; 'I was the bondman of a tyrant who eternally hurl'd the term of scoundrel in my teeth; I murmur'd and was scourg'd – I absconded'. Self-government ennobles, tyranny corrupts.

Harpur's play also addresses another kind of tyranny – the rule of men over women.

> With every maudlin lass about to wed,
> A lover is the pink of all perfection;
> But ask them ere they be twelvemonth wedded
> What proves thy lord? answer, a dog in office.
> Aye, men are tyrants

The debate here is less than serious; Mary's friend Lucy is objecting to Mary's impending marriage and loss of liberty, giving Mary, the heroine, an occasion for some pretty declarations of love. Yet the themes have substance. Lucy warns women to keep their liberty because men are like 'the wild ocean's moods', moved by ungovernable passion. Mary replies that men – especially her man – are too full of 'generous sentiments and kindly thoughts' to play the tyrant. The problem of authority remains, only contained by affection.

In the years to come, Harpur thought that he found a solution to public tyranny in the idea of democracy – a moral, rational people governing themselves. He had no answer to the private tyranny that required a man to rule both himself and his wife, denying her self-government and rationality.

Almost from the foundation of New South Wales the colony had been criticised by penal reformers who hated transportation and all that it stood for. Men like Jeremy Bentham believed that the sentence of transportation supported an unjust system of law, intended to terrify and deter criminals rather than to reform them. He argued that law-breakers could be more efficiently reformed by long terms in prison, where punishment could be made to fit the crime. In Australia the convicts' experience depended on their skills, their usefulness and their luck – or lack of it – in getting a good and fair master. Such arbitrary justice could never make men and women truly penitent.

By the 1830s the English legal system was being rationalised, and prisons – penitentiaries – were being built to shape men's and women's minds as well as punishing their bodies. The new ideas had some impact in the colonies, too, in attempts to make assignment more efficient and secondary punishment more horrible. But critics both in Britain and in the colonies increasingly wanted not to change the system but to abolish it entirely. In 1838 a select committee of the House of Commons recommended that 'Transportation to New South Wales, and to the settled district of Van Diemen's Land, should be discontinued as soon as possible'.

The committee's report described transportation as an abomination, an 'unnatural' system creating a monstrous society. It was unnatural because it was cruel; in the penal settlements it was said that a prisoner 'loses the heart of a man and gets the heart of a beast'. And it was unnatural because it fostered state intervention in relationships that should be private. Assignment was a system of slavery destroying the proper relations between master and servant. It threatened family life by making husbands and wives into gaolers and agents of the state.

The proof of the abnormality of convict society was said to lie in its sexual practice: the shortage of women and the impossibility of marriage for most men, the sexual vulnerability and/or aggression of the women, the frequency of homosexuality and other crimes even more unmentionable among the men. The visible symbol of social disorder was the public presence of the convict women, viewed as they had always been as 'excessively ferocious', 'profligate', 'drunken and abandonned prostitutes'.

Colonists were outraged that their society should be described as corrupt. Landowners argued that 'well regulated' assignment produced not slaves but 'very useful servants'. Emancipists argued that the convicts were not slaves but 'Britons, knowing their rights and jealous of them'. Both agreed that transplanting a man into a society where his work was valued gave him the best chance of reform, however defined. And as evidence of the normality, of the 'naturalness' of colonial society, both offered the modestly successful ex-convict settled on his smallholding, loyal wife at his side and children growing strong at his knee.

The report of the select committee provoked even the conservative men who sat in the Legislative Council in Sydney to a defence of the people of New South Wales. They presented the colony as an agent of reform, producing a 'rising generation of Native-born Subjects ... who in the exercise of the social and moral relations of life, are not inferior to the Inhabitants of any other Dependency of the British Crown'. But the image of the honest currency lasses and lads could not flourish while the convict whore lived. This imagined prostitute influenced the British Parliament's decision to end transportation in 1838, and she has seduced historians ever since.

4 Making Male and Female Worlds

Critics of transportation in the 1830s had a model in mind of a more 'natural' way of creating colonies – the free emigration of British men and women. The penal reformers were also involved with the immigration schemes that effectively replaced convict labour with free workers in the Australian colonies by 1850. Between 1830 and 1850 some 125 000 immigrants arrived in the old convict colonies, and another 60 000 in the new, convict-free colonies of Western Australia and South Australia. In the process the white population of Australia exceeded the black for the first time. The great majority of these immigrants were assisted, their fares paid in whole or part by governments or employers anxious to use their labour to shape their particular vision of a colonial future. But the employers of labour were to find it a refractory beast. Immigrant workers had their own dreams, and they contested their employers' dreams in private and in public.

Hostilities between employer and employee could begin as soon as the immigrants left England. In September 1826 Harriet King – or as she would have expected to be called, Mrs Phillip Parker King – sailed from Plymouth, accompanied by four sons under the age of seven, their nanny, a midwife hired in case Mrs King's pregnancy came to term before the end of the voyage, and a governess, a Miss Charlotte Waring, engaged by Mrs King on behalf of her sister-in-law, Mrs Hannibal Macarthur. In her husband's absence Mrs King was returning to New South Wales to take charge of the family estate, acquired by Governor Phillip Gidley King in 1806.

Visitors observed that, along with the platypus and the kangaroo, one of the oddities of New South Wales was a local aristocracy produced in just one generation. As a member of one of the 'ancient' landholding families of the colony, Harriet King expected deference from her social inferiors. She was soon 'very much disappointed' with Miss Waring; 'she is very different from what she ought to be, or we expected'. 'We had not been 2 hours on board, before I saw she was flirting with Mr. Atkinson, and ere 10 days were over – she was engaged to him'. Mrs King told Miss Waring that 'she did not act with propriety'. The governess replied that her engagement would not interfere with her duties to the Macarthurs, but 'she must be mistress of her own actions'.

Charlotte Waring was a woman of spirit equal to her employer. She married James Atkinson in September 1827, after working for what she believed was a sufficient time for the Macarthurs. Atkinson was already established in the colony as a large farmer and successful author. Seven years and four children later Atkinson died. In 1836 Charlotte married George Bruce Barton, who shortly became insane. Charlotte supported her family by writing the first children's book published in the colony, *A Mother's Offering to Her Children*, bloodthirsty tales of shipwreck and murder made moral by occasional references to providence.

> Teach us to quit this transitory scene,
> With decent triumph and a look serene;
> Teach us to fix our ardent hopes on high,
> And having lived to God, in him to die.

Charlotte Waring-Atkinson-Barton had an excellent understanding of 'propriety', and of 'decent triumph' as well.

Battles between mistresses and ordinary servants took place across a wider class divide, and power lay mostly with the mistress. But the humble had weapons to hand, if they had strength to use them. Fanny Bussell gave a mistress's view of the war, from the Swan River Colony in 1834. 'Emma is behaving better and we sometimes entertain hopes of rendering her a useful respectable girl but she has great faults I had nearly said incurable. An indentured servant is at all times a most dangerous speculation.' In this case, too, conflict had been endemic since the Bussells and their young servant, Emma Mould, embarked for the new Australian colony in 1832.

Emma Mould had signed an indenture in England, 'contracting and binding herself' to 'faithfully serve' the Bussell family in the

Swan River Colony for five years, during which she would 'employ her whole time in or about their proper Business'. Breach of the contract would mean imprisonment, perhaps with hard labour. Hundreds of men and women without work or property did the same thing. Young adults like Emma contracted themselves; heads of families contracted their wives and children as well. Sometimes they knew their prospective employers, but more often contact was made through officials in charge of poor relief, anxious to move their parish poor to the colonies.

For their part the Bussells promised to pay Emma's passage, 'to find and provide' for her during her employment, and to pay her a small sum annually. The promise of cheap and docile labour was made doubly attractive to employers because land was granted according to capital invested in the colony; a general servant landed in Swan River was worth 200 acres of land to his or her employer. Land was still the basis of the political and social power of the English ruling class – the gentry – and families investing in Swan River hoped to make of themselves a new colonial gentry. The Bussells were the children of a clergyman, well bred but impoverished. Other settlers were well-to-do farmers and tradesmen with more money than status. In coming to Swan River they rejected convict labour as unnatural and degrading; rather they would build a life of gentlemanly leisure for themselves and their families upon the device of indenture.

The colony in western Australia did not prosper; by 1840 the white population was little more than 2000 men, women and children. The failure of indenture was central to the colony's woes. Land could not be brought into production fast enough to feed the servants who were meant to work it. Employers unable to fulfil their side of the contract were forced to release their servants from indenture, either voluntarily or under pressure from government. Men and women who had come to the colony to live by the sweat of other people's brows found themselves doing physical work unknown to them in England. Gentlemen laboured in the fields, clearing and ploughing. Gentlewomen were felt to suffer more acutely, being obliged to wait upon their brothers and husbands – a 'distressing and laborious' fate for women used to 'the common comforts and plain cleanliness of genteel life'.

Servants no longer bound by indenture left for other colonies.

Those who stayed demanded high wages and worse – the same food as their employers. Some took up small plots of land and claimed a nodding acquaintance with their former masters and mistresses. John Wollaston, an Anglican clergyman, wrote angrily in the 1840s that 'the common people in general sent out, come with their heads filled with the most extravagant and unfounded notions and expectations of worldly aggrandisement (in short, to be made ladies and gentlemen of)'.

Emma Mould fought the Bussells's authority from the start. On the voyage out she took up with a sailor. The Bussells considered sending her back to England, but decided to 'make the best of her', hoping she would 'reform' away from the ship. The family took up land 200 kilometres from Perth, in dense redwood forest on the banks of the Vasse River. When Emma continued to be 'troublesome and insolent' they punished her with 'solitary confinement' in a small hut built for that purpose across the wide river. In the end Emma made them cancel her indentures by becoming visibly pregnant to one of the Bussell sons. Mrs Bussell wrote circumspectly home: 'Emma has taken her departure from my service. She is the most abandoned creature. She has violated every commandment. But I did not send her away; she would go'.

Thus ended the Bussell women's hopes of remaking Emma as 'a useful respectable girl'. The phrase is revealing. To the Bussells Emma could never achieve their level of respectability – could never, for example, think of marrying the father of her child. To them her respectability was measured by her social usefulness.

Emma's understanding is harder for us to reach. Clearly, like Charlotte Barton she wished to be 'mistress of her own actions', and like Barton this led her paradoxically to marriage, and the taking of a master. In 1836 she married Thomas Sweetman, a seaman turned settler, and bore him eight children in fourteen years. Sweetman became a public schoolteacher in Guilford, near Perth. Emma Sweetman seems to have become a thoroughly respectable wife.

Indenture had been used to limit the freedom of colonial workers for more than 200 years, since the foundation of the North American colonies, and it was the first resort of Australian employers unable to get convict labour. The Van Diemen's Land Company was founded in 1825 with a royal charter, 350 000 acres of land in north-west Tasmania, and an expectation of first choice of convicts from the colonial government. When Governor George Arthur supplied only a small part of its requests for skilled and docile convicts, the company signed seven-year indentures in Britain with about ninety rural workers – mostly shepherds, but also ploughmen, carpenters, masons, blacksmiths, bricklayers and one dairy woman. Forty of these men also signed over the labour of wives and children.

The experiment was not a success. The colonial management complained that the indentured servants would not work as hard as the convicts, and that their wives and children would not work at all: 'the freemen all come here with the full belief and expectation that Van Diemen's land is the true Eldorado, every ploughman expects to be an overseer, his family to be kept for nothing by the company'. The servants complained that their food and accommodation were no better than the convicts', that skilled men were put to unskilled work, and that their wages were half what they could get on the open market.

By the 1830s the Aborigines had been killed or driven from Tasmania, and most of the fertile land had been given over to cultivation and grazing. By settling the far north-west of the island, the management of the Van Diemen's Company hoped that isolation would ensure 'discipline and subordination' in their workforce. But in 1832 twenty men left the company's settlement for Launceston, crossing rough country and flooded rivers to get there. In that town a liberal lawyer, Joseph Tice Gellibrand, found a flaw in their indentures that effectively released them – and the many absconders after them – from the company's control. By 1835 those who stayed in the company's service were being paid at market rates.

Gellibrand was a speculator, one of the men busy inventing capitalism in the colonies. He and liberals like him believed that government interference in the market was politically, economically and morally wrong. The greatest good for the greatest number could be achieved by removing all restrictions to the sale of land and labour. Edward Gibbon Wakefield prophesied in 1833 that a community of enlightened capitalists would be 'the happiest state of society consistent with private property'.

Wakefield intended his ideal society to be a colonial one, created by bringing Britain's surplus population and capital to work on Australia's unused land – unused, that is, except by the Aborigines. In the early 1830s Wakefield proposed to the British middle classes a new way of looking at immigration: no longer 'a squalid traffic of convicts' but a 'solid opportunity and a civilising mission'. British society would be renewed in the colonies by using the proceeds of colonial land sales to import the labour needed to bring that land into production. And ideally for every working man imported, the funds would provide a wife, also as a worker but primarily as a mother, an essential part of that 'civilising mission'.

South Australia, founded in 1836, was planned by men influenced by Wakefield's theories. The planners talked a lot about the idea of the free market, in both land and labour – though never of course in marriage. Indenture was rejected as an unnatural interference in the labour market. Workers accepting free passages were promised easy access to the land that would transform them from 'labour-power' to 'capitalists' – especially if their wives worked beside them. But in effect the price of land was carefully set so high that 'the labourer would be indirectly compelled ... to sell his labour' for many years – as effectively, said William Molesworth, as the slave was compelled to work by the lash.

The planners also talked about the proposition, ignored by colonists elsewhere, that the land on which their prosperity would rest belonged to the Aborigines. They promised the Colonial Office, newly concerned with the rights of indigenous people, that they would protect the Aborigines of South Australia 'in the undisturbed enjoyment of their proprietary right to the soil, wherever such right may be found to exist'. They also promised to feed all Aborigines voluntarily giving up their land and to promote Christianity among them.

After settlement the rights of capital outweighed competing ideas. A few colonists believed that some compensation was owed to 'the people whose territory they [had] usurped', but only Robert Cock, a Quaker, chose to pay rent for his use of the Aborigines' land. Most preferred to believe that while the Aborigines might have some 'moral right or interest in the soil', it could not be seen as 'an exclusive property'. The appointment of a Protector to dispense rations and Christianity was generally supported in the colony, but more in charity than in justice. The Aborigines found themselves received as strangers and supplicants on their own land.

The idea of the free labour market got even shorter shrift. An 'Act for the summary determination of all disputes between Masters and Servants' was the third law passed in the colony, within a week of the proclamation of South Australia as a province in December 1836. The law was 'highly popular' among the masters of the colony. It enforced all agreements between masters and servants, both indentures made in Britain and contracts made in South Australia. Servants could sue defaulting masters for damages under the act, and masters could sue other masters for 'enticing away' servants. But during the two years that it remained in force, the act seems to have been used only by masters to prosecute servants who neglected or left their work. The magistrates, masters themselves, almost invariably found for the employers, and sentenced runaways to gaol for periods of up to three months.

'Gaol' was hardly the word for it. Samuel Westlock, William Power and William Angill, sentenced to three months imprisonment for absconding from the South Australian Company's fishing station, petitioned Governor Hindmarsh in June 1837 to remit the rest of their sentence. During the day they were chained to trees in the 'parklands' around the mushrooming town of Adelaide; at night they slept in the 'soldiers tent'. The prisoners were without coats or blankets; they told the governor that if the weather turned cold again they feared they would be 'Quite Unfit for Ever after being Able to Obtain a Living by Hard Labour'. Most of Adelaide's population still lived in tents at this stage; Hindmarsh was housed in a two-room slab hut, unlined and without glass in the windows. But the governor had been 'daily shocked' by 'the miserable condition' of the men, and advised their release.

Such public humiliation may have discouraged would-be absconders, but the rewards were great. Indentured servants had agreed in Britain to serve their masters for some 20 to 25 pounds a year, with rations – say 9 shillings a week. In the fast-growing colony the shortage of labour was so acute that workmen arriving unengaged could earn 8 or 10 shillings a day, 12 or 14 if they were skilled. By August 1837 the South Australian *Gazette* reported that the breaking of work agreements was a 'daily occurrence'. Prosecutions under the act can have made little impact. South Australia's 'enlightened capitalists' had dismissed the idea of the free labour market, only to discover the force of the reality, acting in the interests of labour.

The workers' advantage was short-lived. A great increase in assisted immigration meant that by the end of 1838 workers were chasing jobs. By 1841 an economic depression affecting all the Australian colonies put 15 per cent of the South Australian population on government relief. Workers across the country were convinced that private battles with individual employers had to be translated into combination in the public sphere.

The ideas of the systematic colonisers affected land sales and immigration in the older colonies too. In 1831 the British government ruled that colonial lands held by the crown should no longer be given away, but sold – initially at 5 shillings an acre. They suggested to the legislative councils of New South Wales and Van Diemen's Land that the revenue be spent assisting immigration to the colonies, in the first instance of skilled artisans and unmarried women. Men were chosen for their usefulness as skilled workers, women as domestic servants and wives. Several thousand women were sent by 1836, and several hundred men.

Ungrateful employers in the colonies questioned the quality of these immigrants, believing that British authorities were sending out the poorest, least capable and least wanted of the population. Certainly Australia, four months from home, was not a popular destination, and assisted immigrants, like indentured ones, tended to be those least able to refuse the assistance. Families labouring in county poorhouses, men and boys in one mean dormitory and women and girls and babies in another; women washing laundry in charitable institutions in London and Dublin; these people came as much in despair as in hope, with little more choice than the convicts.

From 1837 the colonial governments and employers took the recruiting of immigrants into their own hands, and tried to match the skills of the migrants more closely to colonial needs. Influential men in the colonies – landowners and pastoralists – tried to end the assistance to women and children, in favour of unmarried men able to do general farm work. Governors and officials had to override the advice of the leading citizens on their advisory councils to maintain a small surplus of women among the assisted immigrants. They took a longer view than the employers, arguing that a balance of men and women in the population was essential to the growth of a civilised society.

In a learned joke, Governor Gipps told his superintendent in Port Phillip, Charles La Trobe, that 'so long as we belong to what Botanists call the *Pentandria Monogynia* class of colonies, I doubt whether we should diminish the introduction of Women' – a reference to the reproductive power of the five men (*pentandria* or five stamened) present in Port Phillip for every woman (*gyno*). Port Phillip District and its town of Melbourne had been founded in 1836 as a base for pastoral expansion, and was growing at an even faster rate than Adelaide. Its land sales generated a generous flow of assisted immigrants, but never enough single men to satisfy the squatters.

Colonists tended to be hostile towards the boatloads of single women immigrants who arrived during the 1830s. Their work as domestic servants was seen as unproductive, though mothers of large families may have disagreed. Feeling against them turned mostly on simple prejudice against women immigrating independently, without the 'protection' of a husband or father. Such women were seen as both vulnerable and uncontrolled, at once potential victims of sexual aggression and dangerous aggressors themselves. A few of the immigrants had worked as prostitutes in the cities of Britain, and went on to set up lucrative businesses in Sydney and Hobart. But the great majority were concerned, like Emma Mould and Charlotte Barton, to exchange their sexual favours for the more permanent economic support of marriage.

One morning in 1842 Caroline Chisholm got up an hour earlier to find a wife. An ex-convict farmer had written asking Chisholm to select for him 'a desent servant, that can wash and cook and make the place decant', and care for his four-year-old son; marriage might follow if both agreed. Believing that the best wives rise early and cheerful, Chisholm searched the Immigrant Home and its adjacent rows of tents, and found 'a girl at the wash tub' working 'with spirit'. After consulting the records of the voyage out and the matron of the Home to make sure of her 'decency', Chisholm sent the young woman to the country under the care of a married couple, with letters of introduction to several potential women employers living near the farmer concerned. One of these engaged her at once, but not for long. The farmer wrote thanking Chisholm that 'you have suited me exactly; and, as soon as our month is up, we are to be married'. We have no evidence of how well the young woman felt herself to be suited, other than her decision to marry.

Caroline Chisholm had established the female immigrants' home in 1841 to give new arrivals somewhere to live while looking for employment. Before Chisholm persuaded Governor Gipps to allow part of the old Immigration Barracks to be used for this purpose, women whose passages had been paid by the government had to find work and lodgings unaided. Her motives were philanthropic and religious; on Easter Sunday 1841 she vowed herself to the task: 'I was enabled at the altar of our Lord, to make an offering of my talents to the God who gave them ... I asked only to be enabled to keep these poor girls from being tempted by their need to mortal sin, and resolved that to accomplish this, I would ... [not] consider my own wishes or feelings, but wholly devote myself to the work I had in hand'.

Chisholm believed that her 'poor girls' were led into sexual sin by evil men – a judgment they may have resented as denying their right to choose for themselves. But they were grateful for the shelter she offered, and the contacts with employers. As the depression worsened in 1842, jobs in Sydney became almost impossible to find. Chisholm herself often rode into the country looking for work for the immigrants, taking with her drayloads of single women and families and signing them up as domestic servants with 'suitable' employers.

Historians concerned with the exclusion of women from public life at this period have criticised Caroline Chisholm for her ready assumption that all women needed the protection of home and ultimately of husband. Chisholm reported the case of the woman at the wash tub as 'the only girl I ever sent into the country with a direct matrimonial intention', but she placed all that she could in jobs where she thought they would have 'a fair chance of being well married'. And she recommended that women's wages should be kept 'on a lower scale than men's'; 'high wages tempt many girls to keep single while [they] encourage indolent and lazy men to depend more upon their wives' industry than upon their own exertions thus partly reversing the design of nature'.

Certainly Chisholm endorsed the notion of 'separate spheres' for men and women, men properly acting as breadwinners and women as dependants, and inferiors. She saw women, especially working women, as vulnerable and needing a husband's protection from poverty and from the sexual aggression of other men. In Chisholm's stories she often describes single men as dangerous to women, but she sees intending husbands as made tender by goodness and love. One is cited as declaring 'I would like to have a woman that could talk to the children about being good ... if she is pretty, well and good, if she is not, I shall [still] love her'. Another promised that a woman who would 'make my home happy ... need not work more than she like'. Clearly these men assumed that they could command a wife much like a servant. But Chisholm was not worried by this unequal relationship because she believed that women – good women – had the power to civilise men through love.

Since the founding of New South Wales, marriage had been endorsed as civilising both men and women but the idea that women could make men good was new. Its main advocates were the men and women campaigning against the misuse of alcohol. During the late 1830s temperance societies were founded in all the colonies by clergymen hoping to make men moral and employers hoping to make workers sober. The women attracted to these societies were not those ladies of first rank who ran schools and orphanages for the children of the poor; they were the wives of shopkeepers and skilled artisans, and the targets of their reform were men. Sarah Crouch of the Hobart Town temperance society converted a neighbour to temperance and persuaded him to stop beating his wife, making them again a 'loving couple'. This civilising mission held power for some women.

Relations between husbands and wives of course varied across kinds and classes of colonist. Working men, emancipist and immigrant, were not always the tender husbands that Chisholm assumed. Court records show that some men believed they had a right to beat wives who denied their authority, and their neighbours accepted that right. During 1837 Elizabeth Power several times denied her husband's authority by fleeing from his cattle farm in Windsor, New South Wales. Her neighbours tended her cuts and bruises and took her back to her husband, apparently agreeing with him that scolding and blows were 'nothing between husband and wife'.

Well-to-do men, landowners and officials, were less ready to impose their authority by force – or better able to conceal the fact from posterity. But they seem to have expected their word to be obeyed. They were supported in this by the law, which denied married women any legal identity, and by the churches, all of which held that marriage was indissoluble and that women were morally bound to obey their husbands. Literate single women sometimes admitted to their diaries doubts about such submission. Louisa Clifton of Australind, in the Swan River Colony, had a 'strong prejudice' against marriage in her youth, believing it 'an unhappy state for a woman'. But in 1841, still single at twenty-six, she wrote with perhaps a touch of irony: 'as years have rolled on and I have increasingly needed a prop and support, a kindred heart, I have at times thought that [marriage] ... is a state in which I might have found the dependent happiness I have longed for'. The search for the 'kindred heart' who might make dependency happy was to preoccupy most Australian women for the next hundred years.

Louisa Clifton married a little more than a year later, and bore seven children in eight years. She wrote no more in her diary, and we cannot tell how she managed the contradictions of being a dependant and a companion. The great majority of white single women in Swan River chose the same contradictory solution during the 1840s. Most married earlier than Louisa, at about twenty, finished their childbearing later, at about forty, and commonly produced several more children. Patterns of marriage and childbearing were very similar for women in the eastern colonies, with the white native-born women of New South Wales perhaps the most fertile of all. In the village of Camden women marrying before they were twenty-one bore ten children on average, and commonly twelve.

How much choice had women in the passages of their lives? In the decision whether or not to marry, not much. At all levels of society families seem to have expected adult daughters to move out of home, leaving perhaps the youngest to care for parents in their old age. The only paid employment thought suitable for women, service in another woman's house, was seen less as an alternative to marriage than a prelude to it. Certainly in promoting marriage Chisholm was helping restrict women to the private sphere. But existing assumptions about men's and women's work already made economic independence very difficult for women to achieve in the

1840s – much more difficult than at the beginning of the century.

In the decision when and whom to marry, women had clearer choices to make – perhaps the clearest choice in their lives. Like the labour market, the colonial marriage market generally favoured the weaker party to the contract. With two unmarried men to every unmarried woman in Sydney and Hobart, the five to one pentandria lurking in Port Phillip and much higher ratios in the bush, women had plenty of suitors to chose from. Most married young, two or three years earlier than their cousins in Britain. Probably they were wooed more urgently than women at home, but they do not seem to have been reluctant to marry. Many immigrant women married as soon as possible after arriving in the colonies, often men they had met on board ship; others waited and chose from a wider selection. But few waited more than a couple of years.

The question of choice becomes more difficult in looking at these women's reproductive lives. Men's sexual desires were commonly believed to be more pressing than women's. Some held that women had no inherent desire at all. Men initiated, women merely responded. The diaries and letters of the literate show these beliefs translated into action. The diary of Alexander Brodie Spark, 'a respectable Sydney merchant' and banker, records his wife's menstrual periods in the first years after their marriage in 1840, and laments them; he writes of 'a pain in the side, extinguishing late hopes ... fond hopes illusory'. It also celebrates all of her six pregnancies and deliveries, even those coinciding with the depression and his bankruptcy, a disaster that Spark took as a sign that his God had deserted him. Maria Spark's fertility was the proof of her husband's potency, 'a token of better things to come'.

Clergymen and doctors at this time argued that women's ability to bear children kept them both less rational and more spiritual than men, closer to nature and to God. This was particularly so in the dangerous moment of childbirth. Spark wrote of the birth of his fifth child: 'Exactly at 10 o'Clock the distressing sound ceased of that strange agony, the doom of women since the fall, and was instantly succeeded by the interesting cry of infancy on its first introduction to the world ... I had shortly before prayed earnestly to the Almighty, that he would preserve my wife in the trying hour of nature's sorrow, and I felt the delicious glow of gratitude at so blessed an answer to my petition'. Women were more prosaic.

Maria Spark told her husband as she went into labour that 'it was no joke now'.

Literate women rarely wrote directly about matters of the body. Modesty denied them the freedom of expression and perhaps the knowledge allowed to their husbands. The wives of gentlemen were commonly five years or more younger than their husbands, and much less experienced in the practice of sex. It seems likely that most accepted their husbands' superiority in bodily matters. Sophie Dumaresq wrote more frankly than most women of her class. After describing to a friend how skilled her husband was at 'holding out' their baby boy when he woke in the night so that 'the young man' might 'perform what is required of him' – 'Where would you find another Papa to do as much?' – she remarked on her own readiness to talk of such things, and attributed her frankness to her husband. 'I am really now downright impudent, almost improper, which you know was not the case once ... it is all my husband's fault; Stories he used to tell and make me blush at, I now enjoy extremely and think very good fun.'

Women marrying working men were perhaps less modest and certainly more experienced. The best evidence we have of this lies in the numbers who were pregnant when they married: in the 1840s one in five in all the colonies except South Australia – where at one in ten, chastity before marriage seems to have been more valued. Not that this suggests a general carelessness about sexual activity, merely that for many couples commitment, marriage and sleeping together did not necessarily happen in that order.

The case of Mary Ann Charker of Camden shows the interaction between these events, and the power a woman could exercise in the timing of marriage. In 1848 Mary Ann, a nineteen-year-old domestic servant, paid four months wages for a marriage by licence. She had been going for a year with a fellow servant, James Watson, but her father would not let them marry. Marriage by licence allowed her to marry quickly without his knowledge. The Watsons's first child was born a little under nine months after the marriage. Mary Ann may have known she was pregnant when she married, but more likely the relationship had come to a point where she knew that pregnancy could not be long avoided.

Mary Ann Charker's decision to marry gave her immediate power over her life, more perhaps than most ladies ever achieved.

But she was intervening in a game where men made the major moves. Working men as much as gentlemen seem to have assumed their right to begin and set the pace of courtship. And once any woman contracted to marry, a husband's authority was assumed by law and church to extend to – even to be enshrined in – the right to initiate sexual intercourse. Wives may have welcomed intercourse, or feared its consequences; legally they could not avoid it. The steady sequence of pregnancy, birth and renewed pregnancy that shaped most women's lives was accepted fatalistically, as something beyond control – except that the intervals between births could be lengthened by breastfeeding.

Such fatalism about the connection between intercourse and conception was new. Earlier generations of English men and women had not assumed male sexuality to be so imperative in its demands, nor female sexuality to be so passive. For centuries English couples had limited the size of their families to suit their circumstances. Women used herbs like pennyroyal and the mould that grew on black bread to abort unwanted foetuses. Men used self-control to withdraw before ejaculation, or couples abstained from sex altogether. The disappearance of such practices in the nineteenth century is hard to explain. Knowledge and means may have been lost when young people left home, for English cities or for the colonies. But the non-use of withdrawal, probably the most significant contraceptive before the invention of the pill, must have been due to men's reluctance to limit their fertility and their pleasure, and to women's inability to deny them.

There were women in the colonies who believed that large families were not inevitable, and bewailed the ignorance of those who thought otherwise. Annie Baxter was the wife of a struggling squatter in the New England district in northern New South Wales. She was an unusually strong-minded and forthright woman, both in her life and in her diaries. News of a neighbour's 'accouchement' when 'her poor children have positively scarcely a mouthful to eat' moved her to exclaim:

Why do they have any more? I remember telling my pretty little friend Mrs. C. F. that she must not have any more children – She answered quaintly, 'But how is it possible for married persons to avoid it?' Just as if the bare ceremony of matrimony was to be the cause of myriads starving!

Baxter was probably thinking of abstention. When she discovered her husband having sexual intercourse with an Aboriginal woman – a common practice in the outback – she made him swear to 'consent to take for ever one bed, and I another'.

Perhaps women less forthright than Baxter may have been equally strong-minded. Louisa Clifton of Australind, who sought a 'kindred heart' in marriage, bore her seven children in eight years and then no more. About one in five mothers in Western Australia were like Louisa in finishing their childbearing well before menopause. There could be many reasons for this relief, including gynaecological problems. But some women may have found the strength to ask their husbands to restrain their desires in the interest of health, or economy, or love. Perhaps they were assisted by the new idea that Chisholm was helping to make popular, that good women were the agents of morality and civilisation – 'God's police'.

While demography and ideas about 'women's sphere' kept women at home, men were creating a new sphere of public action from which women were excluded. In the 1830s and 1840s governors came to share their power with elected councils of the wealthy, and in the 1850s were abruptly replaced by a masculine democracy. The period sees the creation of new space for men to act in, on stages such as courts, newspaper columns, mechanics institutes, trades societies, public meetings, political associations and finally the ballot box and parliament. Men discovered a new way to think of themselves, as political citizens with a voice in their own government. Those women who tried to speak on their own behalf were told that their role was to be governed.

When Thomas Paine declared in 1791 that 'every man is a proprietor in government' he was drawing on a traditional understanding of politics that was essentially masculinist. In his *Rights of Man*, Paine argued that care of the public interest should be entrusted to the elected representatives of practical men: farmers, manufacturers, traders, merchants. Paine's defence of 'equal natural right' began by including women: 'And God said, let us make man in our own image. In the image of God created he him; male and female created him them'. But as Paine moved from religious to economic argument he slipped into the old Whiggish habit of identifying the citizen with the independent householder and family head. Women were neither household heads, proprietors nor practical business people; Paine could easily forget them.

Mary Wollstonecraft wrote her *Rights of Man* shortly before Paine, and her *A Vindication of the Rights of Woman* shortly afterwards. She was moved to the first by enthusiasm for the universal freedoms promised by the French Revolution, and to the second by her sorrow when the revolutionary councils denied these freedoms to women. Wollstonecraft argued that women, being created equal, should not be ruled by men either in marriage or in the state. She wrote with a nervous determination that reveals just how outrageous her suggestion was: 'I may excite laughter, by dropping a hint, which I mean to pursue, some future time, for I really think women ought to have representation instead of being arbitrarily governed without having any direct share allowed them in representations of government'.

Paine's work, banned by the authorities, was read like a bible by radical thinkers and working men anxious to make the government of Britain subject to the will of the people. Wollstonecraft was read in radical circles, but her ideas made little impact in the wider movement. In the 1830s the great Chartist agitation collected hundreds of thousands of signatures demanding in the first instance universal suffrage, but the claim was rapidly narrowed to manhood suffrage alone. Women activists dropped out of the Chartist Movement as it became less local and more professional, and tradesmen who feared that women and machines were taking their jobs increasingly argued that women's place was in the home.

The growth in assisted immigration to Australia during the 1840s followed the British Parliament's rejection of the Chartists' demands and the sometimes violent repression of trade union activity. Working men carried to the colonies some of the anger of these years. Many came with a sense of their rights as workers and as citizens, and a faith in the power of union to achieve those rights. In the colonial towns and cities these ideas quickly took form in trades societies and protection associations, organised both for mutual support and public action.

In the depression years of the early 1840s, men pursued their rights as workers more urgently than their rights as citizens – though in the colonies the two could coincide. The colonial governments' involvement in immigration and the labour market made workers' concerns more immediately political, more the concern of government than was the case in Britain. In 1842 a large body of male labourers marched through the streets of Melbourne behind a loaf of bread mounted on a long pole in what the Port Phillip newspapers called 'open rebellion against the laws and peace and safety of the people'. The men were newly arrived immigrants, working on a government project intended in the absence of other employment to keep them and their wives and children alive – women, of course, not being seen as breadwinners. The marchers contested a government decision to cut their wages. When the mounted police arrived the marchers dispersed, though one cried that it would be 'better to fight and die, than live and starve'.

Other movements lasted longer, and were more self-consciously directed towards influencing the state. Agitations against master and servant legislation were organised by tradesmen in Sydney in 1840 and by labourers in Melbourne in 1845. In 1843 the Mutual Protection Society was formed in Sydney, 'protecting' workers by assisting the families of unemployed men, and by lobbying against assisted immigration. In 1844 the society tried to take a stand on political issues like the tariff and control of government lands. But members were not clear where their interests lay, and the society did not survive the year.

The stage upon which the great issues of the colony were decided was still closed to most of Sydney's working men. In 1842 an act of the British Parliament transformed the legislative councils of the older colonies from advisory bodies to powerful councils able to make laws and to reject governors' decisions. Membership of the council was reserved for large landowners, and electors had to own or rent a house worth 20 pounds a year, a figure excluding about four men in every five in Sydney. But even without a vote, men of little property took an active interest in colonial politics. On election day for the new Legislative Council in 1843, rival bands of partisans roamed the streets of Sydney, beribboned in Irish green – for the Catholic candidate – or in 'true Australian blue' – for the old defender of the emancipist cause, William Wentworth. Fighting broke out at polling booths, and the intervention of a crew of whalers armed with harpoons and blubber spades made matters worse. Rioting crowds took over the city, with much damage to property, many injuries and one death. Women took part in the excitement, though how many we cannot say; one woman wearing a green ribbon was run over by a mounted policeman, who in turn was assaulted by the angry mob. Riots were common at British elections, though not perhaps on this scale; the historian of this event blames 'the angry frustration of men deprived of the vote'.

   The next election in 1848 saw an intervention by working men into the political process. Several weeks before the election a public meeting in the Royal Hotel elected a committee to support a popular candidate for Sydney. Those involved were so new to colonial politics that they neglected to book the room for their meeting in advance, and had to wait around for three-quarters of an hour while they took up a collection to pay for its hire. All of those involved were men. Had women wished to take part they would have been prevented by the venue; respectable women were not to be seen in pubs. Nearly all were young immigrants, recently arrived in the colony. Most were skilled artisans or shopkeepers. Henry Parkes, elected as one of the secretaries to the committee, was typical of those present. He was a Birmingham man, trained as an ivory turner, and educated politically in the reform movements of that city. Parkes had arrived in Sydney with wife and child in 1839 and worked as a labourer and a very humble civil servant before setting up as an independent craftsman, selling goods of his own making and other trifles in his 'Ivory Manufactory and Toy Warehouse'. In 1848 the rent that Parkes paid for his premises gave him the right to vote; probably most of his fellows were in the same position. Their foray into politics had been planned in the back parlour of Parkes's shop.

   If committee members could vote, they lacked the 2000 pounds worth of property required to stand for election, and they probably felt that they also lacked the gentlemanly accent and bearing appropriate for the Legislative Council. They chose as their candidate Robert Lowe – perhaps the most aristocratic man in New South Wales – a young lawyer and a fiery popular speaker. He kept his distance from his new supporters, agreeing to take the seat if elected but refusing to campaign. The committee set up groups working for Lowe's election in every ward of the city, calling on 'the working class' to fight against privilege in the council. When he won his seat they claimed the victory in the name of 'the people'. Parkes hailed the moment as 'the birth-day of Australian Democracy' – a very masculine birth.

Over the next few years Parkes and his fellow radicals laboured to create 'the people' as a self-conscious political force. Parkes wrote of working men as ideal citizens in a new land, toiling 'By labour, wisdom, unity,/Their country to advance and free'. His friend Charles Harpur sang of 'the Tree of Liberty', and 'the men who shall defend/Its glorious future righteously'. In a later verse women gave thanks to the tree for their blessings.

Making this masculine 'people' required action on two fronts. Men had to be persuaded to seek their rights as citizens, and constitutions had to be changed to allow men to exercise those rights. Working men were more easily moved to action by threats to their livelihood than by abstract questions of suffrage and citizenship, and the radicals took on the task of teaching them to see bread and butter issues in terms of a struggle for political power.

There were various ways of understanding this struggle. The native-born poet Harpur looked back to a literary tradition of individual revolt against tyranny, translated by him into an Australian rejection of the values of the old world. In Europe the fruits of his 'Tree of Liberty' 'were ever sold, and only to the few'; but here all men could enjoy them. Other radicals looked to the current socialist revolutions in Europe and defined 'the people's rights' in economic as well as political terms. The *People's Advocate* took for its motto the declaration that 'Political economy ... must now occupy itself about the distribution of wealth; so that the labourer may no longer be left without his fair share of the produce'. But the most popular understanding among the recent immigrants of Sydney was probably that argued by Henry Parkes. Parkes looked back to the rhetoric of the American revolution and invited his audiences to understand their rights as those of 'freeborn Englishmen endangered by the tyranny of British politicians'.

The transportation of convicts gave Parkes an ideal issue. The British Government's decision to renew transportation to the Australian colonies appalled respectable immigrant townsmen. In 1849 the radicals met the first ship carrying convicts to Sydney with a huge protest meeting on the wharves, probably the largest political gathering to that time in the colonies. The meeting passed a protest motion linking issues of citizenship to those of self-respect. 'The free and loyal subjects of Her Most Gracious Majesty' complained that 'it was incompatible with our existence as a free colony, desiring self-government, to be made the receptacle of another country's felons'. Their conclusion neatly linked public and private conviction; they made their protest for 'our duty to our country, for the love of our families'. Men were taking political action on behalf of their wives and children.

In the event it was not colonial agitations but the oddities of British politics that gave colonial legislatures the power to draw up new constitutions and later to amend them freely. It was a vote of the English House of Lords that gave the vote in the colonial capitals to men paying 10 pounds a year rent, effectively to most male heads of families. As a result in Sydney in 1851 almost 50 per cent of men had the vote, a figure that rose spectacularly over the next few years as the gold discoveries pushed up rents in the city. By 1856, 95 per cent of men could vote, and men like Parkes could get themselves elected. When the new parliament set about amending the constitution in 1858, manhood suffrage passed without the need for any pressure from the radicals. Historians considering the movement for women's suffrage, which took place much later – in the 1890s, have claimed that it was granted without a struggle, that women got the vote 'given them on a plate'. That judgment can be more truly made of working men in New South Wales.

In the Port Phillip District, newly separated from New South Wales as the colony of Victoria, the story was different. Pressure for the suffrage came less from Melbourne than from the men on the gold diggings. The discoveries in Victoria proved richer than the New South Wales finds, and by 1854 some 80 000 men were on the fields, most of them new immigrants. They came from a variety of countries and of political traditions: American republicans, Italian nationalists, German revolutionaries, and British Chartists of several persuasions. The failure of the last great Chartist demonstration in London in 1848 had left the movement split between the 'moral force' men, mostly English, who believed only in asking for political reform, and the 'physical force' men, mostly Irish and Scottish, who believed in taking it. In the words of one

Scottish digger, 'Moral persuasion is all a humbug,/Nothing convinces like a lick "in the lug"'.

From the first 'rushes' in 1851, alarmed conservatives had reported a fiercely democratic, even revolutionary spirit among the diggers. The prospect of wealth and independence made men forget their duty to their social betters. Tales were told of working men refusing to carry a gentleman's bags, and offering him sixpence to clean their boots. On the goldfields a strong back counted for more than an educated accent, and a masculine appreciation of 'manly toil' cut across social distinctions.

From 1851 diggers protested to the government about the administration of the fields: about the state of the roads and the mail, about the corruption of the police and the prevalence of crime, about the scale of the licence fees required to dig – at first 3 pounds a month! – and the brutal way they were collected. Public meetings, deputations and mass refusals to pay brought some improvement, but the Victorian Government was in debt and continued to see the diggers primarily as a source of income.

By 1853 political opposition was well organised on the fields. Public meetings were called by the lighting of bonfires on the previous evening. Groups of diggers marched to meetings behind flags and banners, accompanied by drums, bugles and bagpipes; it was reported that at one meeting of 10 000 or 12 000 people in Bendigo

> the Germans, in particular, seemed determined to come out strong on the occasion, having ordered some splendid new banners for that purpose. The English nation were well represented by royal standards and union jacks, and the Irish ... provided themselves with a very beautiful flag, with the harp in the centre, supported by the pick and shovel: but the one that attracted the greatest attention was the Diggers Banner.

Protest associations were formed. Petitions were signed, and sent off to the government in Melbourne by dogcart; one was 40 feet long, 'mounted on linen and bound in green silk'. Women were not present at these volatile meetings, but their skills made possible the pageantry and display.

In 1854 the newly appointed Governor Hotham ordered twice-weekly licence hunts on the diggings. The fiercest response came from the Ballarat field, where anger at a specific case of corruption set off a series of protest meetings. The influence of a number of experienced Chartists shaped this movement into the Ballarat Reform League, with a more radical political program than the goldfields had seen. A mass meeting in early November demanded from the government an end to the licence system and the disbanding of the goldfields police force. And to ensure that the people's voice would be heard the meeting adopted the six points of the British charter, including manhood suffrage, payment of members of parliament and an end to property qualifications.

The deputation that took these demands to Governor Hotham warned him that to deny them would bring 'the spilling of blood' by 'infuriated men'. Hotham was not averse to the spilling of blood. He seems to have believed that the crushing of an armed revolt would end his problems on the fields and make him a hero with the rest of the community. He refused the demands of the delegation and sent all available troops to Ballarat. The democrats counselled patience, but the diggers responded by voting to burn their licences. The commissioner in charge of the fields responded with a licence hunt and took half a dozen prisoners. That afternoon, Thursday, hundreds of the diggers took up arms and enrolled in companies, swearing solemnly 'to defend their rights and liberties'. They set about drilling, raising a rebel flag and fortifying a hilltop with pit-slabs from the Eureka diggings.

The rest of the tale is an anticlimax. Organisation within the stockade was chaotic, and volunteers were deterred by the lack of guns and supplies. The moral force Chartists called upon the men to disperse, and their resolution began to weaken. By Saturday night only about 150 men remained. When 400 troops and police attacked early on Sunday morning they easily overran the stockade, capturing more than a hundred diggers and killing about thirty.

Hotham's strategy misfired. By Monday a Chartist-led meeting supported the cause that the diggers had died for. In Melbourne a pro-government meeting was taken over by dissidents and a huge gathering addressed by politicians and radical working men proclaimed 'the beginning of the history of the colony' as a democracy. On the goldfields men wore the Chartist red ribbon with a black ribbon added; quiet resistance made the licence system inoperable.

In the months that followed no jury could be found to convict the men captured at Eureka.

Most of the diggers' demands were granted by the government. The monthly licence fee was replaced by a 'miner's right' costing 1 pound per year, and entitling its bearer to vote. Later this provision was to ease the passage of manhood suffrage; when any man could buy a miner's right it was hard to deny that all should have the right to vote. There is irony in this outcome; the 'liberty' pursued by most of the Eureka men had little to do with voting or parliaments. But the belief that blood had been shed to bring about democracy in Victoria was to support a dynamic popular movement in that colony and to confirm the essential masculinity of politics.

Manhood suffrage was achieved in 1855 in South Australia, 1857 in Victoria, and 1858 in New South Wales. The fact that most men already had a vote or could easily get one made it hard to oppose the abstract principle of male suffrage. Opposition came mainly from conservative members of parliament who believed that citizenship should be reserved for men of property and heads of families. James Macarthur, the son of Elizabeth and John, argued in New South Wales that reform 'would take away all the influence of the family man, for he would be put on the same footing with the idle and dissolute stranger'. Macarthur's attack upon 'mere manhood' as a qualification for citizenship led him to argue that if single men could vote, there was 'no justice in withholding the electoral franchise from single women'. But his was a lone voice.

Most men seem to have assumed that men were so absolutely different from women that arguments about men's rights did not apply to women. Men could earn their citizenship by improving their economic status or their intellect; not so women. In 1853 the tradesmen and artisans of Perth, meeting at the Swan River Mechanics Institute, spent three nights debating the topic 'whether Women do or would possess the same amount of Intellect as man if they had the same advantages'; they decided that they didn't and wouldn't. The debaters believed that women's lack of intelligence justified men's rule over women in public and in private: women 'are incapable of equalling the man and taking the rules of Government into their own hands, and of ruling over the men – domestically or otherwise.

If women resented their exclusion from the great world of

politics they rarely said so publicly. A few letters published in the *Sydney Morning Herald* in 1857–58 claimed to speak for educated women. One was against democracy, fearing that as humble men gained political power, ladies of rank would lose 'what little influence we have in the social scale'. Others accepted the rights of all men to political and social equality, and asked for the same for all women. The writers denied that sexed bodies made for sexed minds; to restrict women's rights was to apply 'a physical condition as a test of moral fitness'.

Educated women rarely challenged the idea that men were their intellectual superiors. Letters and diaries and novels often show women deferring to male opinion merely because it is male; 'you will smile no doubt', wrote one intelligent young woman, Jane Ryrie, 'at my attempting to argue!'. A few women were less humble. Menie Parkes was a talented writer whose stories and poems helped keep the family when her father's ventures failed, as they often did. Henry Parkes respected her political advice. At eighteen years of age Menie wrote: 'I cannot think that all things should be held subordinate to the purpose of fitting myself for married life ... ought I not rather, to fit myself to pass through the world unaided?'. But such confidence was hard to maintain. Three years later Menie was deeply depressed to find 'how mediocre the one talent which I possess is in reality, how little I can expect to do with it, and in effect how almost worthless my life is ... I find I cannot achieve in the path I have chosen and I have not the heart to step back into a woman's beaten track'.

The wives and daughters of working men had less opportunity than Menie for intellectual and economic independence, and probably less desire. During the 1850s some 600 000 immigrants were drawn to Australia by gold and the prosperity it created. About two-fifths of these were women. Many single women came with their passages paid by colonial governments still anxious to balance the numbers of men and women in their populations. Many more came as members of families, and like earlier generations of immigrants the single women seem to have married as soon as they could. Given that domestic service was still the only waged work open to women, marriage and work within the family was probably their best option.

In 1852 Lucy Hart wrote to her mother in England, describing how she and her husband had struggled during their first years in South Australia, depriving themselves 'of many things they might have had' so that John Hart 'should not allways work under a Master'. Her husband's labours together with her own – taking in washing and ironing, keeping a cow and poultry and selling their produce – had earned them 50 pounds, and a lucky strike on the Victorian diggings had earned 200 pounds more. John Hart bought horses and a dray and went into business taking stores to the diggings. Lucy Hart also achieved economic independence of a kind, the only kind available to a woman without much education. She wrote proudly to her mother: 'now I consider myself well off in the world so I do nothing but my own work now'.

Marriage was equally necessary to men. One observer noted that 'the English immigrant, when he acquires money, increases his personal and domestic comforts' – and such comforts included a wife and children. Working men carried their concern for family life into the public world that they inhabited as citizens. The trade unionists of the 1850s were more ready than men in the previous decade to confront their masters over control of the workplace. The issue was not wages but hours of work. Masons and other workers demanded and won an eight-hour working day, two or three hours less than they would have worked in Britain. They spoke of the pain of working long hours in the colonial sun, and also of the need for 'time to improve themselves and their children, and to attend to their social and moral welfare'. The *Argus* believed that 'the really industrious and active-minded artisan' would rather lose a day's pay than forgo 'the peaceful pleasures of home ... digging in his garden, feeding his poultry, milking his cow, teaching his children'. The ideal householder-citizen of English political tradition is born again as the colonial working man digging his suburban garden.

It needs to be stressed that the *Argus* had in mind 'a pleasant, patriarchal domesticity'. Recent students of political thought have discovered a historical connection between the idea of democracy (the rule of the people) and the idea of patriarchy (the rule of men over women). The idea that all men have equal rights in governing the state seems always to have included the idea that individual men have absolute rights to govern their families.

The politics of democracy in New South Wales provide a nice

example of how this link worked in practice. In 1857 the British Government passed a law establishing a divorce court in England and Ireland. Before that time an act of parliament was necessary for divorce. The new law made divorce much easier for men than for women. The British Government called on the colonial parliaments to pass similar laws, to keep legislation uniform within the empire. Victoria and South Australia promptly agreed. But the New South Wales Government declined to act.

A recent study of divorce in New South Wales has shown that these new politicians – mostly 'selfmaking' immigrants like Henry Parkes – were vulnerable to attacks on their respectability and political legitimacy. Conservative members could discomfort them by suggesting that men of little education like themselves – shopkeepers, hotel keepers, auctioneers – had no right to be in politics. To introduce the topic of divorce into parliament was doubly dangerous to these men; it invited an attack on their personal lives, and it threatened marriage and men's position as household head.

The artisans of the Swan River Mechanics Institute were certain that women were not fitted for the political world that they themselves were attempting to enter. 'Women never have had and never can have the same ammount of Intellect and no one among us considers his wife is superior in Intellect to himself or superior in Governing powers.' The defence of masculine democracy, the power of all men to govern all women in public, went hand in hand with a defence of patriarchy, the power of individual men to govern individual women in private.

5 Man's Space, Woman's Place

In the early 1860s Caroline Chisholm, her energetic mind still focussed on the problems of white colonists, delivered a series of public lectures in Sydney. Some people, she observed, spoke 'as if they thought that no woman ought to have any opinions whatever as regards politics', but she had experience and insight to offer. Why should her good ideas die with her? Someone needed to speak out, for example, about the growing difficulties for so many city people who crowded together in 'small, ill-ventilated, and filthy domiciles which were not homes', sharing small yards with their cows, fowls and dogs, and paying, even so, high rents. Too many men abandoned wives to chase the goldrushes, too many little children died. Housewives in the city were grossly overworked, because their husbands opted out of their share of the labour and often spent their nights out drinking. Shop assistants toiled fearfully long hours. Domestic servants were another oppressed group, kept toiling away in their evenings when they should have free time. Vulnerable women were often sexually exploited in a society that offered them scant protection, yet made them victims while letting their male seducers off scot-free.

Caroline Chisholm had a remedy to offer. What else would better lead to improved life chances for colonists than the opening of squatters' leased lands to free selection for smallholding? The men stranded in dwindling goldrush areas, the urban workers who wanted cottage homes 'with armchairs for their aged parents, and with cradles for their young children', the innocent children who needed 'fresh air, plenty of room in their father's own cottage, and plenty of fresh milk', the wives who needed men wholeheartedly engaged in promoting the family's wellbeing – all hopes could be met by the opportunity to start afresh with homes of their own, on land of their own. In a lecture entitled 'Free Selection Before Survey', delivered to several hundred people at the Pitt Street Temperance Hall in 1860, Caroline Chisholm aligned herself firmly with the land reformers of the colonies, and in particular with John Robertson, who was leading the campaign in New South Wales. Colonial men had to stand up to men of property and wealth, she asserted, and take advantage of the recent democratic changes (which were working splendidly, overall) to wrench privilege from them. The squatter opposed smallholding in a fashion that was ruthless and unprincipled, as Caroline once discovered herself when she promoted cooperative agricultural communities for unemployed men and their families. The rich were to be feared, not respected: the true future of the colonies lay with ordinary working men and women.

Caroline Chisholm was highly unusual in this era for her capacity, as a woman, to command public attention for her forthright views, but her representation of the best course for colonial society was scarcely idiosyncratic. The issue of 'unlocking the lands' held by squatters was one of the colonial radicals' key policies and was rapidly gaining political momentum. But more pertinently, Chisholm spoke from a woman's particular perspective. Dominant voices have portrayed the economic development of the colonies, both in Chisholm's lifetime and since, as the concerns of white men in their exploitation of natural resources, their utilisation of new technology and of imported finances. Caroline Chisholm, as a white colonial woman, understood that economic choices were also choices about the character of colonial people and the fundamental gendered structures of society. She knew that the distinctive development of the colonies would revolve not only around geographical mobility and production, wealth and poverty, but also around sexuality and marriage, families, kinship and communities; she also saw that the areas of production and reproduction were interrelated. The territorial and economic expansion of the colonies in the decades from the 1860s to the 1890s continued to be spearheaded by white men, certainly. But it is important to capture at the same time the place allotted to white women, who may have played a less obvious, though still significant, part in these transformations.

First we should consider the experiences of white colonial men, and their search to satisfy their longings and needs. The near million and a half people of European origin who were settled in the colonies in the early 1860s clustered, for the most part, in port cities and in towns and rural areas radiating out from the coast. The exceptions were miners at isolated goldfields and the squatters who, with their families and labourers, occupied large tracts of land further afield, carved out of Aboriginal territories despite spirited resistance. The men already in the colonies, however, and the British men who continued to arrive seeking new livelihoods on this imperial frontier, were in no mind to limit their expansion territorially or their profits materially. Many men simply reacted with hope to new openings, while others sought new opportunities more aggressively. A major stimulus to this search was the acute economic need, experienced intensely by the 1860s, that arose in the wake of the goldrushes of the 1850s.

Gold had brought a very large influx of Europeans to the colonies of Victoria, in particular, and to New South Wales. As the ready alluvial gold diminished, this population looked for other employment, and as they married and produced children, their offspring also needed livelihoods once they reached thirteen or fourteen years of age. Many men in urban areas, too, chafed at their limited work options and wished to avoid a life of waged labour by some opening for independence on the land. Either there would be an exodus back to the lands of their origins (and some did return), or there must be intensified exploitation of the colonies' natural resources. The new male colonists had not come so far to suffer patiently penury and privation. After all, they had been enticed from home in the hopes of making a good living, and for married men this included the capacity to support wives and young children.

When men pressed for the opening up of land for smallholding, for example, it was in the name of independent livelihoods. As one radical paper spelled it out in the early 1860s, there would appear in the bush

the homes of an independent yeomanry, opening new sources of employment for their trade. Let the land be unreservedly opened, that they will see towns, not canvas ones, rise along the line. The gilded spire of the village church shall rise above the gum trees where the kangaroos now find a home, and the voice of happy children shall be heard ...

The homes, the church, the village, the children were predicated upon the presence of white women, yet the 'independent yeoman' was presented as the key figure.

A mill worker wrote to the *Argus* in 1863 of his situation as a husband and father of five children, 'none of which have as yet earned a penny'. As a wage earner getting no more than thirty hours of work a week, his need was for land, perhaps for cotton growing:

> often when speaking to my wife on the distress, does she try to make things look cheerful, but the half-stifled sighs which I hear, tell me it is but assumed cheerfulness. Oh, would that I could get to Queensland or some other cotton-growing country. What with my own labour or my three sons ... I should be able to repay the expenses.

With the attainment in the 1850s of democratic political forms, such men had some capacity to influence the legislatures towards the land reform spoken of so often over the previous decade. Politicians were urged to introduce legislation allowing the selection of land for small farms, to be carved out from the squatters' leases, preferably before survey. More, they were asked to provide lenient financial terms, so that new selectors could take up the land with loans to be repaid in instalments. Radicals also expected men in power to provide the necessary infrastructure that would make the new ventures viable: railways, roads and bridges, the new telegraph, port facilities among them.

The visions of both colonial radicals and liberals coincided in this goal. The two groups pressed for closer settlement for intensive agriculture and opposition to the squatters' hegemony, both economically and politically, and were prepared to combine their forces politically. Radical men did not draw antagonistic lines between themselves and all owners of property or employers of labour. As long as middle-class men earned their living by genuine personally performed work, be it in modest areas of industry, commerce, on the land, or in the professions, their interests could be seen to merge with those of urban skilled labourers, rural workers or diggers. It was the rich, those who exploited others' labour, those who manipulated resources, finances and banking, and who gained undue power from their ill-gotten gains, who were to be opposed, and the squatters loomed large in this group. In turn, liberal men contested the power of a landed pseudo-gentry against their own urban bases of wealth, and resented the squatters' keen interest in cheap labour, which they were willing to import under indentured contracts if necessary, as convict labour was slowly cut off. In theory, liberals stood for free enterprise untrammelled by the intervention of centralised governments. But in the case of the desire for land, they also saw that their attachment to equal rights could only be realistic if politicians acted against the current leaseholders' dominance. Liberal members of colonial legislatures became the spokesmen for the radicals, as well as themselves, on the land question.

Starting with Land Acts successfully promoted by William Nicholson in Victoria from 1860 and John Robertson in New South Wales from 1861, the eastern colonies witnessed legislative efforts to break up the large pastoral estates to allow selection of land and occupancy by smallholders. The precise nature of the legislation varied from colony to colony. For the most part selectors could peg out any crown land that had not been 'improved' by squatters, up to around 300 acres, for which they made an initial payment, with the remaining amount to be paid off in instalments over a period of years. Selectors were required in turn to 'improve' their land, to build houses, live there, and invest in developing the farm. Women as well as men were, under certain conditions, allowed to select land – in Victoria, if they were single and eighteen years or over. Those who did so usually operated as part of a family enterprise: a widow might select with grown sons, a young woman might claim a block beside those taken up by a brother, or father, or fiance. This movement was essentially driven by male initiative.

Squatters, too, were permitted to select in proportion to the improvements they had made to their properties. But squatters would seek far more devious means of retaining or acquiring back their domains; selection areas became sites of male struggles as squatters and selectors asserted themselves not only to gain a living from the land but to protect their turf from incursions by the other. In terms of resources, expertise and networks of support it was a decidedly unequal battle.

Meantime, more men with sheep and cattle pushed out the

boundaries of European settlement by venturing further into the interior to make new claims on large leases, subduing Aboriginal resistance in sickeningly similar fashion to earlier colonists. The new squatting initiatives resulted in exploitation of land northwards in South Australia, westwards in New South Wales, north and north-west in Queensland, and north and north-east in Western Australia. By 1890 the frontier of white settlement had been pushed to its outer limit, in terms of land that British-Australians could utilise productively, or climates they could endure.

As pastoralists moved into the Aboriginal lands they named the 'outback', so too did successive waves of miners. The decline in alluvial mining set in quite swiftly in the areas of the first gold strikes in Victoria and New South Wales, and the numbers living in those areas declined accordingly through the 1860s. Some miners stayed on as wage labourers for mining companies, when entrepreneurs financed the equipment to exploit gold at deeper levels in such places as Bendigo. Their lives came to resemble those of workers in the older coal-mining areas such as Newcastle. But fresh gold strikes further north into Queensland saw new rushes, to Ravenswood in 1868, Charters Towers in 1872 and Palmer River the next year. The path of discoveries traced an arc to the north, then westwards across into the Northern Territory, until the final major discoveries of the 1890s in the west at Coolgardie and Kalgoorlie. And there were other mineral discoveries: silver lead at Broken Hill, tin at Mt Bischoff in Tasmania, in New England and in northern Queensland at Herberton. Copper, too, was mined, notably in Wallaroo-Moonta and Kadinga in South Australia. The need for finance for investment in steam engines, pneumatic rock drills and dynamite soon created societies divided into owners and workers, since only a few men had the capacity to raise the necessary substantial capital. Further encroachments on Aboriginal territory occurred along the northern coastlines where white men engaging in maritime occupations, fishing, pearling, or catching bêche-de-mer, proliferated.

Other white men followed the initial pioneers. They built railways, laid cables and sank shafts; they managed stations, felled trees, slaughtered animals, dug dams and erected fences; they trapped rabbits, mustered cattle and shore sheep. In country towns other men ran shops and small businesses, and offered services such as policing, medicine and banking.

Much of what in the opening of the American West was achieved by private capitalist ventures was accomplished in the Australian colonies by government initiatives. Men in government continued to create the conditions that made other white men's livelihoods possible, and which, as a consequence, robbed the indigenous peoples of their livelihoods. Governments fostered this development not only by making and enforcing new laws and by providing transport and communications, but by creating the infrastructure for the growth of towns and cities. Politicians provided finance for roads, streets, bridges, electricity, gas pipes, water, and eventually sewerage, and encouraged further immigration to supplement the labour force. They also played a key political role in facilitating the inflow of foreign capital, which made possible a great deal of this development, and the construction of public works by local councils.

The combination of increased production in the interior and governmental provision of a commercial infrastructure stimulated the rapid growth of urban centres. Heavy industry employed men to process primary products, especially from the expansion of pastoralism and the new agriculture. Male entrepreneurs established industries to provide the materials needed for railways, road-building and bridge-building, for farming equipment and mining. Men established industries to provide the needs of the growing local population for clothing, boots and shoes, foods and drink.

And the burgeoning towns and cities themselves stimulated further industry, through the construction of public buildings, schools, hospitals, churches, housing. By the 1880s colonial cities, especially Melbourne and Sydney, had grown into impressive metropolises with splendid public buildings, efficient public transport, theatres, parks, galleries, museums, zoological gardens, and outer suburbs of garden-surrounded detached houses. There was a wealth of work for men to do, a wealth of schemes for men to dream up and initiate, and, for the luckiest, real wealth to be made. Men built houses; fired metals; performed accounting tasks in banks and offices; traded and sold goods; serviced other settlers' bodies, teeth and souls; settled secular disputes, and taught the elite in universities. As local councillors, justices of the peace, church wardens and magistrates they organised, admonished and controlled the population. Men made spaces for themselves everywhere as they took full possession of the continent.

The very absence of women from certain spaces since the beginning of white settlement had been and continued to be a significant factor in colonial relationships. Where numbers of men were congregated together for any length of time – at a goldrush site, for example – or were left without female partners on pastoral properties, they coped with their sexual and material needs in ways that could be stoical and disciplined, but could alternatively be destructive and negative. In these cases Aboriginal women bore the brunt of white male sexual cruelty, particularly as their vulnerability and increasing destitution exposed them to abuse. Further, for every reserved, self-sufficient bushman or digger there were others whose absence from what Chisholm termed 'domestic influences', and from familial responsibilities, left them incentive, time and energy for drinking and gambling, and fighting among themselves – or against Aborigines. The raw male frontier thereby contributed to the construction of one style of colonial masculinity which valorised all-male company and pursuits, which mocked family ties, and was essentially hostile towards women.

White women did, however, filter into frontier spaces, and their presence in growing numbers was critical to the social transformations of these decades. Men posed as providers for women as they pressed for livelihoods, often obscuring the fact that white women were essential to the economic expansion of the colonies, although in more complex and varied ways than were men. Women, the bearers of white colonial babies and the sexual partners of white men, also attended to the personal and material care of young and old, which enabled men to devote themselves single-mindedly to productive labour. Women laboured, too, in economically significant ways, on the land, in public waged employment, or within the domestic arena. They often undertook the work that men avoided because it was repetitive and monotonous, or because it brought small returns, or because it meant dealing with tiresome sick people or the young or old. Women of course benefited from men's primary labour, if sometimes fitfully and arbitrarily, dependent on male whim. With their own wellbeing linked to male enterprises, women themselves became central to the shaping of notions of class during these crucial decades. Female agency underlay the character of the economic transformation of the colonies, just as the possibilities of the exploitation of colonial resources in turn helped shape the relationship between women and men.

Virtually everywhere that men went in the colonies, women eventually went too. The European settlement of Australia was necessarily a female as well as a male enterprise. It would not have been accomplished had not women consented, gladly or reluctantly as the case might be, to accompany men on their ventures just as they, or their mothers, had done initially from Britain. Men might move temporarily to what they perceived as unsettled areas to exploit resources for economic gain. They remained residents isolated from women in remote places, however, only by default. European settlement occurred when white women were present to live with men, sleep with them and bear the children who would form the basis of a new community. Women established the families that would be the rationale for the economic endeavours of men, justifying their labour and stimulating the trappings of 'civilised' life in towns and cities.

When male relatives of the hardened pioneer squatter Patrick Durack were planning to move to property in the Kimberley region of Western Australia, Patrick was surprised to find them delaying taking wives to the area. 'It's no country for white women, Patsy', the men said. 'Just now women and kids would be nothing but a handicap.' Patrick's reply was a telling reminder of original pioneering ethos: 'But a country without women, I cannot picture it! It will be a sad, barren place until they come'.

Patrick Durack had certainly witnessed enough of the sufferings of white women and children exposed to the harshness of landscape, climate and distance. He arrived in New South Wales in 1853, with parents and a large number of younger siblings, following his father's brother in this hopeful trek from hunger-ridden Ireland. When his uncle was killed before his eyes in an accident with a cart, Patrick found himself responsible for a large number of dependants, as well as for the impoverished Irish relations whose migration he continued to sponsor. Initially family members settled on small farms in Goulburn. But Patrick was tempted to gamble on a pastoral property in western Queensland in 1867, at Thylungra on Kyabra Creek. Patrick and his wife, Mary, had two very small children; Mary's brother, his pregnant wife and small son accompanied them. Mary's parents went too, reluctant to be so distant from their two grown children since they had lost four children who died on the voyage out to Australia. It took the Duracks three months to reach Bourke, still some way short of their destination. Patrick and Mary's two-year-old nephew died on the journey in a fever, calling for water, and was buried in a rough, shallow grave marked with a wooden cross. The Durack women shared all the hardships of white pioneering in the outback as the station was slowly established on an economic footing.

Most men expected female relatives, whatever their health or circumstances, to share tents, bark huts, wattle and daub cottages, as well as sturdier homesteads. Similarly in towns and cities, wives and daughters lived with men in rented rooms or shared houses, in tiny cottages off lanes and back alleys, as well as in substantial homes. While many women reaped some of the benefits of economic development and the prosperity it eventually generated they also faced hardship and deprivation to be with men, and to share their lot. The colonies are often described as though the need for marriage and reproduction was women's alone, shaping their choices and addressing their specific needs. On the contrary, the construction of male sexuality and men's sense of masculinity were often connected with possessing a female sexual partner and children, as well as relying on women for other services. Men's need for women was a driving force in the patterns of economic exploitation of Australia and in the geographic movements of men.

For those who would want later to portray white colonial settlement as a tale of male courage, or endurance, or adventure, the undoubted masculinity of the early years of the colonies added validity. Yet in reality, through the later decades of the nineteenth century, the predominance of men slowly but surely decreased. The excess of men over women began diminishing in New South Wales and Victoria after the 1850s goldrushes partly because of the immigration of single women, but mostly because the sexes were equal in number among the colonial born, who constituted 53 per cent of the white population in 1871 and outnumbered migrants even in adult age groups by the 1880s. Whereas in 1861 there were 138 white men for every 100 white women, by 1891, with the population now over three million, the ratio had changed to 119 to 100 white women. These women were, of course, more likely to live in urban areas, and indeed they came to outnumber men in some pockets of the older cities. Even so, women lived almost everywhere in the country, and the relatively low proportion of white women in the outback diminished slowly but surely as the century proceeded.

At the same time as the white male/female ratio in the population slowly evened, so did the number of single men decrease. The higher likelihood of a white colonial woman marrying by the time she reached her mid-forties remained true. But by the early 1890s at least three in every four colonial men were also married by that age, and in Victoria and most notably South Australia the proportion was higher: in the latter case, the figure was nearly 90 per cent in urban areas. For women, the reverse was true: a slightly greater proportion of urban women remained unmarried by their mid-forties than their country sisters. For reasons discussed in the next chapter nearly one white woman in ten in urban New South Wales was single in the early 1890s. During the decades from the 1860s to the 1890s the majority of white men, rural or urban dwellers, did marry, even if single men, more than single women, remained a notable feature of the social structure. This was partly due to the higher age at marriage of men, some five years later than for women.

The increasing likelihood that adult men were married or would marry in the not too distant future gave further substance to the valorisation of the respectable, prudent family man fostered in the colonies before 1860. It was a model of masculinity distinctly at variance with the rough-hewn independent white male of the frontier myth, and competed with this representation quite forcefully.

This working man's vision of manliness invested in domestic responsibility found a counterpart among the urban middle class in a romantic elaboration of the separate spheres appropriate to men and women. Although this model took fresh shape in the colonial context it was essentially as derivative of English social beliefs as was the working-class model of respectability. Traditionalists portrayed men as the active sex, defenders of the home, those who fought the public battle for the family, and were potentially roughened by it. Women, in contrast, were the keepers of the home, the guardian of the family's moral and spiritual values, and, so long as they kept to their allotted sphere, the consciences of men. As the Anglican Bishop of Melbourne, James Moorhouse, asserted to his flock, woman was not an inferior kind of man, any more than man was an inferior kind of woman. Both taken together fulfilled the ideal of humanity. He hurried to add, however, that this difference in nature and function carried with it a kind of subordination.

Man, the fighter and toiler, occupies, as he must, the more prominent, though by no means more important position. Woman, on the other hand, the nurse, the comforter, the sanctifier, can only do her work if she keeps out of the din of battle and the glare of publicity. Her delicate qualities wither and die beneath the glare of publicity.

And so the bishop cautioned against any rash voices that might be raised seeking the same rights for women and men. 'Fanaticism would ignore these eternal natural distinctions', he said. 'Aiming at dull, mechanical equality, which abolishes the rich variety of nature, it would make man more effeminate and woman more manly, thus deteriorating each.' Did this seem contradictory in the light of Christian teaching on the religious equality of men and women? Not a jot. The woman was the religious and social equal of man. Indeed, she might well be his moral and intellectual superior. But 'when two people live together as heads of a family, the position of leader must be assigned to one of them. Nature has marked out man for that position by awarding to him the preponderance of the active powers of life'.

As long as wives were notionally in a situation where their lives were constrained and directed by their husbands, and where husbands and fathers took ultimate responsibility for the economic viability of the group, the fiction of the separate spheres could be maintained. And with it was sustained the assumption that women's functions were personal, obscure, secret, in the private world of existence. Men, it seemed, inhabited the public world, the arena of truly significant undertakings. The paternalism of the masculinity embedded in the male assumption of headship of a family suppressed public acknowledgment of women almost as effectively as that other style of masculinity which derided or bypassed them.

Life for women was not, however, so readily compartmentalised. The substance of women's work within the family varied according to rank, but all wives carried out labour that was significant materially or ideologically. First, consider their childbearing. There was a continuing high colonial birthrate that was based, not so much on an eager desire of women to bear children, as on the absence of effective means of preventing conception. As one woman, Christiana Blomfield, wrote home to her niece, 'You ask me in one of your letters if you have any more cousins'. Apart from the three older boys, there was now a little girl aged eighteen months – 'a very fine child and beginning to be very interesting'. But what a surprise to be able to relate that shortly there would be another baby, to be named Louisa Matilda if a girl, and Barrington if a boy. 'I think your Aunt Matilda will say we stock our house too fast now, but in this colony we are only considered very moderate folks. Most people add one to their family every year.' Parents sometimes spoke hopefully of setting the baby clothes aside for some time, as did Joseph Elliott in a letter in 1860 from his Adelaide home to his mother in England. Joseph was father to three children aged five, three and seventeen months (another baby had died in infancy). He described the furnishings of their family home, including a chest containing 'Baby Linen put away I hope for a long time'. But this did not turn out to be possible: his wife Rebecca, bore six more children, four boys during the 1860s, and two little girls, Ethel and Daisy, in 1872 and 1875 respectively.

In the three decades from the 1860s to the 1890s, white women like Rebecca Elliott continued to bear children in considerable numbers. Wives who were born in the late 1830s (1836–41), many of whom began childbearing in the early 1860s, bore on average seven children (where all marriages were taken into consideration). Around 60 per cent of these women bore six or more children. The wives of the birth cohort of the late 1850s (1856–61), many of whom began childbearing in the early 1880s, bore almost six children on average, and almost 50 per cent of them bore six or more children. The slightly lower rate can be accounted for by a slow increase in never-married women, and a slight rise in the age of marriage.

Women's burden in reproduction is scarcely captured by the mere recitation of statistics, especially since stillbirths were not counted and, as well as known offspring, a woman might have experienced as many as two or three unproductive pregnancies. Bearing a lot of children and rearing most of them to early maturity was an enormous investment of energy, effort, and anxiety. Women knew they faced death in childbirth. The mother of the novelist Rose Praed, Matilda Murray-Prior, when pregnant and isolated on a station in outback Queensland, nearly died giving birth to her first baby. As a nineteen-year-old bride, she contemplated the impending birth: 'Having neither doctor nor nurse, and knowing that I might die before there was any hope of medical assistance, I endeavoured to prepare my mind for leaving this world'. Many a first-time mother shared her trepidation, and few women ever contemplated childbirth without fear.

The dangers were manifold. Medical intervention by doctors might relieve some difficulties but also sometimes caused puerperal fever, a greater danger than the actual birth itself. Midwives, often comforting, kindly women who had borne children themselves, frequently managed births unaided, but they were not trained in the use of forceps, which were crucial in difficult births. Mismanaged births could also leave women with a variety of gynaecological ills, such as prolapsed uteruses, damaged cervixes and perineal tears, that could bedevil them all their lives.

This prolific childbearing meant that the white colonial populations were young populations; babies and children were everywhere, and their presence made a considerable difference to the character of colonial society. As the English visitor Richard Twopeny noted of the colonies in the early 1880s, nurses were expensive and hence babies much in evidence. 'Consequently, baby lives in the family circle almost from the time of birth.' Babies, whom he felt were much indulged, accompanied mothers as they went about their household tasks, and even when they received visitors.

But the middle and lower classes of Australia are not content with baby's supremacy in the household. Wherever his mother goes, baby is also taken. He fills railway carriages and omnibuses, obstructs the pavement in perambulators, and is suckled *coram populo* in the Exhibition. There is no getting away from him, unless you shut yourself up altogether. He squalls at concerts; you have to hold him while his mother gets out of the omnibus, and to kiss him if you are visiting her house.

To suggest that white women were significant in the colonies as sexual partners to white men and as bearers of white children leaves unaddressed their further importance in the work of social reproduction. Wives' rearing of children, their work of transforming raw materials into the necessities for living, or purchasing goods, or organising the household's work, or performing income-earning labour themselves all contributed to their own and their families' style of living. Women's labour underwrote the economic transformation of colonial Australia; women's labour was a major component in the character of the distinctive white society that began to emerge; women were central to colonial class formation.

Rosa Praed, the novelist who wrote reminiscences of growing to maturity in outback Queensland, had a keen eye for the ways in which women were central to rural enterprises, and the styles which women stamped upon family endeavours in rural Australia. She spoke as a member of an élite group, despite occasional irony. There was her own educated mother, who had written with such fear of her first birth, and found herself as a young mother working on one failing property after another, trailing after a would-be-squatter husband. Matilda Murray-Prior utilised Aboriginal women's labour, but Rosa portrayed her as also performing, as did other women on properties, menial duties amidst the dust, flies, heat, drought and bushfires; similarly their menfolk, despite pretensions to gentry status, salted beef, milked cows and fetched wood and water when Aboriginal labour and white workers alike were not available. The Murray-Priors's educated neighbour had no household help at all, and seven children to care for. 'I call it just slavery, working all day and never feeling tidy', this overwrought wife complained; 'washing pots and pans and cleaning knives, which is what I hate most – the brick dust gets under one's nails. I just loathe my hands!'.

Yet Rosa traced how through it all these wives from middle-class backgrounds sustained a semblance of genteel standards, educating their children in manners and skills appropriate to their class, fitting out their homes with 'good taste', sustaining rituals of meals, dress and entertainment that signalled their true station in life, however temporarily obscured. Rosa herself scoured milk pans, cleaned weevily flourbins, exterminated cockroaches and spiders, bound saddlecloths, made pie-melon jam and shelled corn. But she was still prepared for gentility and marriage to the appropriate suitor. Rosa had no trouble distinguishing quite early in her life the essential differences between her own middle-class family and the families of local selectors eking out a spare living as they struggled to build up their small farms. Typical of such a family was the strapping fifteen-year-old selector's daughter who seems to have helped Rosa's mother around the house. Rosa describes her as a girl inured to the fatigues of physical work by her experiences shepherding her father's sheep barefoot under the Queensland sun. Unlettered, unabashed, curious but unawed by the pictures in the drawing room and the new sewing machine, Rosa conceded that the selector's daughter gave amiable service until she married 'Barcoo Bill', a stationhand from Rosa's father's property, and left to prosper on a new selection.

Down in the local township of Boonah, the keeper of the hotel (a 'two-tiered pine-box with ill-joined partitions and a zinc cover') was a widow who had once known better days, and who controlled with equanimity her loud-mouthed, heavy drinking male customers. 'They recognise that I'm superior', Rosa Praed had the widow asserting; 'if anyone gets rowdy, it's enough for me to say the word, the others will back me up and call out, "Don't you hear the lady talking to you?"'. It wasn't, she conceded, the life she would have chosen, all things being equal. Women in rural areas might find themselves translated into uncertain and difficult arenas but the acquisition and maintenance of status, authority and social power did not rely solely on men's access to wealth. Women, too, were central actors.

Miles Franklin, another educated woman writer from a propertied background, described her mother's family home of Talbingo in western New South Wales. In most successful squatting families wives had been at first, as was Miles Franklin's grandmother, important to the working arrangements of the property. Slowly she had adapted to the more subtle, though by no means less important, undertaking of displaying the taste and refinement, and sustaining the social networks among their kind, which transmuted a husband's labour and money into an enviable style of living, to be perpetuated through daughters' felicitous marriages and sons' openings to landed or business careers. Such a transformation could occur in one generation. The charming homestead at Talbingo, the orchards and gardens, the hospitality and entertainments, the intricate pattern of broader kinship interaction: Miles Franklin captured its delights in *Childhood at Brindabella* and *My Brilliant Career*, as well as the role of her grandmother and aunts in making it so.

Both women and men on smallholdings faced obstacles to gaining secure tenure, and had to confront the many ways in which squatters tried to retain land, or acquire it back from selectors. One such example is Ellen Kelly, mother of a large brood of seven children including the eleven-year-old Ned. Ellen was widowed in 1866 and, as a single woman, took advantage of her opportunity to select 88 acres of land for a small farm near Greta and Benalla in northern Victoria. For close on thirteen years Ellen, illiterate and poor but resilient, fought with the help of her older children to keep the farm afloat in the face of the depredations of local squatters. Among other strategies to harass selectors, squatters often took the farmers' stock if animals wandered on to their land. As Ned Kelly explained in his Jerilderie letter in 1879, 'Whitty and Burns not being satisfied with all the picked land on King River and Boggy Creek ... impounded every beast they could catch even off Government roads[;] if a poor man happened to leave his house or a bit of a poddy calf outside his paddock it would be impounded'. Ned and his brothers retaliated with behaviour that rapidly brought them to the attention of the law.

Once put in court for 'furious riding in a public place' (through a street in Benalla), suspected of selling sly grog to supplement the family income and with a keen eye out for an alternative male provider, Ellen Kelly was the mainstay of the family's resistance to dispossession and destitution. In the autumn of 1878 Ellen apparently hit Constable Alexander Fitzpatrick with a shovel when he came to the farm to arrest young Dan on a charge of horse stealing (she admitted she had a 'damned bad temper'). The squatter McBean presided on the bench at her trial, and she was sentenced to three years' hard labour; Ned Kelly said the thought of his 'poor little brothers and sisters' left motherless made his 'blood boil'. When Ellen was released in 1881 her sons Dan and Ned were both dead, the latter for the murder of a policeman at Stringybark Creek, an act that was to entrench him in colonial mythology. His mother's feisty defence of her family went unremarked in folklore.

But struggles with squatters were just the worst of the selectors' problems. Some farmers had never worked land, in Britain or the colonies; some had been farmers, but had no notion of how to clear and use Australian land. Droughts and floods, rabbits, insects and moulds faced them, as well as the insecurities of fluctuating prices and uneven demand for their produce. There was the added problem of transporting the goods quickly, or cheaply, to city depots. The farmers were not people hoping for peasant-style subsistence, but producers wanting a decent surplus, using distant markets. But though they worked hard to attain that security of tenure and income, perhaps as many as half of the hopeful agriculturalists and dairy farmers did not survive on the land to see the day when they had paid off loans on properties and became freehold landowners.

The small farmers who did succeed were often those who had acquired larger holdings, an effort in which the leases taken out by family members, including women, not infrequently contributed. The presence of a competent, hard-working woman was crucial to this growth. Women milked cows and made butter, kept fowls and tended gardens to obtain some cash income, as their older children worked alongside their fathers, removed from school at peak rural work times to do so.

Consider the contribution of Ann Currie, a Gippsland dairy farmer's wife who kept a careful work diary over several decades of life on their small holding. The whole family worked hard. Husband John was out on the property day in and day out, performing the heavy physical labour of breaking in scrub-covered terrain, of tending cows, ploughing, sowing crops, harvesting and haymaking as the seasons passed. Sons Tom and Bert were from the age of ten out of school and helping with a range of tasks including cutting scrub, grubbing roots, clearing stumps and felling trees; so too was their sister Kate. The boys took other paid work at times: Tom on the railways, Bert at age twelve managing a milk-round. Only the little girls, Fernie and Rose, were exempt; they walked alone to school over several miles of rough country roads. One little toddler had drowned in the well, when unattended for a few moments. Ann herself, sometimes with Kate's help, performed the household tasks, including making preserves and syrups from farm-grown fruit. In addition she made sausages and hams for sale. She bred fowls, ducks and geese, and sold eggs and poultry. She assisted with the milking, and churned butter for sale, somewhere between 10 and 18 pounds each week. She also made cheese for the family's use.

For Ann Currie even social occasions entailed the performance of useful household chores. When she visited a neighbour one afternoon Ann noted: 'I took a Dozen pillow slips. We nearly finished them'. It was no wonder that she would say at times: 'I am not half well[;] hardly able to crawl about[;] took a Dose of Senna tea'. John Currie was known as the farmer yet without Ann's work the resources of the family would have been spare indeed.

The work for small farmers' wives could be grinding without the modest outcomes that the Curries enjoyed. Mary Gilmore, a champion of the lot of poor rural and urban women, in *Old Days: Old Ways* described a Riverina selector's wife, Mrs Ricklys, whose efforts were crucial to the family's economic fortunes, one woman among many where families paid the price of land in the wife's premature ageing through overwork coupled with childbearing. The family ate possum and crows, owned few animals, and planted only a little wheat as money for seed was scarce. It had been 'the man and the woman who, as horses, had pulled the harrow over the seed when it had been sown', wrote Gilmore; in the first wheat plantings in Riverina, many harrows were handpulled, and sometimes, as in the present case, women had to do it.

If Rosa Praed had been an eager interpreter of the place of wives in establishments on the land, the novelist Ada Cambridge, wife of an Anglican clergyman, wrote similarly from the perspective of an urban member of what was snobbishly termed 'the better class of people'. She described the town of Wangaratta in the early 1870s as containing 'a highly-civilised society', headed by a police magistrate and two doctors and their wives, one of whom even managed to employ a Swiss nurse: her children chattered in 'baby French'. After them came the bank managers and their wives. One such couple, who belonged to 'two substantial colonial families of high repute', held pleasant parties headed by the 'lady', a 'charming woman and hostess'. Admitted into this circle were 'leading tradesfolk, between whose class and that conventionally supposed to be above them the line of demarcation is always very thin'. Ada Cambridge continued:

I keep in affectionate remembrance the wife of a stationer who was like a mother to me, the wife of a general storekeeper who often sat with me when I was lonely and needed looking after, and the wife of a chemist with whom I was in particular sympathy at that time.

And then, there were the 'cottage people' who, however, did not consider themselves to be 'the poor', even if beyond the social pale according to Ada's scale of values.

In the cities of Sydney, Melbourne, Adelaide, and increasingly Brisbane and Perth, the families of wealthy business and professional men were living in decidedly greater splendour than their country town counterparts. Like the squatting families with whom the urban wealthy became intertwined, through marriages, through commercial dealings and increasingly because of contiguity, the wives put their considerable talents towards sustaining standards of gentility, and measuring whom from the aspiring members of the newly arrived would be admitted to the ranks of genteel society, whose menfolk dominated politics and property. The group claimed access to the circle of governors and governors' wives as their touchstone of recognition. Their large, lavishly appointed homes displayed their attachment to the material trappings of high status.

Ada Cambridge herself – without the necessary wealth but with all the social capital for nice distinctions – demonstrated the success of mothers in inculcating appropriate values in their young. One son had been a boarder at Geelong Grammar School. After Ada and her husband shifted to Melbourne they asked the boy to transfer to being a day boy at Melbourne Grammar School. Having been over four years at Geelong, and his boat having been Head of the River most of the time, he responded: 'I would sooner kill myself'. Such pecuniary savings could therefore not be contemplated! 'I think the Boat Races and Speech Days have furnished the keenest joys of my Melbourne life', Ada confessed. She fought off 'the thieving little town-boys' who persisted in stealing her fruit, having the audacity to tear off palings in the fence to enter. (One of her growing sons occasionally boxed their ears.) She commended her young domestic servant, a devout Roman Catholic, for never inconveniencing the Cambridge household because of her religious observances. The maid would do washing in the middle of the night in order to get to morning services, and would leave mass to put the potatoes on to cook for Sunday lunch, 'and trot back again'. A treasure indeed for a family prepared to benefit from her poorly paid sacrifices.

The majority of middle-class urban wives like Ada Cambridge sustained comparatively modest establishments with the help of one maid and of older daughters once they had completed their schooling. The servant undertook the heaviest work, but wives with several growing children had continuous involvement in child care; with lighter household duties such as sewing, ironing and preparation of desserts or preserves to keep up household standards, such wives were well occupied a considerable portion of the day and week. Take, for instance, Alice Johns, wife of Reynell Johns, who was clerk of the court of petty sessions and deputy coroner for Fitzroy, Collingwood and Carlton in the 1880s. The Johns, with their five children Harold, May, Nell, Arthur and Clare, lived in a comfortable two-storey terrace in North Fitzroy; Florrie, their young servant, also lived in. The children did not appear to perform many of the chores in Reynell's painstakingly detailed diary. The adults catered for their needs. Reynell was a fond husband and father, who hastened home from his work each evening and each Saturday afternoon ready to garden, or mend broken furniture and toys, or occasionally help mind the baby or entertain his visiting relatives. He was an enthusiastic natural history scientist, with a modest but interesting collection of artifacts neatly shelved in the parlour, which he cleaned out and dusted once a week to save others the trouble. Clearly, however, most of the labour of keeping a household of eight people operating smoothly fell on Alice's shoulders, with Florrie's assistance. Florrie undertook the physically onerous work of heavy cleaning and the laundry, as well as some food preparation and washing up. Mostly, however, Alice worked alongside her during much of the day. On Florrie's day off, or when she was on holiday, Alice was busy indeed. The children were to be cared for, the older ones taken to and from school, the little ones breastfed, carried about and soothed. There were outings for them all, to church and dentists, to beaches, parks and to relatives. And there were countless nights of broken sleep as one child after another suffered colds, coughs, earaches, diarrhoea, measles and mumps.

Poor Alice had had 'a bad day', Reynell Johns noted on one

occasion. 'Harold came home early with a headache, Arthur fell and cut his lip deeply, and May and Clare have bad colds, which makes the latter very troublesome.' Reynell could go to work each day, as did so many other professional men, secure in the knowledge that wives at home were organising their households with considerable dedication, allowing their husbands to concentrate on furthering their careers.

Urban wives could as occasion allowed be found assisting husbands more directly in their economic concerns than could Alice Johns. Wives of clergymen, as Ada Cambridge saw with dismay, frequently offered themselves as second, unpaid labourers in the parish cause. (It was not the parson who 'bears the burden and heat of the day', she remarked caustically, but 'the uncomplaining drudge who backs him at all points' and all too often made him 'selfish and idle by her readiness to do his work as well as her own'.) Wives of small businessmen or of professional men such as doctors, shopkeepers, councillors or politicians might work alongside their husbands; husbands and wives not infrequently taught in schools together. Other wives offered services from home, as teachers of music, dancing and French, or by undertaking sewing, millinery, feather cleaning or mantua-making. Numbers of middle-class wives continued such work, or took it up, when husbands were incapacitated, or died. In *The Getting of Wisdom* the writer Henry Handel (Ethel) Richardson described how, after her father died in 1879, her mother worked as a country postmistress, thereby supporting Ethel's education at the Presbyterian Ladies' College in the city.

The domestic labour and child care undertaken by urban working-class wives made a significant contribution to their families' ability to maximise resources. Boiling water for heavy laundry; cooking over wood or coal-fired ranges, where they were not fortunate enough to acquire gas cookers; coping in small houses with large families; carrying shopping; struggling to keep children clean and husbands fed; all represented crucial and often physically demanding labour, particularly for working-class women, who laboured without benefit of paid help. Indeed, the performance by men of waged work for long hours at sites distant from home was predicated on the personal, unwaged labour of wives, whose worth was often recognised fully when illness or death deprived the family of their services. The poorest took in outwork from factories; or performed washing, ironing or cleaning services for other households; or found ways of selling goods such as newspapers, rags and bottles, and old clothes to obtain meagre rewards. In their resourcefulness they resembled poor women across the rural and urban divide, who used their wits and commandeered child labour to keep their families from starving.

The poorest women kept their families afloat through appalling difficulties. Elizabeth Rogers of Adelaide, for example, became the breadwinner for her four children, herself and her husband when he became a chronic invalid in the late 1880s. By taking in sewing from a sweater factory and working from 7.30 a.m. until midnight or 1 a.m. she could earn 14 shillings a week. 'I am not all the time at my machine', she explained to an inquirer. 'I have my family to attend to. That is why I work such late hours at night. There are dozens around me who have to do the same.' When Rose Hussey in Brisbane left her husband because he ill-treated her, she took two of her three daughters aged nine and eleven to sell newspapers with her on street corners, by which they earned altogether 9 shillings a week; in addition Rose scrubbed out a Wesleyan church once a week for an additional shilling. When a charity worker pressed her to put her daughters in an orphanage, since they were getting no schooling, Rose replied: 'I am very delicate, and it is only my children who keep me up. I should not like to part with them all'. Also of Brisbane was the widow Mrs Wilson, who had six children to provide for, and who similarly told her story at an inquiry in 1888. The two oldest boys, one only eight years of age, found jobs, the mother joining the younger at a jam factory; sometimes she received weekly wages, sometimes she was on piecework. She trudged the 5 miles to and from the factory and home each day by foot; her work hours were from 7.30 a.m. to 5.30 p.m.; she never made more than 12 shillings a week, unless she was on piecework. The contribution of such women to sustaining the economy of colonies was undoubtedly marginal but, even if colonial statisticians found such work difficult to quantify, their nearest and dearest certainly appreciated its significance.

In urban areas there were male fields of work where some women – mostly single women – were increasingly to be found. These women were the daughters of urban workers, from homes where the girls' as well as the boys' earnings would be a welcome addition; or of farmers who could no longer provide for grown children of either sex; or of middle-class homes where girls wanted horizons beyond the domestic round of assisting their mothers. Demographically the number of single women in towns and cities was increasing. Waged work was being created that women could do. While women worked within the family, even where they undertook heavy work or male tasks, dominant ideas about the family kept such actions from breaching conventional concepts of masculine and feminine. When women left domestic arenas for waged work, not simply in other people's homes, but in open, public spaces shared with men with whom they had no family ties, a challenge was issued to these normative values. Over the decades 1860 to 1890 women's waged labour became the centre of a debate in the colonies. The issue fuelled movements for social reform over the relationship between the sexes, and over the character of waged and unwaged labour in and out of the home. Men had invaded colonial spaces, and tried to define the place of women within them. But women in the colonies were not to be readily and neatly confined. The years that saw the occupation of the continent and its economic exploitation also witnessed bids to change the social order as it applied not only to rich and poor, but to male and female.

6 Sex, Violence and Theft: 1830–1910

The white frontier of 'settlement' was perceived by many Aboriginal people as a frontier of mayhem and destruction. It was a place of fear and desire, of struggle and survival where indigenous people and colonisers came into contact, interacted and clashed. Along with intimate pleasures, warm friendships, exchanges of goods and knowledge, for many Aborigines the frontier experience was one of rape, cruelty and murder, accompanied by new diseases and moral strictures and increasing criminalisation. British male immigrants wanted land and resources and Aboriginal women. At the same time most feared the Aborigines' unfamiliar culture. If not initially wary, Aborigines soon learnt the terror of the white men's guns, though they also came to desire some of their goods, including food – such as flour – tomahawks and glass. Very few black men and fewer white women acted upon sexual desire across the colonial divide. White men pillaged Aboriginal women as part of the conquerors' spoils and murdered black men to 'protect' white women.

After the invasion of coastal areas, the British gradually ventured inland in search of new country for grazing and agriculture. Over the decades from 1830 to 1910, a large proportion of Aboriginal land was taken over, curbing if not crippling local hunter–gatherer economies. With economic considerations paramount to both individual colonists and governments, sheep and cattle were given priority over the indigeneous population. Aborigines were murdered and dispossessed and forced to negotiate new means of survival. White men needed to enlist black assistants as trackers; without Aboriginal survival skills and knowledge of the bush, white exploration and pioneering would have proceeded much less rapidly. Aborigines became part of a long line of native peoples who were victims of British imperialism, of colonial greed and callousness, of what is euphemistically called 'frontier expansion'. But they were also agents: they fought the Europeans, often effectively, and in other circumstances attempted to cooperate with them. Aborigines, however, were on the side that had most to lose.

Colonial struggles can be perceived as battles between opposing forces but we must not assume unanimity within each of the two categories. The colonisers differed according to gender, ethnicity and class and often had competing or conflicting interests. Their various economic activities also affected their attitude to Aborigines. Some were of a humanitarian or even missionary bent. The colonised also had a range of conflicting and competing interests. At the time of white settlement the original inhabitants did not see themselves as a distinct people. Rather, numerous Aboriginal clans were responsible for tracts of land throughout Australia; they usually only interacted with clans or land-owning groups on bordering or near bordering territories, and distant peoples were feared as strange. There were therefore hundreds of Aboriginal groups, just as there were over 500 languages. Aboriginal Australia may have been a kind of nation, but not in the sense we understand today, when information and a sense of collective consciousness is disseminated via the written word.

It is debatable whether we call whites 'invaders', 'intruders' or the more neutral 'newcomers'. To Aborigines, the British fitted each of these categories. They were usually armed, and intent on invading Aboriginal lands and territories. The British saw themselves as a sort of official forward party sent from England or the settled areas; their colonising mission was approved by Christian dogma, by the state and by contemporary scientific ideology. To the Aborigines the whites were trespassers on the land, lacking the permission of its custodians, potentially angering both people and spirits.

Initially the coming of the whites presented an intellectual puzzle for Aborigines; they appeared friendly and proffered strange gifts. Were they ancestors? Did they possess human bodies? Unfamiliar with western weaponry, and viewing the newcomers from a safe distance, Amy Laurie's great grandparents thought the guns they carried were actually long fingers which pointed, coughed and killed. The creatures were explained by Aborigines in various ways: they might be kinspeople reincarnated, cousins or brothers whose skins were bleached white on the long sea voyage back to the living world. Their inability to understand local languages was explained as a form of amnesia due to trauma. Yet their magic might be superior. After a time Aborigines recognised they were a different group of people from some distant earthly plane and intent on staying permanently. It seemed logical therefore that they could be fitted into the indigenous world, and be taught to conform to its law and authority.

Once their human status was decided, it was important to ascertain their gender. Aboriginal kinship rules demanded special propriety and avoidance etiquette when dealing with the opposite sex. Gender established identity, protocol towards others, permissible places to visit. Age and kinship could be ascertained next. White men were almost always the first newcomers appearing in the world of Aborigines. This was sometimes interpreted as a hostile contingent, for where were their women?

At the outset, the conflict between Aborigines and Europeans was not just about violence and the essentials of survival: resources and livelihoods. It was also about ways of life and philosophies, about cultural priorities, ways of reading or thinking about the land and the development of new explanatory frameworks, laws and behaviour.

The frontier is usually understood as the boundary of white settlement before the establishment of white institutions. But for Aborigines the frontier was defined and represented not just by a definable line on the landscape, but by contact. White and black often inhabited the same area of land. They frequently met, confronting each other face to face; in a whole variety of ways their lives became intertwined. The frontier was highly flexible, for it was not always a physical or even a cultural boundary. Rather it was a meeting place of two very different worlds, and often a coming together. This could be cooperative or tragic.

The land had been declared *terra nullius* or a land unoccupied by the British, as the nature of Aboriginal residence was not considered to constitute occupation. The legal correctness of this was recently rejected by the High Court's Mabo decision, and past British motives and understandings of Aboriginal land use remain under scrutiny. Adoption of the concept of *terra nullius* meant that the land was officially to be settled rather than conquered; no official treaties had to or could be negotiated with the indigenous peoples. When the land developer Batman arranged a dubious treaty with Port Phillip District Aborigines, signed at Geelong in 1835, it was declared invalid on the above grounds. Aborigines often did negotiate with Europeans, though the agreements were not necessarily honoured. In Tasmania, Aboriginal conciliator George Augustus Robinson arranged an unwritten treaty with the indigenous people for them to move to Flinders Island. Elsewhere many Aborigines negotiated to stay on or near their land by agreeing to cease hostilities and by working for the whites.

Aboriginal women and children, being less mobile than men, could not leave the war-zone, even if they wanted to. Many Aboriginal groups were devastated. Banggaiyerri, or Jack Sullivan, explained the tension between the two sides in north-western Australia:

See, in those days I would be frightened of you and you would be frightened of me as to who would get in first ... In those days you had to have a squirt [a gun] in your belt all the time because bad blackfellers could meet you anywhere and drive a spear into you; so a white man when he met a blackfeller would pull the gun out and shoot him. One had to win out on one side, the white or black ...

When the whites had hold of a bit of land, they would 'quieten' the blacks, and 'tamed' them for work. They were also engaged to fight the other blacks who refused to cease hostilities; 'they put a bullet in them'. Grant Ngabidj told of a brutal encounter near Ningbing station in the Kimberleys, where a group of his Gadjerong people were chained up and about twenty of them shot by Billy Weaber and Topsy, a 'Queensland girl' from the Gulf country. Some women were shot but of those saved, Grant's sister became the 'boss's stud'. Aboriginal women's stories also stress the practice by white frontiersmen of saving some of the 'pretty dark ladies' as sexual partners. These sexual hostages would later be used as intermediaries in helping to 'tame' those blacks who continued a bush lifestyle and occasionally speared cattle.

In the earlier and more rapidly settled regions of Tasmania and Port Phillip, warfare was often intense and swiftly destroyed the local clans. Tasmanian farmers were constantly on the look-out for

SEX, VIOLENCE AND THEFT: 1830–1910

sudden attack. In Tasmania in 1830, Aborigines killed forty-three Europeans. On the Macintyre River on the Queensland–New South Wales border in the 1840s, stockworkers were always fully armed; one man would keep watch while others carried out milking and other tasks. Frontier conflict was often prolonged: thirty whites were killed on the Macintyre over a year between 1857 and 1858, and in some areas conflict extended to a decade or more. In the second half of the nineteenth century, an average of fifteen to twenty whites were killed each year. Throughout Australia, at least 3000 Europeans died and another 3000 were wounded in conflicts with Aborigines.

Violence against Aborigines took a greater toll. One of the most notorious massacres of Aborigines occurred in 1837 at Myall Creek in New South Wales when twenty-eight Aboriginal men, women and children were dragged half a mile from a homestead and shot or hacked to death. Even very small children were killed, with two young girls spared as sexual hostages. Word got out, and seven white men were hanged for the murders in 1839. Among whites there was a belief that killing a black was not really murder; it was the hanging not the massacre that caused outrage in the white community. From this time on, attacks went unreported; murder of Aborigines became a more discreet affair.

Despite earlier pastoral intrusions, it was the discovery of gold in Victoria that finally 'squashed' local Aboriginal groups off their land. Aborigines were poisoned, shot, hung, drowned and flogged. Phillip Pepper recalled the desperate situation that faced his ancestors when the missionaries moved into the Gippsland area in 1858:

Only for the missionaries there wouldn't be so many Aborigines walking around today. They're the ones that saved the day for us. Old Hagenauer took them sick ones in and gave them medicine and food too. And they learnt to be Christian. Their tribal business was messed up before that.

Missionaries like Hagenauer intended to change Aboriginal identity into a Christian one. Pepper remembered Naming Days when all the Aborigines at Ramahyuck would stand in the square and state their chosen white name, or Hagenauer would give them one. A pair of twins were called Adam and Eve.

Aboriginal resistance was sometimes directed against introduced animals or against individual white men. Sometimes it was on a larger scale: the fights put up by the Wiradjuri in New South Wales and the Kalkadoons in north Queensland have indeed been classed as wars. Individual whites were killed in retaliation for specific acts committed by themselves or their kind, often relating to transgressions against Aboriginal laws. Some murders of whites were undoubtedly offensive attacks; others were retaliatory punishments. It is impossible to judge which Aboriginal clans were most warlike towards Europeans. Unlike North America, where the Cheyenne, the Apache and Sioux became known for their successful battles against colonials, Aboriginal attacks on whites were generally not large-scale affairs.

The British and local authorities labelled all such acts as hostile, however, suggesting a state of warfare existed on frontiers. As the land was officially alienated, Aboriginal actions were classed as criminal, and white retaliation was frequently out of all proportion to the 'crime'. Killing of sheep or cattle for food was usually matched by murderous raids. Occasionally the colonial police would be brought in to detain offenders, who were chained up by the neck or ankle and had to walk long distances to jail. More commonly frontier retaliation was instant, with frontiersmen expected to look after their own interests. In defending their newly appropriated land colonists defined Aborigines as the enemies, the law-breakers. The invaders considered they had the right to conquer, and would not be impeded in their task.

The state did little to quell the anti-Aboriginal violence. Indeed colonial police forces had been set up in response to settlers' requests for protection from blacks, who were portrayed as the main threat to law and order. Governments could excuse atrocities on the grounds of the remoteness of frontiers, though the police role in crushing Aboriginal resistance was well known. Aborigines were recruited to native police forces at Port Phillip, New South Wales and Queensland, and while the violence meted out by the southern forces may have been exaggerated, the later Queensland native police force was brutally effective at wiping out black resistance. In 1861 a government inquiry found evidence that black police in the Burnett district had slaughtered local Aborigines because they had eaten station cattle and, in another case, merely because they refused to hand over their blankets. Existing rivalry and fears between Aboriginal groups were brutally exploited as a colonising strategy.

Where governments intervened to prosecute and punish, Aborigines had equally poor prospects. Hundreds died when sent to Rottnest Island in Western Australia. Consequently prison authorities thought confinement of Aborigines a poor solution as they did not survive in gaols. Police had legislative power to move Aboriginal camps, and government control over rations and employment reinforced Aboriginal vulnerability.

Tasmanian convicts had no sympathy for Aborigines, and the colony's rapid settlement and intensive sheep-farming exacerbated the rapid decimation of the island's Aboriginal population. Tasmanian blacks were also sent across to the Port Phillip frontier by men like George Robinson to assist in gaining the acquiescence of local Aborigines. Port Phillip's intensive settlement, and concomitant conflicts with explorers, overlanders and pastoralists, had a particularly destructive effect. In Queensland and northern Australia, later expansion enabled frontiersmen to use advanced weaponry such as Winchester revolvers that was more effective than gunpowder or the slow-loading muskets of the earlier nineteenth century. In addition, they had more experience of guerilla resistance and Aboriginal strategies. To offset this, Aborigines were better prepared and had recovered from the worst onslaughts of introduced disease. Yet no matter how good their fighting technique and spirit, throughout Australia at least 20 000 Aborigines were killed in frontier warfare.

Along with their weapons, numbers and relative unity, one of the Europeans' key strategic advantages in their battle for domination was the diseases they had inevitably introduced into the previously isolated continent. In 1788 there had been at least 750 000 Aborigines throughout Australia, but this number dramatically declined after British takeover. Smallpox alone may have wiped out between 30 and 60 per cent of the original population. The very young, the elderly and pregnant women were all extremely susceptible to the disease. Outbreaks were known to have occurred in 1788 at Port Jackson and 1829–30 along the Murray River, at Port Macquarie and north to Brisbane and across the Liverpool plains. The old men said the disease outbreaks followed the rivers, leaving so many bodies it was impossible to bury them all; they remembered the stench of rotting flesh. Smallpox pustules attacked the hands and feet very severely, causing painful cracking and swelling and making it impossible for hunters and gatherers to obtain their food. Various white travellers reported that whole groups were wiped out. Clans usually had to confront the invaders in a seriously weakened if not devastated condition.

Unlike the ever-growing white population, Aboriginal populations continued to decline severely throughout this period. As Aborigines were not systematically counted in the official census of the colonies, available population figures were often based on loose estimates, and definitions of Aboriginality varied. Sometimes only 'full-bloods' or those living a traditional lifestyle were counted. Nonetheless, there is little doubt about general trends. Tasmania was one of the most tragic examples: from an original population of between 1000 and 10 000 people at white settlement, by 1836 there were only 106 Aborigines on Flinders Island and fifty classed as 'wandering' elsewhere. By 1861 only eighteen remained on Flinders Island. Aborigines of mixed descent were apparently not included. Economic historian Noel Butlin suggests the Victorian pre-contact population was between 50 000 and 100 000; an 1835 estimate put them at 15 000, declining to 2500 by 1852, and further to 643 by 1911. Queensland's Aboriginal population plummeted from an estimated 120 000 in 1788 to 22 508 in 1911. The Northern Territory Aboriginal population did not suffer its greatest declines until after commonwealth takeover in 1911, partly due to later white settlement and partly because earlier contact with Macassans meant that they were already resistant to some diseases.

Dramatic population declines throughout this period led to great grief and desolation, and necessitated major adjustments including new clan amalgamations. In most areas, Aborigines began to mix with local Europeans relatively soon after European settlement, usually after a 'wild time' or period of violence or warfare. Sometimes both occurred simultaneously. Aborigines performed various jobs around European houses and farms, and in more remote regions where labour was scarce they were essential to the establishment and maintenance of the enterprises. Often they were paid only in rations, though in some occupations and areas, like sheep-shearing in Victoria and New South Wales, they received equivalent wages to white workers. Aboriginal families were also permitted to live on the larger pastoral stations. When agriculture expanded on the northern New South Wales coast in the late nineteenth century, more Aborigines were moved off their land, and only workers were permitted to stay during picking season.

Many women worked as prostitutes or were coerced into sex with white men. Sexual pleasures with the women were in strong demand by the predominantly male population. Shepherds, hut-keepers, whalers and sealers, pastoralists and landholders enjoyed sex with Aboriginal women on a casual basis, as mistresses, or in *de facto* relationships. Yet even in the 1830s, white male observers conveniently blamed Aboriginal men for the 'awful and alarming extent to which the females are prostituted'. Consent was rarely an issue; if Aborigines resisted sexual demands, white men stole and raped the women anyway.

Not all relationships were forced. Some Aboriginal women, like Charlotte of Berrico station, who lived with the convict James Brigg, had negotiated a mutually acceptable arrangement. When local Aborigines raided the station for sheep and attacked Brigg in 1835, Charlotte saved Brigg's life. Other Aboriginal women collaborated with each other to murder their white male partners while some gained notoriety as outlaws or accomplices to male felons. Charlotte's daughter Mary Ann Brigg went into hiding with her bushranger friend Thunderbolt, or Fred Ward. Mary Ann's skills were indispensable, as the outlaws lived off stolen beef, wild yams and wattle gum. Ward held a white woman hostage to help Mary Ann and her three children.

The Aboriginal population crisis was only exacerbated by interracial sexual relations. By 1841 the Moreton Bay Aborigines, noted as still more populous than southern counterparts, were already decreasing: 'intercourse of the aborigines with the white people invariably tends to the shortening of their lives, and the less frequent occurrence of births among them'. The number of children was also extremely small compared with adults, and there were over one-third more men than women. At the Wesleyan Mission at Port Phillip, many of the children born were of mixed descent and a high proportion of these were killed at birth. Only two 'purely native children' had been born in the region in the previous year and it was therefore believed annihilation was imminent. Influenza outbreaks had affected the women badly and, within a year, the population had declined by 15 per cent.

In a society where Aboriginal women normally had only one or two children, the prevalence of venereal disease drastically curbed fertility rates. Venereal disease contributed to infantile and post-partum infections, thus increasing early infant mortality. Poor nutrition and the effects of depressive illnesses further lowered birthrates and increased miscarriages. Widespread sexual relations with whites led to a greater proportion of lighter-skinned children, frequently killed by the women at birth. Such infanticide was commonly reported in the 1840s in the Murrumbidgee area and other parts of New South Wales, the Swan River Colony as well as Port Phillip. The women probably believed the children would not survive or were associated with evil spirits, though we cannot be sure of their precise motivations. They disposed of their offspring in the bush, away from European eyes. The need for group viability eventually led elders to accept lighter-skinned babies.

Income from prostitution was often essential to Aboriginal survival. In many cases Aborigines attacked white men who dishonoured an understood contract or mistreated Aboriginal women. Aboriginal men also tried to resolve the crisis caused by a shortage of available women by taking them by force from neighbouring clans. Besides the personal suffering involved for the women, new tensions arose between men of neighbouring clans, resulting in revenge killings. Some Aboriginal men actually requested that white male 'Protectors' of Aborigines intercede on their behalf for the return of their wives.

Authorities often recognised sexual interaction with whites as the most immediate and far-reaching problem for Aborigines. The government's suggested solution to what they saw as the inevitable annihilation of Aborigines was to isolate them on missions or government reserves, away from the general white population. There they would be enclosed and 'protected', and mix with supposedly 'good' whites.

Aboriginal children were in demand for training by missionaries and on government settlements. Baptism of children soon became a measure of civilisation. In 1840 the Wesleyans at Port Phillip reported that the boys were doing well, manifesting 'an aptitude for learning equal to children of European origin'. Promise was also displayed by the girls, who were taught sewing by the missionaries' wives. However, their 'frequent wanderings' prevented their improvement. The same pattern occurred in Western Australia, where families would not permit girls in the Perth Aboriginal children's home to stay with Europeans after they reached ten or twelve years old. Local Aboriginal law required that at this age they begin to live with their future husband. If they did not leave, the Europeans believed that illness or some calamity would strike them or close kin. The male elders therefore sent more boys to work as domestics and live with the Europeans to replace the girls.

The colonisers believed they had to 'civilise' Aborigines, so they took it upon themselves to interfere with their customary practices, often via Christian missionaries. One of the first targets was to prevent their 'wandering habits'. Although only recently arrived themselves, white settlers believed that only sedentary folk could be civilised. As a result they attempted to break Aboriginal people's desire to hunt and gather and visit relations by providing a regular supply of rations. Aboriginal economic independence was thus discouraged. They also tried to inculcate the work ethic and to stop what they termed Aboriginal 'idleness' and 'begging'. Aborigines were told to stay in one spot and cease their traditional activities then were later accused of being lazy. The Aborigines' demand for supplies was partly a response to the fact that Europeans were occupying their land, taking their women, and getting them to do what they requested. Their requests for food, condemned as begging by Europeans, followed Aboriginal principles of mutual resource provision among those they considered kin and also revealed the Aboriginal view that whites were indebted to them.

Missions were often the only places where Aborigines could obtain a rudimentary education and the basis of an independent income. At Poonindie in South Australia, Aborigines farmed successfully and were self-sufficient by 1865. The Ngarrindjeri people of the Lake Alexandrina area, South Australia, tried to re-establish their community in the wake of violent frontier conflict. They became skilled saddlers, blacksmiths, carpenters, stone-masons and bakers, but there was little employment available. Several Ngarrindjeri people including Napoleon Bonney and Henry Lambert acquired their own blocks by 1870, about thirty years after initial contact, and their descendants continued to successfully farm the area.

Missionaries taught 'gender-appropriate' work, and European-style marriage. They abhorred the practice whereby older men married much younger women and had multiple wives as 'against nature and against common sense'. Missionaries thus commenced an ongoing intrusion into Aboriginal marriage arrangements, which were a crucial facet of social organisation and inter-clan relationships. Young women were betrothed to young husbands, generally mission-educated boys. When setting up the Bathurst Island mission in 1911, Bishop Gsell 'purchased' 150 young Tiwi women to prevent their promised marriages, and also to get a contingent to justify a mission. He became known as the 'bishop with 150 wives'. Elsewhere it was common practice for missionaries to make all marriage arrangements, not only selecting the couples without any consultation with partners or their relations but also by arranging mass weddings and performing the ceremony. Bessy Flower was a gifted Aboriginal girl who attended an exclusive girls' school in Sydney. At the age of sixteen she went to Gippsland to teach; her interest in a white male friend was vetoed by the missionary Hagenauer who instead married her off to a less educated Aboriginal, Donald Cameron. Hagenauer then tried to instil in her a sense of wifely subordination. Her later unhappiness is not surprising.

Aboriginal men found it increasingly difficult to obtain wives. Women's cohabitation with white men meant fewer women were available. Population decline also strained Aboriginal marriage practices, where polygamy was common. For the period 1830 to 1910, Aboriginal men significantly outnumbered women throughout Australia. It is not known whether this pattern was a result of colonialism or existed prior to contact. The imbalance was worse in 1891 than 1910. The differential impact of diseases and application of food taboos that affected women's protein intake, along with the stresses of pregnancy and childbirth, contributed to the low numbers of women. It is not known whether frontier violence had a worse impact on women than men, and no statistics exist on the rape and murder of Aboriginal women.

Mission marriages damaged the status and the survival chances of the man anticipating his promised wife, and they had wide-reaching consequences in eroding the authority of Aboriginal elders, both men and women. Young men became more powerful and their disinclination to listen to male elders was one of the reasons many turned to unrestricted drinking of alcohol. The older men also indulged in their new access to alcohol, sometimes to wipe out the pain of the past. Yet in trying to obliterate memories of violence, alcoholics also forgot some secret rituals. Bush drinking-styles focussed on binges and such white cultural habits were adapted by Aboriginal men. Although women also drank, Aborigines saw the practice as less acceptable for women than men. Dispossessed of their land, Aboriginal men lost their traditional basis of power, and were often unable to continue their hunting economy. Many men obtained work from Europeans, though women were often favoured by male employers because of their sexual role. Responsible for the staple food supply, women fulfilled their obligations through prostitution. They also continued their reproductive and child-nurturing roles, except where white male partners expelled their children.

Irish, Dutch and German men were more likely to marry Aboriginal women than the English. In the case of Irish Catholics cohabitation with Aboriginal women is testified to by the shamrock/Aboriginal names prominent among Aboriginal families today. Some white fathers recognised and brought up their children, but perhaps Jimmie Barker's experience reveals how this could be short-lived. Jimmie was born of a mother of Muruwari descent on 28 July 1900 in Cunnamulla. Bocher, his German father, who had anglicised his name to Barker, managed Gerara, a property on the Queensland border. Jimmie's brother Billy was born in 1903. When Jimmie was five, his mother confided that she was not getting on well with Barker and they had to leave. From then on life was a struggle. Jimmie did not 'remember having any Christmas that year'. In about 1906 their mother took the children away to Mundiwa on the Culgoa River, a camping reserve for Aborigines which consisted of tents and old shacks. There they lived in a tent about 12 feet square, receiving only irregular rations of flour, tea and sugar, but no baking powder or meat. Their mother made beds out of bush timber supported by forked sticks, and stuffed possum skins with emu feathers for their pillows and kangaroo skins with reeds for their mattresses. Life was a daily struggle for the family. After a few spasmodic gifts during the first year, Jimmie's father stopped visiting and sent no further assistance. In 1908 the family moved to Milroy, a station about 40 miles from Brewarrina, where their mother had a job at the homestead for

7 shillings and 6 pence a week. The station butcher could supply daily meat and Mrs Armstrong, her boss, was said by Jimmie's mother to be kind. Their parents had been divorced by this time and once the father remarried, this was the last they saw of him.

Such material poverty was commonplace for Aboriginal families. Local whites were complacent about black living standards, and charity was meagre. Aborigines were often expected to leave towns at sunset. It was difficult for them to find a permanent place to stay, for their 'unsightly camps' were often moved away from towns and creek beds.

White women's presence on frontiers has often been blamed for exacerbating conflict, for disturbing the supposed harmony that men had created. Such claims are highly debatable, not least because violence was a part of frontier life, but also because white men's rule was premised on sexual exploitation of Aboriginal women. White women were urged to be 'respectable', which meant personally monogamous, and to uphold Christian values relating to sexuality, marriage, nakedness and cleanliness. It was in their interests to ensure that their husbands did not infect them with venereal diseases such as syphilis or gonorrhoea, or spread these diseases among their domestic workers. It was also in white women's interests to ensure that white men fathered white babies. Wives' tenuous rights to property via their children's inheritance were theoretically challenged by the birth of illegitimate offspring, as was their economic security through marriage. Competition was threatening, and most women probably felt that there was no reason to allow men to enjoy extramarital affairs prohibited to white women. At least for Annie Baxter of Yessaba it provided an excuse to reject a husband she already disliked. A wife whose husband had been found making love to a 'lubra' had a socially approved justification to cease the duties of the marital bed.

White women generally stood in the relationship of employer to black women, who performed a wide range of domestic labour for them, including cooking, waitressing, cleaning, gardening. Other types of interdependency and friendships occurred between Aboriginal women and white. White women provided medical help for local Aborigines, while black women sometimes assisted in such areas as childbirth. After her marriage, Emmalin Macarthur went to live with George Lesley at Canning Downs. In the late 1840s, she bandaged up a seriously injured Aboriginal woman. While she was nursing her back to health George Lesley was secretly preparing for an assault on Aborigines who had 'stolen' stock on their traditional lands. As Emmalin wrote: 'I knew nothing until their return, though I had asked why they were cleaning guns and filling powder-flasks'.

Killing blacks, like having sex with black women, was men's business. Diaries and letters from many other white middle-class women, including Jeannie Gunn, imply that they were largely kept ignorant of the murdering business. Perhaps it was feared that women's concern for other women and children or their Christian beliefs might lead them to tip off their best servants; or perhaps, like all warfare, it was considered men's domain.

While not all white women were pacifists, they rarely killed Aborigines. When they did so it was more likely to happen when their husbands were away, or when in direct danger. In the 1850s a group of Aborigines approached Coochin Coochin station, and started to set its buildings alight. Two women and their young babies were alone at the station: 'Mrs Lister took down her gun and shot every black she could see'. At Yambuk in the 1840s Annie Baxter went looking for Aborigines who had been spearing stock. She was equipped with a pistol, though she only used it to threaten a man, using her horse to intimidate them as well. Some white women had regular revolver practice and never travelled beyond their door without a revolver in their belts.

Mutual respect often developed between Aborigines and whites on stations, and particularly between women. Mary Ogilvie encouraged her children to learn local languages, which were to prove a useful negotiating tool. At times Aboriginal women generously shared their skills with white women; in the absence of white doctors and midwives, their knowledge of childbirth, wet-nursing and child care were especially important. Sarah Castles of the Burraberongal and Warmuli was a respected midwife of the Plumpton area, who had delivered numerous local children. (She was a descendant of Maria Lock, the outstanding student at the Parramatta Native Institution, who had topped the Parramatta exams, in competition with a hundred European children.) When Lizzie Mildren moved to Lucyvale station in 1863, Big Bella, the matriarch of the local clans, taught her native cures, including an ointment of stinging nettles and beeswax and a liniment of deadly nightshade, a burr broth for stomach ailments, and a thistle vegetable dish. Bella explained dreaming stories and gave gifts of fish to Lizzie, suggesting that she had been accepted into a kinship relationship with reciprocal obligations. Aboriginal women played important roles in rearing white children, teaching hunting skills and stories of country.

Aboriginal women often enjoyed learning the new skills offered by missionaries. Louisa of Maloga in New South Wales learnt crochet from mission co-manager Janet Matthews; Sarah made bread, and Harriet quickly learnt to make a dress with frilled bodice and sleeves. At Coranderrk mission, the women enjoyed learning European women's crafts, and one girl crocheted a collar with such technical perfection it was sent as a present to the Queen. Learning such refined arts and dressing like Victorian ladies, did not dim these women's assertiveness, for they sent a petition to the Victorian Parliament and wanted to send a delegation to speak directly with the government. Demand for black children's and women's labour sometimes broke up Aboriginal families, though this applied more commonly to those on missions or in towns rather than on pastoral stations.

In less settled frontier conditions, Aboriginal women also played the part of intermediaries, and white men's dependence upon them enhanced their power relative to Aboriginal men's. This in turn enabled them to negotiate on their own and their communities' behalf. Aboriginal women tended not only to have closer relations with white men through intimate sexual rapport, but they could also have close liaisons with white women as black women were helpful, sometimes took a close interest in their children, and were less likely to turn around and spear or shoot them.

Aborigines shared important knowledge with female ethnographers such as Kate Langloh Parker, who gathered much information about New South Wales peoples. The Bibulman or people of the Ooldea region played host to Daisy Bates, a journalist who travelled to Australia in 1899 to undertake an investigation for the *Times* and ended up staying there for thirty-five years. She subscribed to the view that Aborigines were 'remnants' of a destroyed race and that she was there to observe their inevitable passing.

By the late nineteenth century most anthropologists endorsed such theories; they believed that Aborigines would inevitably lose in the struggle for survival of the fittest. Expounded by Charles Darwin, this theory was then extended to apply to various human groups by Herbert Spencer, and neatly fitted colonial ambitions. In response to the doomed race theory, the Queensland Government introduced the Aborigines Protection and Restriction of the Sale of Opium Act of 1897, which was premised on the rounding up of Aborigines into large-scale reserves where they could be protected from the ravages of venereal disease and vices such as opium and alcohol. These reserves had the additional benefit of serving as labour pools and paving the way for more homogeneous, neater-looking white Australian townships. The idea of protection, with its inevitable handouts of blankets and food, may have appealed to white humanitarians, but for Aborigines it meant loss of residential freedom, including the right to live near traditional lands. Many people were removed to islands or areas where they could no longer live off the land; many, like those shipped off to Queensland's Fraser Island, died of disease and desolation. The reserve system opened the way for greater control of Aborigines' wages, employment and family lives.

Sexual violence and the handling of rape cases clearly demonstrate some of the dynamics of colonial power relations. In the 1830s white men of all classes were accused of 'bad conduct' and 'vicious connection' against Aboriginal women. However, since Aboriginal testimony was not accepted in all courts, and as non-Christians, Aborigines could not swear on the Bible, lack of proof became an excuse against state interference. When a child and three sleeping Aboriginal women, including one in late pregnancy, were shot dead near Mt Rouse in 1842, the alleged perpetrators were found to be educated Christian men who worked at a nearby station. In general, Europeans were more likely to be acquitted or receive light sentences for such crimes, unlike the Western Australian Aborigines who murdered a settler's wife. Dojib and Barrabang were the first two people in the colony to be judicially executed.

In Queensland from the mid-1860s to 1900 more men were executed for rape than murder. These cases all related to the rapes of white women; while they indicate the seriousness with which rapes of white women were treated, rape of black women was considered inconsequential. Rape legislation addressed a crime against another man's property; all white women were the property of white men, a symbol of power and dominance. The callous attitude to the rape of black women suggests that many white men viewed Aborigines as another category altogether: considered there for the taking, they were the property of all white men, undeserving of protection or respect. To justify this attitude, colonial ideology tarnished Aboriginal women as universal whores, a reputation reflected in their treatment by the judicial system. Questions of Christian morality were also influential, and as Aborigines were not thought to have any sexual ethics they were considered implicitly immoral. Aborigines in fact had very strict laws relating to appropriate pairing, and were horrified by the absence of order in the western-style arrangements: to them whites could mate with anyone, just like dogs.

In rapes involving white men and women, the woman's reputation was generally raised by the defence, especially if she was working class. But where the rapist was black and the woman white, her character was rarely called into question, whatever her class. The belief that black men were customarily brutal to their women was widely promulgated. This put white men in a secure position to justify violence or ill-treatment of Aboriginal women, on the basis that the women were better off with cruel white men than their own husbands.

Rapes of white women by Aboriginal men, however, were often followed by public hysteria in the white community and, invariably, the advocacy of lynching. The white women also suffered as though defiled or tainted. In Queensland and other colonies throughout the 1860s and 1870s, there was much talk of white women's special need for protection against blacks. The massacre of the women of the Fraser family and their employees at Hornet Bank, Queensland, in 1857 reinforced these beliefs. The women's rapes exaggerated the outrage that had been committed, and all Aborigines were subsequently considered a threat to white women. It was argued that 'hanging is the only thing that brings home to them the terror of the law'. The prerogative of mercy was also much less likely to be applied to convicted Aboriginal men. This was in spite of evidence that the attack was in retaliation for the rape and cruelty against Aboriginal girls by the Fraser sons and employees, of which Aboriginal elders had earlier complained to Mrs Fraser. Numerous events including molestation of women by visiting native police, poisoned food and being kept off traditional land had compounded the tribe's grievances. For the deaths of the eleven whites, as many as 200 Aborigines were shot dead in reprisals, including people who were tied and handcuffed together.

Some Aborigines, like the Governor brothers of the Mudgee area in the 1900s, and Johnny Campbell, fought their own wars of reprisal. Trucaninni, once alleged to be the last Tasmanian Aborigine of full descent, had a tragic life, but she bravely resisted domination. She was the daughter of a chief. Sealers stabbed her mother and abducted her sister in 1828, and her fiance was drowned trying to save her from abduction by sawyers. In 1839 Trucaninni accompanied George Robinson to Port Phillip, but she took advantage of the situation, raiding and looting settlers' huts, and then tracking down her sister's abductor and shooting him.

When released in 1879, the Aboriginal outlaw Johnny Campbell reportedly proclaimed that he intended to treat white women in the same way as white men had treated black women. Judging by the evidence against him it seems he may have carried out this threat. He was a proud man, with a reputation as a courageous horseman, and spoke excellent English. When asked by a white man in Gayndah if he would hold the man's horse he replied: 'Hold your horse? What do you take me for? As you think I am a blackfellow no Sir, stand by and hold him yourself'. Unlike remorseful 'mission blacks' such as Isaiah Jennings of Victoria, who received reduced sentences of imprisonment, Campbell received a death sentence for raping a white woman. The unrepentant Campbell was hanged in Brisbane gaol on the morning of 16 August 1880. That afternoon the Russian naturalist Baron Nikolai Miklouho-Maclay, who had witnessed the hanging, removed Campbell's brain. The following day he commenced the pickling of the body, immersing it in saltwater, arsenic and other chemicals and pricking it to lessen swelling and encourage fluid absorption, so that it could be shipped to Berlin as a specimen for dissection and further observation. Other Aboriginal bodies were treated with similar disrespect. Skin was turned into tobacco pouches, and scientists kept ears, noses or armpieces, hands or feet. After Trucaninni's death in 1876, British scientists demanded her skeleton, which was displayed by the Royal Society, and subsequently placed on public display from 1904 to 1947.

By 1910 Aborigines of full descent were declining in number, while Aborigines of mixed descent increased. The presence of Europeans and their pastoral and agricultural activities had meant a drastic reduction of Aboriginal hunting areas and severe economic hardship. Although the intruders had some attractive items like alcohol and tobacco, it was the necessity of finding new means of subsistence and forging new access rights to their land that led many Aborigines to perform casual work, including prostitution, for the settlers. By 1910, in many areas of Australia, Aborigines' economic and social base, the land, had been totally wrenched away. Aboriginal women, the suppliers of staple foods, had also been snatched from their communities or departed as a survival strategy, while many others had died from disease and malnutrition. The sexual imbalance within Aboriginal communities had created conflicts between Aboriginal men and women, which sometimes led to violence between them. Men's increased competition for wives also led to inter-tribal conflict. Aboriginal women and men thus had to negotiate new relationships within and outside their communities.

White Australians did not envisage a place for Aborigines in their new nation. Indeed, with the 1901 federation of the Australian states, the constitution specifically excluded Aborigines from the census and, unlike other ethnic groups, from the exercise of commonwealth powers. Nor were Aboriginal women to receive a maternity bonus to encourage or assist them in reproduction. Aborigines were relegated to the past, to be displayed in museums, part of the history of the evolution of modern man but certainly not as part of the future nation.

At the same time Aborigines began to experience the beginnings of a sense of common identity arising from shared historical experiences and ongoing struggles. They started to resist colonialism in a range of different ways. Activists like William Cooper of the Joti-Jota people and William Barak of the Yarra Yarra people fought for Aboriginal people to be recognised as humans, to obtain some independence and to receive security over the land they had worked and improved. In 1907 the holdings of the successful Cumeroogunga farmers were revoked. But as Cooper lamented, seeking justice was like trying to get 'blood from a stone'.

7 Contested Domains

In the 1880s and in the following decade of the 1890s four remarkable men and women, William Guthrie Spence, William Lane, Louisa Lawson and Bessie Harrison Lee, were among notable colonists who took public stances on issues of social justice in colonial society. Their personal histories were particular to themselves, but the causes they espoused reflected the concerns of thousands of their white peers.

The two men rose to prominence in the thriving union movement of the prosperous 1880s. In 1882 William Spence became secretary of the Amalgamated Miners' Association, which grew rapidly over the next four years to a membership in the Australasian colonies of close to 25 000 workers. In 1886 he became president of the Amalgamated Shearers' Union, initially combining the local branches of Ballarat, Bourke and Wagga, but soon incorporating shearers across the colonies of Victoria, New South Wales and Queensland. The ASU had been strongly influenced by colonial craft unionism, which emphasised the 'harmony of interests' between workers and employers, and a cautious, moderate approach to industrial conflict. Spence counterpoised this with a militant challenge imbued with a socialist understanding of class antagonism and the need for a unified labour movement to demand more equitable treatment.

Spence, of Scottish origins, had been brought in 1852 as a child of six to the Victorian goldfields at Creswick. His brief schooling terminated abruptly when he was thrust in early youth into a series of unskilled jobs, but he worked himself into a career as an engineer. In 1871 when he was twenty-five years old, Spence married Ann Jane Savage, a young woman of Northern Irish extraction, in the Presbyterian manse at Creswick. Ann Spence gave birth to four daughters and five sons over the years when her husband, a

Christian and a temperance man, was developing his strategies for strengthening unions. Spence's exceptional organising ability inspired new unions of transport workers, maritime workers and wharf labourers, where both the numbers and strength of union sentiment led to searching questions about the sources of resentment of white waged workers in these new societies.

William Lane similarly made an important contribution to the shaping of the labour movement through his work as a journalist and propagandist for socialism in the papers he edited, the Brisbane *Boomerang*, and the Sydney *Worker*. In 1883 Lane arrived in the colony of Queensland where he found work writing for radical Brisbane papers. He had been born in 1861 in Britain, son of a Protestant Irish father who worked in a plant nursery. During his early years Lane's brood was very poor and he witnessed his mother's struggle to raise her large family in penury. In time his father's earnings improved enough for Lane to attend a grammar school for a few years, before his mother died and the boy was sent to work in an office. His father was a heavy drinker, and William Lane, who had dearly loved his mother, was alienated from him. At the age of sixteen Lane sailed for North America and found work in both Canada and the United States, where he came into contact with the fledgling labour organisation, the Knights of Labor, and with utopian socialist ideas. Lane entered an early marriage with a Scottish professor's daughter, Anne Macguire, whom he met on the job with a Canadian newspaper where he worked first as a compositor and then as a reporter. William and Anne Lane eventually raised seven children, five daughters and two sons – a large brood, like the Spences's.

Once established as a political journalist in Australia, William Lane pressed for the formation of a Brisbane Trades and Labour Council, which soon attracted seventeen unions, while he vigorously urged the workers' cause with his pen and voice. He looked forward to an Australia that would be a utopia, as he saw it, of 'manly men' and 'virtuous women', ideas he elaborated later in his novel *The Workingman's Paradise* published in 1893. Losing hope for major change within Australia, however, he departed to found a socialist community named New Australia in Cosme, Paraguay, with Anne Lane, their children, and various friends: a total of forty-five adults and twelve children initially.

The other remarkable figures were two women, Louisa Lawson and Bessie Harrison Lee, who became prominent at the same time in a second significant social cause, the movement for women's civil liberties. Louisa Lawson gained public recognition in 1888 with the first edition of her journal for women, the *Dawn*. 'Men legislate on divorce, on hours of labour, and many another question intimately affecting women', she wrote, 'but neither ask nor know the wishes of those whose lives and happiness are most concerned'. The *Dawn* would provide a space for women's voices, and promote women's causes: 'nothing concerning woman's life and interest lies outside our scope'. Louisa Lawson was born in 1848 at Guntawang, near Mudgee in New South Wales, the second daughter of English migrants, Harriet Albury and her husband Harry, a carpenter who eventually opened a public house on the road to the nearby gold town of Eurunderee. From a life of hard work in her parents' business, Louisa Lawson was transported to the hard work of a wife on the goldfields, and subsequently to becoming a selector's wife, by her marriage at the age of eighteen to Peter Lawson, a Norwegian seaman who had jumped ship to chase colonial gold. She eventually gave birth to five babies, one of whom died as an infant. Lawson found her married lot an unhappy one and in 1883 moved to fend for herself and her children in the city of Sydney after both Peter's ventures and the marriage failed. She worked at a variety of tasks and trades to keep a roof over their heads. Louisa Lawson experienced, therefore, a woman's perspective on labour, both unwaged and waged, from which she responded to the radical views she encountered in the city, and became a protagonist for women's emancipation.

Further south, in Melbourne, another notable writer and speaker, Bessie Harrison Lee, twenty-eight years of age in the year Lawson began the *Dawn*, joined the newly formed Woman's Christian Temperance Union, becoming president of the Richmond branch. Bessie Lee was born in 1860 in Daylesford, the daughter of a butcher. Her childhood was seared by the early death of her mother, and her subsequent relegation to an aunt and uncle, alcoholics, who beat and terrified the young child. Like Louisa Lawson, through an early marriage, at nineteen years of age, Bessie Lee escaped a hard-working, isolated and loveless existence in a remote settlement, a mining village near Enoch Point south-east of Lake

Eildon in Victoria. Her husband, Harrison Lee, was a Melbourne railway worker. In the industrial suburbs of Footscray and then Richmond, Lee became a church worker, a teacher and preacher, and eventually an advocate for women's rights. In an environment where both male drinking and male domination of wives were commonplace, Bessie Lee reacted in horror at the abuse of women and children perpetrated with impunity by hard-drinking men. People said that the hand that rocked the cradle ruled the world, she preached. Let women have the vote then, and put that faith into practice. Women had tried too long to fit their sons for the world; let them now fit the world for their sons.

Urgent voices had begun to advocate sharp changes in direction for white colonial society, not only in what would become years of sudden, drastic depression in the early 1890s but beginning during the period of widespread but uneven affluence in the 1880s. Undoubtedly, white colonists heard the constant descriptions of the much vaunted high living standards of the Australasian colonies, and of their egalitarian character in comparison to the rigid British class system. For radicals, these very representations made more overt and insupportable the inequalities and difficulties that faced considerable numbers of the white population.

The appalling and tragic omission from this plethora of reform agendas was the plight of Aboriginal Australians. Indeed, even worse, the very character of the radicals' programs would involve to a greater or lesser extent hostility to Aborigines and all peoples of non-European origins. One must weigh that scar against the undeniable characteristic of the period when fresh visions of colonists' rights and responsibilities, and energetic reappraisals of customary white social relationships, were expressed through associations of like-minded citizens. The late 1880s and early 1890s, in particular, was a period in which certain colonists agitated for reform, and found that the sudden onset of hard times gave urgency and renewed impetus to their varying demands.

At the core of the debates about the direction that a reformed white society should take were the constructions of the spheres of public and private, of waged work and unwaged domestic work, and of the place of men and women in each. Certain men, wage labourers, who found their lives dominated by the needs and power of a small group of wealthier men who controlled production, challenged the practices of the workplace and the structures of its distribution of rewards. Certain women perceived their domestic labour and access to waged labour as dominated by men, the more powerful sex, and found their personal autonomy restricted accordingly. Hence they challenged the practices of both workplace and family from a different perspective. The so-called 'public' and the 'private', the world of waged work and the world of the family, became contested sites, as groups of men and groups of women sought to translate their reform ideas into realisable political goals.

The politicisation of the conflicts embedded in white colonial society, which crystallised by the late 1880s and early 1890s in the public activism of organised protest movements representing labour and representing women's interests, was part of a questioning of social transformations that was taking place with varying degrees of intensity in industrialising western nations of the north. The British debate was obviously influential, since most of the white population and a continuing stream of migrants were British or Irish in origin, read British papers and journals, and brought ideas with them from home. The American debate was also important for Australian colonists, since in some respects the American social context more pertinently mirrored colonial situations; in particular class differentiation was less overt, rigid and entrenched there than in Britain. Social conflicts were represented as revolving around two axes. The first debate posed the problem that some men, and their dependants, were denied access to the secure share of the resources that their honest labour created, by a few elite men who monopolised wealth and power. The second contended that women of all social groups were denied access to a secure share of the family's resources, to control of their sexuality and childbearing, and to social power, by men who appropriated those aspects of women's lives for their own empowerment. Colonial newspapers referred to these twin issues as 'the social question' and 'the woman question'.

Liberals in the colonies had not sustained the same stress on individualism as characterised British liberal thought in the nineteenth century. Liberals everywhere urged the removal of all barriers to individuals' rights to develop their personal capacities to the highest level to which talent and ambition might take them. In a context of equality of rights, many liberals in Britain held that those deserving of comfortable livelihoods would rise to the top; the lazy, the incompetent, the ignorant, would justly fail to prosper. Interference in this process was unjust, inappropriate and, ultimately counterproductive. Colonial liberals tended instead to recognise social, as well as individual needs, and to allow the state to qualify rights derived from property. This had made their alliance with radicals possible and, in the short term, fruitful. All drew upon the promise of the workingman's paradise that they believed could be created under colonial conditions.

Increasingly in the 1880s a political vision stemming from socialist thinkers offered another explanation for material inequality while at the same time sustaining that conviction of the optimism about the colonies characteristic of the earlier period. There was variety in the new strictures from, among others, utopian socialists, Christian socialists and Marxists, whose views came to dominate the European socialist movement only in the later years of the nineteenth century. For socialists, access of individuals to a share of a society's resources was structurally created by the capitalist system in which the owners of production, the employing class, controlled the wages and conditions of work and hence the livelihoods of workers in the interests of their own profits, not in the interests of the good of the whole society. Socialists looked to collectivist solutions generated by workers themselves to overcome this injustice, in inevitable opposition to the employers, and owners of wealth. Whether this would entail forcefully pressing the wealthy elite to change their ways, or the total overthrow of the capitalist system, was a point of contention.

Where did adult women fit into these political reform agendas? Increasingly as the century progressed it became difficult to ignore the 'woman question'. Too many women were entering waged work, too many began acquiring more advanced education, and reformers began raising their voices to articulate women's discontents. Within liberalism, it was the respected male philosopher John Stuart Mill who offered the first systematic challenge to the prevailing view: adult women's interests, he wrote, like children's, were unfairly and unhappily subsumed within the interests of the male head of the household. In 1869 he published his essay *The Subjection of Women* in which he argued that the supposed appropriateness of the separation of women to the domestic sphere and men to the public was no more than a mechanism by which men dominated women, and made women's interests subordinate to their own. Being born female in practice constituted a disabling factor in terms of civil rights and economic interests, similar to other traditional oppressions that were based in ascribed status arising from family, religion or racial difference. What position women could attain on the basis of talent remained unexplored, Mill said, since from birth women's whole upbringing and education were aimed towards shaping styles of personality and ambitions geared to eventual marriage and household activities. Mill's stance legitimated the position of the handful of women working towards the so-called 'emancipation of women', and attracted others, both men and women, to reformist ideas.

But the woman question inevitably was intimately entwined with the social question. If middle-class women were straining to gain entrance to appropriate avenues of respectable work, single working-class women were already in employment, but in menial unskilled work characterised by poor conditions and low pay. In industry they posed some threat to male employment opportunities, a situation that demanded some response. Should the working man aim at wages that covered the needs of all women in his family? Should the waged work of women be supported as an avenue to women's personal independence from male authority? Were working women oppressed and exploited by capitalists, by men, or by both? Again, these issues were raised increasingly by women in sex-specific groups but also by men within existing socialist labour organisations.

In the colonies, it was that branch of the labour movement committed to the 'new unionism' inspired by Spence and Lane that spearheaded the discussion of the social question in the late 1880s. The woman question was thrust into prominence by more disparate groups of organised women in suffrage leagues, including Louisa Lawson, and in the Woman's Christian Temperance Union, including Bessie Harrison Lee, where the goal was the twin one of fighting the use and abuse of alcohol and improving women's status. The labour movement and the women's movement mediated radical ideas common to western societies within the specific experiences of white colonists, and within their own personal experiences of colonial life. For many white colonists – probably for the majority – life was by and large satisfying, and their difficulties were perceived as having been caused by personal ineptitude, poor choices, or sheer bad luck. But those colonists who discerned structural disadvantages underlying individuals' troubles, be it as workers or as members of a particular sex, and who promoted paths to change, became increasingly influential and persuasive as the 1880s and early years of the 1890s proceeded. First, we will consider the debate arising from the insecurities of working-class male employment and working-class women's situation within domestic and waged work, and the responses of the labour movement.

In 1887 William Lane's socialist paper, the *Boomerang*, published a stinging indictment of a working man's burden in the land that ought otherwise be the birthplace of free men and virtuous women, under a heading 'Men Must Work and Women Must Weep'. The man in the story, a driver, worked from dawn to midnight to earn a pittance, scarcely enough to keep his wife and children in barest poverty. Daily at his place of work he faced the insolence of the supervisors who enforced the brutal rules of the company, so that he felt 'used as a dog by a soulless and impalpable master'. His sad and weary wife coped at home in the absence of her husband, who kissed his sleeping children goodbye when he left for work, and found them asleep again when he returned. The woman was not, however, stoical in her response to her husband's exhaustion, for she spoke angrily of his situation with eyes blazing and fists clenched. The author of the story posed the question: 'Were we to repeat in the Southern land the misery and the mistakes of the North? Was progress to mean with us poverty, and was Queensland's greatness to be cemented with the tears of millions who must weep and toil?'. And Lane pondered sadly upon the course of 'our Australia', whether 'we ... were to pursue the course which has wrought already such countless misery, whether we were to leave to any man or men the power to oppress and enslave a brother'.

The story encapsulated key resentments of working-class men that became increasingly evident in labour rhetoric. The central thrust of the union agenda remained in some ways as it had been from the start. Working men combined to convince employers that their wages were not simply for themselves as individuals, but that they constituted a social wage, covering the needs of their dependents as well as themselves. As for hours, working men were also family men, who needed time to act as fathers to their children and companions to their wives. In the 1840s, 1850s and 1860s many men in waged labour had been employed by other men with small industrial or commercial concerns, who often knew their workers and their families personally, and indeed might work daily alongside them. Small workshops remained common through the 1880s, but very different work situations were also appearing. Factories employing fifty or more hands were no longer uncommon; some were much larger. But in rural industries too, miners, pastoral workers and seasonal workers more often found employers distant strangers, whose way of life was alien to their own. Increasingly it made more sense when employers were described, in derogatory and exploitative terms, as the 'fat men' who harvested ill-gotten gains by extracting the last ounce of energy from working men, who in turn were kept subservient by their unfair lack of resources. No longer were unionists hopeful that by steady persuasion they could convince employers of their need for secure and safe conditions and the moderate hours, nor for the increase in wages essential if men were to provide for wives and children.

The avenues of support for white colonists who were unable to sustain employment or who were not provided for by a relative's income – usually a father or husband – were few, and unattractive. The state was not to be called upon. Colonial governments had been forced to finance much of the infrastructure for economic development. In the 1870s they ceased funding denominational primary schools and set out to create a comprehensive centrally controlled system of state primary education: if there was to be democracy, the population needed to be educated. Governments maintained gaols for criminals, hospitals for the mentally ill or the indigent poor, and they paid police, magistrates and judges to keep colonists safe from criminals. Benevolent asylums took in a small number of abandoned children and the friendless elderly. Governments, however, did not see it as their task to give direct assistance to needy individuals in ordinary circumstances, although they might countenance modest work creation schemes during periodic downturns in the economy. Instead, governments preferred to subsidise modestly the funds raised and services given by churches and charitable organisations.

The churches maintained a range of institutions for the poor or defenceless: orphanages, lying-in hospitals, refuges and inner-city missions. In place of the English system of parish relief, associations of middle-class women in ladies' benevolent societies and other similar parish or secular groups, were at the forefront in providing assistance at the local level. These activities provided affluent women with an engagement that occupied some leisure time and gave them a sense of agency commensurate with their status. Less affluent middle-class women also found such work important for their identity. Although this was heavily class based, at the same time the women's activities undoubtedly afforded some help to desperately needy colonists. The attitude of benevolent society women as of other workers for charitable networks towards supplicants, however, was alienating for prospective clients. The so-called 'deserving poor' were separated from the 'undeserving poor', as applicants found themselves subjected to humiliating questioning and inspection. The Lying-in Hospital (later the Royal Women's Hospital) in Melbourne, which was established to provide a place where poor women could give birth, provides one such example. The committee of affluent women that set up and ran the hospital's affairs, presided over by Mrs Frances Perry, wife of Charles Perry, the first Anglican Bishop of Melbourne, kept a sharp eye on affairs, and on the morality of those admitted. Stories came down from the early days about Frances Perry's presidency of the Committee of Management: 'of the pointed toe of her buttoned foot probing under beds for what may be there; of mittened fingers sliding along window sills for signs of dust; of parasol-poking behind curtains for evidence of domestic sloth or carelessness'. Another story is recorded by a diarist, Curtis Candler, on 23 September 1867:

Mrs. P examining a candidate for the lying-in Institution. 'Who is the father?' – 'I don't know his name ma'am?' – 'Not know his name?' – 'No, Ma'am: he was a thin gentleman with gaiters and a shovel hat and an apron on: I met him one night near the Fitzroy Gardens and he seduced me – I have never seen him since'. It is said that Mrs P. had substantial reasons for disbelieving the girl's statement.

The ability to produce 'marriage lines' was very important if a woman wished to be admitted to the hospital; in fact, some unmarried women borrowed friends' certificates in their need. The committee even asked the registrar-general for permission to search for the registration of marriages in cases of doubt. As women who wished to uphold publicly the dignity of the marriage state, separate treatment of the respectable poor from those presumed to be unrespectable, perhaps even prostitutes, was mandatory.

The stories of the people who came to charities for help were heart-rending, mocking the rhetoric of colonial prosperity, pricking the bubble of colonial success. The help that charities finally offered in the face of such needs was short-term, access to it varied geographically, and in a depressed economy the pool of affluent donors, whose contributions sustained charitable activities, tended to decrease in size, shrinking the funds available for redistribution. Only a few men demonstrated a kind of restricted mutuality through joining benefit societies to shield themselves and their dependents in adversity.

The majority of white colonists relied on their families, both close relatives and a wide network of kin, to assist them through bad times. The politics of liberals and conservatives alike were based on the assumption that when trouble struck an individual, it was to their own family that the unfortunate person should turn. Just as the family was supposed to cater for the young, the sick, the disabled and the elderly under usual circumstances, so it should cope from its own resources with its members' crises of unemployment, bereavement, injury, sickness and homelessness. To a surprising degree (surprising for a migrant society, where Europeans had severed ties with family to sail for the colonies in the first place) white colonists could often find someone to turn to in distress. Settlers usually sustained ties with relatives who lived in the colonies, and those who had come as children, reached maturity and married, often themselves raised large families. Even if the search for economic opportunities eventually saw relatives widely scattered, ties of sentiment and duty might keep them in touch.

When settlers first arrived in the colonies, it was to relatives they looked, where possible, for temporary shelter and, hopefully, employment opportunities. It was to relatives they looked first when livelihoods failed, and breadwinners died. Female relatives were invaluable in times of childbirth and illness; they cared for the children of bereaved husbands; they boarded country nieces and nephews who needed schooling; they prepared wedding feasts, and laid out the dead in times of mourning. Sisters offered housekeeping duties for bachelor brothers, as Rachel Henning did for her brother Biddulph on his New South Wales station, running his home and taking charge of the bookkeeping. Bessie Bussell performed similar tasks for her brothers in Western Australia. Bessie was, her sister wrote, 'an admirable girl and equal to anything. We hear from the boys that she is working wonders, reducing our savage brothers to some kind of order'. The meaning of such ties was well expressed in Jane Caverhill's reminiscences of her aunt, Mrs James Austin:

she was always good to us and loved Mamma very truly and in all our many money troubles Mamma always went to her and she always helped her to the utmost in her power. I am telling you this so that if it ever lies in your power to do a kind act for any of her grandchildren you ought to do it for your Mother's sake who will always love her for what she was to her much loved Mother.

Yet for most of the population most of the time, a family, of parents and children, functioned as an economic unit and this meant essentially having a male breadwinner, fit, well and willing to provide the basic labour or wages on which the rest of the group relied. But in this need, even in the generally prosperous times of the 1880s, people were by no means secure.

The utopian colonial vision articulated by so many radicals in the 1850s and 1860s, of a future of self-sufficient independent farmers tilling their soil, with wives, children and aged parents contentedly ensconsed in rural cottages, failed. Obviously some venturers succeeded on the land in small farming, and more people were being supported by a livelihood in agriculture by the late 1880s than had been the case in 1860. The people who succeeded because they started out with greater resources or skills, or were luckier, usually had been able to increase their holdings to a more economical size. But drought, failed harvests, debt and threatened destitution forced many selectors off the land – perhaps half, or more, of those who tried farming – to join the ranks of people seeking other avenues of employment in towns and cities.

One example is enough to indicate the tenor of these pleas: the letters of Charles Bernnell, clearly an original native of the English southern counties, who clung desperately for years to a 210-acre selection at Nullan in the Wimmera. In October 1879 he asked the Minister for Lands for more time to pay his rent, as he had had a very poor year; he took only 70 bags of wheat from 58 acres 'so it leaves me very prest[;] i hav too yong horses and if i cold sell them i cud get strate'. But he could not get straight, and in May of the following year he wrote again to explain his continuing arrears:

i av had sum illness in my family [;] thear iss nine i av too support out of wat i can make with one pair of hands[;] my father and muther is too old too woork now[;] iff you will give mee a littele time that i can get sum muny that i have too ree serve for striping weet for sum of my nabours ... at present i hav too wate for it.

But his neighbour's crop was mortgaged to stores in Donald, and yet another year on, Bernnell's prospects remained gloomy: 'i can not get sum of my dets in from those that i was striping for and my children as been very bad wich one dide[;] wich thru mee back in getting my weet a way wich i am dooing now as fast as the wether per mits mee.' His crop had amounted to no more than two bags per acre from 80 acres, but a year later he had averaged less, only 96 bags from 100 acres: 'i had 23 akers eaten by the rabetts on a place that i took from Mr Darke and the ribts iss bad thear ass the land iss unocupide next to it[,] soo it is noo use one tring too keep them down.' There were no more such letters. On 3 May 1884 Bernnell applied to transfer his lease to one Patrick Bergill. The unequal struggle was at an end.

Among those families who hung on to land but with difficulty, it was, as we have seen, the supplementation of the household's resources by family members through periodic or seasonal waged work that was critical. The hopes of a future independent living on the land had well and truly faded for most urban landless and savings-less people by the 1880s. Pastoralism still dominated the rural economy, and pastoralism provided independent livings for very few; instead it offered openings for waged labour. Mining, too, had swiftly shifted from an occupation for individual prospectors, to company-owned enterprises employing waged workers. The growth of cities continued to provide livelihoods for self-employed men, and for professionals and officials on good incomes. But here, too, waged labour in industry, transport and construction swiftly became dominant. By the 1880s, an even higher proportion of people than in 1860 were living in one of the major seaboard cities, dependent on their own or someone else's wages for a living. In a colonial population with its economic interests geared towards supplying Britain with raw materials and importing manufactured goods in turn, waged labour had become the lot of more than half of the adult male population, and of these, a substantial number were unskilled or skilled workers subjected to conditions of work laid down by men of the employing class.

In the best of times male breadwinners were unconfident, and in the worst, incapable, of sustaining a wife and numerous children in the absence of other resources. In country towns and on the margins of cities, families still had the opportunities to acquire 'free foods' such as fish or rabbits, free firewood, a plot of land on which to keep a cow or hens, or to grow some vegetables or fruit trees. In inner-city areas, everything had to be purchased, and purchased with ready cash. Growing food was difficult, and local councils instituted fines for those who persisted in rural ways with their goats, cows or hens sharing cramped yards or, worse, roaming streets. Men's seasonal labour, their frequently temporary work situations and the liability of the economy to sudden inexplicable downturns were even sorer trials in these environments.

Evidence from South Melbourne, an industrial inner suburb of Melbourne, suggests that for most of the boom period from the 1860s to the early 1890s life would have been a struggle for working-class families. In 1870 a labourer, his wife and three children might have had a margin of 7 shillings after paying for food, fuel and rent; by 1880 this margin would have grown to 12 shillings, and by 1890 dropped to 10 shillings. From this margin the couple had to purchase clothing, keep up a lodge subscription, replace furniture, household utensils and work tools. If men indulged in alcohol or cigarettes, their habits would have bitten into this small pool of disposable income. Skilled artisans brought in higher wages but even here earnings could be seriously depleted by gaps between jobs or reduced hours, both common occurrences. Probate records show that at the end of the boom almost three-quarters of South Melbourne residents owned no more than the clothes they wore, the household utensils and furniture they daily used and, at the very most, a few pounds invested in the local savings bank.

Urban work, like rural labour, could be hazardous, and able-bodied men in full wages with steady employment could plunge their families into dire straits when an accident brought injury or death. Unless they belonged to the prudent few who contributed to union or friendly society funds as a protection against hard times, men knew that unemployment, or their deaths, could leave wives and children reliant on a wife's resources and skills, or on the low wages of older sons or daughters. For a poor widow with a family, living above basic subsistence was almost impossible. Clothing factories were one of the major employers of women. No detailed wages lists on such factories exist for South Melbourne, but records for Collingwood and Carlton suggest that women's wages seldom exceeded more than 25 shillings per week in the late 1880s. On the other hand the cost of food, fuel and rent for a widow and three young children was 20 shillings in 1870, 21 shillings in 1880 and 26 shillings in 1890. And in South Melbourne widowhood was by no means rare. Of the men who married in 1881 at the age of 25, for example, 7 per cent would die before their thirty-fifth birthday, and 12 per cent before their fortieth birthday.

Few colonists seemed to contemplate seriously an alternative to the emerging gender division of labour that would have rendered adult women less vulnerable to insufficiencies in male labour. The prospects of reliance on women's work, on the contrary, posed a particular threat to male workers. As long as women worked within a home or family context, however hard or however numerous the tasks, man's paramount position as head of the household was not challenged. But waged work for women was another matter.

Even the waged work of single girls involved difficulties. To send off a daughter to earn wages as a servant was one thing – to see young women entering new work using machinery or recent inventions was another. In the first place where would the dividing line fall between women's work and men's work in such situations? And what other arenas might young women invade, to the detriment of male employment prospects? Some socialists tried to be progressive in this respect, welcoming the independence that waged work could give single women. A column written by William Lane under a female pseudonym applauded Chicago 'girls' who earned their own living and considered it the proper thing to do. 'And there were lots of things for willing girls – telegraphing and telephoning, proof-reading, typewriting, copying, and a hundred things, enough to suit every taste.' There was no doubt that in modern America a 'girl could be something else than a dressmaker or a servant-girl or a shop-girl. She could be independent and respectable, and that meant a lot'. Even in this passage, however, it was notable that the type of work described was potentially 'feminine' – but is that where women would stay, especially since employers could secure their work at lower cost?

But then, too, some of the workplaces that young women entered willingly, or wives more often of necessity, were highly exploitative, with low wages, long hours and poorly ventilated premises, clearly detrimental to women's health. There were stores of food-processing factories where acids from fruits and vegetables slowly destroyed the skin of women's hands. There were tales of cartridge factories where explosions put women workers at risk of injury or death, and of clothing factories where girls not yet in their teens crowded together for pittance wages, the air thick with lint and dust, the provision for meal breaks or lavatories exceedingly inadequate. One factory inspector complained in 1889 that whereas men were generally ready to speak out and contradict their employer if he made an untrue statement in front of them, 'with women it is different. But even if the statements made by the employees are found to be true, they would be most difficult to prove as the girls have great objection to going to Court'. The reason? The girls and women feared dismissal, either because they had no other support than their own wages, low as they were, or had others partially or fully dependent on them.

The prospects of such circumstances for their own kin were hardly a source of pride for a male breadwinner, and often a source of anxiety and anger. In good times, and when other family members were not reliant on their earnings, young women could take the chance of moving from place to place seeking better conditions. Others were very dependent on keeping their work, and more exploitable because of it. Meantime if widows found waged employment, they clung to it despite the strains of the double day on top of uncongenial conditions.

Not that waged domestic labour was easy by comparison. There had been little improvement in technology within the home except for the few people able to acquire gas for cooking or electricity for lighting. Washing, ironing, cleaning, shopping, cooking, washing dishes, cleaning houses, heating water and rooms, all took a toll on youth and energy. For unwaged housewives with no domestic help, the toll on energy was heavy. And the home environment for the poorest was drafty, crowded, poorly aired, insanitary: a source of ill health at best and life-threatening illness at worst. Much of this work, however, was less remarked, because it was apparently private, subject to some individual control, and apparently for love and duty, not for a stranger's profit.

Anger at the economic conditions that working men faced in their efforts to provide for families in decent security, combined with fear at the growing incursion of women into waged labour as rivals of male workers, shaped the stance that moderate and militant wings in the labour movement adopted in the 1880s. From the first, union leaders from the building and manufacturing industries asserted that the fair and decent reward that they expected for a good day's work was an amount sufficient to cover the needs of a wife and family. Union leaders sustained this stance as they encouraged the growth of unions in a variety of work arenas in the 1880s, and fostered links between unions with intercolonial conferences and affiliations.

Such sentiments shaped, too, the rhetoric of the militants whose approach to labour–employer relations reflected socialist and other radical influences, including two Americans: Henry George, advocate of the land tax, and utopian socialist Edward Bellamy, author of *Looking Backwards*. William Guthrie Spence and William Lane organised workers with the inspiration of 'new unionism'; for the first time male workers organised on the basis of shared work, rather than craft skills. As militant leaders energetically trumpeted forth their views of the inequities of the current oppression of the 'have nots' by the 'haves', true colonial manliness was aligned with standing up to the boss, and striving for wages that forestalled the need for their wives and older children to seek waged labour. Unionism, as Spence described it, involved a loyalty to fellow workers that went to the root of a man's virile character: the man who 'never went back on the Union' would be honoured as no other was honoured or respected, he declared. The women who appeared in Lane's *The Workingman's Paradise* were the 'weary sex' who had lost their womanliness, oppressed by the 'struggling toil that never ceases nor stays', just as men were oppressed by tyrannical and greedy masters. In the new order, the degradation of humanity would cease as men pulled together as mates and worked for what was best for all. Unionists promoted manly identity through mateship allied to proper responsibility for women and children. Men joined unions on an increasing though still limited scale, and as the 1880s drew to a close, industrial confrontations became more common in key industries. Some women strove to form their own unions, but for the most part they were largely absent from union ranks. If excluded from this determined and loyal brotherhood, however, women were crucial in unionists' representations of women's needs.

For many male waged workers, the key problem for decent life chances may have been articulated as the inequities of their relationship with employers, and the insecurity in sustaining wives and children in decent circumstances. For some colonial women, however, the problem in their pursuit of decent life chances came to be seen as a problem of inequities in their relationship with men, and the insecurity this constituted for their material and psychic wellbeing. These tensions, which the women's movement, through activists Louisa Lawson and Bessie Harrison Lee, brought to the fore as the 1880s proceeded, stimulated another sharp critique of injustice in white colonial society.

At one level, the colonial women's movement was driven by perceptions of certain middle-class women about their economic situation compared with that of men. While single working-class women were being thrust into uncongenial workplaces with little choice, numbers of single women from better-off families were prevented by convention and lack of appropriate training from entering workplaces at all, since this would mean entering work occupied by men of their class. If white colonial men trumpeted loudly the egalitarian nature of colonial society, what of the laws relating to marriage and the organisation of sexuality, to divorce, to guardianship of children, to a wife's right to hold property, all of which placed women – rich as well as poor – in a subordinate position? And what of the exclusion of women from the right to vote for representative bodies including colonial parliaments, or to stand for election? Women whose family backgrounds instilled in them some self-confidence, and who experienced particular tensions arising from the different relationship of women compared with men – to education, work, marriage or political power – interpreted pragmatically within their own contexts current ideas about women's rights to social equality.

Louisa Lawson and Bessie Lee had clearly experienced a range of such tensions. Lawson was frustrated in her desire for education, in her marital relationship and in her struggle to earn a living when necessity imposed this on her. Bessie Lee knew alcohol abuse as a child and later observed the helplessness of wives to protect themselves and their childen from a husband's power – or of other women to help them – given women's legal and economic position. These notable women, just two among many who appeared at the forefront of colonial life, personified the competency of women when permitted a broad arena of social involvement. Both promoted women's causes within a social environment often dismissive of, or indifferent to, the urgency of their claims.

Feminists in every colony alerted inquirers to a range of inspirations for their advocacy of women's special needs. The novelist Miles Franklin was expected in her youth to marry and become a privileged member of a pastoral elite, or to remain a maiden aunt assisting relations with domestic tasks in times of need. However, she wanted an extended education, broader life experiences, a circle where she could be taken seriously as a writer, an independent income – and she defied convention to seek such avenues of fulfilment. Rose Scott, growing up in a wealthy Sydney family, developed a sensitivity at an early age to the incongruent status of women in her world. This was intensified when she noted the male derision of the New South Wales legislature that greeted such issues as raising the age of consent for girls. Scott claimed for herself a serious involvement in learning, an engagement in deliberations on public policy, and the right to undertake political lobbying for her own sex as on other concerns.

Catherine Spence demonstrated in Adelaide the capacity of women to earn an independent living when, as a novelist and journalist, she aired progressive views on a range of pressing issues, the position of women among them. Vida Goldstein of Melbourne, raised by liberal Christian parents who encouraged their daughters' education and professional activities, first became concerned about women's needs when she became involved with her mother in the anti-sweating movement which resulted in the first Victorian Factory Act regulating women's waged work. She joined the United Council for Women's Suffrage, as a close collaborator of the union organiser Lilian Locke and the suffragist Annette Bear-Crawford. These were but a handful of middle-class colonial women seeking broader horizons and self-fulfilment by engaging in waged work, or social reform, while at the same time lobbying for public policy changes that would also improve the status and life chances of other women.

In 1869 John Stuart Mill wrote to Catherine Spence that there was unlikely to be organised protest about women's social position in the Australian colonies because so many women were married and preoccupied at home with domestic duties. He clearly saw the English women's movement as driven by the need of single middle-class women for professional and white-collar work, and the training essential for this. In terms of the colonies, Mill miscalculated. There were more single women seeking work than he imagined. In the cities in particular many women did not marry until their late twenties, and certain educated middle-class single women wanted waged work concomitant with middle-class status. Quite a few such women remained single all their lives by choice, not wishing to relinquish their social or sexual autonomy for a husband's dominance. But other women, married as well as single, inspired with an evangelical Christian imperative to right the anomalies of society, sought respect as social activists rather than the rewards of waged work in itself. They perceived that within a patriarchal society, for themselves as for less fortunate women, female avenues for social action were effectively blocked. This potent tension was as pertinent in the colonies, and if white colonial society was less deeply divided by class, and democratically more advanced than England, this only made the anomalies in middle-class women's lives more glaringly apparent.

The pressure for change in women's social position began modestly. In 1869 a Melbourne woman, Harriet Dugdale, responded to Mill's *The Subjection of Women* (as did so many other women throughout the western world) by raising her own voice in favour of women's emancipation in a letter to the *Argus*, ideas which she subsequently elaborated upon in 1883 in a short utopian book entitled *A Few Hours in a Far-Off Age*. Dugdale was a freethinker, who added the dominance of men over women to the evils resulting from organised religion. The 'vain, unjust and brutal' image of God revealed 'his MAN origin', she asserted. An advocate for rational dress reform, who designed a costume with a divided skirt and wore her hair short, Dugdale joined with Annette Bear-Crawford in 1884 to form the Woman's Suffrage Society, the first of a number of small pro-suffrage organisations in the various colonies. Louisa Lawson's Dawn Club followed in 1889 and two years later, also in Sydney, Rose Scott, with Lady Margaret Windeyer, wife of a prominent liberal judge, initiated the Womanhood Suffrage League. The women who joined these associations invariably had supported, as they continued to support, a range of initiatives. The earliest reform movement was the effort to establish an academically oriented secondary education for girls, and the right of women to enter universities, including enrolment in such professional courses as medicine, and the acceptance of women as waged professionals. C. H. Pearson, who claimed the acquaintance of John Stuart Mill, was one of many prominent liberal men who facilitated such innovation. Such men were essential to the cause, for although women themselves needed to urge action, agitation was of little practical use unless men within the halls of power promoted their agenda, and saw to it that reforms were implemented. C. H. Pearson vigorously supported academically oriented secondary education for girls and became the first principal of the school he helped found, the Presbyterian Ladies' College in Melbourne. The University of Adelaide, which opened its doors in 1874, permitted women to attend lectures and, together with the universities of Melbourne and Sydney, admitted women to degrees in the late 1870s and early 1880s. Later in the decade medical courses were made available to women. University degrees may have been of immediate concern to just a handful of women, but they were symbolically important in slowly transforming representations of women's nature and capacities. In the early twentieth century the first female graduates would in turn contribute to a more progressive climate for acceptance of new ideas through their independent work, their management of complex lives when they did marry and, occasionally, by becoming themselves directly involved in the women's movement.

Of particular concern to a wider number of women were the legal changes in the position of married women set in train by alterations to the laws on divorce, property and guardianship of children. Colonial parliaments in the nineteenth century had generally followed British legislation in these respects. From the late 1850s divorce, for example, was allowed, but on unequal terms: men could divorce their wives on the grounds of a single act of adultery; women needed to prove adultery compounded by cruelty, or failure to provide for the household. The misery a woman might face before she finally attempted to end a marriage is appallingly revealed in the case of Emma Clark who in December 1870 filed for divorce from her husband, James Clark, a coal and timber merchant, on the grounds of adultery and cruelty. They had been married for seventeen years, during which time Emma bore ten children, six of whom were living. Meanwhile James had had an adulterous affair; had once attempted to have intercourse with a servant in the presence of Emma; had frequently assaulted his wife, once leaving her face 'one black mass of bleeding punctured flesh'; had once tied her to a dray being shaken by 'a violent untamed and gibbing horse' while he 'enjoyed her agonies'; had 'approached' Emma soon after the birth of her last baby, and 'although well aware of her condition', seized her 'by her private parts and pulled at them violently for some time causing her pains and suffering more agonizing than those in childbirth at the same time attempting sexual connection with her'. When asked why she had endured such treatment, Emma said that she feared the 'exposure of her said husband's conduct would operate to the prejudice of their children', and that James had threatened to 'quit the Colony and leave her to die in an Asylum and their children to rot in the Orphanage and Industrial Schools'. She had had, she agreed, a most unhappy married life.

By the late 1880s and early 1890s advocates of the women's movement had pressed sufficiently for liberalisation of the laws to see significant new arrangements enacted, despite the churches' vocal opposition. In the *Dawn* in 1888, Louisa Lawson supported the divorce extension bill before the New South Wales Parliament: 'There are few questions so important for the consideration of women as those of the laws of marriage and divorce, since full half the sorrows of women rise from marriages foolishly made, or from nuptial ties, which being made cry out for severance'. How could male legislators, she asked, not respond to the sight of 'a woman bound by ill-made laws, and by the crude pruderies of public opinion to a life of hourly sorrow and perennial torture'.

Even where couples were comfortably suited to each other, laws and conventions that made it difficult for wives to have independent sources of income brought an element of tension to many women's situations. Where husbands failed to provide, where they deserted families, or were verbally or physically abusive, wives were trapped in appalling situations. In seeking an end to their plight, women were constrained by existing legal provisions as well as by their inability to find alternative financial support for themselves and their children (who were in law their husbands'). Changes to the colonial divorce laws in New South Wales in 1889 and Victoria in 1890 widened the grounds for access to divorce, and at the same time made access more equal for women.

As was the case with the former laws, only a small minority of wives were in a position to take advantage of the new ones, however, because of convention, cost, and their lack of viable alternative economic avenues for support. For many female reformers the answer to victimised wives went far beyond the issue of changes in the law, or indeed broadening access to waged work, to a challenge to the consciousness of men about their dominance of women, socially, physically and sexually, and the preparedness of some men to exercise that dominance in highly oppressive ways.

The women's association that confronted this area of discontent most directly was the group to which Bessie Lee attached herself, the Woman's Christian Temperance Union. The WCTU began in the American West during the 1870s, when bands of praying women invaded saloons and bars, entreating men to stop drinking and publicans to stop selling alcohol. It swiftly became a lobby group of formidable strength, deriving energy from resentment at the consequences for women of widespread alcohol abuse by men, not only in frontier communities but throughout urban society. Men drank: women, and their children, were deprived of needed income. Women faced physical abuse but legally they had little recourse to assistance. Under the leadership of a Christian socialist, Frances Willard, the WCTU swiftly connected this male drug abuse with a broad range of anomalies in the relationships of men and women, a perception that was readily adopted by the Australian women who founded the association in the colonies.

From a firm beginning in 1887, the WCTU saw branches formed in many suburbs and country towns, as membership grew rapidly, recruited in the main from adherents of Protestant churches. 'Social purity' became a central goal, as the temperance women sought to bring to open public debate delicate issues. They deplored the exploitation of women's vulnerable and impoverished situation in prostitution, and the double standard of sexual morality that punished women for sexual transgressions – and branded their offspring illegitimate when pregnancy resulted – while leaving men untarnished and free to repeat their behaviour at will. They responded, too, to government attempts to remove the civil rights of women suspected of prostitution in order to control venereal disease. And so, along with their campaign to redeem drinkers for a drug-free existence, to educate the young to the dangers of alcohol, and to lobby governments to restrict the accessibility of alcohol, the WCTU reformers joined the suffragists to address a range of women's issues, including the laws and conventions surrounding sexuality, as well as women's civil liberties and access to waged work.

At the outset of the decade of the 1890s, therefore, a large male labour movement, and a smaller, dispersed but energised women's movement, were poised to pressure fellow colonists to recognise the urgent need to adopt various aspects of social equity. The first group fought for adult men disadvantaged under capitalist economic organisation, and made claims also for those men's dependents. The second group fought for the female sex, almost half of the population, but made claims that their reform would also benefit the other sex, men. These were wide-ranging agendas.

Towards the end of 1891 signs became ominous that the long period of a buoyant and expanding economy was coming to an end. Falling prices for raw materials meant reduced export incomes, while speculative excess had to be serviced by higher capital charges. The building boom of the 1880s had faltered; building societies crashed, banks failed, businessmen went bankrupt, British loans for colonial legislatures and local councils dried up. The prosperity of the colonies relied on the British economy, which had now entered a depression. There had been many speculators, whose money-making machinations had pushed up the price of land and housing artificially. Heavy industry, especially the construction industry, was hardest hit. Men lost jobs, and women too, although their low-waged work in factories and in the provision of services had more continuity through the depression. Families were plunged into desperate straits when a sole breadwinner was thrown out of work. Even where older children in a household managed to retain work, the small wages that had once supplemented the family income could not now replace a father's earnings.

Men, women and children trapped in poverty in cities and towns kept themselves from starvation by whatever strategies they could. Some colonial governments looked to the perennial hope of putting families on the land in agricultural settlements. Many men left the most depressed areas in search of rural work, or went to the goldfields of Western Australia. Bert Facey was one young lad from the eastern colonies whose father took off for the Western Australian goldfields in the 1890s depression; Bert's mother followed alone, and in time also his grandmother took Bert and his siblings to the West, only to find their father dead, and their mother remarried. At Kalgoorlie, living on the diggings, Bert's Aunt Alice (with Uncle Archie and the older boys absent earning money chopping wood for the mines at Boulder) made money from the empty tins discarded by prospectors. She, Grandma and the youngest children collected the tins and burned them in a brush fire. Thereupon Aunt Alice melted the fragments in an iron pot, cooled them in moulds and sold the sticks for 5 shillings per pound in the town. 'All this used to help, and, as Aunt Alice said, it gave them something to do', Bert Facey laconically reported.

The hostility between employers and working men in militant unions intensified as anxiety and distress mounted, and as pastoralists and businesspeople felt the pressure of declining incomes. Industrial disputes flared, the rights of male workers to combine were restricted, and there were disputes over control of the work process. In 1890 maritime workers struck and were soon joined by wharf labourers, shearers and miners. Confrontations were strident, fierce at times, but the forces were unequal. Unions covered only a small proportion of the workforce. Desperate need meant hungry workers who would take the place of strikers. The employers had police and governments largely on their side, as well as the resources to sit out periods of low production. Strikes were broken; unions lost members at a debilitating rate. In the aftermath of the depression, many unionists turned to the political wing of the labour movement to improve their conditions. And they looked to the state for greater protection for the poor, and for those smitten by ill fortune and ill health.

Activists in the women's movement sought their rightful place, along with men in making decisions for a better society. Their numbers were even smaller than the unionists', but their success came earlier. The first colony to grant women a place in the political process was South Australia, which in 1894 legislated to allow women to vote – following New Zealand in 1893. White women, it seemed, would gradually be involved in the process of sorting out the needs of the population, alongside colonial men.

8 Gendered Settlements

The trauma of the depression of the early 1890s stimulated a spirited debate about the character of the new society that white settlers were constructing in the colonies, and about the way forward into the new century. Many writers and speakers participated in attempts to define who an Australian was, and how Australians should organise politically to bring out the desired characteristics: the act of definition was at the same time an act of prescription. It was a debate that had many vocal participants, and many contested positions. Each was either explicitly or implicitly underwritten by understandings about men and women and about how they supposedly already related, or should ideally relate, to each other and society at large. The important new social structures, such as the family wage, that were in place by 1910 were essentially gendered settlements to the conflicts and tensions of the new white nation that resulted from the federation of the colonies in 1901.

The way in which the essential character of Australian society was described in the years of the 1890s and early 1900s fitted frameworks derived from political movements common to all western democracies, but they developed in particular ways within the Australian context. Constructions of race loosely based on Social Darwinism were particularly important. A foretaste of the political impact of such racial reasoning was offered by C. H. Pearson's *National Life and Character* published in 1893, in which he addressed the pressing issue of the ethnic composition of Australia's population, and in particular a Chinese presence in the colonies.

Australia is an unexampled instance of a great continent that has been left for the first civilised people that found it to take and occupy. The natives have died out as we approached; there have been no complications with foreign powers; and the climate of the South is magnificent ... The fear of Chinese immigration which the Australian democracy cherishes, and which Englishmen at home find it hard to understand, is, in fact, the instinct of self-preservation, quickened by experience. We know that coloured and white labour cannot exist side by side; we are well aware that China can swamp us with a single year's surplus of population; and we know that if national existence is sacrificed to the working of a few mines and sugar plantations, it is not the Englishman in Australia alone, but the whole civilised world, that will be the losers ... We are guarding the last part of the world, in which the higher races can live and increase freely, for the higher civilisation.

Pearson was participating here in a significant and increasingly urgent debate. It centred on a definition of white settlers in relation to people of non-Anglo-Saxon origins, and was aimed particularly at those nations closest to Australia's shores. The indigenous Aborigines were presumed to have been defeated, with the survivors, in the most populous colonies, thrust on to mission stations and government reserves. But what of the threat of the victorious settlers themselves suffering an invasion from the large populations crowding neighbouring countries to their north? The Australian colonies would be white, not bi-racial, with a declining indigenous dark-skinned remnant who would, many whites hoped, die out. Meanwhile Aborigines of mixed descent would, so it was believed, merge with the white population. But the threat to the white settlers' racial identity was now perceived as powerfully present from another source.

From the time of the goldrushes, white colonists had demonstrated their concern for preserving the new southern lands for their own stock, not only by their ruthless dispossession of Aborigines, but by their hostility to Asian immigrants, notably the Chinese who sought quick gains alongside Europeans at the diggings. Anti-Chinese sentiment abounded through the 1860s, 1870s and 1880s, and Chinese migrants found themselves sustaining a life in the colonies under highly oppressive restrictions. From the 1870s Melanesian labourers were brought to Queensland to work on the sugar plantations, but were contracted with the stipulation that they return after a period of years to their islands; there was no intention that they become permanent settlers. Kanakas were numerous, however, and a visibly different presence, alarming to white racist eyes. The history of white settlement had already been a history of attempts at white exclusionist policies, but by the 1890s and early 1900s concern to sustain the land for white inhabitants reached a new peak, when the preservation of the continent seemed under serious attack.

One reason for this intensification of racist sentiment was the ready acceptance by many white colonists of Social Darwinist ideas about the survival of the fittest. If at a grassroots level white settlers found a multitude of reasons to reject people unlike themselves, Social Darwinism offered a pseudo-scientific rationale for their narrow and ungenerous responses. The white races were supreme, so the claim ran, because of inherent exceptional qualities that promoted them to dominance among the world's societies. African, Asian and other non-white peoples were legitimately subjugated by whites because they were behind in the evolutionary scale, and hence had remained at the bottom of the human order. Imperialism by white nations was justified; settler societies like Australia concomitantly had the right to retain a distinctive character and exclude other races. Adherents to such views demonstrated the same arrogance that had once rationalised invasion of Aboriginal lands. The activities of other imperialistic European nations in the Pacific, particularly Germany, sharpened white settlers' fears of their vulnerability as a small group of expatriates clinging to a huge, if largely arid, continent. It also intensified their pride in their British origins and their affinity with British values. The white settlers' search for some sense of separate identity as Australians, then, was inextricably intertwined with a sense of themselves as Anglo-Saxon and fundamentally superior to other 'racial types', but most particularly to those who lacked that supposed badge of superiority, fair skin.

Social Darwinism also gave a pseudo-scientific basis to the negative attitudes of conservative and mostly wealthy colonists towards the working class. As in other industrialising countries, especially the United States of America, it also gave a new impetus to elitism. The idea of the survival of the fittest could be readily adapted to applaud the talents of the rich and could legitimate disregard for the needs of the poor, 'deserving' or 'undeserving'. Such a creed lent weight to wealthy colonists' claims for a lion's share of resources derived from the productive capacity of the colonies.

But there was also a positive and optimistic reading of Darwin that prompted other middle-class thinkers and activists in progressive liberal directions. They argued that humans, unlike animals, had the capacity to change their environment. Rather than displaying a fatalistic resignation to poverty, disabilities, slums and crime, human beings had the capacity to intervene and change the conditions that produced much of this misery and deprivation. Liberal Christianity interpreted such possibilities in the light of a social gospel, urging government intervention to ease the plight of the disadvantaged as appropriate for the followers of Christ in the new age. Given the importance of Protestantism among the middle class, those who promoted this liberal agenda went part of the way to negating some of the organised churches' conservatism.

Such an interpretation of Darwin was also critical to a second major debate on class relations. The terrible depression of the early 1890s set in train an intensified discussion about the character of the political system underlying colonists' social relations. The suffering and deprivation of so many people shocked some settlers, previously complacent about their prosperity and good fortune, into a realisation that greater measures of social equity would be needed if the life chances of a wide section of the working class were to be more satisfactory. While readings of Darwin's theory united most white colonists in racist dismissals of people of non-white origin, therefore, and legitimated conservative antagonism to impoverished white settlers, an alternative reading of the implications of Darwin for class divisions opened the way for some liberals and labour supporters to begin a reappraisal of the relationship of the state to those white citizens disadvantaged under a capitalist system.

The other major intellectual and political force shaping bids to define a special identity for Australian society was similarly imbued with racist superiority but, in terms of the white population, also sustained radicals in a conviction that a progressive will could eliminate much of the misery and poverty endemic in urban and rural communities alike. Fabianism and progressivism were the most influential doctrines, relying on notions of guided evolution, and the need for new ways of handling powerful historical trends. Labour now entered politics as a significant force, engaged not just in direct industrial activism, but bent on influencing mainstream political culture. Once again, this was not a new phenomenon. Liberals had engaged to some extent in state interventionist policies since the 1860s. Now, interventionism seemed more pressing. The union movement had consistently supported individual working men's efforts for election to legislatures through the 1870s and 1880s. With the failure of the massive strikes of the early 1890s, and the decimation of unions in the wake of the depression, leaders placed far greater confidence in the political efficacy of labour parties. The ballot box seemed to hold the answer, at least in part, both to the broader problem of working-class living conditions, and to waged workers' unequal negotiating position with employers. Here, too, Australia mirrored the European situation where labour and socialists within (male) democracies had looked with hope to the state as an instrument of benevolent change. The Australian Labor Party (ALP) slowly took shape.

As the colonies slowly agreed, over the decade of the 1890s, to federate, and as the new Commonwealth of Australia began to establish a specific political culture on a national scale, the political debates on race and class raged. It was within such political debates that bids for a say in defining the national character, and of promoting images of what Australia might become, were made. Considerations of gender were fundamental to understanding debate about race and class within Australian society in the 1890s, and the solutions to national problems that, by 1910, had been slowly put in place.

The key to understanding the extent to which the debates were about the relative power of men and women is the issue of motherhood, and the implications of women's essential function as mothers for the allotment of social roles for women and, by contrast, for men. For many vocal colonists, if white Australia was to be secure, white women needed to mate only with white men to produce the future desired citizens. For many vocal colonists a fair and equitable Australia meant that married white women needed to be freed from waged work to become mothers, and single white women in the waged workforce needed protection from rampant exploitation that might diminish their health and fertility. These ideas had preceded the new formulations of race and the new liberal and left-wing initiatives, but events in the 1890s and early 1900s gave such views renewed impetus. The women's movement made a determined effort to spearhead the debate about motherhood in an effort to present what they maintained was 'a woman's point of view', aware as they were of the dominance of the male voice in such discussions. Other political forces in the 1890s were male dominated, but none of them could ignore women and all were forced to respond not only to changing conditions for women, but specifically to this effort by a group of activists to insert women's situation into public male consciousness. First, let us turn to the women's movement.

The women's movement now intensified its effort to gain greater autonomy from men, both in the home and in public affairs, by an increasing emphasis on motherhood as a basis for women's acceptance as full citizens. It was not that all women were mothers, but that the 'motherhood principle' (nurturing; altruism; care for the young, old and needy; peacemaking; judicious good judgment) were promoted as the characteristics of women as a sex because of their biological difference from men. It was women, endowed as they were with these fine attributes, who would help develop the policies and practices in every avenue of life that would guarantee a fair, decent and honourable Australian nation. Leaders of the women's movement eulogised motherhood as the basis of their campaign to empower women socially, not intending to prescribe domesticity for all women, nor to restrict women's right to end a poor marriage, nor the right to enter waged work on an equal basis with men, nor to keep them from mainstream political engagement, but as the legitimation of all these things. The following piece of verse exemplifies their reasoning:

> Queen of Home, true friend and help meet.
> Guide and mother of the race;
> Wide her sphere, and great her mission.
> Naught her influence can efface.

The way in which activists in the women's movement described national characteristics is a useful guide to their reform goals. Bessie Lee's fictional sketches of colonial life were intended to persuade readers of the claims of women to a place in public life and simultaneously assert a representation of white colonial women as part of an emerging national tradition. Sally Pumpkin, the main protagonist in Lee's columns and pamphlets, was an able selector's wife, who could turn her hand to everything from making butter, curing hams or driving pigs out of the clover. By contrast, she refers to men as 'terrable useless critters in a house, though they may be some kind of count in a kricket ground or in parlyment, where there's nothen to do but play and tork'. When Sally Pumpkin's granddaughter, a member of the WCTU, promotes the women's vote, Sally is at first hesitant: would this demean women to the level of men? But then she reasons that 'when a lot of wimmin make up their minds like that, they'll move mountains'. And Sally's husband, Bartholomew, has no hesitancy about the entry of women to parliament, for to him this was merely a natural extension of the useful partnership of wife and husband. Bartholomew addresses Sally thus:

I consulted you about the schoolin' for the girls and gettin' married to you more'n fifty years ago ... Consulted you about the trades for the boys ... Consulted you about buyin' that there selecshun ... I reckon I never did one thing that mounted to anything in life without consulting you, Sarah ... and for my part I must say, if Parlyment ain't a fit place for my wife, it ain't a fit place for me.'

Sally Pumpkin emerges as a practical, energetic and competent woman endowed with an informed and shrewd common sense. She could in no way be described as oppressed by men, but cherished her sense of femininity as empowering. She sustained a right to hold a critical stance towards the opposite sex, and to point to the weaknesses to which they could so readily succumb without the benign influence of wise women. She was intended to be an exemplary figure.

Bessie Lee, like many others in the women's movement in the colonies and abroad, did not herself suggest that wives best served their nation by bearing large numbers of children. Many in the women's movement increasingly saw, in fact, an inverse relationship between good mothering and having numerous offspring. Decent, hard-working women, Bessie believed, were suffering shattered health and premature death from repeated childbearing. In this, her ideas meshed with those of certain freethinkers and rationalists, who promoted smaller families as the way for working people to avoid poverty. They advocated the use of 'preventatives', such as condoms, cervical caps and soluble pessaries, as the means to this end. In a landmark judgment in 1888 Mr Justice Windeyer of the Supreme Court of New South Wales had upheld the right of a free-thought lecturer and bookseller, charged with obscenity, to sell works containing such information, which the churches, the medical profession and respectable opinion uniformly viewed as disgusting and degenerate. 'Information cannot be pure, chaste and legal in morocco at a guinea, but impure, obscene and indictable in a paper pamphlet at sixpence', Windeyer ruled. One such rationalist, Mrs Brettena Smyth, a chemist in North Melbourne who stocked contraceptives and who was a well-known speaker on birth control, pointed out that Australian men worried enough about breeding their sheep and cattle. Why couldn't they concern themselves more with their wives' reproduction? 'Every woman should say so many and no more, and when she will have them. Marriage should protect her freedom, not make her a slave', Brettena Smyth wrote in her manual *Limitation of Offspring*.

But rationalists and feminists parted company over how best to bring about reduced childbearing: most feminists advocated abstention. In a work entitled *Marriage and Heredity*, published in 1893, Bessie Lee discussed 'voluntary motherhood', declaring that wives should choose when they were ready to bear a child, rather than remain at the mercy of husbands' unrestricted sexual needs. Louisa Lawson echoed these sentiments. What is woman's God-appointed calling, she asked?

Is it to minister to the passions of men, passions cultivated by generations of excess, and bear silently the untold sufferings that result to her? Is it to bring into the world large families of wretched human beings, in some cases knowing that they must suffer want ...?

Not in the least. Motherhood should be an elevated task, and this had both personal and broader social implications.

Keep your thoughts and body pure for the use of the sacred functions of motherhood, for which use alone these functions were given; and devote your surplus strength to the elevation of womanhood to this standard. Follow man no longer as his slave; step forward as his peer; advance, and if he does not keep pace, be his leader in progress.

All that was needed was a 'few more turns in the great wheel of evolution' and women would recognise their inherent power to develop 'the highest possibilities of the race'.

Having brought the issue of elevated motherhood to the forefront of debate, the women's movement in the 1890s turned its attention to the enfranchisement of women in the colonies and in the coming federal state. There was a victory for suffragists in South Australia in 1894, and in Western Australia in 1899. Although in both colonies the suffrage passed the legislatures with a combination of unexpected manoeuvrings by male politicians anxious to reap the benefit of the women's vote, the success was nevertheless heartening. Still more exciting, however, was the passage in 1902 of the act allowing women to vote in the federal elections. Rose Scott saw women thereby bringing a new element into the nation's political life.

Remember that a woman's mission is to inspire man and to help him build up our young nation upon all that is righteous. Brute force and intellectual force have in the past dominated the world. Let us contain both these forces with moral force. The safeguards of the nation will then rest on the individual conscience of its women.

Feminists stressed motherhood even more than wifehood as the core of women's claims. As the mother moulded the child, she should now aim to mould, purify and exalt national life. The hand that rocked the cradle had been degraded in status, since 'subject' mothers 'never did, and never will, produce a race of free, well disposed, liberty loving, justice practising children'. Men could not rise above the mothers of the race, but the next generation would be children of free women, not any longer of bondwomen, a writer in the WCTU journal, the *White Ribbon Signal*, declared.

The women's movement, then, offered a vision for an improved Australian society which would be based on social equity between men and women, enabling the mother-force of women to suffuse all avenues of human interaction, apparently humble or overtly powerful, with the fine qualities that women possessed. Family life would be improved when women had opportunities for dignified occupations as alternatives to loveless marriage; mothering would improve when women could control the number of children they bore, and could rear them well; political life would be cleansed by the presence of women; society would be governed far better; and measures to assist poorer women and children to a fairer and happier life would be set in train. The feminist agenda proved an effective means of alerting other women, and men, to the need for change, and by the turn of the century the women's civil rights campaign and economic policies were clearly gaining ground.

But many other groups were talking about the new Australia to be created from the pain of the depression in ways that represented the relative position of men and women in distinctly different ways. These groups, too, valorised motherhood, and thereby offered women agency within the new Australia, but their vision contrasted in significant ways from that of the feminists. This was deliberate, not by chance: it represented their own response to the changing place of women in urban society, and to the claims of the women's movement; it revealed their own particular orientation to the political implications of that change.

One of the most significant bids to describe the new Australia emerged from the male-dominated labour movement. The Australian nation would be white; it would be democratic and egalitarian; women would be equal citizens but inevitably and justifiably excluded from public roles of status and power because of their capacity for motherhood. The most notable of these labour definitions of Australia emerged from the group of writers associated with the *Bulletin*, the Sydney radical journal edited by J. F. Archibald.

The pages of the *Bulletin* evinced a powerful antipathy to political women, those leading advocates of women's causes, and in particular the WCTU women whose spirited espousal of sobriety, domesticity, companionate marriage and sexual purity seemed most at variance with the *Bulletin*'s representation of the Australian – in reality, Australian masculinity – aligned with the carefree, freewheeling man, who abhorred the constraints of family life. WCTU activists were portrayed as hard-faced, aggressive, shrieking cockatoos, freaks of nature, and ugly; women who had missed out on all the sensual joys of life and hoped to make their deprivation universal. Bessie Lee came in for particular vilification, with her sceptical views of male sexuality and the need for abstention if wives were to gain some control of reproduction. The *Bulletin* reacted scathingly to Lee's depiction of ideal marriage as a 'union of souls, a sweet companionship, a mutual help and sympathy ... We are told that in Heaven there is neither marriage nor giving in marriage. A cynical man will admit that that would be Heaven indeed.' Linking feminism with another emerging fact – that the birthrate was indeed declining – the *Bulletin* declared:

Marriage plays too important a part in the life of the modern civilised man. He is cramped and coffined in on every hand ... He is forced to look to the home, to conventional marriage, for all his character-culture, his higher excitements as an intellectual being, and he finds it bitterly inadequate.

The *Bulletin*'s position was aligned here with many men who had no egalitarian pretensions, like the members of the Legislative Assembly in Victoria who warned that 'Woman's suffrage would abolish soldiers and war, also racing, hunting, football, cricket and all other manly games'.

The tactic of denigrating marital bonds – wives were nagging, depressed, burdensome creatures – and celebrating the ideal of the 'man alone', the bushman, pervaded the stories and poems of the *Bulletin*'s best-liked contributors, including Henry Lawson (son of Louisa Lawson), 'Banjo' Paterson and Ted Dyson. Their heroes inhabited a male world, where some conquered the frontier, while many simply endured or negotiated it with stoicism and humour. Whichever way, this experience, and these qualities, defined Australianness: women were excluded from their constructions, or existed in an uneasy marginality in relation to them. The bush was no place for women, particularly mothers, and most, like the drover's wife whom Henry Lawson sketched, were oppressed, dehumanised and defeminised by it. The drover's wife stood in marked contrast to the effective, capable Sally Pumpkin, that second selector's wife, Bessie Lee's creation. These writers' means of confronting the challenge of the gendered transformations of late colonial life was to deny agency to women, whether as spinsters, wives or mothers, and to portray the archetypal Australian as the type of male whom they espoused as the true Australian.

Writers of the *Bulletin* school were not the only men attached to the labour cause who represented Australian identity in ways significant for women. 'We may reform industry all we like, but unless the race-blood is warm the race is dying out', wrote William Lane in his significant work *The Workingman's Paradise*. He proclaimed with conviction that women were 'race-mothers'. The labour movement as a whole could not ignore women in their bid to define a national agenda, and women – especially women in their capacity as mothers or would-be mothers – were certainly included. The debate was male-dominated in terms of whose interests were addressed and who had the right to speak for the group. But male unionists could not ignore that women were indeed waged and unwaged workers. For many members of a key union, the Australian Shearers' Union (later the Australian Workers' Union), the work of women as small farmers' wives promised a far greater hope for prosperity for the man, and the family, than the wifeless bachelor could expect. For urban male workers, women were an established fact in the waged workforce, and it was imperative that some policy towards them be devised. In addition, socialist-feminists within unions, and socialist and labour groups more generally, brought specific attitudes to women into the central arena of discussion. The pages of the labour journal *Tocsin* in the late 1890s provides a useful illustration of the scope of alternative labour movement attempts to represent Australian masculinity and femininity.

The *Tocsin*'s chief writers, in contrast to those of the popular *Bulletin* magazine, supported the civil rights campaign of the women's movement with considerable conviction: few causes which feminists raised at the turn of the century in respect to political and legal change went unnoted, and unapplauded. Labour women, of course, would reap the benefits of emancipation along with their middle-class sisters, and they were urged to begin organising immediately in support of issues associated with the labour cause. The wives of labour men, however, the *Tocsin* hoped, would not work for women or women's civil rights issues alone, but for the general political and social welfare of the community – working-class women and children in particular but their menfolk too. These labour men were prepared to call the new labour-oriented Woman's Political and Social Crusade (once its members understood this message fully) 'a plucky, useful, and vigilantly democratic society'. Men were portrayed, however, as the movers and shakers of the activist labour movement, whom wives and sweethearts were urged to support and nurture: 'This is peculiarly your work – work which only women can do – to cheer, to inspire, to stimulate, shed around the men who are away at the front the aroma of your love'. There were alternative voices. One column headed 'The Agitator's Wife' portrayed an activist's wife complaining that her husband's own children barely recognised their father: 'this "revolutionist", the man who talks of "planting the flag of the future upon the barricades", but turns white with fear if I ask him to hold the baby whilst I run a message'. Labour wives and mothers could sustain a low-key but useful activist role themselves, as auxiliary supporters of men's labour agenda, though with a specific and useful brief for their own sex.

The activism *Tocsin* legitimated was voluntary work. There was profound dismay at the thought that girls' and women's current incursion into waged labour was a permanent phenomenon:

The TOCSIN does not believe that women should be compelled to take part in what may be called the outside struggle for existence, and does not think that she would do so of her own notion if the fruits of man's outside toil were fairly and equitably allotted to him.

And again, forecasting a utopian future:

Given the power to maintain and educate a family decently, men will so perform their natural duties to women that very few women will need to come into the outside world of competition at all. And the TOCSIN believes very strongly that that's how it should be.

Overall, thought the *Tocsin*, only harsh exploitation awaited women in the workforce, where their blood was poisoned, their ears deafened and their bodies crippled. Women's instincts surely were towards wifehood and motherhood, whereas foul and dangerous workplaces withered these hopes. One columnist went so far as to describe female waged workers as 'spayed women', such was the destructive quality of the environment for these potential bearers of children. As true democrats, the *Tocsin* knew that socialist men should accept a woman's right to enter any sphere of work she chose, but 'whether it is in the best interests of the race that she should have to assert her undoubted right is a somewhat arguable question' – even though they knew well that some women were sole breadwinners for children, or for unemployed parents.

This stress on the ill effects of workplaces on women's capacity for motherhood stood, of course, alongside men's many expressions of fear at the capacity for low-waged women to undercut the male wage. The danger that the cheap labour of women would replace that of men in work which people could perform regardless of sex had surfaced urgently in the painful years of the depression. Women, fearful men noted, were every day becoming more skilled and more competent in all manner of trades. Hence it was not to be wondered at that it was common 'for married women machinists, fitters, etc., to take employment in the boot factories from which their husbands have been turned away owing to the depression. They are taken on because they will work for less than their husbands will work for'.

Socialist-feminists urged, by contrast, that all women should unionise, and fight alongside working men in the common cause. *Tocsin* writers mostly preferred to make chivalrous noises about mothers at home, or waged mothers-to-be whose health and fertility were being steadily undermined.

What of the lives of these working-class mothers in their own domestic workplaces? There was some acknowledgment, and deprecation, of the fact that selectors' wives and daughters undertook heavy work:

> tens of thousands of the mothers and future mothers of the Victorian people are daily, and have been for years past, compelled ... to bullock their way through life ... Such work will, no doubt, develop masculine muscles in these women, but it will also, and assuredly, unsex them. And we have no right – we in the towns – to be parasites on an unsexed country womanhood.

Urban working-class mothers, however, were portrayed as carrying out light chores in the home, albeit in an environment of housing depressed by greedy landlords' neglect, and by greedy capitalists' avarice in denying fathers decent wages – seldom was the exploitation of husbands mentioned. The path to a satisfying life was monogamous marriage and legitimate – and frequent – childbearing. The *Tocsin* was shocked at the discovery that became obvious in the 1890s, that the birthrate was in decline, since this struck at the core of their social vision. There was no problem, they assured readers, of too many children – merely a problem of unequal distribution of wealth. Contraception struck 'a foul blow at the sublime instincts of motherhood and paternity: it would transform marriage literally into sanctified prostitution, and undermine and destroy the sacred institution of the Family for ever'. A woman writer responded with some annoyance that it was all very well for men to speak of the duty of wives to bear children:

but the fact remains, and a sad fact, too, that the conditions of life for the average wife are so hard that ... the joy of motherhood has turned to bitterness, and she is putting aside the 'duty', laying down the burden, reluctantly for the most part, not because the love for motherhood is less, but the struggle has become so great 'she just can't bear it'.

But for the *Tocsin*'s principal writers, as for others who opposed neo-Malthusian notions of restricting population growth, motherhood was sacred. They applauded such sentiments as those voiced by Nellie, the central character of William Lane's *The Workingman's Paradise*, who shrank from the barrenness 'that was coming to be regarded as the most comfortable state and being sought after ... by the younger married women'. She renounced any possibility of marriage, however, until the 'serpent' of Asian immigration had been expelled from the garden. Nellie was made to ask, in terms that combined Lane's protagonism for a strong working class with his racism: 'What were they all coming to? Were they all to go on like this without a struggle until they vanished altogether as a people, perhaps to make room for the round-faced, bland-cheeked Chinaman?'.

Concern for preserving a white society, and for fostering white motherhood, were key motives serving to integrate colonies within which otherwise so much contestation was evident between classes and people of differing religious persuasions and geographical areas.

The prime movers in the bid for federation, the men who assumed the task of persuading the many sceptical colonists across the continent, were swift to see this. Alfred Deakin, a doyen of those pushing for federation, said of Australia's racial character:

> the question of white Australia touches all colonists' instinct for self-preservation – for it is nothing less than the ... national future that [is] at stake ... no motive power operates more universally ... and more powerfully in dissolving the technical and arbitrary political divisions which previously separated us than did the desire that we should be one people, and remain one people, without the admixture of other races.

Deakin and the other 'founding fathers' of Australian federation needed such an integrating force. While many people saw federation as an opportunity for colonists to pool their skills and resources in the interests of promoting their collective wealth, as well as defending their shores, others in the labour movement were suspicious of those who might benefit unfairly at the expense of the less fortunate; some colonists, located far from the key population centres in the south-eastern cities, feared domination from a distance. The racial exclusionist appeal in the debate was conducted in masculinist terms, a further factor in enhancing a sense of common destiny, this time for Australian men. As one politician proposed:

> As a true federationist, I believe that the only federation that can be effective is a federation of the manhood of Australia – a truly representative federation. It is not a question of federating acres and wealth; it is a question of federating the spirit of the manhood of Australia, and that is what we should seek to do.

Many politicians who might otherwise have shown little enthusiasm for the cause were forced to concede that within this masculine federation women would have to be citizens, since two states had already granted them the franchise, and women of these states should therefore be offered similar rights in the federal constitution. A few were chivalrous enough to welcome women's political participation; others did so by stressing, not the improvement in political life heralded by the women's movement, but white women's common links with their menfolk. Said one politician:

> I know that numbers of women have taken part in this movement, and when we are speaking in terms of praise of the efforts made by the young men of the colony, we should not overlook their sisters, and, perhaps, also their mothers.

No one would ever regret the wide liberty offered all the people of Australia under the new constitution, he continued, referring to white women's and men's racial affinity, since 'the utmost liberty may be given the Anglo-Saxon without any fear of his abusing it'.

When politicians did promote women as important participants in the new Australia, women's main contribution was not forecast as active citizenship, but prolific childbearing. The first act of the new Commonwealth of Australia was one restricting non-white entry. Australia's spaces would be filled instead by pure white babies. But it was soon apparent that, in pressuring women to propagate, those vocal public men opposing fertility control were fighting a losing battle. The decline in the white colonial birthrate already noted in the 1890s, was acutely registered in the 1901 census. Later, the drop would be seen as part of a marked shift common to all modernising societies, from a demographic profile of a high birthrate and high death rate, to a low birthrate and low death rate. Several explanations are plausible. On the one hand, wives' expectations of better health and some freedom from unremitting domestic toil were rising with the spread of women's movement ideas. At the same time, the accelerating shift of population into urban areas, compulsory schooling for children and their need to stay longer at school to gain credentials, gave many couples incentives – despite the opposition of all churches, the medical profession and politicians – to limit their families. Children were now a greater financial burden than in the past, and rearing children and adolescents in cities was increasingly a strain on mothers.

One churchman in 1901 applauded certain doctors' pronouncements about the 'population problem' and the responsibilities of women as cutting 'deep into the canker which is eating the very heart out of our Australian society'. His suggestion was a regular meeting between the clergy and medical men to deal with the problem, so that 'two great vital forces would thus be directed against what everyone admits is a growing evil and menace to the State'.

Such a meeting did take place in 1903, when so concerned was the state government of New South Wales about the steady decline in the birthrate that it established a royal commission under Justice Charles MacKeller to investigate the reasons for this apparent act of 'race suicide' (as President Theodore Roosevelt had termed a similar decline in the United States). The commissioners found that such factors as a rise in the age of marriage could not of itself account for the decline in births. Instead they pointed to:

i An unwillingness to submit to the strain and worry of children;
ii A dislike of the interference with pleasure and comfort involved in child-bearing and child-rearing;
iii A desire to avoid the actual physical discomfort of gestation, parturition, and lactation; and
iv A love of luxury and social pleasures, which is increasing.

Federal and state governments set about devising ways to restrict the advertisement and sale of contraceptives, and the circulation of materials informing people of ways to control fertility. Ideas about 'social purity', about encouraging chastity and monogamy, underwrote other legislation raising the age of consent for girls, and opposed the double moral standard implicit in legislation to control venereal diseases and prostitution. Law enforcement agencies also began to intervene more actively in such concerns as abortion, the foster care of babies, and the conditions of lying-in hospitals and orphanages, to help prevent deaths. New legislation removed some of the stigma from illegitimacy, and allowed those parents who subsequently married to legitimise children born prior to marriage.

Married couples seemed to challenge the strong external pressures placed upon them to breed prolifically. Women did not necessarily restrict conception when first married, but bore fewer children after the age of thirty-five years; also fewer women bore more than four children. Later some younger wives in their twenties waited a space after marriage for first births. These practices appeared more swiftly in urban areas, where information was passed on more readily, than in rural areas: but within a decade, there was little difference between the two. Stronger regulation of fertility appeared more quickly among middle-class than working-class wives, and among Protestants than Roman Catholics or Lutherans: but again, there was little to distinguish them within a decade or two.

The situation in the inner suburban area of South Melbourne demonstrated the urban pattern. Between the years 1871 and 1891 there was a drop in marital fertility in women aged thirty-five to thirty-nine years from 235 births to 149 for each 1000 married women. In the decade of the 1890s the age-specific fertility of women between twenty-five and twenty-nine years was halved, a dramatic and rapid decrease. The wives who struggled to restrict their fertility may have seldom been aware of feminist ideas, but the demand of the women's movement that married women should have the right to control their own bodies was by no means unimportant for wives' slowly increasing capacity to do so. The decline in conception was effected as much by abstention from sexual intercourse, as by the new mechanical devices.

But if women were winning the right, and learning the means, to control their fertility, the dominant construction of women as mothers, which feminists had tried to co-opt for their own purposes, prevailed in other important aspects of their life experiences. As time proceeded fewer children by no means implied a parallel lessening of women's publicly represented identification with home and family. Feminists had hoped that women could have both specific empowerment on the basis of biological difference from men, and civic equality on the basis of shared humanity with men. Negotiating the two proved a difficult task in the face of the strong forces from the right and the left that portrayed adult women outside the competitive arena of waged work and politics, sustaining social stability at a crucial turning point for the country by maintaining the family's emotional and physical needs.

Women activists most certainly intended to play a vital part in the political processes of the new nation. Louisa Lawson spoke for most when she wrote in optimistic terms about women's capacity to utilise democratic processes for female concerns. Given the fact of imminent enfranchisement, she said, it was every woman's duty to think seriously of her new responsibilities:

deep down in the heart of every woman lives the desire to make better moral conditions for her husband and children, and the full development of this desire can only be achieved by the fullest freedom to exercise her God given aspirations. So while men are engaged in the weightier matter of legislation, such as the military (and who craves peace more than women), and the tariff (and who knows more about its effects than women), and so on, Give her, for God's sake, the broom and the duster, and let her clean up the sanitary and moral conditions of the country.

She continued with characteristic intensity:

Yes, there is plenty for her to do; and when men have struck off the shackles which now bind her, and have thrown down the barriers of suppression, she will no longer sit at home and suffer, but will go out and battle, as only a wife and mother can, against the immorality of the age, and the temptation and dirt which assail the moral and physical well-being of her loved ones.

Women were present, indeed, as the various groups who had assumed the right to define Australianness jockeyed after 1901 for the right to set in place the structures that would signify the new nation's identity. But the route they negotiated for themselves kept women marginal to mainstream politics. At the same time the political agenda they espoused thrust them into collusion with other interest groups on policies, in a way that tended to suppress women's separate and specific voice. Over the first decade of national life, male representations of appropriate femininity and women's social space gradually took precedence. Many Australians were politically involved in defining motherhood in ways that legitimated their own sectional interests. Politically active women continued their policy, successful as it had been in gaining civil rights, of asserting motherhood as socially empowering for women. It proved a useful – but also ultimately confining – strategy for sustaining an authoritative voice in the body politic.

Women activists were swift to organise once the vote was won, but whereas in pre-suffrage days there had been considerable unity around that central goal, there was now diversity in their practices. Some veterans of the women's movement remained in feminist groups or formed new ones: Vida Goldstein in Victoria, and Rose Scott in New South Wales, for example, remained central to separate feminist endeavours. Vida Goldstein distinguished herself by standing for the Senate in 1903, and campaigning forcefully as a politician representing women's issues. She did respectably in the polls, but was unsuccessful in this and further attempts to join mainstream politics directly. Other women sought a place in the ranks of the major parties. Women were admitted to the various labour parties as full voting members by the mid-1890s. Separate women's auxiliaries formed in each state, offering women some space for gender-specific endeavours, although these auxiliaries remained tightly woven into class-based politics. Liberal and conservative women – some of the latter had earlier staunchly opposed the granting of votes for women – formed the Australian Women's National League, ostensibly a non-party women's organisation, but in fact promoted by liberal and conservative men who now had every reason to wish their womenfolk organised on an anti-labour platform. Contrary to expectations, however, patterns of voting at the first federal elections revealed that the women's vote split, as did men's, on the basis of economic interests and party political divisions.

The feminist non-party organisations sent delegates to branches of the National Council of Women (NCW), established in each state and open to all women's groups except those with avowedly political party affiliations. There were professional women's groups and charities, women's sporting organisations and religious associations, with the Young Women's Christian Association and the Australian Women's National League among the most prominent. At regular meetings women from this varied range of endeavours discussed and developed policies that they then pressed upon the appropriate authorities, at local, state and federal level, with letters, delegations, and printed literature to back them up. The NCW epitomised the political activism of women post-suffrage. Within a political party such as the ALP women did have influence, but they did not reach executive positions or leadership positions, and certainly did not get selected to represent the party in winnable seats at general elections. For some women the alternative was working within a separate lobby group.

Women's political influence was predominantly exercised – rather as it had been in the past – by joining forces to promote gender-specific issues. Increasingly, mainstream politics came to be seen as the clash of men representing the conflicting economic concerns of working men, of business, and of farmers. 'Women's issues' were seen as marginal to these central conflicts, and women sought to intervene in the political agenda through lobby groups, rather than becoming integrated into the political system as parliamentary representatives with electoral responsibilities. Yet, to a surprising extent, both liberal and labour women began to advocate policies that, while motivated by different class orientations, converged to a considerable degree. The effort to improve the life chances of working-class women and children emerged as the focus of much women's activism. Feminist issues about the relative status of men and women were promoted by a minority and then somewhat apologetically, or self-consciously. Many of the women now active in political lobby groups never had been, nor were now, feminists, though protagonists for women they well might be over specific issues. Slowly, a feminist voice became submerged by welfare orientations.

For liberal women activists, the needs of poorer women seemed pressing. Most working-class mothers were decidedly better off, liberals thought, caring for their children and their homes than in the workforce. The environment for mothering needed reform, in housing, food and milk supplies, and the provision of parks and recreation centres; working-class mothers needed instruction in caring for infants, centres where the health and wellbeing of young children could be monitored, and kindergartens to provide periods of supervised, safe play away from the dangers of the streets. In the workforce, waged women needed protection from dangerous environments, they needed decent pay and hours, with inspectors to see the law was carried out. As an alternative to factory labour, working-class girls could be trained for domestic labour, preferably beginning in schools. If such girls later married, standards of housework in working-class homes would benefit; until they married, the young women would provide a pool of much-needed, efficient assistance for middle-class wives who had the wherewithal to pay.

With these policies, middle-class women activists became part of a conscious process of modernising, of correcting behaviour now apparently anomalous beside new sensibilities about the expected organisation and conduct of a 'progressive' and 'enlightened' people in an industrialising society. Professional women, educated women, women with the necessary skills and credentials to carry out and monitor reforming structures were poised to benefit from new employment opportunities. Wherever there were women as clients, as victims, as pupils, as patients, as inmates of institutions, educated women won a place in the expanding ranks of the 'helping professions', as social workers, doctors, psychologists, nurses, inspectors, teachers, institutional visitors and matrons. Their participation was at first modest, but would increase slowly but surely as the century proceeded, since such work was eminently suited to women whose whole public presence was justified, not on the basis of some abstract notion of equality, but on the basis of maternal ideologies.

Labour activists, too, saw that working-class mothers and their children would gain much from this same reform platform even though labour activists' motives were driven more by empathy for poorer women with whose interests they identified, than by humanitarian concern deriving from liberals' guilt at their own privileged social position. Working-class women, after all, did need better living and work environments, better health and better life chances for their babies and children. There were major obstacles to mothers undertaking waged work, and the conditions of such work itself were often highly exploitative. Some of those working-class women who were in waged employment supported the socialist-feminist call for male unionists to welcome women as comrades and equals, to support equal wages for women's work and confront employers as a united group, but such women were a minority.

This male suspicion of women workers was often presented in public forums as disinterested concern for the exploitation of women in the workforce, for the need to protect the weaker sex and future childbearers from permanent injury to health and fertility. Clearly women workers often laboured under extreme difficulties. The key issue was, how should this be coped with.

The combined political force of liberal politicians and labour movement leaders, backed up by the reforming impulse, saw to it that in the new commonwealth working-class women as well as men received some degree of industrial protection. In Victoria, the movement to assist workers in their unequal battle with employers had begun as early as 1896 with the establishment of wages boards. The boards enabled unions to register and subject their industrial needs and disputes to the deliberations of a tribunal at which workers, employers and government were represented. New South Wales set up industrial and arbitration courts with a similar goal, a structure carried through into national legislation after federation. In a number of ways women in particular benefited considerably from the opportunities that this new legislation opened up. Whereas previously unions, virtually all male, had won some important concessions from employers through direct industrial confrontation, women had been largely outside unions, and their position had been particularly dire. Even for men, though, the depression had led to a severe depletion of union membership.

Now there was a strong incentive, underwritten by state action, for women, as for previously unorganised men, to establish unions and use this new bargaining opportunity. The numbers of unions increased swiftly. Women for the first time were awarded minimum wages and some improvement in hours and working conditions. This was only of use, of course, where the legislation was enforced and employers abided by the law, but it certainly gave women in unionised industries some leverage. That the Australian state pioneered ways to intervene on the part of the working class to offset the dominant power of the employers attracted Australia (and New Zealand) considerable attention from reformers and labour in the United States and Europe. Women workers were seen as the major beneficiaries.

But the new system also held disadvantages for women both in their capacity as workers and as a sex. For much of what underwrote this settlement of the relationship of labour, capital and the state was a concern to protect men as wage earners, and through them, protect those adult women who were unwaged, dependent workers, the wives caring for men's homes and children. This was registered most patently in the Harvester Case judgment brought down by Justice Higgins in the Commonwealth Industrial and Arbitration Court in 1907, a finding that became a landmark in Australian labour history. Higgins sought to describe a fair and reasonable remuneration for workers to meet 'the normal needs of the average employee regarded as a human being living in a civilised community'. His determination decreed that a minimum wage for a man should reach 7 shillings per day, to cover the basic needs of rent, food and fuel for himself, a wife and three children. As Higgins decreed a year later: 'A wage that does not allow for the matrimonial condition for an adult man is not fair and reasonable, is not a "living wage" '. So men's wages were set as a 'family wage' and in many ways this was a progressive and humane concept now passed into law. Higgins clearly viewed the compulsion of impoverished wives to be breadwinners as a burden to be avoided, and saw no reason to ask employers to indulge with high wages young single women, who were presumed to contribute only towards their own keep within a family household. And so women's capacity to earn a fair wage, judged by criteria of equity and individual needs, was dealt a sore blow, which would bedevil their fortunes for decades. At the same time, the formal demarcation of men's and women's jobs was institutionalised.

The relative benevolence of the state, therefore, and the relative victory of labour and liberal reformers in gaining some security for waged workers, was a gendered settlement. Men were enshrined through these processes as the accepted breadwinners for the family group, and hence were offered higher wages and greater legitimacy as workers. Many men were in fact single, separated or widowers – and some, of course, though married, failed to share their earnings at all willingly with their families. Women, moreover, were enshrined in this settlement as workers who were marginal, temporary, young and maintained in part by a father's or husband's resources. The typical female worker was the housewife. Most adult women were indeed housewives, but the period was one in which some fluidity in what was considered men's work and women's work seemed possible. Now a place for some women was confirmed in waged work, but, ideologically, traditional values had won through.

This situation was repeated in the other legislation that made Australia notable in these years. Through income tax, the state began some modest distribution from the rich to subsidise improved facilities, education and welfare for the poor. Old age pensions and widows' pensions assisted the elderly, and bereaved wives, especially those without alternative family support, to lead penurious but independent lives. When it took over government in 1910, the first national ALP administration elected with a parliamentary majority, headed by Andrew Fisher, confirmed this direction, of a supposedly benevolent state intervening to assist those disadvantaged under a capitalist system. But for women, there were costs, too, in these other efforts towards social equity. Help given in pragmatic fashion to assist the poor served at the same time to reinforce the conviction that adult women's place not only was usually in the home, but ought to be in the future. Working-class family life, because of social equity measures and the concerns of reformers, shifted a little further towards the style of family life cherished by the middle class. While working-class women sustained a substantial presence in the ranks of unskilled and semi-skilled labour, and while a small but important minority of mostly single middle-class women was entering professional and white-collar work, the dominant representations of gender, family and work denied the radical force of this social transformation.

Two small items in the Church of England *Messenger* of the period could be seen as straws in the wind. Some Anglican women, and some women in other Protestant denominations, had been moving modestly to the fore in church affairs during the 1880s and 1890s, not only in traditional parish work but beyond it. There was talk of giving women the vote in parish and synod elections. There were plans afoot to revive the ancient order of deaconesses. But the prized initiative was the Mothers' Union: 'To awaken in mothers of all classes a sense of their great responsibility in training their boys and girls (the future mothers and fathers of the Empire)'. Would this at least prove an opportunity to organise more women for church work? Not in the least. 'For although we have rightly called it a Church society', ran an editorial in the *Messenger*,

it is not an institution for the furtherance of Church work ... indirectly, indeed, every department of Church work would be immensely benefited ... by the spread of the principles which this association seeks to promote, but the sphere of the Mothers' Union is the sphere of the Woman, and that is not the Church, but the Home.

Women were to be encouraged into associations in order to reinforce their place in the home.

And again, look at the speaking position of Sister Esther, a deaconess, appealing for women volunteers for charitable work in a speech 'Woman's Work in the Church' delivered to a church congress. Even she, a woman in a position of responsibility, felt obliged to admonish:

Let us not forget to remember that no active Church work should be undertaken at the expense of home duties. We have every right to sacrifice ourselves; we have no right to sacrifice others, or to fail in our duty to those whom God has given us to love and cherish in our home life.

Was it any wonder that by 1910 the Archbishop of Melbourne, Henry Lowther Clarke, was bewailing the lack of sufficient female volunteers for active church assistance to those in need: Anglican women who were single could train and seek waged professional work; the married women, still responsible for the family's young, for the elderly, the sick and the handicapped as well as for their husbands' needs, had been clearly told that their duty lay with their individual homes.

Lost opportunities would be 'the scourge of the Church', the archbishop told his diocese, and the scourge of the Australian community more broadly, we might add on later reflection. Women seeking reform in their social status would redouble their efforts to assert motherhood as an empowering concept, even as the 1911 census confirmed the continuing reduction of the numbers of children each woman bore.

9 Giving Birth to the New Nation

In the winter of 1906, at the age of twenty-five, Jane Daley entered the Women's Hospital in Melbourne to give birth. The bringing forth of a new life into the world might have been an occasion for communal celebration and thanksgiving, a source of womanly pride and joy, but this would not be so in Jane Daley's case. In a patriarchal society that deemed the children of unwed mothers illegitimate, the birth of such a baby was surrounded by secrecy, shame and anxiety. Not only did the mother and child suffer ignominy and ostracism (while the father went unremarked), but society was organised in such a way as to make motherhood and child support – breadwinning – almost impossible to combine. The despair of women in this situation had led some to kill their babies – to suffocate them or throw them in the river – but that, too, was against the law. Jane Daley was more fortunate than many single mothers in that her own mother and father were still alive and were prepared to support their daughter and new grandchild. She returned with him to the refuge of her family home at Wallacedale, in western Victoria, where her father worked as a shearer.

Jane, now known as Jean, went back after a time to live and work in Melbourne, leaving her son in the care of her parents. She found work as a confectionery maker, cook and caterer. By 1910 she had become involved with her trade union and also joined the Women's Organising Committee (WOC) of the Political Labor Council, which concerned itself with the conditions of women and children, at home and in the paid workforce. In September 1912 the women of the WOC were moved to pass a strongly worded resolution expressing their 'utter detestation at the foul slanders levelled at our class' by a deputation to Labor Prime Minister Andrew Fisher, who had protested at the extension of the proposed maternity allowance to unmarried mothers. Poor women, the deputation had told the prime minister, would be induced to 'sell their honour' for the 5 pound payment. The WOC further resolved to express its appreciation of the prime minister's 'noble and wise act' in 'conferring this instalment of the mother's maternal rights' and its hope to also have a child pension. For Jean Daley this protest signalled the beginning of a long campaign for a cherished goal: the economic independence of mothers.

Prime Minister Fisher's avowed intention in introducing this payment to mothers on the birth of a child was 'to protect the present citizens of the Commonwealth and give to coming citizens a greater assurance that they will receive proper attention at the most critical period in their lives'. 'Statistics show', he said, invoking a parallel that would become popular, 'that maternity is more dangerous than war'. He proposed a one-off payment of 5 pounds (the equivalent of four weeks wages for a woman in a factory) to mothers upon the birth of a baby and the issuing of a medical certificate, thus encouraging women to use their money to pay for medical attention. The prime minister justified the expected annual budget outlay of 400 000 pounds as a judicious investment for a developing nation: 'The more young Australians we have the wealthier the country must be'. Women thus had a central part to play in economic growth – women in their capacity as mothers.

Not all mothers were deemed eligible for the maternity allowance, however, and the categories of women excluded tell us much about the racial constitution of the Australian nation. Women who were 'Asiatics' or 'Aboriginal natives of Australia, Papua or the islands of the Pacific' would not be paid the allowance. This discrimination drew sharp criticism from non-party feminists who deplored the exclusions as the White Australia Policy gone mad. 'Maternity is maternity whatever the race ...' Few other voices condemned the colour bar. Labour women, strongly committed like the parliamentary representatives of their class to White Australia, were more concerned to defend the extension of the payment to unmarried (white) mothers. This was by far the most controversial aspect of the legislation, provoking an emotional debate in the press. The prospect of the government condoning the 'immorality' of women giving birth to 'illegitimate' children generated widespread community criticism. In South Australia, the state branch of the Woman's Christian Temperance Union thought its application to mothers of illegitimate children would encourage an evil already too prevalent. Male opponents argued revealingly that offering public monies to 'those who would be mothers before they have become wives' threatened 'marriage as a contract' that was the 'necessary foundation of national welfare'. One correspondent of the press complained that the state was bestowing a civil right upon transgressors of its law – the 'divine and human law'. The stridency of the critics suggests that the law being broken by these women was the law of male control – exercised through the 'ties of marriage'. The government's proposal would 'belittle' this key institution.

Though there was fierce disagreement over the categories of women eligible for state assistance and indeed the wisdom of making any monetary payments to women, all parties to the debate were agreed that Australia needed a bigger (white) population. As immigrants to a 'new found land' and the dispossessors of the original Aboriginal custodians, British Australians were anxious about the future of their race and their ability (and perhaps, at an unconscious level, their right) to hold the continent. The long coastline and 'vast empty spaces' heightened the young nation's sense of vulnerability. Their proximity to the numerous peoples of Asia simply accentuated their sense of isolation and the insecurity of this outpost of empire.

The keystone of the national policy of defence and development then was a large increase in white population, and the implications of this policy for the lives of all Australian women were vast. Aboriginal mothers would be systematically deprived of their children as state authorities throughout Australia took their offspring away and placed them in state or church institutions or private employment. For white women, meanwhile, motherhood was lauded as their grandest vocation. Within this context they were able to achieve an identity and status that proved to be simultaneously beneficial and confining. As mothers, women lobbied for and were granted special services for themselves and their children. As well as the maternity allowance, there were new infant welfare centres and women's hospitals. State 'boarding out allowances' enabled deserving widows and deserted wives to keep their children. But as unpaid civil servants and wealth producers, women were also subject to increasing surveillance, responsibility and blame. And, defined as mothers or potential mothers, women were often denied entry to alternative vocations, often refused the right to paid work and a living wage of their own. As mothers, said the *Australian Medical Gazette* in 1912, women should devote their lives to 'the breeding of a stronger and sturdier race'. For forty years or so white women worked for their advancement within and also with difficulty against this powerful identity as mother.

While most public policy identified women with motherhood, women's actual experiences and opportunities were more diverse. In rural industry, still the principal employer of Australians in 1912, women worked alongside men in many occupations. Closer settlement policies and irrigation projects had promoted a wider range of primary industries, producing butter, fruit and meat for export as well as local consumption. Closer settlement offered men freedom from wage slavery on the understanding that their families would provide the unpaid labour required on the family farm. Women in the country supplemented family incomes by picking fruit, vegetables and hops, by milking cows and selling produce such as eggs and cream. In Mildura, in northern Victoria, industrial trouble occurred as a result of women's employment in grape picking. Men feared women's cheaper wages were depriving them of jobs and the case went to the federal arbitration court. In the landmark Rural Workers' Case of 1912, Justice Higgins ruled that when women engaged in competition with men in men's jobs they should be awarded equal pay. When the work was 'women's work' they need only be paid half that rate, enough as Higgins said, to meet the 'normal needs of a single woman'. Although he recognised that up to one-half the male workforce did not in fact have dependants to support, he felt he could not discriminate between married and single men. The solidarity of working men was thus maintained at the expense of proper remuneration to those women who struggled to maintain themselves and/or dependants on a single woman's wage. Of women turning thirty between 1912 and 1917, 14 per cent never married. A still larger percentage of women contributed to the support of dependants.

In 1912 the Australian non-Aboriginal population reached 4.5 million. Although rural production still accounted for the bulk of Australia's overseas earnings and employment, the population was drifting to the cities. Government leaders recognised that the development of secondary industries was, nevertheless, severely impeded in Australia by the small local market and the expectation of high living standards. Central to the policy of national development was the strategy of 'new protection', whereby manufacturing industries were offered protection from foreign imports in return for their provision of the basic (living) wage. Factories making tools, machinery, electrical goods, furniture, car bodies and components, as well as food, drink, clothing, shoes and textiles expanded in the fifteen years after 1912, assisted not just by the protective tariff, which was extended with the establishment of the Tariff Board from 1921, but also by women's and children's low wages. By 1916 it was estimated that one in every three factory workers in Victoria was female; one in every four in New South Wales. At the outbreak of World War I, the basic (men's) wage stood at 2 pounds 8 shillings per week. 'If all the women workers in the ready-made clothing business were to get 48/- a week and the tariff remained as it was it would mean there would be no factories in Australia', warned a male trade unionist, faced with women's demands for equal pay. The growth of many manufacturing industries depended on women's cheap wages, which were in turn justified by women's primary identity as mothers.

Women's march 'out to work' put working men in a dilemma. On the one hand they did not fancy forgoing the benefits, power and status that went with their higher wages as breadwinners; on the other hand, they feared the possibility that women with their lower wages would take over men's jobs altogether, rendering them redundant and undermining their very identity as men. Their solution was to press for the segregation of women into women's jobs through submissions to wages boards and the arbitration court.

The national policy of defence and development called onto the national stage two key players, the citizen soldier and the citizen mother. From 1911 all boys from fourteen to eighteen were liable to train as cadets. Thereafter, until the age of twenty-five, they would serve as part of a citizen defence force. Training took place on annual camps. The career officers in charge came from the Duntroon Military College, also opened in 1911. Though still expecting protection from the mother country, the young nation spent much effort and income on the manly business of self-defence. The growth in military expenditure in the first years after federation was dramatic – from 780 260 pounds in 1901–2 to 4.3 million pounds by 1913–14, when it comprised a third of all commonwealth spending.

When not engaged in preparations for self-defence, boys and men fulfilled their obligations as citizens through engagement in paid work, which guaranteed their independence – the assumed prerequisite for citizenship – and formed the underpinning of manhood. Work, observed Justice Piddington was 'the energetic tissue in a nation's virility' and he commended the establishment of BHP's steelworks, which began production at Newcastle in 1915, as 'specifically deserving of encouragement' because of 'the masculine character of industry itself'.

But paid work was often a necessity for women as well as men: the wage system was many women's only source of income. As more middle-class women entered the paid workforce – in teaching, office work and journalism, for example – some heralded their historic 'release' from their 'specialisation' in domestic duties and began to argue that work was a human right as well as a necessity. Most women were more cautious in their claims. When formulating their arguments for a living wage, labour women were careful to attend to men's fears of displacement. Equal pay, they insisted, would preserve men's jobs.

In September 1913 the Victorian Trades Hall Council convened a Women's Industrial Convention in Melbourne, presided over by Mrs Withen, a Labor stalwart who had travelled for the occasion from the Mallee in northern Victoria. A few male trade unionists (representing women's unions) were admitted, but the majority of delegates were women, representing unions of workers such as the Hotel and Caterers, the Office Cleaners and the Tobacco Workers. It was time for women, having been admitted to the 'dignity of citizenship', to organise politically and economically. There was much discussion of the meaning of 'equal pay'. It was recognised that as so many women worked in women's jobs, there was no male rate for the majority to aspire to. Sarah Lewis, a single woman and committed trade unionist, argued that all women needed to be paid the living wage and that a law should be passed embodying the principle. Under existing legislation wages boards were required to determine rates specifically taking age and sex into account. The character of the work, rather than the sex of the workers, should be the basis of pay rates – 'a rate for the job' (not the sex). Women in general, it was argued, had the same responsibilities as men: 'whatever was fixed as a decent living wage for a man should be paid to a woman'. The convention passed a resolution asking that the Labor Party proceed with legislation, at the federal and state levels, to delete the term 'sex' from legislation covering award determinations.

Though women in paid work were thought by some to deserve and need a living wage, it was assumed that most adult women would find security and reward in marriage and motherhood. Women were expected to devote themselves to the nurture and protection of their children. From 1914, however, with the outbreak of war, mothers were suddenly expected to deliver up their sons to do battle for Britain. Women were praised for their capacity for self-sacrifice – first sacrificing their 'selfish' interests to perform the national duty of motherhood, then sacrificing their sons to the military authorities. At war, their sons might make the 'supreme sacrifice', but their collective death would bring forth life, the birth of the nation.

Britain declared war on Germany on 4 August and the dominions were automatically committed to a European war. Most Australians had, initially, few regrets about Australia's involvement in support of the mother country. Britishers and Australians at the same time, their double identity was reflected in the name given to the first national expeditionary force of 20 000 men, the Australian Imperial Force. The most vociferous opposition to Australia's participation in the war was voiced by international socialists and pacifists, men and women.

The declaration of war took place in Australia amidst a federal election. The previous year Fisher's Labor government had been narrowly defeated; Joseph Cook became prime minister, but effective government was impossible as Labor still commanded a large majority in the Senate. A double dissolution was obtained and the parties were in the middle of their campaigns when news of the war came through. The leaders vied with each other in expressions of imperial loyalty. Fisher, who won the election for Labor, promised to support Britain to 'the last man and the last shilling'.

The men rushed to volunteer. They were activated by patriotism, the attraction of commitment to a greater cause, restlessness, the chance of travel and adventure overseas and the opportunity to escape domestic difficulties. 'Moving on' was customary practice for many Australian men, underscoring their independence. Army authorities complained about the number of men who gave false names upon enlistment. Married men were required to allocate part of their pay (6 shillings a day) in separation allowances to their wives and children and some assumed a new name to avoid this obligation. The government also pledged to pay pensions to soldiers' dependants in the event of death or disability. The state thus undertook the obligation to assume men's patriarchal responsibilities as breadwinners, in order to release them to fulfil their higher patriotic duties to the state itself.

Although men travelled in their thousands from all over Australia to enlist, the British authorities' demands soon began to exceed the supply. In April 1915 Australian men in company with the British, French and New Zealanders went into battle at Gallipoli. Newspaper reports celebrated the Australians' 'blood sacrifice' and 'baptism of fire'. The issue of reinforcements acquired new relevance as the relatives and friends of those killed and wounded struggled to come to terms with their anxiety and grief.

In mid-1915, in response to imperial calls for further reinforcements, the states launched official recruiting drives. Social pressure on unenlisted men to prove their manhood increased as myriad means were devised of shaming the reluctant into stepping forward. Women, assumed to exercise a disproportionate influence on male relatives, were identified as potential unpaid recruiting agents and the unmarried were urged to refuse their favours to 'shirkers'. One Brisbane woman recommended:

At our social functions when a gentleman asks may he have the pleasure of a waltz or any other dance, how would it be if the question were politely asked: 'Are you a recruit or a reject or a returned soldier?' If answered in the negative the reply 'No, thank you' should follow, and it might bring a sense of duty into the blushing shame of the shirker.

Some women, however, were troubled by what they saw as a contradiction between the life-preserving vocation of motherhood and the destructive pursuit of war. Vida Goldstein, member of the Women's Political Association and first president of the Women's Peace Army, formed in 1915, asked: 'what can a boy think of the mother who teaches him one thing, and then countenances this legalized murder? The time has come when the women, the mothers of the world, shall refuse to give their sons as material for shot and shell'.

Goldstein toured Australia in 1915 with Adela Pankhurst and Cecilia John, setting up branches of the Women's Peace Army in Sydney and Brisbane as well as Melbourne. John often opened meetings by singing the rallying anti-war song 'I didn't raise my son to be a soldier' – which was deemed to be so effective a statement against war that it was outlawed under war precautions regulations as 'prejudicial to recruiting'.

Although thousands of Australian men continued to volunteer in the first months of 1916, their numbers still fell short of the reinforcements demanded by military authorities. The level of slaughter on the battlefields of Pozieres and the Somme was unprecedented. Prime Minister Hughes visited the front, conferred with imperial authorities and returned to Australia convinced of the necessity of conscription for overseas service. In the referendum on the question in October 1916, the proposal for conscription was defeated as it was again in the following year, in December 1917.

The campaigns around conscription were marked by passion and disorder. Meetings were frequently disrupted by opponents and speakers were attacked on platforms and in the press. Returned soldiers and women anti-conscriptionists were especially noticeable in their confrontations over issues of free speech and public space. Arguments for conscription stressed the military necessity and democratic fairness of conscription; arguments against stressed the right of men to choose for themselves whether to fight in a war, whether to kill and face death. Both sides addressed Australians' deepest insecurities. Arguments for and against conscription invoked racial fears: those for compulsion warned that without British victory Australia would be overrun by the numerous hordes of Asia. The prime minister cautioned:

On our very borders are teeming millions, jostling each other for space, striving virtually for a foothold on the earth's surface ... the White Australia Policy keeps them back ... if the Allied armies were defeated they would come in their millions.

Those against conscription also invoked racial fears arguing that a 'no' vote would keep Australia 'clean and white'. The imposition of conscription, it was argued, would lead to a dearth of white men, opening the way for an influx of cheap coloured labour. The recent arrival of some Maltese was identified – despite protests by their supporters that they were 'not Asiatic pagans, but good European Roman Catholics' – as the advance guard of the coloured invasion.

Both sides of the debate addressed women as mothers. By 1916 women constituted a majority of registered voters in many metropolitan electorates, and much of the propaganda was directed at women. The anti-conscriptionists appealed to women's assumed maternal instinct to preserve life, but women's identities as nurturing mothers did not necessarily lead to an anti-war stance. Quite the contrary could happen. By 1916 hundreds of thousands of women had sons or brothers or husbands at the front. Their motherhood – or their familial identity – undoubtedly led many of them to support compulsory reinforcements to support the boys in the trenches. At a meeting in Melbourne one distressed pro-conscriptionist woman, 'nearly in tears addressed the small group of oppositionists – Oh, you Yarra-bankers! God help you! Send your boys to help ours!'.

Anti-conscriptionists portrayed a 'yes' vote as 'the Blood vote'. In a particularly lurid leaflet a woman was pictured living the nightmare of condemning a man to death:

> I heard his widow cry in the night,
> I hear his children weep,
> And always within my sight,
> O God! The dead man's blood doth leap.

Advocates of conscription feared that women's family ties would interfere with their duty to the state as citizens. Were motherhood and citizenship in fact compatible? Would women act responsibly as citizens when faced with 'the greatest question of all'? The prime minister launched a special 'Call to the Women of Australia' in which he suggested that women voters were on a sort of probation: 'Women in this Commonwealth are endowed with the full rights of citizenship; they are the equals of men'. They had to recognise that liberty was born of sacrifice and put the nation's interests first. But in case the duties of citizenship did not weigh heavily on women, in case they responded to his opponents' 'sentimentalism', Hughes, too, resorted to the plea that women act to save their boys, that they refuse 'to abandon [their] own brave Australian boys to death'.

Conscription was ultimately defeated by a narrow margin, but there were 'yes' majorities in Victoria, Tasmania and Western Australia in 1916 and again in the latter two states in 1917. Statistical analyses of voting patterns have concluded that industrial workers and Catholics (persuaded by the strong anti-war stance of Melbourne Archbishop Daniel Mannix) voted 'no', whereas women and farmers voted 'yes'. Such conclusions do not, however, take into account people's multiple identities: the divisions between people of sex, class, religion and ethnicity are also divisions within individuals. How did Protestant male factory workers or female Catholic farmers negotiate these difficult issues?

By 1917 some 300 000 enlisted men had left Australia. In the vacuum thus created women moved into increasing political, economic and social prominence. From the early days of the war, some women had sought to play an active part in the prosecution of war itself by joining rifle clubs, raising patriotic funds, establishing Red Cross branches or enlisting as nurses. In the absence of men, women became increasingly important in the politics of the home front. The overwhelming vote in favour of the early closing of hotels in referenda held in most states in Australia during 1915 and 1916 was attributed to women's disproportionate electoral influence. Powerful groups such as the Woman's Christian Temperance Union had long campaigned for restrictions on alcohol consumption as a means of improving the position of women, of protecting the home from sexual and domestic violence and the effects of poverty. Supported by other temperance, women's and church groups, the war gave them their chance of success. Drinking was said to be undermining the nation's economy and efficiency, seriously detracting from the war effort.

Women also took action as housewife consumers against rising prices. The drought of 1914, the disruption of trade occasioned by the war and the commandeering of wheat and meat for military supplies had led to a soaring cost of living. By July 1917 the price of food and groceries had risen in Melbourne by 29 per cent. Wages had risen by only 15 per cent in the same period. Conservatives initiated thrift campaigns, but working-class people grew resentful about policies that deprived them of basic foodstuffs. As during the conscription referenda, women were especially prominent in direct action – condemning 'profiteering' – and were urged on in their demonstrations by stirring speeches from Adela Pankhurst and Jennie Baines, who were both arrested and gaoled.

Thousands took to the streets in 1917 against food shortages, high prices and profiteering. As the providers of food to families, women's political action grew out of their responsibilities as mothers and wives. As a housewives' petition to the New South Wales Government had pointed out in 1914:

It is always upon the woman that these things fall most heavily. It is her duty to try to make the limited allowance stretch over an unlimited increase; it is she who has to scrape and screw and continue to keep the family properly fed and decently clothed.

Excluded from many institutionalised political forums and channels of influence (women were still ineligible to stand for some state parliaments), working-class women drew on the older political traditions of the food riot and the mass demonstration to express their grievances. Middle-class women formed new organisations such as the housewives' associations established in Melbourne and Sydney during the war, to set up cooperative distribution centres supplying members with produce at cost price.

Meanwhile thousands of Australian men continued to be killed and injured on the Western Front, and their places were taken by new volunteers. Few homes were left untouched by the high casualty rate. Though enlistments slowed during 1917, overall the extent of men's engagement in that distant war was remarkable. Over 400 000 men – or one in every two eligible – enlisted in the AIF. Their departures created much grief and resentment, but also pride. They also resulted in widespread employment vacancies.

The war accelerated the migration of women workers away from domestic service into new openings in shops, offices and factories. The increased visibility of young women travelling to and from work, their presence in streets and parks – their sudden liberty –

alarmed many and led to calls for their protection. Women's groups such as the National Council of Women argued that the new industrial conditions that were forcing women from 'the security of their homes' necessitated the appointment of women police. The first women officers were sworn in in Sydney in 1915 and Melbourne in 1917. As their daughters entered the world of men, mothers feared for their safety. They argued for the establishment of a wide range of new positions to ensure that girls would not fall into men's hands. In Sydney the *Woman's Voice* called for the appointment of women as 'investigators, inspectors, medical officers, councillors, guardians, health visitors ... lecturers, teachers and matrons'. The 'future of the race' depended on the further development of this work of protection. Women would chaperone their daughters as they entered the public sphere and began to be appointed to new positions as welfare supervisors and medical officers in factories and large department stores.

Women moved into occupations, such as clerical positions in banking, insurance and the public service, where they had never worked before. There was much resistance to these developments – in the case of the Australasian Bank only direct orders from London overcame local opposition to the employment of women – but ultimately women were accepted, because contained. In developing new occupational identities in typing, shorthand and routine clerical work for women, employers reaped considerable financial rewards and men were channelled into specially designed career paths that marginalised 'female' skills. Although by the mid-1920s an arbitration court judge could conclude that banking had 'very definitely become a woman's occupation', women's progress was very strictly limited. One social group who thought women had trespassed too far already was the Returned Soldiers' and Sailors' Imperial League of Australia (RSL), formed in 1916 to protect the special interests of Australia's heroes, the returned men, or Anzacs.

'Returned soldiers' began to arrive back in Australia from 1915. Their exemplary citizenship was also rewarded with special privileges and preferences. A generous pension scheme – benefiting both soldiers and their dependants – had been inaugurated in 1914. From 1916 returned soldiers (and nurses) were offered farms on generous terms with state credit, as well as special access to education and training. In addition legislation guaranteed them preference in employment. Returned soldiers were also provided with generous loans to purchase War Service Homes. Their official body, the RSL, was granted direct access to the prime minister and in 1919 a war gratuity (calculated according to the number of days served) was paid to every returned soldier.

The special achievement of these richly rewarded men was that they had given birth to the nation. From the first anniversary of the invasion of Turkey – or the 'Landing at Gallipoli', as it was mythologised – public leaders paid tribute to the men's courage, endurance and mateship. It was 'a feat of arms unparalleled in history'. Nations and men had to be proven and war was the ultimate proving ground of both. The achievement of Australian manhood was the achievement of nationhood. Although the military campaign had been a failure resulting in an inglorious retreat in December 1915, Gallipoli was hailed as the nation's birthplace. Australia had had her 'birth and her baptism in the blood of her sons'. 'A nation was born on that day of death'. Anzac Day – April 25 – institutionalised as a public holiday by a federal act of parliament in 1923, became Australia's *de facto* national day. The metaphor of men's procreation involved a disappearing act. In this powerful national myth-making, the blood women shed in actually giving birth – their deaths, their courage and endurance, their babies – were rendered invisible. In determining the meaning of men's deeds – their Landing at Gallipoli – women's procreative capacities were at once appropriated and erased. Men's deeds were rendered simultaneously sacred and seminal. Though women gave birth to the population, only men it seemed could give birth to the imperishable political entity of the nation.

World War I, like most wars, had contradictory outcomes for gender relations. Women had won a new measure of independence and had trodden new paths. A New Woman had emerged, posing far-reaching challenges to relations between the sexes. The Melbourne *Age* suggested in 1919 that the influx of women into commerce and industry was 'the greatest and perhaps the most threatening social change worked by the abnormal conditions of almost five years of war'. Yet all agreed that it was men's status that had really been enhanced by the war. *Lone Hand* proclaimed:

The Australian comes out of this great war looking the most virile thing on earth. The tasks other men could not do, he went into with a laugh, and though the laughter died in the bitter strain of the front trenches in the rush across 'no man's land', his achievements remain ... Australian manhood is our chief asset.

This very celebration, however, meant that the solidarity that traditionally secured white men's privileged status was under threat. War had enhanced the position of some men – the returned men – at the expense of others, the 'stay-at-homes'. Labour men had already suffered a series of defeats at the hands of avenging conservatives. The war had enabled political radicalism to be linked in conservative propaganda with foreign subversion, as distinctions between Hun, Sinn Feiner and Bolshevik blurred. The Industrial Workers of the World had been declared illegal, its leaders gaoled. Men who participated in the 1917 general strike were victimised. Socialism, once as Australian as mateship, now came to be seen as just as foreign as Bolshevism.

New conflict erupted over the spoils of war in the postwar order. Strikes spread and men confronted each other and sometimes women over their competing rights to work. Unionists confronted so-called loyalists; returned soldiers were encouraged to take the place of striking unionists on the wharves. Different groups of men claimed masculine privilege. Returned soldiers claimed preference in employment at all times (much to the alarm of some employers who championed 'business principles' and 'efficiency'). Fathers argued that as breadwinners they had greater rights to the dwindling pool of jobs than single men, returned or not. Labour men pointed to the tradition of preference to trade unionists.

One of the men to emerge victorious – if only temporarily – from the turmoil of the Great War was Prime Minister Hughes. Defeated on the issue of conscription, Hughes had won a decisive victory in the Win-the-War election of 1917. In 1919 he hastened to the peace talks at Versailles where he insisted on rewards for Australia's part in the war effort: rule over German New Guinea and a refusal of support to Japanese resolutions in favour of racial equality on the basis that this would jeopardise the White Australia Policy. His preoccupation with Australian security and the maintenance of a White Australia earned him unfavourable attention at the conference and in some quarters at home. 'There is nothing to celebrate', wrote E. Dwyer Gray, editor of the Tasmanian Labor paper the *World*, 'except a triumph of paganism, hate and territorial greed'. Hughes had asked for heavy reparations to meet the Australian cost of war. He was confident in making such claims, for, as he told the Australian Parliament: 'Australia became a nation ... We had earned that, or, rather our soldiers had earned it for us'.

But had Australians witnessed a stillbirth? There were grave fears for the nation's future. During 1919 thousands of lives were claimed by an influenza pandemic. In the turmoil unleashed by the war, however, nothing was so terrifying to conservatives as 'that ugly monster, Bolshevism'. Loyalty leagues and other conservative political organisations rallied to stamp out the Bolshevik, who was often represented as posing a particular threat to women. War propaganda had invoked images of German men as rapacious Huns. Conservative women's groups such as the Australian Women's National League (AWNL) in Victoria and the Women's Reform League in New South Wales drew on the same repertoire of images to represent the horrors of Bolshevism. The formation of the Communist Party as an Australian section of the Third International in 1920, with its attempt to apply Bolshevik principles to Australia, increased alarm. The new family code of the USSR was cast as a direct assault on women and their domain, the home. A critique of male sexuality had been central to feminism since the nineteenth century: it was women's treatment as 'creatures of sex' that was responsible for their degradation. In their reported proposals for 'free love' and the abolition of marriage, the USSR emerged as some women's worst nightmare – a state based on sex slavery or the wholesale prostitution of women. Women's organisations warned that 'Not only was capital thrown overboard, but religion, marriage, the family and respect for women'.

This political strategy clearly struck a responsive chord among many women. The AWNL was the largest political organisation in Australia at this time and one of the most effective, delivering tens of thousands of women's votes to the conservative Nationalist party. By 1920, the AWNL had 200 branches in Victoria, two organisers, eight field officers and an office staff of five. The understanding of male sexuality and militancy as threatening and aggressive, and of the home as women's sanctuary, led many directly to the anti-Bolshevik camp.

GIVING BIRTH TO THE NEW NATION

In 1919 Hughes led the conservative Nationalist forces to another election victory. The promised royal commission proceeded to inquire into rises in the cost of living and the efficacy of the basic wage in covering these. Members of the Housewives' Association were called upon as expert witnesses. After extensive investigations of working people's budgets, the commission concluded that the basic wage fell short by about 30 per cent of the cost of living for a breadwinner, his wife and his family of three children. Labor women such as Muriel Heagney stressed that even the minimal standard of living enjoyed by working-class families was made possible by the never-ending unpaid labour of wives and mothers. They worked the longest hours for the least income. As a result of rising prices during the war, many working-class people now had to go without such items as new clothes. Heagney gave notice of women's intention to lobby for motherhood endowment.

The Chairman of the Royal Commission, A. B. Piddington, observed that the cost of families could influence many men to remain single. Unmarried men could afford to spend so much more on their own comforts and entertainment. The implications for the future of the nation were grave:

> Such a position may easily result in discouraging marriage and the growth of families. No reflecting mind can picture any one influence more inimical to national welfare, nor any country that can less afford to foster such an influence, than the encouragement in Australia of single life (if for selfish motives) with its waste of wealth, its impairment of character and its unmanly distaste for the national duties of husbandhood and fatherhood.

A wide-ranging debate ensued on matters of political economy, on how best to organise and distribute national income to guarantee national welfare and to achieve the highest standard of living for society as a whole. Increasing the basic wage for men to the required standard was deemed an economic impossibility. In any case, perhaps it could not be justified. Piddington pointed out that the large majority of men either supported a wife but no children, or no one but themselves. High wages were paid to support an army of phantom wives and children. On the other hand, there were large numbers of women who did have dependants to support.

In his memorandum of 1920 Piddington set out his solution of a living wage supplemented by a scheme of child endowment. The basic wage should be set at the level required to support a man and his wife; child endowment collected from a levy on employers would be paid by the state to support actual children. As a result of his recommendations, the commonwealth public service adjusted the wages of its own officers to take account of the children supported by male wage earners.

Piddington's scheme aroused enormous interest among women in the labour movement who had advocated motherhood endowment for some time as a means of freeing women from 'sex slavery', women's sale of their bodies, in marriage and out. Drawing on feminist discourse, they extended the socialist critique of dependence to formulate a critique of men's power in the working-class family. Labour women proposed a platform of three interrelated planks to secure women's independence: equal pay, motherhood endowment and child endowment. They aimed for a version of economic justice that addressed the differences between men and women, as well as the differences between women themselves. The wage system as a means of income distribution was seen to discriminate against those with the capacity and the desire to give birth and nurture. Motherhood endowment was a popular demand among women, because it promised independence, while also allowing them to maintain their base in the sanctuary of the home.

Motherhood and child endowment were conceptualised as distinct demands: motherhood endowment as payment in recognition of women's work that would also secure their independence from individual men; and child endowment that would pay for the costs of raising children. Although the Labor Party adopted the plank of motherhood endowment from 1919, it consistently interpreted it to mean child endowment. In labour debates women's arguments for independence and economic reward for their particular work were lost sight of; childhood endowment to ameliorate family poverty became Labor policy. As in later years it was evident that the national conscience was stirred more readily by children's poverty than women's poverty. Labor men expected that all men should retain the higher male living wage and they expressed strong opposition to any plan that involved a redistribution of income from men to women, from the wallet to the purse. There was a refusal to accept that payment of the wives' and children's portions of the family wage directly to the intended recipients logically involved a reduction in men's wages.

The independence of women remained an elusive goal. In 1927 the New South Wales Government, following the appointment of Piddington to the New South Wales Board of Trade, introduced a limited form of child endowment. The male living wage remained in place, however, and women's wages were set at about 54 per cent of the male rate until World War II. Women's dependence on men became a self-fulfilling prophecy and, as a result of unequal pay, numerous women and children suffered hardship. Of sixty women in the printing industry interviewed by Dr Ethel Osborne in 1924, twenty-seven had 'serious financial responsibility' for dependants. Many unfortunate women earned much less than half the basic wage, especially those who washed and cleaned or undertook piecework for the clothing industry at home. With the spread of mass-production methods in association with the rise of large department stores in the 1920s, outwork in the clothing industry flourished anew. Some women accommodated the irregularity of their own or their husbands' incomes by developing survival strategies based on the selective use of charity, or credit – available in new forms in these years – or by visiting the pawnbroker. Before the introduction of unemployment benefits by the commonwealth government in World War II, most married women were forced to develop a wide range of income-producing strategies.

Those who were relatively free from the responsibility for the care of dependants could seek work beyond their homes in shops, offices and factories in cities and towns, or in the country. As manufacturing expanded and diversified in the 1920s – with the growth of the printing, metals, rubber, electrical, clothing and food industries – so the number of women (especially young women) in industry increased. The expansion of manufacturing, as well as the expansion of clerical work, meant new possibilities (however limited) of economic independence for some women. Though manufacturing was afforded tariff protection to protect men's standard of living, the real beneficiaries in terms of employment, as many noted sourly, often seemed to be women. The proportion of women among factory workers grew steadily so that by 1923, according to some estimates, men constituted only 48.3 per cent of the factory workforce in Australia. The preponderance of women was particularly marked in Victoria where men were only 35.1 per cent of (registered) factory workers. Many of the women were employed making the very goods – processed foods, clothing and electrical goods – that allowed them to imagine that emancipation from a life of household drudgery was at last possible. But the work itself was often unpleasant, monotonous and injurious, and the condition of young women and girls in factories became a major preoccupation of women reformers. The harmful effects of industrial work were especially worrying, said Ethel Osborne, because of the need to 'keep prominently in the foreground the importance of the conservation of the health of the young women workers for their future motherhood'.

The promotion of manufacturing through the use of tariff protection was geared solely to import-replacements; little thought was given to the development of manufacturing as an export industry. Locked into the imperial division of labour and a condition of colonial dependency, policy makers assumed that Australia was a primary producer, that rural industries should do the work of providing Australia's export income. A few entertained alternative visions. Greeting the disruption to trade caused by the war as a golden opportunity, enthusiasts for new industries sketched plans for decentralised export-oriented manufacturing towns, to be located on Australia's natural harbours and exploiting Australia's abundant coal deposits. Some saw the 'chance of a century' which might never come again. Not for another fifty years would political leaders give serious attention to turning manufacturing into an export. It was the wealth of the land that gripped most Australians' imaginations in these years, a wealth extolled by journalist and labour man E. J. Brady in his book *Australia Unlimited*. Travelling across the continent, Brady reported on 'wonder, beauty, unequalled resource. Under the arid-seeming plains I saw possibilities of marvellous tilth. Barren hills poured out a golden recompense in minerals. The whole continent has proved to be a vast storehouse of mainly undeveloped wealth'.

The development of rural industries was thought to produce not just economic benefits, but a sturdier stock, a stronger racial fibre. The lands beyond the cities, it was believed, were the 'breeding grounds for health and wealth'. This dual project would become the work of Australia's family farms. Discussions of national prosperity and greatness were increasingly informed by eugenicist interest in the quality of the breeding stock. The 'drift to the cities' which had prompted the appointment of a Select Committee in Victoria in 1917, was contributing to 'racial degeneracy'. 'Will anyone tell me', asked Queensland Labor Senator Stewart in federal parliament, 'that a young woman who has spent her life from fourteen years of age ... in, say, a draper's shop, where the atmosphere is vitiated, is likely to be as good a mother, and produce children as healthy as a young woman brought up on a farm?'.

And farmers were also the economic mainstay of a new country: the prosperity of this country, it was often asserted, depended upon the prosperity of the farmer. Land settlement was promoted to secure economic and population growth. 'Primary industries', said the *Age*, 'involve our export trade not to say the physique and fibre of the Australian race'. The war had made the problems more urgent. 'Much virile power would be lost to the manhood of the continent through losses on the battlefield', warned the banker and historian H. G. Turner. Regeneration, politicians liked to believe, would best take place on the land.

Australian policy makers formulated their economic objectives within the constraints of imperial imperatives, in the context of an international division of labour whereby Britain exported population, capital and manufactured goods to the dominions which in turn exported food and raw materials to the mother country. During the war, as some dreamers contemplated the possibilities of developing Australia's embryonic manufacturing industries into export earners, the imperial stategist Sir H. Rider Haggard arrived to persuade governments to include British ex-servicemen in postwar schemes for soldier settlement. Agencies in Britain would impress upon British soldiers 'the advantages accruing to them, and to Imperial interests, from them making their future homes in the Dominions'. When some premiers warned about the proven perils of land settlement on a grand scale, an impatient Prime Minister Hughes made the imperial bargain clear: 'Our chances of getting money largely depend upon the extent of the facilities we will offer British soldiers to take up land in Australia'. British soldiers duly became eligible and in the 1920s, as loan followed loan for Australia's development and interest accumulated, the overseas debt soared.

Soldier settlement was the major element of World War I repatriation policy. About 37 000 settlers including servicemen's dependants and ex-army nurses, as well as hundreds of British ex-servicemen took up land throughout Australia. The profound desire for independence was, however, no match for the overwhelming economic hurdles. As the majority began farming with little or no capital, they were rapidly weighed down with impossible debts. Plummeting commodity prices from the late 1920s exacerbated their poverty and drove thousands to leave their farms after years of backbreaking labour, but not before they had won substantial concessions and debt relief.

Australian governments also promoted schemes for civilian land settlement in the 1920s, in conjunction with expansive British immigration programs. These were largely the work of Stanley Melbourne Bruce, the English-educated Melbourne businessman who had succeeded Hughes as Nationalist Party prime minister in 1922, when Earle Page, leader of the new political force, the Country Party, had refused to form a coalition with ex-Labor Hughes. The major ingredient of Bruce's recipe for national prosperity, like that of national leaders before him, was more people. As the prime minister told the 1923 Imperial Economic Conference: 'Australia's aim above everything else is to populate her country and advance from her position of a very small people occupying a very vast territory'. There was generally a preference for the locally born product (if white), but also a recognition that the local supply was unreliable. The birthrate in the 1920s was about half that of the 1880s. If population increase were to take place steadily and with speed, the numbers would have to be supplemented through immigration – British immigration, if possible. At the 1923 Imperial Conference Bruce negotiated a 34 000 000 pound deal with the British Government to provide assisted passages to British migrants. People from other countries – such as Italy and Greece – made their own way to Australia in this decade. Altogether, some 300 000 assisted and unassisted migrants arrived during the 1920s, boosting the overall population to 6 million by the end of the decade.

Prime Minister Bruce expressed his economic strategy in the catchphrase 'Men, Money and Markets'. Money was needed as capital to invest in production, markets were needed for Australia's rural products and men were needed as the workforce to develop

Australia's natural resources. Nowhere were women mentioned in this national policy formulation, but their work as mothers (as population producers) was a crucial underpinning of this economic strategy. Hence the conclusion of the royal commission appointed in 1925 to inquire into the national health that the high maternal mortality rate posed 'a grave national danger'. In outlining national policy, Bruce also insisted on the importance of efficiency as the guiding principle for industry, for producers primary and secondary. Women's work as mothers and housewives would not be exempt: they too would be subjected to the new regime. Maternal instinct no longer sufficed: women were to be instructed in scientific, efficient and economical practices by experts trained in the new fields of infant welfare and home management.

As a result of extensive voluntary work by women's groups, infant welfare centres and 'mothers' schools' were established before the war. Women lobbied successfully for state funding for the development of a network of clinics, so that ultimately all mothers would have access to free guidance and assistance. In Western Australia, infant welfare centres, a hospital for women, and women's rights became major concerns of Edith Cowan, President of the Western Australian National Council of Women from 1913 to 1921 and the first woman elected to an Australian parliament. She entered the Western Australian Parliament in 1921 as an endorsed Nationalist candidate for West Perth; her friend Ada Bromham who stood as an independent 'woman's candidate' for the seat of Claremont in the same election did not fare so well. Her defeat and that of Vida Goldstein in previous Senate elections suggest how difficult it was for non-party women to secure political power in a system organised around the interests of capital and labour. Edith Cowan lost Nationalist Party endorsement and was defeated in the elections of 1924 and 1927. Increasingly in the 1920s, Australian women looked abroad to non-party international forums such as the League of Nations and British Commonwealth League to exercise influence and achieve reforms.

Women's bodies and reproductive processes, once the concern of community nurses and midwives, became increasingly subject to the authority of the male medical profession, authorised by state regulation and legislation. Initially women doctors and nurses had envisaged infant welfare clinics run for and by women independent of the male medical establishment that ruled the public hospitals. Their proposals initially received some government support, but were successfully opposed by the medical profession, which directed that the treatment of sickness and disease be removed from the auspices of infant and maternal welfare clinics. Infant welfare sisters were required to refer all cases of illness to a local doctor or public hospital. Despite such restrictions, women reformers regarded the establishment of the clinics as a major achievement for women.

Girls began to be prepared for scientific motherhood and efficient housewifery in new domestic science courses in schools, while rural women during the 1920s acquired the new knowledge from talks arranged by the Country Women's Association, which attracted thousands of members by the late 1920s. In Victoria, the Better Farming Train's special mothercraft carriage also carried the message. Posters, leaflets and films, all emphasising the modern scientific ways, were distributed throughout the community.

Women were encouraged to think of themselves as citizen mothers, but citizenship interpreted as motherhood became a heavy responsibility with few social rights or public rewards. The responsibilities were awesome. 'The problem of right or wrong feeding and nutrition in early infancy determines the health and fitness of the being throughout life and largely determines the fate of the race', declared Truby King, infant welfare expert. With the exception of the maternity allowance of 1912 there were no special allowances or disability pensions, rehabilitation centres, retraining provisions or public holidays for mothers.

Aboriginal women did not even receive the maternity allowance and were often excluded from maternity hospitals. They grieved over the loss of their children to state authorities, who insisted that they were better off with white strangers. Many white women, meanwhile, sought the means to avoid motherhood altogether. One report on the Women's Hospital in Victoria stated that admissions for abortion trebled between 1910 and 1920 and doubled again in the 1920s. Feminists drew on the popular understanding of men's and women's different capacities as citizens – as soldiers and as mothers – to argue for better conditions and for economic independence for mothers. Just as society applauded the Anzacs, so should it 'honour and make much of the women who through desperate travail and suffering bring their children into the world'.

Women activists such as Muriel Heagney, Jean Daley, Irene Longman, Jessie Street and Edith Cowan argued that citizen mothers, like citizen soldiers, should be rewarded with an income. Citizenship entailed rights as well as responsibilities. An independent income was seen as a means of disconnecting motherhood from the demeaning status of wifehood. Arguing for the payment of motherhood and child endowment, Heagney drew a parallel between the travail of the mother and soldier:

Every mother, like Hercules in the quest of Alcestis, has been down into the Valley of the Shadow and wrestled there with death in order to bring a young life into the light of day. Twenty-four centuries ago, a mother, in the play Medea claimed that her lot was harsher than even a soldier's. 'They say we women live a sort of sheltered life in the home while men go forth with the spear. They reason ill. For I would rather thrice confront an enemy with my shield than once bring forth a child'.

Heagney pointed out that by 1926 the cost of war services in Australia amounted to at least 627 596 308 pounds. The introduction of child and motherhood endowment would cost a small fraction of this. Despite the relentless lobbying of labour women and non-party feminists, however, the 'right' to motherhood endowment was never achieved.

10 Depression Dreaming

In 1926 Dr Vera Scantlebury Brown was appointed foundation Director of Infant Welfare in Victoria. As she had recently married, she was required to take the public service position on a part-time salary. During the next few years her commitment to the job, combined with the mothering of two small children, left her physically and mentally exhausted. As a professional mother in a double sense, Scantlebury Brown was both architect of and subject to the new imperatives concerning infant welfare. She recorded the daily stresses of her double life in her diary:

I had to make the Rice Jelly twice (it burnt the first time!) Mothercraft in earnest!

A *vile* day at the office ... The posters and the leaflets had to be sent out and so it was all very trying and headachy and on top of it the babe was a little upset and I am ashamed to say how my stomach seems to turn upside down when he is not perfect. It is difficult to be reasonable.

Dr Scantlebury Brown chided herself: her emotion as a mother seemed to be at odds with the reason required of the professional.

Born in 1889, Vera Scantlebury was raised in a comfortable middle-class home, adjacent to her father's medical practice. She attended Toorak College, a small private school for girls, and went on to the University of Melbourne, where she, too, studied medicine. She graduated in 1913, worked briefly in the Melbourne and Children's hospitals and then travelled to London in 1917 to take up war work. Back in Melbourne after the war, Vera Scantlebury was unable to find a practice and so accepted a position as medical officer to the newly established Baby Health Centres Association. When she married fellow professional Edward Brown, Associate

Professor of Engineering at the university, she was thirty-seven years old, more than a decade older than the average woman marrying at that time. The delay allowed her to consolidate her career, but the contradictions of wifehood (followed by motherhood) and career remained unresolved.

The infant welfare movement created new career opportunities for professional women at the same time as it rendered motherhood more demanding. As a result of the conscientious work of people like Dr Scantlebury Brown herself, motherhood had by the 1920s come to be seen as a grave responsibility and an exclusive, full-time occupation.

Mothers took their work seriously. They put themselves in the hands of experts, entering hospitals in unprecedented numbers for the birth itself. They submitted to medical supervision, consulted the new manuals on a daily basis – one woman referred to hers as her 'bible' – and visited the new infant welfare centres that opened in cities and country towns throughout the 1920s and the following decade. There were known to be a rebellious few who ignored the new imperatives, but for the most part mothers did their best to incorporate the new knowledge of hygiene and nutrition into work schedules already heavy. Getting children and home irreproachably clean was hard and ceaseless work. The use of soap increased by 3 pounds per head per annum in the 1920s. Germs were declared to be a woman's deadliest foe, all the more worrying because invisible. The dangers known to be lurking in milk, dirt and dust generated new anxieties and insecurities, rendering women responsive to advertisers' promises about novel products such as flysprays and disinfectant soaps. In the new rural settlement areas, the pursuit of cleanliness was especially frustrating. One woman recalled that her mother lived in a bag humpy with dirt floors and 'a dirt floor means that everything in sight is dirty too ... She battled to keep everything clean ... And there wasn't even running water, it was carted in a kero tin! It was all so hopeless. It took a strong toll of my mother.'

Women's cleaning work was imbued with imperial significance. In the context of White Australia it was cast as a form of racial hygiene. Cleanliness was associated with whiteness in advertising that equated feminine white skin with racial purity. Aboriginal women were thus made to feel dirty; when employed as domestic servants in white homes, kitchens and bathrooms could become sites of a colonial form of domestic violence as white mistresses scrubbed Aboriginal women's skin with pot scourers or pushed them into scalding baths. Leading Aboriginal activist Margaret Tucker recalled that as a punishment for failing to master the new hygiene regime, she had dirty baby nappies rubbed in her face. 'For the first time I felt a deep resentment.'

The house in which Margaret Tucker was employed used a copper to heat water over a fire. In the new postwar suburbs improved housing made it easier for mistresses and servants to meet the new standards of home management. Space, sewerage, ventilation, hot running water, connection to gas and electricity supplies – all made women's work more feasible. But the new standards made housework and child care more time-consuming, not less. Increasingly, with the gradual disappearance of household 'help', the absence of husbands at distant workplaces and the raising of the school leaving age, housewives were left to do it all alone.

The burden of new responsibilities and workloads was perhaps felt most keenly by mothers who also performed, by necessity or by choice, other jobs as well. Commanded to watch over their children, women feared leaving them unattended. The injunction to breastfeed infants kept mothers close to home. Not surprisingly some labour women, familiar with the terrible toll of the double workload on many working-class mothers, formulated the slogan 'One Woman One Job', in conjunction with their campaign for motherhood endowment. In a 'properly organised social system where the economic independence of women was fully recognised and assured', said Lilian Locke-Burns, President of the Women Workers of New South Wales, a mother would not be 'expected to combine half a dozen occupations to the serious detriment of herself and of the children she is rearing'. Similarly, rural women campaigned for the right to be 'only housewives'. Women on farms were faced with contradictory demands: constituted by national policy makers as the 'breeders of health and wealth' they still felt compelled to justify their single-minded devotion to infant welfare. 'My children being so young I'm unable to go to the shed therefore have to keep a lad' explained an apologetic soldier settler's wife to city officials. Some attempted to do it all. 'I have also milked with a baby in the pram', wrote a correspondent to the *Countryman*,

man, 'and a toddler in a little wire-netting yard by the bail, and then bumped the pram home with the two in it, and a bucket in each hand'.

Well-educated women too, such as the author and book reviewer Nettie Palmer castigated themselves, if ironically, for being 'bad mothers'. During the 1920s Palmer combined work as a freelance reviewer and essayist with her work as mother and teacher of her two daughters and wife to novelist husband Vance. Author of the prizewinning *Modern Australian Literature*, published in 1924, she perhaps did more at this time than any other Australian writer to introduce the reading public to new Australian novels, a majority of them by women. Between the wars was the golden era of the woman novelist. Eleanor Dark published *Slow Dawning* in 1932 and *Prelude to Christopher* in 1934, the partnership of M. Barnard Eldershaw published *A House is Built* in 1929 and *The Glasshouse* in 1936, Jean Devanny published five novels between 1926 and 1945 including *Sugar Heaven* in 1936. Katharine Prichard also published several novels and collections of stories, including *Working Bullocks* in 1926 and *Coonardoo* in 1929. Significantly, most of the women who built successful careers as writers in the 1920s and 1930s remained single or childless and some – Miles Franklin, Christina Stead, Henry Handel (Ethel) Richardson – felt the need to leave their kin and country altogether to achieve the independence thought to be necessary to develop their art.

Nettie Palmer was aware of the way familial bonds limited all women's freedom. In her essay 'A Nation of Charwomen: Does Housework Get Us Down?', she argued that the all-enveloping domestic labour of Australian women too often prevented them from exploring their creative potential. Palmer worked hard to provide encouragement to writers, introducing them to each other and commenting at length on their writing. Her provision of a network of support and serious criticism was warmly acknowledged. 'More than any other critic', wrote Marjorie Barnard in 1931, '[more] than anyone else – you make us feel welcome'.

Middle-class women who combined domestic work with professional occupations and thereby enjoyed an independent income, usually depended on the employment of some domestic assistance. Nettie Palmer, Vera Scantlebury Brown and novelist Eleanor Dark all relied on paid domestic help. In 1936 Dark, a mother of two and a doctor's wife, wrote to Palmer that 'three months of maidlessness' had forced her to put a half-finished novel away and 'grapple with brooms and pots and pans'. Working-class women (who often were the maids) faced either the exhaustion of a double burden of laborious work or the oppression of financial dependence. Thus motherhood and child endowment were advocated as feminist strategies especially appropriate to working-class women. Muriel Heagney referred to the old belief that a nation's greatness may be measured by the status of its womanhood and observed that 'much remains to be done with regard to working mothers'.

Women's arduous and conscientious work for their children paid dividends for the emergent nation. The white infant mortality rate began to fall dramatically in the second decade of the century. From 74.8 deaths per thousand in 1910, it fell to 69.1 in 1920 and then almost halved in the following twenty years. Ominously, however, the maternal mortality rate began to rise. And as commentators noted, the white birthrate continued to decline.

For many – perhaps most – women, children were their chief joy and solace, but motherhood had also become a burden, best limited or even avoided altogether. It was becoming clear that many women were prepared to risk their lives to limit their families. A continuous stream of reports from the mid-1920s had drawn attention to Australia's high maternal mortality rate and the role of abortion in contributing to this. A number of women's groups in New South Wales formed a Standing Committee on the Reduction of Infant and Maternal Mortality. Millicent Preston Stanley, founding member of the Feminist Club in Sydney, member of the Nationalist Party and in 1925, the first woman to be elected to the New South Wales Parliament, made maternal mortality one of her main concerns. In 1928 Professor Marshall Allen of the University of Melbourne presented his report on Maternal Mortality and Morbidity in Victoria and two years later Dame Janet Cambell, Senior Medical Officer for Maternity and Child Welfare for the Ministry of Health in England presented her report on Maternal and Child Welfare in Australia. Campbell noted that the maternal mortality rate had climbed in Australia since 1922 and was consistently higher than in England and Wales. Between 1919 and 1928, 7012 mothers had died giving birth in Australia. The evidence led her to conclude 'the incidence of fatal abortion appears to be higher in

Australia and accounts in part for the higher total maternal death rate'. The other major factor was thought to be the higher incidence of hospitalisation and attendance by doctors at childbirth in Australia, which resulted in higher levels of puerperal infection. Campbell also made the point that 'for every woman who dies as a result of childbearing many others were injured more or less seriously, more or less permanently'. She judged that this 'physical disability and the resulting loss of health and strength is an even more serious matter than the actual mortality'.

Motherhood involved risk of death and permanent injury and yet at the same time imposed ever more demanding work standards on women. Deteriorating economic conditions in the 1920s and the continuing casual, seasonal nature of much work in Australia, resulting in irregular income, made it even harder for women to meet social expectations. This was the argument put by numerous female witnesses to the Royal Commission on Child Endowment or Family Allowances in 1927 and 1928. Jean Daley, member of the Women's Organising Committee of the Victorian branch of the Labor Party, said that 'the mothers of Australia find it impossible to bear the burden of rearing children'. She explained women's resort to abortion: 'The position at the present time is that the women of Australia are not able to have children, and consequently they are not having them; as a result they are endangering their lives, and the nation is losing valuable children'. For Muriel Heagney the irregularity of men's work strengthened the demand for an independent income for mothers; the wellbeing of women and children should not be dependent on men's good luck. She painted a picture of 'poverty and destitution hanging like a spectre over thousands of Australian homes during the period when a young family is dependent upon the breadwinner'. Did she really think that was the case in Australia, asked an incredulous commissioner. 'Yes', replied Heagney, 'in the home of the casual worker; a very large class in Australia'. The seasonality of much work in Australia – whether on the farm, at the port, in factories and shops – together with the effects of sickness and accidents meant continuing insecurity for numerous families and increased responsibilities for women.

Similar evidence had been presented to the Royal Commission on National Insurance in 1926 and 1927. The commissioners noted the prevalence of unemployment in some industries and some seasons and the piecemeal, inadequate response by the state to the occurrence of unemployment. Affirming the principles 'that every person in the community should have the right to work, and that if a man is willing and able to work and work is not forthcoming, then the Government should provide full sustenance for him and his family whilst he is unemployed', they recommended that the government introduce unemployment insurance, a national health scheme and extended maternity benefits. The conservative Bruce government, already committed to reductions in public spending, declined to act on the recommendations. The Royal Commission on Child Endowment or Family Allowances itself declined to recommend their introduction, saying that a federal scheme was neither legally nor economically feasible. A minority report by John Curtin, the Labor representative, and Mildred Muscio, the President of the National Council of Women, did recommend a system of childhood endowment, but agreed that motherhood endowment was not desirable as it would substitute a contract between woman and the state for the sexual contract between husband and wife and thereby 'revolutionise the organic unity of the family'.

In drawing its conclusions, the Royal Commission on National Insurance pondered the causes of underemployment in Australia. The high standard of living (the commitment to the basic family wage) and Australia's failure to develop new industries were seen as related, contributing factors. Australia exported raw materials and imported manufactured goods. The 'enormous and increasing volume of imports' was thought to generate unemployment. Given Australia's natural advantages as a 'great primary producer', it seemed unfortunate that all the required manufactured goods could not be made locally: 'more than three quarters of the value of the wool clip is paid away for imports of apparel, textiles and manufactured goods'.

Soldier settlement was emblematic of the Australian plight. Suggestions during the war that repatriation be made the vehicle for the development of Australian manufacturing industry had been impatiently rejected. Instead vast amounts of borrowed money had been poured into a scheme to promote primary production. Advances to settlers had been generous and indiscriminate. Inflated prices were paid for land, much of it unsuitable for farming. A faith in yeomanry ideology, in the efficacy of industry and honesty, blinded most to the realities of capitalist farming. Women and children were expected to provide the farm labour even as other voices commanded them to concentrate on home and school. As markets faltered, settlers' debts accumulated and failure threatened, further monies were spent in an attempt to render the holdings viable, to provide daily sustenance and to finance debt adjustment. State royal commissions and the commonwealth inquiry conducted by Justice Pike stressed the need for settlers to be allocated 'living areas' that would afford the returned men on the land the same standard of decency and comfort promised to city dwellers by the 'living wage'.

Soldier settlers were beset by feelings of failure and betrayal. Many men felt they had failed doubly, as farmers and as breadwinners. 'I left the place', one settler explained to his bureaucratic supervisors, 'because there was not sufficient money coming in to enable me to keep my wife and family'. Women shared these understandings of masculinity, the equation of manhood and breadwinning. One woman, angry at her own exploitation, charged that her husband wasn't 'man enough to maintain his wife and little ones'. Settlers hit out, sometimes at their families, sometimes at politicians and bureaucrats. They grew bitter, concluding they had been used and duped. Their resentments fuelled the membership of the Country Party and the RSL during the 1920s, and effective political campaigns were waged on their behalf. Settlers demanded political intervention to have their tenure extended, concessions granted and their debts cancelled. One wheatgrower wrote to RSL headquarters in Melbourne:

After wasting 10 years of the best part of my life on a proposition which the Commission admits is hopeless from a wheatgrowing point of view I do not want to be forced out with a debt chasing me. Simply because I was an 18 year old hero in the war and upon my return had sufficient faith in human nature to believe the lies told of the Mallee.

The soldier settlers' considerable political influence – as Anzacs, as lifegivers to the nation – achieved significant reductions in their debt, often its total writing off. This gift to the soldiers added materially to the burden of debt to be paid by all Australians. The

Pike report of 1929 had estimated the Australia-wide loss on soldier settlement at 23.5 million pounds. The following year the Victorian Government announced a deficit of 1 172 870 pounds. The year's losses on soldier settlement had contributed 607 000 pounds to this amount. In all states land settlement had become a heavy drain on revenue.

The weakness and vulnerability of Australia's economy became increasingly evident as the decade passed. One could easily mistake the gloss of modernity in the 1920s for general prosperity. Families living in squalor on soldier settlement blocks looked enviously at the apparent affluence of city life, and certainly some sections of the community enjoyed novel comforts. The building of new suburban villas with indoor bathrooms and running hot water, the tenfold increase in cars, the availability of consumer goods, the spread of mass-produced fashions and modern cultural forms, such as advertising, moving pictures, the wireless and the phonograph, created an impression of general affluence. The advent of consumerism as a lifestyle and the proliferation of commodities undoubtedly fuelled desire – and a related sense of deprivation.

The modern style of affluence seemed most evident in the figure of the 'flapper'. Engagement in paid work allowed young women of all classes to indulge conspicuously in the exciting, unchaperoned recreations of motoring, dancing, drinking in public and smoking. Their youthful hedonism led them to picture theatres, where largely American films further incited the desire to desire. Commentators worried about the effects of the expensive tastes of these materialistic girls on future husbands' pay packets, and feminists such as Vida Goldstein and Rose Scott condemned young women's trivial pursuits and flaunting of sexual desire as a betrayal of the advancement and independence they had long championed for women.

The frivolous flapper was not the only New Woman to attract attention. Another appeared with 'cane, monocle, cigarette case, Eton Crop hairstyle, straight figure ... thoroughly masculine'. She might pursue a 'literary life', fly planes, or like Alice Anderson, in the Melbourne suburb of Kew, turn a passion for motor cars to account, and set up a garage and chauffeuring business. Women claimed masculine privileges in dress and recreation. Hairstyle could denote sexual style. Some women passed as men and claimed the ultimate masculine privilege of sexual access to women. Lesbian desire led some women to assume a masculine identity – Eugenia Falleni masqueraded as Harry Crawford until her murder at the hands of a lover blew her cover. As paid work came to be taken for granted for unmarried women – in banks, in schools, in department stores, in factories – it became easier to contemplate a life without husband or family. Jean Daley, who worked as an organiser for the labour movement, defended the choice not to marry in terms of the alternative social and political vocations available. Referring to a spinster friend who worked for the cause of peace, she remarked: 'She has needed no marriage to develop the capacity to aid and understand her fellows – which, after all, is the greatest thing in life'. For some women marriage seemed inappropriate because of their love for a woman. Such love was evoked in the poetry of Lesbia Harford, who fantasised a life as Sappho:

> Greece my land, not this!
> There the noblest women,
> When they loved, they would kiss.

In the case of other women, their consuming love for each other was understood as spiritual and a gift from God. The increasing sexualisation of love in the context of an insistent heterosexuality began to make some women wonder, however, whether their strong feelings for each other were, in fact, 'natural'. Lesbianism was stigmatised as the ideas of sexologists, such as Havelock Ellis and Freud, circulated more widely. For many women in the 1920s and 1930s, friendships and political commitments to women nevertheless remained intertwined.

The cost of independence for those who lived on a single woman's wage was usually relative poverty. Most households, however, especially those with children, lived precariously in the 1920s. Cars, washing machines and other symbols of modernity were beyond their reach. Unemployment hovered around 7 per cent, rising steeply at the end of the decade. Real wages increased modestly in the 1920s, but thousands of workers were displaced by new technologies, the restructuring of industries and associated reskilling. Work was irregular, people moved in and out of employment and many would have agreed with the bush worker who exclaimed 'Depression! I never knew nothing else! The 1920s was just as bad'.

Australia moved deeply into debt in these years. Whereas in 1913, 9.5 per cent of export earnings was required to service the overseas debt, by 1923 it had reached 16.2 per cent and by 1928, 19.5 per cent. Prices for rural export commodities faltered. Export income growth peaked in 1924–25 and stagnated until it fell dramatically from 1928. Australia slid into a depression.

Encouraged by 'expert' economic advice and directives from Britain, political and business leaders attempted to cut back on government expenditure and the costs of production, especially the costs of labour. Following a commonwealth arbitration decision in 1927 granting engineers a 44-hour week, Prime Minister Bruce and his advisers became convinced of the necessity to radically reform the arbitration system, to end its role as protector of the Australian working man. The government introduced a range of penalties for industrial action and provisions requiring courts to take economic conditions as well as the needs of men into account when making decisions. New awards incorporating attempts to drive down wages and increase the working hours of waterside workers and timber workers produced prolonged and violent industrial disputes. In the coal industry employers themselves led the assault on working conditions. One miner was killed in the resulting conflict. Bruce's introduction of legislation to abolish the federal arbitration system altogether (which was defeated in the parliament) became a major issue in the 1929 federal election. The conservatives were defeated, the Nationalists were ousted from government and Bruce lost his own seat of Flinders to the Secretary of the Victorian Trades Hall Council, E. J. Holloway. The new Labor government, led by James Henry Scullin, was sworn in just one week before the Wall Street crash.

A trading nation, heavily dependent on overseas loans and markets, Australia was thrown deeper into crisis as markets collapsed and capital inflow ceased. Unemployment rose from 9.3 per cent of registered wage earners in 1929, to 14.6 per cent in 1930, to 25.8 per cent in 1931. By mid-1932, around one-third of wage earners were recorded as out of work, but that official figure was undoubtedly an underestimate of the real extent of unemployment. Most basically, loss of jobs meant that women and men were unable to feed, clothe and house themselves and their dependants. Children were forced to leave school early to supplement the household income, leaving many Australians with a long-lasting sense of deprivation. Schooling was also disrupted by constant moving. Unable to meet rent and building society payments, families fled from house to house in the dead of night or stayed to face eviction. Just as men felt their failure as breadwinners, so women agonised over their failure as 'good mothers'. The eviction became a powerful communal symbol for husband and wife of their joint defeat as homemakers and an effective focus of community protest. Women and men joined together in neighbourhood networks of resistance, often activated by the Communist-led Unemployed Workers' Movement. The losers in these battles with landlords and the law often had little choice but to move to one of the shanty settlements that sprang up on the outskirts of cities and towns. In the nightmare of the depression the dream of home ownership acquired new power.

People were forced to beg, to steal, to sell from door to door, to live on charity and rations. Men and women had to deal with the trauma of men stranded at home. Whereas men suffered the humiliation of idleness, most women worked harder than ever to put food on the table and make clothes to cover malnourished bodies. Single men were pressured by government authorities to move on, to travel in search of work. They took to the track, jumped the rattler and tramped the bush looking for a job. Some state governments provided men with the dole or rations or sustenance, increasingly in exchange for intermittent labour on public works. Unemployment and receipt of the dole were experienced by many men as emasculating. Equality, independence and activity – the attributes of men – had been ignominiously snatched away and they felt keenly their sudden inferiority. Housed in 'Parkes Barracks' in Canberra, one group of men pleaded with the prime minister for work: 'We feel very acutely that "inferiority complex" that "dole relief" is surrounded by and cannot emphasise too strongly how demoralizing each successive week becomes in enforced "idleness"'. Breadwinners who retained jobs or worked short hours lived in constant fear of dismissal.

While most people adjusted to lower incomes and many lived on rations, some women had no resources at all. The implications of the official definition of women as dependants became painfully clear when they were deemed ineligible for the dole and rations.

The proportion of female breadwinners in the female population over fifteen had increased from around 26 per cent in 1921 to 33 per cent in 1933. Women's organisations provided relief – food and clothing – while labour women set up special work depots. In general, however, women in paid work were less likely to lose their jobs and more likely to regain them sooner than men, because their industries – food, textiles, drink, clothing and services – were less severely affected by the depression than masculine industries such as heavy metals, building and construction. Unemployment seemed to become a permanent condition for many men, and the sight of women – any women – in paid work revived old complaints that women were stealing men's jobs.

In responding to the depression, Prime Minister Scullin drew on traditional Labor policies. Immigration was stopped and tariff barriers substantially increased. He was also persuaded, however, that public expenditure and the costs of production needed to be reduced. Wage and salary earners suffered a cut in income as a result of an arbitration court ruling reducing award rates by 10 per cent in 1931 with the implementation of the Premiers' Plan. Prices also fell, however, so that some groups, for example those in steady private sector employment, had higher real wages. The arbitration court ruling represented the first significant challenge to the principle that in Australia 'men's needs' should determine wage rates, setting in its place the new principle of 'industry's capacity to pay'. Economists, employers, bankers and judges convinced the federal cabinet of the wisdom of Bank of England emissary Sir Otto Niemeyer's judgment that Australians were living beyond their means. On the recommendation of a committee chaired by economics professor D. B. Copland, public service salaries and social service payments would be reduced by 20 per cent. War pensions were cut more severely than other pensions. Ex-servicemen lobbied strenuously against the reductions, reminding Australians of their debt to their fighting men and pointing out that 10 000 returned men already suffered the shame of unemployment. Their suggestion that the widows' and children's pensions be reduced leaving the basic male pension intact was rejected by the government. The RSL was more successful in resisting plans by the Scullin government to substitute preference to trade unionists for preference to returned soldiers in employment. Many young men felt they missed out on work in these years because of the continuing discrimination in favour of returned soldiers.

By the 1930s Australian working men were divided against each other and on the defensive. The formation of the Australian Council of Trade Unions (ACTU) in 1927 promised more coordination in unions' campaigns for better pay and conditions, but their position was undermined by the concerted attacks launched by government and employers. With the appointment of more conservative judges to the arbitration court in the late 1920s, the consensus that had protected men's wages was breaking down. Workers faced an intransigent coalition of forces determined to cut back on what they believed to be privileged conditions. Arguments about single men's unjustified receipt of the 'family wage', made familiar by feminists, were seized on by conservatives keen to cut costs. Thus the arbitration court judgment of 1931 defended the reduction of award rates in part by arguing that a 'basic wage to provide for the average needs of a man, wife and three children, extended to all single men and to men who have no children, is admittedly beyond the capacity of industry'.

Working men translated their grievances into political action, rallying first to Labor leader Scullin (against Bruce), then to populist, more confrontational heroes such as New South Wales Premier J. T. Lang, whose advocacy of the repudiation of British debts led to new splits in the Labor Party. They embraced conspiratorial theories about the 'money power', or if on the right of politics, the subversive intentions of Communists. Rendered powerless and vulnerable by economic forces beyond their grasp, Australian men responded to the depression by shows of strength, by marches and demonstrations, by re-forming army units into paramilitary organisations such as the New Guard, by militant displays of manhood.

Whereas men's worst fear was unemployment, women were also tortured by a terror of a different kind. 'The wife's fear', wrote Daisy McWilliams, 'was of what so many of the women of Australia suffer from and is affecting their health – the fear of having more children when they have no way of keeping them'. Irregular income or unemployment brought increased anxiety and distress into family life. Exhorted to raise their children the scientific way, paying attention to hygiene and nutrition, thousands of mothers in the 1930s despaired over their children's failure to thrive.

As the dejected witnesses of their children's hunger, their shabby, cast-off clothing, illness and death, women felt that they had failed at motherhood – and that the nation had failed the birth-givers. ' "Populate or perish" we are told', one woman raged, 'but let those who cry out loudly put themselves in the same position as we are today'. Many women also began to conclude that in the battle to care for large families, they themselves were 'pulled down', incapacitated, destroyed. One woman, commenting on political leaders' pronouncements, responded succinctly: 'I populated and I perished'.

Some women literally perished in their attempt to terminate a pregnancy. There was little information about, limited access to and no money for, artificial contraceptives. Most probably relied in these years on abstinence or withdrawal. As one Port Melbourne woman explained: 'Well, you see in those days, me husband and me, we used to take a ticket to Coburg and get off at Brunswick ... the stop before ... you know. Very unsatisfactory state of affairs ...'. Little versed in prevention, women thus frequently had to resort to the cure of abortion. Another woman who raised her three children in the 1930s on the 'susso' recalled: 'Somebody would say, "why don't you get rid of it?" You could go anywhere and pay for somebody to get rid of them. It was illegal, backyard abortions, that's what they were. You had them without an anaesthetic or anything and I'm telling you it's damned agony'. Many women also attempted to terminate pregnancies themselves using a syringe or coathanger, often inflicting injuries that led to hospitalisation. 'Whenever I have been a patient at the hospitals', recalled Daisy McWilliams, 'I have seen rows of beds with women suffering from internal troubles, which in many cases are the result of illegal operations'. The incidence of terminations again rose: at the Women's Hospital in Melbourne abortions became so common that it was estimated in 1935 that one abortion was admitted for every two confinements.

Living in fear of pregnancy, women still had to negotiate their husbands' sexual demands in a situation where many men felt the need to prove their manhood. Tensions between husband and wife escalated. 'After my first child was born I found that fear of becoming pregnant again too soon stopped me from co-operating with my husband which naturally led to disagreements and quarrels.' In the case of another, 'the overtime of uncertainty' made her 'a nervous wreck' and 'household conditions strained'. 'Where there is continual fear of pregnancy', wrote another, 'it is bound to cause discord.'

In this situation men's decision to leave home, to travel in search of work, afforded relief from domestic tensions – as did the increasing availability of contraceptives. From the 1930s, family planning clinics – significantly named Racial Hygiene Clinics – began to appear in the capital cities. Many advocates of birth control were eugenicists, more interested in guarding the racial stock from deterioration and contamination through indiscriminate breeding than in women's emancipation. One such exponent was Dr A. V. Wallace in Melbourne, who made birth control information his specialty. Contraceptives, such as diaphragms and pessaries, were hailed by many women as the answer to their need. The depression had instilled a dread of pregnancy into women of such proportions that the white birthrate dropped to the lowest levels yet recorded.

People sought escape from the grim reality of everyday life in sporting spectacles and picture theatres. In 1930 crowds flocked to witness the arrival of a modern heroine, who had descended from the skies. On Empire Day – 24 May – Amy Johnson landed her plane in Darwin, completing a remarkable solo flight from England that almost broke Bert Hinkler's record time for the journey. In cities and outback towns throughout the country huge assemblies paid homage to her gallantry and heroism: hers was pronounced 'one of the most wonderful feats in history accomplished by a human being'. Australians, for whom isolation was a preoccupation, had followed developments in aviation with interest, welcoming the aeroplane as the most exciting and comforting harbinger of modernity.

A special significance attached to Amy Johnson's flight. She was a modern heroine, her achievement pointing to future possibilities for women. It was hailed as a 'triumph over sex': women might join in the adventures of men. The threatening implications of an obliteration of sexual difference were evident in the frequent reassurances that the aviatrix, whose preferred nickname was Johnnie, was not a woman of the masculine aggressive type, but of fine features, frail and feminine.

For years women activists had sought to improve women's condition on the basis of women's difference and sought to elevate their status as mothers. They had argued for decent remuneration, working conditions and state services for all women, and a say in the ordering of social and political life. Women campaigned to make motherhood a condition of dignity, honour and independence, but their partial victories had confined them ever more closely, reinforcing their dependence on men. The home had become a workhouse and a place of solitary confinement. Women's arguments about the national importance of home and motherhood were turned against them. In the labour movement women's campaigns for motherhood endowment were cast as an attack on the interests of working men. Activists began to reformulate their demands. Gradually talk of human freedom and equal rights replaced references to women's special vocation. Amy Johnson's amazing flight and the more general visibility of the technologies of mobility – the car and the aeroplane – were timely: they captured women's imagination and signalled new possibilities of movement and freedom.

The aviatrix rendered the 'spinster' an anachronism. The new identity required a new name – the 'bachelor girl' made her appearance. Modern and stylish, confident and free, she enjoyed a career in law, medicine, dentistry or commerce. She could live happily without a husband or male relative. 'Among the outstanding triumphs woman has succeeded in gaining', observed a writer in the best-selling *Australian Women's Weekly* in 1933, 'the improvement in the prestige of the single woman is undoubtedly the most important'.

In depression dreaming there was a new day dawning. Daughters who grew up in the late 1920s and 1930s resolved not to repeat their mothers' experiences. 'I am determined never to follow in my mother's footsteps', wrote a teenager in the early 1940s. 'Ailing and disheartened parents are not a good example for the younger generations to see, and who can blame us if we later determine to have empty cradles'. Writing to her doctor about 'family planning' in the 1940s, another woman reflected on the meaning of her mother's life in earlier decades:

Mother used to go out doing different people's washing and ironing also their housework to get some extra money. She used to take the youngest with her while us others went to school then she would have to come home and get our meals, then the work had to be done ...

Contraceptives would enable this woman to avoid her mother's 'terrible struggle'. Another woman recalled that her mother 'died at the age of 43 with her 9th unborn babe and I was 20 with 7 young brothers and sisters to rear'. And another confirmed: 'we have seen too much poverty, ourselves and others, to be selfish enough to have children to suffer what we have ourselves if it can be avoided ... my mother had 10 children luckily 5 died'. Exhorted to devote themselves to home and family, it was women's very responsibilities as mothers, their attempt to feed and clothe children, that drove large numbers to leave their homes, seek out contraceptives, abortions and paid work.

Depression and social disillusionment found an outlet in identifying scapegoats. Working women were an easy target. Their occupancy of 'men's jobs' was seen to be both symptom and cause of the social and economic disorder. But others were also nominated as candidates for blame: Communist agitators, Premier Lang, non-British migrants, returned soldiers and foreign moneylenders. Australian xenophobia became vociferous and attacks on Italian and Yugoslav workers became more vicious in the depression years. In Western Australia, for example, the Australian Workers' Union protested on behalf of unemployed workers against the 'undue influx of Southern Europeans'. The desire to blame turned differences into divisions. Employer groups camouflaged their own interests in talk of the 'national interest' and attacked their opponents' 'selfish' espousal of party, class and ideology. As one conservative spokesperson claimed at a meeting of women's societies in October 1931, the fundamental cause of Australia's deplorable position was 'sectionalism', the selfish pursuit by organised interests of their own advantage. Women, who were accustomed to espousing the interests of home, community and nation, rather than self, had an established tradition of non-party politics to which conservative men could speak. The non-party figure of the housewife came into her own. Schooled in the virtues of good housekeeping, women responded to calls to balance the budget. The National Council of Women (NCW) offered support to the rightwing All For Australia League (AFAL). Women, like experts, businessmen and scientists, could offer disinterested advice, the NCW told a meeting of more than 2000, predominantly women, gathered in the Melbourne Town Hall to support the AFAL in 1931. They argued that what was needed was 'a combined party of honest politicians prepared to work for Australia and not for party, with an advisory board of businessmen, economic experts and a few experienced women to undertake scientific investigation of problems and to advise the government'.

Non-party feminists rallied in opposition to Communism, calling for the party and its literature to be banned. In Sydney, Millicent Preston Stanley transformed the Feminist Club into a branch of the Sane Democracy League. Adela Pankhurst, who, ten years earlier had denounced capitalism for undermining the home and family relations, now the mother of several children, moved to protect these same interests from the imagined assault of Communism. In 1929 she helped establish the Australian Women's Guild of Empire, obtaining funds from the Australian Chamber of Manufactures. Though Pankhurst had moved from the extreme left to the extreme right in class political terms, her preoccupations remained relatively constant.

The very militancy of some men's response to the depression heightened women's sense of threat. Home and family needed protection from masculine violations. White slaver, striker and Communist agitator all partook, in Pankhurst's eyes, of the same essence of aggressive masculinity. These non-party women's organisations attracted large memberships, drawing on the established tradition of cross-class feminine identity. Ruby Duncan, member of the Women's Country Club and independent self-proclaimed 'women's candidate' in the election of 1932, voiced the prevalent fears and the feminine desire for harmony: 'Party politics is a curse to the country ... Instead of unity for common legislation it divides the people and brings about a severe class distinction, while engendering a spirit of bitterness into politics, which should be broad enough to satisfy the whole'. Women's separate claims, however, could themselves be seen as partisan, as divisive and selfish. Ruby Duncan was one of five New South Wales women who contested the 1932 election with the support of the United Associations of Women, formed in 1929: all were unsuccessful. Women still found it virtually impossible to secure representation in Australian parliaments. There were no women at all in the federal parliament by the end of the 1930s.

In Western Australia and South Australia at this time, some feminists reached out to Aboriginal women, to try to rescue them from sexual exploitation. By giving them training and teaching them new skills, they hoped to secure their economic independence. Feminists such as Mary Montgomery Bennett and Bessie Rischbieth of the Federation of Australian Women Voters, formed in 1921, saw the much discussed 'half-caste problem' as an inevitable consequence of white men's perversely primitive sexuality, which if left unchecked would not only bring immense harm to women and children, but would undermine white civilisation itself. In succumbing to their lusts, white men were forfeiting their right to rule. In 1934 Mary Bennett wrote in distress to her friend Bessie Rischbieth of the 'madness' of her fellow whites:

I cannot see how white supremacy in the Pacific can last out this decade even. We, I mean white supremacy, is in the most imminent danger and everybody is blind. In my view, our only chance of survival is to put our 'spiritual' house in order and do it mighty quick.

In rescuing Aborigines, whites were rescuing themselves.

Mary Bennett's work on behalf of Aborigines resulted in official attempts to discredit her as mentally unbalanced; she was said to have an obsession with the natives. Bennett courageously defied such attempts at intimidation, but her work suggests how implicated were such feminist reform efforts in the larger imperialist project.

The feminist concern with sexual morality was shared by Joseph Lyons, the new leader of the triumphant United Australia Party. An ex-premier and Catholic father of twelve from Tasmania, Lyons had defected from the Labor Party with two others in 1931 and joined forces with the Nationalists to establish the new party. His promise to the electorate to adopt sound, honest financial measures and his appeal to people to put national welfare before class drew an enthusiastic response. Scullin's Labor Party was vanquished, its numbers in the House of Representatives reduced from forty-seven to thirteen. The United Australia Party would govern for another nine years. One of its legacies was the banning of thousands of foreign books, especially the work of sexual libertarians such as D. H. Lawrence, Ernest Hemingway and James Joyce. Such a policy spoke directly to the fears of many women, but not all. Women artists, writers and socialists, women self-consciously modern in sensibility, deplored such repression and suffered because of it. Katharine Susannah Prichard, whose novel *Coonardoo* celebrated the sexuality of the Aboriginal woman as 'nearer to the source of things', found it difficult to have the work published and discussed.

As a Communist, Prichard's primary allegiance was to the working class and she would later chastise feminists for their chauvinism, their excessive loyalty to their sex. During the depression, however, the working class was often divided along lines of sex. In Queensland, when trade unions asked the government to legislate against all married women workers, the government reminded them that equality of opportunity was the policy of the Labor Party. In New South Wales, legislation was passed in 1932 to ban the employment of married women teachers and college and university lecturers.

The depression was emasculating. The doctrine of 'masculinism' would be Australia's 'only salvation', wrote Keith Mackenzie in the *Sydney Morning Herald* in 1934. Under the influence of 'feminism's shameless banner' women had stolen men's jobs. In the interests of patriotism women should 'refrain from entering the professions where they compete with men'. This would help the economy because the wages that would be paid to married men instead of girls would be spent on necessities for the family, such as food, clothing and furniture manufactured in Australia. 'We shall spend more on our good home-grown bread and butter and boots and less on imported champagne and caviar and lipstick (not to speak of demoralising films and finery for the women demoralised by them).' Less would be squandered on imported feminine fripperies. Women were unpatriotic as producers and consumers. The graphic contrast drawn between the finery of the working girl and the shabbiness of the man on 'susso' evoked a powerful emotional response and fuelled anti-women campaigns in the 1930s.

For labour journalist Warren Denning, the real problem was thought to lie in 'industry'. Inspired, perhaps, by the doctrine of masculinism, he accused women in manufacturing of being 'in ruthless and relentless competition with men':

What an ironical commentary on our social organization it was in 1933 to find 355 935 men unemployed while there were 136 077 women working in our factories! What a crazy society it is today with nearly 100 000 men *out of work* – many of them youths and young men from 18 to 27 who have *never* had an opportunity to work, and who as potential breadwinners, homemakers and fathers are being *destroyed* [emphasis his].

Not only were women 'destroying' men; they were failing to 'produce in the field they were created to produce [in]'. They were failing to produce the children 'the nation so desperately needed'.

Mindful of contemporary developments in Fascist Italy and Nazi Germany where women had been driven from the workforce, and 'apprehensive of the future in Victoria', women in that state formed the Equal Status Committee, which emphasised 'the unqualified right of women to work when and where they will, on an equal footing with men'. One of the members of the committee, Muriel Heagney, compiled a report on women's employment published in book form as *Are Women Taking Men's Jobs?*. She demonstrated the extreme sexual segregation of the labour market in Australia and argued that if women posed any threat at all to 'men's jobs' it was because they received less pay. But the case of the Equal Status Committee went further: women, like men, had human and civil rights. 'Woman's right to work rests not on the number of her dependants, nor on the fact that she does or does not compete with men, but in the absolute right of a free human being, a taxpayer and a voter, to economic independence.'

Women's rights and freedom, it began to be argued, would be won in the labour market through an emphasis on their equality and identity with men. Women gradually relinquished their campaign for motherhood endowment and jettisoned the politics of difference. There was a renewed and single-minded concentration on the cause of equal pay. In 1937 the New South Wales Clerks' Union convened an equal pay conference that was attended by fifty-three organisations, including trade unions and women's groups such as the Feminist Club and the United Associations of Women. The conference was addressed by John Hughes, Assistant Secretary of the Clerks' Union, who affirmed: 'Equal pay means the establishment of economic independence for women, and provides a basis upon which they can struggle to secure the consummation of full equality'.

Australians emerged from the difficult years of the 1920s and

1930s with twin determinations, with visions of freedom born in the knowledge of fear. Men's dreaming arose from a sense of loss and harkened back to imagined glories: their new social order would be based on a recuperation of the old, the restoration of the power of full employment. Women's dreaming arose from a lack of self-possession and freedom. Women resolved to explore the possibilities of life beyond motherhood. One woman explained her refusal of self-sacrifice:

Personally I am not at all keen on having a baby ... People have written about women like myself and say we're selfish, but I don't think I'm selfish in other ways ... I like what I'm doing – the work as a milliner – I'm not the maternal type ... I like to be able to earn my own living and be independent. I'm very happy ...

Said another, 'I admit to being selfish but there are no medals given out for unselfishness'. Men's desire for work and the nation's need for productivity were commensurate, but between 'national' needs and women's desires a gulf opened up. Women were refusing their social function as national breeders: self-fulfilment beckoned.

In the new social order imagined by men, the keystone of economic and political policy was full employment, supported by a commonwealth system of social security with unemployment benefits to be paid to men as a right and not as a charity. (If both husband and wife were unemployed the benefit would go to the husband.) The working man was henceforth to be protected from emasculating depressions and his political citizenship would be made meaningful by economic security. Introducing his White Paper on Full Employment in 1945 the Minister for Postwar Reconstruction, J. J. Dedman, outlined the necessity for a full employment economy in terms of the pervading fear: 'To the worker, it means steady employment, the opportunity to change his employment if he wishes, and a secure prospect unmarred by the fear of idleness and the dole'.

The depression effectively came to an end with the outbreak of war in 1939. Unemployment was still around 10 per cent in that year, but the call to arms and the requirements of war production soon occupied all available 'manpower'. The experience of economic hardship had generated new visions of self-realisation and freedom among men and women – dreams of economic and reproductive freedom. When events in Europe suddenly plunged Australia into a second world war, it seemed to some that the nation's cause might now also be women's. At its second annual meeting on 16 September 1939, the Council of Action for Equal Pay resolved that when women and girls replaced men enlisting to fight, in any occupation, the full male wage rate should prevail.

11 Freedom, Fear and the Family

In October 1940 Betty Hayles, organiser of the Australian Women's Army Corps, issued a 'declaration of war':

Women can fight just as well in tanks and armoured cars. We are going to get hold of service rifles and machine guns, too, though I can't tell you how just yet. We will do bayonet exercises and train until we are good enough to teach the men about machine guns.

Thousands of women saw the outbreak of World War II as an opportunity for active national service, a chance to prove their equal, full citizenship. Impatient with the waiting role usually allotted to women in wartime, they wanted to exchange weeping for weapons, balaclavas for bayonets.

Britain declared war on Germany on 3 September 1939. For R. G. Menzies, prime minister and leader of the United Australia Party, it followed automatically that Australia was also at war. In the family of nations Britain was still the 'mother country' and Australia part of the 'British world'. As police proceeded to round up aliens for internment during the next few days, it seemed to many that they were about to witness a rerun of the events of 1914, but there was none of the excitement and rush to volunteer that had characterised the outbreak of World War I. Indeed several weeks passed before it was announced that an expeditionary force would be sent abroad and it was not until January 1940 that the second AIF departed, like the first, for the Middle East. The war seemed very distant. Menzies had urged Australians to stay calm, to proceed with 'business as usual' and people seemed to be all too ready to take his advice.

Enlistment had its attractions, however. Unemployment

remained high and the army offered many men their first chance of regular pay in a decade. There was a strong demand to join the new glamour service, the Royal Australian Air Force. In October 1939 Australia was invited to participate in the Empire Air Defence Scheme. By March 1940, 11 500 men had applied to join the RAAF, of whom 184 were in training. A further 56 777 had sought enlistment as ground staff, of whom 5346 had been accepted.

Large numbers of women were keen to fill in the gaps in national defence. Volunteers formed a Women's Transport Corps, a Women's Emergency Signalling Corps and a Women's Flying Club. The latter's training program aimed at equipping members to take over 'men's jobs' in the air force should the necessity arise.

Donning uniforms symbolised women's bid to be taken seriously, but for months the authorities resisted granting them recognition. Condemned for 'playing at soldiers', women defended their sartorial swank. Miss Helen Caught of the Melbourne Militors (khaki shirts and shorts) argued that uniforms helped to create discipline: 'Every girl is more inclined to look up to superiors when she and they are in uniforms than she would be otherwise'. Mrs John Howse, of the Women's Auxiliary Service Patriots (grey with burgundy accessories), declared uniforms were essential if women were to be recognised for 'real war work', while Mrs F. J. Woodward, Commandant of the Women's Auxiliary Training League (blue overalls and navy peaked cap), said they were essential primarily because of their practicality.

To retain some control over the rapid spread of women's auxiliaries and paramilitary organisations (there were 102 in Sydney alone by June 1940), the federal government authorised the Women's Voluntary National Register and the Women's Australian National Services, led by Lady Wakehurst, wife of the Governor of New South Wales, to coordinate and regulate women's training groups. Not until mid-1941, however, did the government, faced with a shortage of male recruits, succumb to women's pressure and establish official auxiliaries to the armed forces. Even then the government was quick to reassure the public that those who entered the Women's Australian Auxiliary Air Force (WAAAF), as wireless and teleprinter operators, were taking over work not wanted by men. The Labor spokesman on defence, Norman Makin, still objected to the enlistment of women as premature: the first duty must be to see that 'full justice is done to the men of Australia'. With thousands of women clamouring to enlist, however, and men not forthcoming in sufficient numbers, the United Australia Party government proceeded to establish the other auxiliary services: the Australian Women's Army Service, the Women's Royal Australian Navy Service and the Land Army. Women's pay rates in the auxiliaries were set at about 60 to 70 per cent of men's, a decision that drew sharp criticism from the Council of Action for Equal Pay (CAEP), which was hoping that the war would be a catalyst for change. Its campaign was strengthened when a special ACTU conference, recognising the implications of wartime mobilisations, resolved to support the claim for equal pay.

Those charged with recruiting during the first two years of war were often dismayed by the cynicism and alienation they discovered in young men. There was a belief that returned soldiers had been let down after the last war; that although Australia had won the war it had lost the peace. Political leaders of both parties began to publicise plans for a new postwar order that would take care of the needs of all Australians. A bargain would be struck with Australia's fighting men: theirs would be a fight for social and economic freedom. In January 1941 the UAP government introduced child endowment, long promised by the Labor Party, to be paid on behalf of each child after the first, regardless of parental income. Harold Holt, the Minister for Labour and National Service, offered the scheme 'as a foretaste and pledge of the full reconstruction that will be possible when we can again turn our surplus productive forces to the purposes of peace'. In July that year the federal parliament appointed a Joint Committee on Social Security to inquire into and report upon ways and means of improving social and living conditions in Australia. The following month Professor Elkin of Sydney University reported on his research into public attitudes to the war. Indifference to the call to arms could be traced back to disillusionment: 'The roots of such apathy and antagonism as there is may be traced in many cases to the depression years ... If they are not responding to the nation's call, it may be because they have not felt themselves to be an integral part of the nation'. The same conclusion was reached by the parliamentary committee on social security: 'There is abundant evidence that economic security is fundamental to the survival of democracy'. Central to economic security was the abolition of unemployment. The state would support the male breadwinners and, in their absence, their dependants. In 1942 the federal Labor government introduced civilian widows' pensions.

Menzies had returned reluctantly from a long absence in England in 1941 to find seething dissatisfaction with his leadership. Pressured to resign, he was replaced as prime minister by Arthur Fadden for a month before two independents crossed the floor and brought UAP–Country Party rule to an end. A Labor government took office for the first time in ten years, with John Curtin as prime minister. Almost from the start his administration brought to the conduct of the war a dynamism and purpose previously lacking.

As 1941 drew to an end, Japan's war of aggression in Asia moved closer to Australia. The situation was rendered suddenly more threatening with the attack of 8 December on the American Pacific base at Pearl Harbor. The newspapers confirmed the grim news the next day: 'Australia is at war with Japan'. The national emergency called for drastic measures. The new phase of the war was signalled by the Prime Minister's nervous public announcement on 15 December of cabinet's approval of the 'extensive employment of women'. The announcement was followed by an 'undertaking', a contract with his fellow men, that such employment would be 'only for the duration of the war' and due attention would be given to the 'prevention of an invasion of men's work by cheap female labour'. The fight for national freedom carried with it the regrettable necessity of drafting women into the public realm.

The Japanese attack on Pearl Harbor produced relief as well as fear in Australia, for it precipitated the United States' decision to enter the war. With the continent itself now vulnerable to attack, and Britain fully occupied in Europe, Prime Minister Curtin made a dramatic appeal for American assistance. His plea was an eloquent testimony to the painful responsibility of nationality and the sense of vulnerability that came from separation from the mother country:

Without any inhibitions of any kind, I make it quite clear that Australia looks to America, free of any pangs as to our traditional links with the United Kingdom.

We know the problems that the United Kingdom faces. We know the dangers of dispersal of strength, but we know, too, that Australia can go and Britain can still hold on.

We are, therefore, determined that Australia shall not go, and we shall exert all our energies towards the shaping of a plan, with the United States as its keystone, which will give to our country some confidence of being able to hold out until the tide of battle swings against the enemy.

Reliance on the mother country had, however, produced a habit of complacency and many still believed that the British base at Singapore would keep Japan at bay. The shocking news that the bastion of British power in the 'east' had fallen came through on 15 February 1942. Four days later Australia was under attack.

For the first time since the British themselves had invaded Australia, wresting it from its Aboriginal custodians, Australians were threatened with attack and invasion. The Japanese landed troops in New Guinea and adjacent islands. As summer came to an end preparations for war in Australia began in earnest. Lengthening nights became even darker as air-raid precautions, including the brown-out, were enforced. Slit trenches and bomb shelters were constructed throughout cities and suburbs. All eligible men were directed into war work and women were encouraged to join the auxiliaries to free men for combat or to take up work in essential civilian occupations, such as the manufacture of munitions.

The prospect of women's wholesale invasion of men's domain proved unsettling and even as the Japanese bombed and shelled Australian coastal towns and cities, an emotional debate impeded the smooth enlistment of women into war production. Unlike the United States and Britain, Australia did not legislate for equal pay for the duration. Some trade unions – such as the Tramways and Omnibus Employees' Union in Sydney – voted to reject women workers altogether. Others opted to protect men's interests by insisting, in line with the ACTU resolution of 1941, that women entering men's jobs be awarded equal pay. Employers on the other hand wished to preserve the cheapness of women's labour, to maintain the profits that flowed from women's lower rates. Both trade unions and employers feared the long-term implications of wartime changes.

Prime Minister Curtin sought to resolve the dispute between masters and men by creating a special temporary tribunal, the

Women's Employment Board (WEB). The board was empowered to award women in men's jobs between 60 and 100 per cent of the male rate, allegedly on the basis of women's comparative productivity. Though possibly more productive, they could not be awarded more than men. Men's performance of work constituted the standard, against which women were assessed as relatively deficient. Few women were awarded 100 per cent; many were granted 90 per cent.

Although less than 10 per cent of all women workers stood to benefit from the WEB's determinations, employers and their allies in parliament resisted the implementation of WEB rulings and higher awards at every step. Despite these obstructive tactics, thousands of women began to receive unusually large pay packets. The discrimination between women in men's jobs and those performing similar work but not in a man's place, produced much tension at the workplace and occasional industrial action. The award of higher wages and generous overtime to women in 'male' occupations only served to emphasise the exploitative conditions and wages of women working in the traditional 'female' occupations of the clothing and food industries. Resentments among women in these latter areas were fuelled by the fact that these were classified as essential industries from which workers could not move.

Large numbers of women were drafted into the metal trades and munitions industry, which had been reorganised under the direction of Essington Lewis, former managing director of BHP. In 1939 less than 10 per cent of munitions workers were women compared with 50 per cent in 1943, when 328 000 women were employed in this field. The demands of war production led to severe labour shortages, especially in the poorly paid clothing, textiles, food and drink industries. Unable to entice sufficient women to take up these jobs, manpower authorities extended their power of industrial conscription in August 1942 to include all 'unoccupied' – single and divorced – women. Although desperately short of labour, the state declined to abrogate the husband's right of domestic government and the wife's duty to family. Nor did the committee on manpower requirements consider the option of releasing mothers from their 'domestic responsibilities' by establishing a nationwide system of creches. Rather, their ambitious plans for the further expansion of war production were eventually shelved.

Wives exercised no comparable jurisdiction over husbands. Subject to state direction in war work, from early 1943 men also became liable to compulsory military service overseas. Prime Minister Curtin, a committed anti-conscriptionist during World War I, persuaded the majority of his party to forgo its traditional opposition to conscription in order to allow Australian servicemen to be sent to fight in the south-west Pacific area. The alliance with American forces, conscripts themselves, necessitated this revision of policy if Australia were to be seen as a real partner in the Pacific war.

The Americans had decided that Australia should be the base from which the Allied army would launch their counter attack against the Japanese. The first of the US troops arrived in Melbourne in February. In May 1942, after a seemingly relentless advance by the Japanese navy, the Allies had their first victory in the Coral Sea. Although Coral Sea Week was later celebrated as the Battle for Australia, the moment when Australia was saved from invasion, Australia's condition of 'unmanly' dependence on the United States disqualified this battle as a milestone in the annals of nationhood. The Siege of Tobruk on the other hand, the defence of the Libyan fortress town by men of the 9th Division of the AIF, became a major event in Australian military history, signifying the national qualities of endurance and determination. In the Pacific, the Allies triumphed again at Midway Island in June and, despite the continued Japanese assault on Australian coastal shipping, the sense of threat eased. The Japanese continued to advance in New Guinea, however, until they were finally forced back along the Kokoda Trail. Kokoda, where the Australians fought alone, would also become an important national symbol of resistance in masculine mythology.

During 1942 and 1943 hundreds of thousands of American servicemen, under the command of General Douglas MacArthur, who was also Supreme Commander of Allied Forces in the south-west Pacific area, arrived in Australia. Initially stationed in Melbourne, the American headquarters then moved to Brisbane, which became a kind of garrison town. The presence of so many American soldiers in Australia's capital cities set in play a series of sexual, social and political dramas whose reverberations would be felt in Australian life for many years.

Encouraged to extend hospitality to their American guests, the Australian people, women especially, became enthusiastic hosts. Young women and girls also grasped the opportunities for sexual romance. The years between the wars had seen the sexualisation of women; sexual pleasure came to be seen as every woman's right. The modern cultural forms of advertising and cinema had redefined femininity as a matter of sexual attractiveness – democratically available to all – rather than a matter of gentility. Class-based emphases on daintiness and refinement gave way to an insistence on sex appeal and allure. Increasingly, in films and advertising, women were incited to seek out sexual excitement. As men once more embarked on the dangerous adventure of war, women were enjoined to go adventuring in the danger zone of sex.

The Americans were men in uniform; their uniformity and foreign provenance gave them an anonymous appeal and encouraged a process of visual objectification. Much was made of the superiority of their uniforms to those worn by the Australian servicemen; their cut and style gave them a certain 'look'. The objectification of the Yank allowed women to position themselves as sexual subjects:

I expressed a desire to silly Jack P. for a Yank boyfriend (Melb. & in fact all Austr. is swarming with them – since Xmas) – & I felt I'd missed life, not having even met one – Else and I spoke to some one night in the dark of Swanston St. but didn't pick them up, as most girls do now.

Women and girls sought out Yank partners and within weeks many couples had applied to marry. Other women enjoyed themselves more promiscuously and began to attract blame for the increasing incidence of venereal disease. National security regulations passed in 1942 empowered police to detain persons suspected of carrying venereal disease, and invariably many more women were targeted than men.

The sexually active woman was portrayed as a symbol and cause of the social and moral chaos unleashed by the war, in the same way that the economically active woman had been perceived during the depression – they were signs of their disordered times. Numerous measures were advocated by groups as diverse as feminists, clergymen, medical authorities and the army to confine these 'out of control' women. Regulations banned the advertising of contraceptives, even as army authorities promoted prophylaxis among the troops. Schemes were devised to deny women access to alcohol and to promote healthy recreation, and feminists joined church leaders in promoting early marriage.

Feminist activity, which had burgeoned in the 1920s and 1930s, became more widespread during the war, culminating in the 1943 Charter Conference, attended by the delegates of ninety-one women's organisations. Their agenda was to formulate a charter for a new postwar social order for women that would secure their economic and political equality. Many of the guiding voices in this movement came from older women, like Jessie Street, who had worked for improvements in women's status for years and who, by the 1940s, were in their fifties. They believed that women's degradation stemmed from their social constitution as 'creatures of sex'. Prostitution they saw as paradigmatic of the female condition. Advancement for women, they believed, meant advancement beyond their condition as creatures of sex into the full citizenship of public life. In a bid to allow women to more fully exercise their responsibilities and rights at citizens, a number of activists organised the Women for Canberra movement. Despite numerous attempts by non-party and party candidates, no woman had yet been elected to the national parliament. In the 1943 election, finally there was success. Dorothy Tangey – ALP candidate from Western Australia – and Enid Lyons – widow of Prime Minister Joe Lyons, endorsed by the United Australia Party and from Tasmania – were elected to the Senate and the House of Representatives respectively. In her first address to parliament, conscious that it was the first time a woman had ever addressed the House of Representatives, Enid Lyons spoke about perceptions of the apparent incongruity of women as political representatives. She insisted, however, that the perspective on public affairs offered by a location in the home and family was just as important and valid as that afforded by masculine domains. Lyons was forty-six years old, an experienced political campaigner and a mother of twelve when she took up her seat. Organisers of the Women for Canberra movement lamented that they were not supported by young women as enthusiastically as they might have been. Instead, young women seemed preoccupied with the pursuit of personal pleasures.

The apparent 'sexual epidemic' occasioned by the war alarmed and distressed feminists. They saw clearly the cost of sexual freedom, in the spread of venereal disease, fatal abortions, rape and murder. The assault and murder of three Melbourne women by the American serviceman Edward Leonski confirmed their view of sexuality as dangerous, even life threatening. His hanging in Melbourne did not alter the fact that double standards punished women while male offenders generally went free. Feminists attempted to extend protection to girls and women, but they recognised too that a generation gap was opening up, that young women had different priorities and were not as responsive as they might have been to feminist initiatives.

While the presence of American servicemen in Australia meant enhanced sexual, economic and social opportunities for women (as well as increased risks), Australian men came to feel acutely disempowered. The greater pay and benefits provided to American servicemen rendered the Australians economically disadvantaged. The obvious preference of many women for the company of Yanks left Australian men feeling sexually impotent. To compound the insult and injury the Americans seemed to be leading the main thrust against the Japanese, arrogating to themselves the starring role in the Pacific war, while Australian soldiers were left with the inglorious mopping-up operations in their wake.

The hostility between Australian and American servicemen erupted in numerous battles and skirmishes in Australian cities. Alert to the tensions, army authorities attempted to effect greater mutual understanding and harmony by arranging special football matches, concerts and other entertainment. Americans were instructed not to embrace women in public places, and not to demand special dishes in restaurants or prior rights to taxis. Australian men attempted to assuage their sense of emasculation by stigmatising the Australian women who went with Americans as prostitutes, 'going jeep' – and by physically roughing up their allies at every opportunity. The anger at America's domination and dispossession of Australian men left a legacy of deep anti-Americanism among some sections of society and supplied the emotional dynamic of later political campaigns, particularly on the left.

By the end of the war, in 1945, almost one million men and women had put on uniform in their country's service. This had been a people's war in which hardly any lives were left untouched. Yet compared to the Russians or Germans or English or Japanese, Australians were relatively unscathed and casualties were fewer than in the first war. Australians were shocked, however, by the return of the survivors of Japanese labour camps, their emaciated bodies speaking of experiences beyond their reckoning. For those servicemen well enough to benefit, there were generous, well-organised rehabilitation, training and education schemes. The universities had a much more democratic mix of students in their postwar enrolments. A determination to avoid the masculine degradations and humiliations of the depression and to reward servicemen for their national service informed the plan of reconstruction, the plan to build a new order guaranteeing economic freedom and based on a secure family life.

The preference accorded soldiers and men in general meant that many women were forced to leave the jobs they had been enticed to enter during the war. Many simply transferred into the new female jobs opening up in domestic appliance factories and the expanding service sector – female employment reached the same level in 1948 as it had in the peak year 1943. The war effort had established a new pattern of workforce participation among married women, which would become more evident after the war. Many women, however, were pleased to leave the workforce, seeking 'fulfilment' instead in the sexual relationship with a husband and the family life that soon followed.

Marriage rates reached record levels during the war and – largely as a result of the increased incidence of marriage, women marrying at an ever younger age and bearing children early in married life – the postwar years witnessed a baby boom. Marriage was more popular, but more unstable. Women entered marriage with heightened expectations of sexual pleasure and personal fulfilment; inevitably many were disappointed. Marriage and the family, rather than being seen as the culmination of sexual freedom, could just as easily be its casualties. The marriage boom was followed in the 1950s by a divorce boom. Statistics on divorce exerted a particular fascination, an enthralling alternative to the official story of happy families. Newspaper readers learnt that the incidence of divorce was steadily rising, from 1954 cases in 1933 to 4686 in 1943 to 8043 in 1953.

Jubilation at the end of the war – tempered by sadness at the untimely death of Prime Minister Curtin on 5 July 1945 and awe at the dropping of the atom bomb – soon gave way to frustration and impatience with the continued austerities and shortages imposed by the war effort. Petrol continued to be rationed after the war. There was a severe shortage of housing and people often exchanged the irritations of sharing with relations for the lack of amenities and community in the new suburbs taking shape on the outskirts of the cities. Having chafed under wartime restrictions, Australians yearned for freedom from rules and regulations, yet nevertheless recognised the Labor government's record of achievement and commitment to a new social order, the 'light on the hill'. In 1942 the commonwealth government had increased its power in relation to the states by taking over complete responsibility for the collection of income tax. From 1944 it began paying unemployment and sickness benefits and subsidising health costs through a free medicine scheme. The following year it set up a national airline, Trans-Australian Airlines, and an Airlines Commission to control civil aviation, and in 1947 established Qantas as a government-owned overseas carrier. The Australian National University was established and access to all universities made easier by a new system of scholarships. Concerned to protect Australians from another depression, the new Labor Prime Minister, Ben Chifley, passed legislation in 1945 to establish the Commonwealth Bank as the central bank and to put banking policy under government control. To achieve rapid population growth, Minister for Immigration, Arthur Calwell, broke with Labor tradition in inaugurating a massive scheme of assisted immigration, but doggedly held to Labor tradition in maintaining the White Australia Policy.

The Labor government's easy victory in the 1946 elections encouraged Chifley to press on with his reforming measures, but people's growing fears about the spread of Communist influence at home and abroad made many more cautious. Large numbers, especially women, were increasingly ready to respond to the alternative political explanations and appeals issued by the recently formed Liberal Party, led by Robert Menzies.

When Menzies and his supporters forged the new Liberal Party from the ashes of the UAP in 1944, they succeeded in persuading the formidable women's group the Australian Women's National

League (AWNL) to forgo its separate identity and merge with the Liberals. Their reward was the high priority given by the new party and by Menzies in particular to women's interests, especially their interests as wives and mothers. In Menzies's political credo *The Forgotten People*, first enunciated in 1943, he appealed simultaneously to women's identification with their children and their lack of social recognition. 'The real life of the nation is to be found in the homes of people who are nameless and unadvertised, and who ... see in their children their greatest contribution to the immortality of the race.' Guided by the women of the AWNL and the first woman member of the House of Representatives, Enid Lyons (elected in 1943) Menzies was able to rally women to his campaign against Communists, unionists and, eventually, Labor. He revived the Communist union leader as a frightening symbol of militant masculinity, threatening the wellbeing of homes and the security of women and children.

The militancy of the Communists, however, also made them effective union leaders, winning for their members better pay and conditions and, by the late 1940s, putting them in leadership positions in the key coal miners', seamen's, waterside workers' and ironworkers' unions. In the winter of 1949 the Miners' Federation went out on strike, impatient with the slowness of the Coal Tribunal in considering their claim for a 35-hour week. As coal supplies quickly ran out, factories and businesses closed down putting half a million out of work. Cities were plunged into darkness, and in Melbourne and Sydney homes were restricted to one hour's use of gas per day for cooking. The disruption caused by the 'evil' force of Communism had entered women's kitchens, the heart of their domain.

The efforts of the Chifley government to lay the foundations for a new order of social justice and economic security for the working man through nationalising the banks and the health service foundered on the conservative opposition of vested interests, but also on the mobilised fears of Communism. Chifley made a bargain with working men that in return for their support they would be spared the humiliations of poverty and unemployment. Labor appeals positioned women as the wives of men, moved by the same anxieties. Menzies went out of his way to appeal to the different subjectivities of women. He espoused a view of the world that in many ways successfully integrated women's experience of the private and the public. Mothering was the work of protection. Just as women in the 1950s had to protect their families from the dangers of germs, polio and comics, so they needed to safeguard their homes from the 'insidious growth' of Communism. Just as advertisers of flywire doors admonished mothers to 'Protect Him. He Can't Defend Himself Against Insect Pests', so political campaigners alerted people to the threat of the Communist, 'a venomous snake – to be killed before it kills'. Homemaking was unpaid work, but offered women autonomy and opportunities for creativity. Socialism was represented as 'government supervision and direction of every phase of family life' in contrast to the liberalism which offered 'Freedom to manage your own family life without interference'. In the 1949 election, just a few months after the disruptive coal strike and the emotional campaign around bank nationalisation, Menzies outlined a policy designed to strengthen women's support for the Liberal Party. In addition to general promises of freedom and prosperity, there were specific pledges to lower income tax, end petrol rationing, ban the Communist Party and (bowing to pressure from Enid Lyons) introduce child endowment for the first child. The Liberal triumph in the 1949 election – the coalition won seventy-four seats in the House of Representatives compared to Labor's forty-seven (though Labor still dominated the Senate) – inaugurated twenty-three years of Liberal–Country Party rule in Australia.

The conservative hegemony in postwar politics was in part a local effect of the Cold War that followed the expansion of Soviet influence in Eastern Europe and the victory of the Communists in China. Australia identified itself as part of the 'free world', but freedom was thought to be precarious. As Professor G. L. Wood of the University of Melbourne reaffirmed in 1950: 'Today the conception of freedom is once again taking on a larger meaning. Our generation is thinking of the threat to freedom which comes from poverty and insecurity'. The Menzies Liberal–Country Party government pledged to provide the desired security through development, industrial growth, educational opportunities, home ownership, population growth, an expansion of welfare benefits and full employment. Individuals would be encouraged to help themselves and their resultant prosperity would be an effective antidote to the appeal of Communism. Australia industrialised, building on the base laid down by war production, and prosperity ensued. Governments both Liberal and Labor, federal and state, were in these halcyon days the lucky beneficiaries of developments that occurred largely as a result of forces independent of government policy, in particular the buoyant world demand for Australian commodities.

Threatened by real and imagined enemies within and without, public leaders rallied to the defence of the 'Australian way of life'. Patriotism demanded conformity and consensus. On Remembrance Day 1951 six Protestant church leaders and six chief justices issued a 'Call to Australia' which was read out in full on ABC Radio and reprinted in all daily newspapers. The country was said to be in danger from a vast array of sinister forces. 'Good Australians' would recognise the need for a 'community of thought and purpose', seeing in differences only destructive divisions and 'evil dissensions'. A different force for conformity and conservatism found voice in the ideals of 'the Movement', a Catholic intellectual and political grouping, guided by a young University of Melbourne graduate, B. A. Santamaria, determined to expunge Communist influence from union and Labor politics. Everywhere in conservative political rhetoric, the mutuality of people's interests and shared identities was stressed – in marriage, the family, the community, the workplace, in the assimilation of 'New Australians' and Aborigines. Those who persisted in speaking of the distinctions of class, sex, race or ethnicity were branded as divisive and subversive.

Women who previously had been accorded the right to speak for the separate and distinctive interests of 'the home', were now invited to share with men the mutual domain and responsibilities of 'the family'. Whereas the 1943 Women's Charter for Equality included a separate section entitled 'Woman as Mother and/or Home Maker', by 1946 when a revised charter was formulated, this had been reduced to a subsection, subsumed under 'The Family, the Home and the Community'. The new emphasis was a response to the ground swell of anti-feminism after the war, which frequently took the form of a virulent anti-Communism, focussed on the leader of the Charter Movement, Jessie Street. In 1945 Street was the only woman in the Australian delegation to the founding conference of the United Nations (UN) and in 1947 she was the Australian delegate to the UN Status of Women Commission. Her appointment was attacked by conservative rivals, such as Bessie

Rischbieth, President of the Australian Federation of Women Voters, and Street became the subject of a national smear campaign in which she was deemed guilty by association with Communists. 'She says she believes in the liberty and freedom of the individual', wrote a correspondent to the Launceston *Examiner*, 'yet she joins with those who do not'. The Labor government bowed to her opponents' demand that Street cease to represent Australian women on UN committees. The shifting currents of Cold War politics left feminists like Street stranded. Caught between leftists, like the novelist Katharine Prichard who increasingly branded the separatism of feminist politics 'chauvinist', and conservative feminists who branded the United Associations of Women and the Charter Movement as communistic, Street quit the country in 1949, going into exile in Britain until 1956.

Previously encouraged to identify with their sex in the collectivity 'women', wives and mothers were henceforth invited to think of their identity in terms of their individual relationships with their homes and husbands and children. The divorcee joined the spinster as a social outcast. 'Today's greater tolerance of divorce', advised the *Sydney Morning Herald*, 'does not necessarily include a divorced woman. A majority had been made to feel, in one way or another, like strange, alien creatures'. The family was the postwar world's discovery, with new books addressing its problems and place. In a chapter on the family in George Caiger's *The Australian Way of Life* published in 1953, W. D. Borrie explained: 'The family is a subject which still awaits serious study in Australia'. The neglect was made good by A. P. Elkin, the editor of *Marriage and the Family in Australia* published four years later. The mutuality of women's and men's interests and needs, emphasised by the dominant discourse on sexual partnership, was expressed in marriage and the family. 'Sex is the true foundation of marriage', said Dr David Mace, marriage guidance counsellor. 'It is a way of expressing and maintaining mutual love and tenderness.' Heterosexuality ruled, but the insistence on sexual fulfilment and self-realisation sowed the seeds of its subversion, as growing numbers of men and women embraced the sexual identity of 'homosexual' or 'lesbian'.

The homosexual was identified in the 1950s as yet another threat to the wellbeing of the Australian way of life. In a classic instance of projection, male homosexuality was portrayed by heterosexual authorities as aggressive and predatory, engaged in the harassment and entrapment of innocent boys and young men. The police responded by persecuting and entrapping homosexuals. Legal and medical intervention in gay men's lives became more brutal and oppressive with the increased use of aversion therapy, psychotherapy and drugs. Such repression, accompanied by the proliferating discussion on homosexuality, was unintentionally productive as well, providing publicity about the existence of a gay subculture and helping to consolidate an emergent homosexual identity. Lesbians were less visible, their desire not rendered public in the same ways. Where there was press attention to lesbians in the 1950s, they were represented in different terms from male homosexuals: lesbianism was portrayed as an exclusive, excessive, antisocial, emotional relationship. Despite the lack of publicity, however, women's attraction to other women did progress from schoolgirl 'crushes' to adult sexual passion, and lesbians too were subject to violent medical intervention. Women nevertheless acted on their desires. The sexualisation of love saw passion as its own justification and sexual fulfilment as a matter of self-realisation.

In the redefinition of marriage as primarily a sexual partnership, children sometimes assumed the identity of interlopers. Children intruded upon the 'privacy' of the married couple as they increasingly expected 'time together alone'. In order to provide education and a better standard of living for their children, and to have more time to attend to their own interests, women practised birth control, increasingly taking advantage of artificial contraceptives. The postwar family was usually limited to two or three children. After 1961, when the contraceptive pill was introduced, the birthrate declined sharply as Australian women became its most enthusiastic consumers.

Women's refusal to bear more children generated much anxiety among public leaders and an official inquiry, conducted by the National Health and Medical Research Council in 1944. In the aftermath of Japan's aggression, population was thought to be Australia's most pressing need. Women's desire for freedom from domestic drudgery – sometimes called selfishness – was thought to be undermining Australian security. National extinction threatened. Australians were warned that they 'must either populate and develop their vast continent or accept the probability of having it taken from them'. Australian babies were considered to be the best new Australians, but if Australian women refused to bring forth enough new citizens, then they would have to be obtained from elsewhere.

Labor and Liberal governments concurred in the necessity for large-scale immigration programs. Their preference was for British migrants, but following an agreement with the International Refugee Organisation, Australia began to accept thousands of 'displaced persons', especially from states occupied by the Soviet Union. Between 1945 and 1952 British arrivals – 360 000 – were slightly outnumbered by non-British – 362 000. Refugees were treated as mobile labour, housed in camps and directed to work on large developmental projects, such as the Snowy Mountains electricity and irrigation schemes. Evidence of these people's professional or trade skills was disregarded. In the 1950s and 1960s an increasing proportion of migrants came from southern Europe and countries such as Italy, Greece and Yugoslavia. To provide for these unsettled foreign men, who might otherwise seek sexual relationships with 'Australian' women, 'bride ships' brought women from their own countries to be their wives.

The building of postwar Australia depended heavily on migrant labour. In the ten years after 1947 the labour force increased by 908 400, of which 678 718 were the result of immigration. Migrant workers were especially significant in manufacturing, over-represented in jobs associated with textiles, metals and vehicle construction, but hardly evident at all in the professional and white-collar areas of management, finance and public relations.

The huge influx of migrants in the postwar years and the greater availability of education financed by the new commonwealth scholarship scheme offered Australian-born men and women unparalleled opportunities for social mobility. Men did not have cause to feel displaced. Work was available to all comers and the unprecedented affluence of families was often based on the new opportunities for overtime. It was not uncommon for men to hold more than one job. Their engagement in long hours of work was in turn made possible by women's assumption of responsibility for family matters. Married women were themselves nevertheless going 'out to work' in record numbers and grew accustomed to juggling the demands of work at home and away. Between 1947 and 1961 the female workforce increased at a faster rate than the male workforce.

Migrant women suffered the greatest pressure. With more need to earn income than most Australian-born women and a greater likelihood that they would be working in a factory, they also struggled to keep families together as the new society pulled husbands and children away in different, foreign, directions. In many ways the custodians of their traditional culture, migrant women, with little time or opportunity to learn English, were least able to 'assimilate' as required by official policy. For them home became a refuge from an alien world, and the political emphasis on home and the family often struck a responsive chord.

The acceptance of migrants in the Australian community in the 1950s and 1960s depended on their demonstrated ability and desire to assimilate, to adopt the English language and the 'Australian way of life'. The government invested considerable resources through the Good Neighbour Council and the Adult Migrant Education Scheme to instructing old Australians in the virtues of tolerance and new Australians in local manners and mores. In 1954 the Department of Immigration asked Gwen Meredith, author of the popular radio serial 'Blue Hills', whether she might 'in a future script ... find some way of reminding listeners of the importance of immigration to Australia and the obligation upon all Australians to adopt a spirit of tolerance and understanding in their everyday contact with newcomers in this country'. Old Australians' acceptance remained conditional. The sound of foreign tongues in public places – at the football or on trams – could excite intense, irrational hostilities.

Married women of all backgrounds were increasingly joining the paid workforce, though often on a part-time basis. In the past, women had been able to make a significant difference to their family's standard of living through the exercise of specialist skills at home: sewing, mending, cooking and gardening, taking in lodgers and other people's children. But by the 1950s it became evident that the standard of living was being measured in terms of commodities, such as refrigerators, cars and television sets, that could not be made at home or obtained through exchange. And the more women invested emotionally in home decoration, in securing a Home Beautiful, the more they needed to seek outside work to pay for it. Incited by advertisers to seek instant gratification, to purchase goods without delay on 'easy terms', women and men became locked into a life of weekly instalments on their credit account. The unleashing of the pent-up demand for homes, cars and consumer goods fuelled the local manufacturing industry (tariffs were high and imports restricted) and the finance industry that expanded to meet the voracious appetite for credit. Home ownership expanded at an unprecedented rate, climbing from a rate of 46 per cent in 1947 to 72 per cent in 1966. During the 1950s the population increased by about one-quarter; the number of cars doubled; and the hire purchase debt increased fourfold. Seventy per cent of the debt was owed on cars.

Since the 1940s more Australians had been employed in the manufacturing industry than in rural industries. By 1959 over a million Australians earned their living in factories, compared with about half that number employed on the land. Moreover, the productivity of the manufacturing workforce outpaced that of the agricultural and pastoral industries in these years. Australia, nevertheless, was still vitally dependent on rural production for export income and fortunately, prices for wool and wheat soared in response to demands set in motion by the outbreak of the Korean War in 1950. In the following year wool exports accounted for more than half of the total value of Australian exports.

Visitors constantly marvelled at the affluence and apparent classlessness of Australian society in the 1950s. Stories of the successful (male) migrant confirmed the image of Australia as the freest country of the free world, a land of opportunity and enterprise. To the American writer James Michener in 1956, the nation was 'a worker's paradise'. Stanton Hope, invoking the same metaphor in the same year, observed in his book *Digger's Paradise* that Australians had 'never been better off'. Australian good fortune and classlessness seemed most evident in their abundant leisure and obvious enjoyment of the beach, sunbathing, swimming, sport and the cinema. Leisure pursuits also focussed attention on the masculinity of Australian culture, which often seemed to centre on the lifesaving club, the RSL, the pub and the racetrack.

As Australia was a man's country according to popular wisdom, so the 1950s seemed to be a man's decade. The long tradition of male solidarity in Australia was reinforced by men's experience as soldiers and prisoners-of-war and the postwar introduction of national service for eighteen-year-olds. Women's difference – their distinctive claims and interests as women – had been eclipsed by their positioning in the family. On the new frontier of sex, heterosexual women explorers often seemed to stumble on barren territory, their desires unreciprocated by men. In his essay on Australian life in the 1950s, J. D. Pringle observed of women: 'They are always conscious of themselves and of their sex, in spite of the fact that the men generally seem quite unaware of their existence'. Girls seem 'quite shameless in their pursuit of young men, while the young men seem downright rude in their indifference'. Sometimes men's lack of interest extended to the offspring of sexual liaisons – exnuptial births increased in the 1960s and unmarried mothers became a much discussed social problem. Most were pressured to give up their infants for adoption, laying the basis for much unresolved grief, while providing a ready supply of babies for infertile couples. Married women were urged to seek pleasure and gratification from home decoration. Some found these things instead in their relationships with each other. Australia in the 1950s was organised around the separate cultures of men and women.

Men seemed to derive solace from the taciturn company of their mates. A proliferation of books paid tribute to men's – especially working men's – role in building the nation, in forging a national tradition. Fiction celebrated the tight-lipped, square-jawed, lean and wiry masculinity bred in the outback, a style embodied by Chips Rafferty in films such as *The Overlanders* (1946), *Bitter Springs* (1950) and *The Phantom Stockman* (1953). Academic titles such as Russel Ward's *The Australian Legend*, A. A. Phillips's *The Australian Tradition* and Vance Palmer's *The Legend of the Nineties* identified an emergent national spirit in the actions and writings of their forefathers, of men of independence and action in the 1890s. Domesticated and suburbanised, men romanticised past freedoms. In Ray Lawler's *Summer of the Seventeenth Doll*, performed for the first time in 1955, a play about canecutters who travelled south each year to see their Sydney girlfriends, critics heralded the beginning of an authentic Australian theatre. In these representations of the true nation, femininity was, by default, cast as unauthentic and un-Australian. Australian gatherings were symptomatic – women left to themselves at the 'other' end of the room, their conversations unheard by men.

The most popular women's groups of these years were those that appealed to women's familial identity: mothers' unions and clubs, new, old and progressive housewives' associations. Yet many women still dreamed of shrugging off the limitations of their sex. The memory of Amy Johnson lingered on. In September 1950, in response to the refusal of the civil aviation authority to allow women pilots to perform an air display, the Australian Association of Woman Pilots was formed, taking the motto 'Skies Unlimited'. A few months later the Feminist Club demanded that women in the armed services be granted equal pay: 'It is time men recognised women have a place beside them, and, up to the moment, a little ahead of them'. Women teachers also protested at the refusal of their claim for equal pay. In 1950 the arbitration court raised the women's rate of pay to 75 per cent of men's, a decision that angered many women's organisations, such as the Australian Federation of University Women and the Australian Federation of Business and Professional Women's Clubs, and inspired them to redouble their efforts to achieve full equality. They were joined in their campaign for equal pay by a new group of progressive women called the Union of Australian Women, formed in 1950.

In the conformist climate of the 1950s, left-wing writers celebrated independence and anti-authoritarianism as Australian and masculine virtues. They promoted a radical, socialist platform against the ruling conservative politics of the Liberal–Country Party coalition, and offered an alternative vision of freedom than the one espoused by America and the rest of the free world. Indeed anti-Americanism was often the main stance adopted by radicals, an opposition to American 'domination' portrayed in the form of strong, virile working men for whom domination was an offence to their status as men. For many Australian men the image of the controlling Yank summoned up painful reminders of past humiliations. The promotion of 'the Australian way of life' was successful at this time, because it differentiated the nation not just from those behind the 'Iron Curtain' and those homelands that immigrants were urged to forget, but it also insisted on difference from America. This became all the more necessary as the population, especially young people, imbibed more and more messages and values from the United States through films, television and, most worrying of all to some, comics. Although Prime Minister Menzies formalised

Australia's military reliance on the United States in the ANZUS treaty and presided over his country's growing economic and cultural dependency on the same country, he largely avoided an image of unbecoming subservience to the Americans by his identification with Britain and professions of love for the Queen.

Menzies led the conservative parties, with leader of the Country Party John McEwen as his deputy, to successive electoral victories. On some issues, however, he was effectively opposed. His proposal in 1950 to ban the Communist Party was narrowly defeated by the people in a referendum. In 1954 he looked in danger of being beaten at the election by the Labor Party, led by the talented and mercurial ex-chief justice H. V. Evatt, when a storm broke around the defection in Canberra of Russian spy Vladimir Petrov. A royal commission was announced and although the election took place before it was underway, rumour and suspicion concerning links between the Labor Party, Communists and Russian espionage ensured that a majority of voters opted for the security represented by Menzies. Labor prospects were further battered by the destructive divisions generated by the activities of the Catholic Movement-inspired Groupers, who had had considerable success in installing fervent anti-Communists in leadership positions in Labor Party branches and trade unions. Their expulsion from the party in 1955 and the consequent formation of the Democratic Labor Party, which assiduously directed its preferences at election time to the conservative parties, helped keep Labor out of office during the next two decades. The Liberal–Country Party coalition came closest to losing office in 1961, when unemployment reached the unacceptable level of 2 per cent.

During the 1950s and well into the 1960s Australians ordered their lives around the touchstones of freedom and the family. It was these fundamentals they had in mind when they spoke of the Australian way of life and returned the Liberal–Country Party governments to office at election after election. The dominant political view positioned Australia as part of the free world and people's mutuality of interests was made manifest in their identity as new and old Australians, members of the free world, members of families. But the nationalist drive towards assimilation was inherently oppressive. By the end of the 1960s 'national liberation' movements challenged the claims to moral leadership made by the free world, women attacked the family and male supremacy as obstacles to the liberation of their sex, and Aborigines and migrants rejected assimilation as leading to the wholesale erasure of their culture and identity. The late 1960s saw the resurgence of diversity and the politics of difference.

12 The State as Father: 1910–60

As we have seen, Aboriginal people were omitted from the concept of the new Australian nation. Denied citizenship until 1948 and excluded from the census and voting for federal elections until 1968, the commonwealth could not legislate on their behalf. Not all Aborigines had come within the power of the colonisers, though; in remote regions, their land and communities were still their own and frontier warfare was not yet over. Class, sex, race and ethnicity were branded as divisive in the new nation, but colonialism located Australia's indigenous people not only in a special position of oppression but also one of danger to the national interest. To acknowledge the separate interests or different history of the Aboriginal people would reveal the extent to which Australia's white settlement was premised on colonial takeover and domination.

Racist beliefs that Aborigines were 'childlike' justified the colour-bar that excluded them from democracy. Via fiction and official national histories, white Australians concocted and absorbed seemingly innocuous mythologies about Aborigines. Schoolbooks portrayed them as 'other', emphasising the 'simple' nature of Aboriginal people, their 'backwardness' and few material possessions. Jeannie Gunn's *We of the Never Never*, published in 1908 and a recommended school text until the 1960s, depicted Aborigines as cute and amusing, but outside the 'real' story of Australia – the romance of pioneering. Gunn's equally popular *Little Black Princess* told of the 'nigger' 'orphan girl' adopted in an act of self-sacrifice by the Little Missus. As Gunn breezily wrote: 'So Bett-Bett found a Missus, and I – well, I found a real nuisance'. The 'nuisance' was in fact the much-trusted domestic servant Dolly Bonson, the model for Bett-Bett, not an orphan at all. Yet the abandoned picanninny image found a place in the home decor of the 1940s and 1950s, on wall plaques and ashtrays.

Overwhelmingly, white society found it comfortable to portray an intrinsically exploitative relationship as Christian benevolence. There were those, such as volunteer foster parents, who were willing to 'help' Aborigines but the extent of the favour was conditional on 'good' behaviour, which meant discarding Aboriginal ways and families and disobeying traditional marriage laws. Whites complained if Aborigines appeared ungrateful for 'kindness', however intrusive.

Government, missionary organisations and some employers took on a parenting-style role. Aborigines were defined by the legislation of various states as a separate category, subject to a range of rules and regulations. Some state governments classed them, like orphans, as wards, at least until they reached twenty-one years old. Aboriginal life chances were also affected by discriminatory practices relating to employment, control over earnings, mobility, leisure activities, land ownership and residence.

Governments changed from policies of segregation and 'protection' of Aborigines on reserves, to dispersal or absorption into the wider community. The policy of protection was based on the premise that Aborigines were a dying or doomed race. Greater controls over individuals were exerted in the eastern seaboard states, while more remote frontier conditions made surveillance difficult. Eugenic considerations were important, with girls and women being more tightly controlled than males.

Queensland 'experts' in Aboriginal protection like W. E. Roth and J. W. Bleakley played influential roles in developing policies in other states. Queensland's large Aboriginal population and greater areas of underdeveloped country enabled the establishment of numerous large government and mission-run reserves. Reserves were tightly managed, with an emphasis on control and discipline. Aborigines were rounded up, transferred from their own areas, and moved onto settlements like Barambar (renamed Cherbourg) where they served the local pastoral industry, or, from 1918, to Palm Island, which Aborigines viewed as a prison. Residents of Palm Island made numerous attempts to swim the 20 miles to the mainland. Inmates, as reserve residents were called, were regularly moved around against their will. Aborigines were forced to live on land not of their own choosing, in communities of disparate clan groups, which often led to rapid cultural breakdown.

Torres Strait Islanders' village lifestyle and Melanesian-influenced material culture gave them superior status in the eyes of white Australians. Their strident demands to run their own councils were heard, allowing greater decision making and a sense of autonomy. Brought under the Queensland act from 1904, separate legislation was drawn up for Torres Strait Islanders in 1939 after they had waged a lengthy strike to demand control over their own wages. Their successful pearling fleet also provided them with a strong economic base.

From the 1830s, Tasmanian Aborigines were moved to reserves on Gun Carriage, Cape Barren and Flinders islands, where they were supervised by outsiders and subject to numerous strictures. The number of days children attended school was closely monitored. 'Improvements' made to land were regularly assessed, yet despite their continued pleas, Tasmanian Aborigines were not ensured any security of land title.

Throughout Australia many Aborigines were forcibly relocated from traditional lands as a result of European farmers' and miners' demands for land and labour. Jimmie Barker's family was thus forced to move from Milroy to a Brewarrina reserve in 1911. Food was so poor that fathers, in particular, were often driven to steal, ending up in gaol, which resulted in even worse poverty for families. In Queensland and New South Wales, offenders were generally banned from their reserve homes after release, and thus doubly punished. The managers could be mean, cruel and corrupt, but complainants risked severe punishment. Protective policies gave Aborigines little ability to move outside missions and reserves – closed institutions that functioned like nations apart.

The right to be treated as an adult or 'exempted' from Aboriginal status was only granted if a man or woman stopped associating with and living an 'Aboriginal lifestyle'. On reserves Aborigines often developed a sense of greater community; new land associations were forged and they collectively resisted compulsory relocation. On the other hand, the reserve system encouraged a culture of economic and psychological dependency on the state that left a lasting legacy.

A variety of Aboriginal groups battled against their humiliating treatment. From the 1920s organisations such as the Australian Aborigines' Progressive Association (AAPA) led by Fred Maynard rapidly expanded. It aimed to improve the material conditions of Aborigines and end political oppression. In 1932 William Cooper established the Australian Aborigines' League, organising a petition to the King for better living conditions and adequate parliamentary representation. During the sesquicentennial celebrations of 1938, Aborigines declared a Day of Mourning and staged a protest in Sydney. The following year, one hundred Aborigines walked off Cumeroogunga reserve to protest against poor food and conditions. Attempts were made to discredit leading Aboriginal militants such as Bill Ferguson and Jack Patton by accusations of Nazism. Due to state powers over Aborigines, those who protested risked imprisonment and harassment of their families.

Although the work patterns of many Aborigines during the 1910–60 period were shaped by government interventions, the majority achieved a certain autonomy from authorities. While many became successful farmers, few Aborigines owned the land or were entitled to security of tenure. This was clearly demonstrated when Cumeroogunga residents were forcibly relocated to Lake Tyers in 1923. A range of recently published Aboriginal autobiographies, such as that of Jimmie Barker, tell the stories of battlers who struggled against the odds and were deprived of even basic facilities like water supplies. Ella Simon, who worked from the age of twelve, revealed the commonplace nature of child labour in rural and urban environments. Ruby Langford tried to eke out a living as she bore her nine children. While attempting to rely on male breadwinners, who got fed up with the responsibility or drank excessively, Ruby was frequently left to her own resources. Even with her partner Gordon employed, and she pregnant with her sixth child, in 1957 Ruby had to milk cows, feed chickens and horses, cook, wash and mind the children, then trap rabbits at night. Again pregnant, deserted by her partner, and with only small children to assist, Ruby had to fell and haul logs to construct their dwelling.

Aboriginal men in New South Wales, Victoria and South Australia frequently worked in pastoral occupations – as stockworkers, shearers, fencers, general labourers and handymen. In rural New South Wales, many Aboriginal pastoral workers lived in station communities, sometimes comprising up to 30 per cent of the workforce. Most men were boundary riders and casual labourers, while women worked as domestics and launderers. Rations were meagre, and Aborigines hunted rabbits and kangaroos for food. In most states, they also engaged in seasonal work, such as fruit and vegetable picking and woodcutting. Many Aborigines made a living through self-employment: fishing, bartering, fencing and carrying out other rural contract work. Others complemented paid employment with possum-snaring, rabbit-trapping, dingo-catching, fishing, timber-selling and other entrepreneurial pursuits.

However, Aboriginal workers were particularly susceptible to fluctuations in the labour market. During the 1930s depression, Aborigines had to compete with white men who had taken up their swags and gone bush in the desperate search for work. Northern Territory Aborigines fared relatively well at this time, for bush food supplies had not been so drastically reduced, and Aborigines were more skilled than others at procuring what was available.

The 1940s and 1950s were times of relatively high employment: labour shortages during the war saw a strong demand for workers, enabling Aborigines in some areas to gain the same wages as whites. By the 1950s less rural domestic work was available for Aboriginal women, but urban employment prospects were expanding, precipitating greater movement to the cities.

Aboriginal seasonal workers were usually employed for two-thirds of the year. A New South Wales survey conducted during 1957–58 revealed that Aborigines had different work attitudes to whites, preferring not to work continuously for long periods. Seasonal labour that required travel was often seen as an advantage as it enabled breaks to visit kin and special land sites. Choice of employment was severely affected by limited access to education and training. Up until the 1960s, only 1 per cent of New South Wales Aborigines were classed as skilled, with over 81 per cent unskilled, and the remainder semi-skilled. The fact that seasonal work was dominated by men and usually involved travel often meant that fathers lived apart from their families for most of the year, and sometimes for years at a time. As emerges in Bill Cohen's autobiography, children missed their fathers and much responsibility fell upon the women.

In eastern Australia, Aboriginal workers were generally paid wages, though not uncommonly at lower rates than white workers. Aborigines were not widely unionised, however, and most lacked the numeracy and literacy skills or self-confidence to argue about employment conditions. If workers came under the jurisdiction of Aboriginal protection boards, their wages were paid into trust accounts, and they required permission to draw upon their own earnings. Employers debited food, clothing and other requirements and when left with little cash after years of labour, many workers suspected fraudulent practice, but could do nothing about it. The system was open to massive exploitation, yet union organisers were banned from supervised reserves.

In northern Australia a particularly large proportion of pastoral workers were Aboriginal – up to 80 per cent on some stations – and they had a reputation for excellence at horsebreaking, mustering and tracking. After serving as a girl domestic, the real Bett-Bett became a stockworker at Bonrook and other stations in the Northern Territory. Aborigines also worked in the pearling and bêche-de-mer industry in the Torres Strait and around Broome, and the buffalo industry in Arnhem Land. They worked in tin mining at Annan River, north Queensland, and in ochre mining in Central Australia. Although ocean-based industries had standardised wages for Aborigines, the pastoral industry was different. While a small cash wage was compulsory in Queensland, in the Northern Territory and Western Australia pastoralists could pay their Aboriginal workers in kind. Aborigines and some of their dependants therefore received only rations of flour, beef, sugar and work clothing.

In both rural and urban Australia, Aboriginal women were viewed as readily available; they were stereotyped as prostitutes and Aboriginal men's views were ignored. The forbidden nature of black women's sexual offerings was reflected in slang terms, such as 'black velvet'. In northern Australia, some Aboriginal women worked as prostitutes for boat crews and around mining towns. While many obtained casual payment for sexual services, others negotiated longer-term arrangements. Aboriginal women were motivated by more than immediate material rewards, however, at times acting as intermediaries and bargaining for favourable treatment of their clan.

Controlled by 'protective' government boards or subject to the exploitation of the open market, Aboriginal labour remained relatively unfree. At times, however, Aborigines were able to obtain a measure of control. In pastoral regions they often agreed to work because they wanted access to traditional land and security for their communities, including those relations not employed by the cattle bosses. Kinship obligations could be met by redistributing their own supplies. White bosses were incorporated into Aboriginal value and social systems, and as they were generally single men, they were frequently offered 'promised brides'. Isolated white men sometimes fulfilled their obligations under this system, but the tensions in negotiating a path as coloniser and colonised often proved untenable.

Aboriginal workers of both genders lacked access to the full award available to white male employees. Sometimes Aborigines protested against bad conditions, as in the Pilbara strikes of 1946, but they lacked the muscle of trade union membership. During the 1920s and 1940s white unionists opposed the cheapness of Aboriginal labour in commonwealth arbitration cases concerning the pastoral awards, but their primary concern in doing so was to increase employment opportunities for their white members. It was not until the 1960s, that unions substantially supported Aboriginal agitation for better wages.

Army employment during World Wars I and II enabled Aborigines to compete on more equal terms. From 300 to 400 Aborigines enlisted in World War I, one-third of whom lost their lives. Despite this, they were excluded from digger legend, dependent as it was on the evolution of a virile white manhood. During World War II, 3000 Aborigines and Torres Strait Islanders enlisted and another 150 to 200 *de facto* servicemen were employed in the coastwatch. Overall about one in twenty Aborigines directly contributed as servicemen, servicewomen or labourers. At about one in four, the participation rate of Torres Strait Islanders was even higher, outstripping the commitment rate of white Australians. Despite official fears that the 'half-castes' or other blacks would betray their country to the Japanese, it was remote Aborigines who warned ill-prepared troops of the first attacks on Darwin. For many Aborigines, the army offered better pay and conditions than they had previously experienced. Many were also caught up in the patriotism and adventure surrounding war. For Bill Cohen, enlisting was one of the few things he could do without having to seek any special permission from Aboriginal authorities. War became associated in his mind with proving his manhood to the world.

As I lay in bed, thoughts began to probe my mind, saying I was a coward ... so my weekend off I rode on home to the Aboriginal Reserve where my wife and family were ... I broke the news to my wife of joining the army which she wasn't at all pleased about, so I had another week with my family and kids ... women could never control me. Whatever I had in my mind I'd do.

Several Aborigines rose in the ranks: Reg Saunders became a lance corporal within weeks of enlistment and was then promoted to sergeant and commissioned officer. Kamuel Abednego, a Torres Strait Islander, served as lieutenant in the United States Army, operating small ships in the waters between Torres Strait and Papua New Guinea. Some Aboriginal soldiers spent lengthy periods as prisoners of war, were maimed in battle, or killed in action. Tim Hughes and Clive Upright won the Military Medal for outstanding courage in battle. Oodgeroo Noonuccal (Kath Walker), who served as a signaller in the AWAS, explained: 'in the Army they didn't give a stuff what colour you were. There was a job to be done ... and all of a sudden the colour line disappeared'. Sometimes white Australians mixed with Aborigines for the first time, and came to see them as equals. Many stories imply a sense of cohesion, brought about by the conformity of service: the uniforms, haircuts, drill and new social hierarchy replaced the racially based one of civilian life.

While the war enhanced agitation for Aboriginal civil rights, the returned servicemen's associations ignored Aborigines. Army achievements such as Reg Saunders's outstanding leadership qualities and sporting skills were ignored in civilian life, where he could only obtain employment in poorly paid jobs such as foundry worker, tally clerk and tram conductor.

Poor education facilities on missions and in schools in areas with substantial Aboriginal populations also ensured that few gained literacy and numeracy skills, and certainly not with any degree of proficiency. Such basic skills were essential to other Australian adults, and Aborigines were thus particularly vulnerable to exploitation by individuals and government agents. Local racial bigotry was also influential: white parents frequently prevented Aboriginal children from attending school with their children. Minor complaints would be used as a pretext for black children to be barred from attending. 'Poor hygiene', blamed on such common problems as nits and scabies, was one such ground for exclusion. The sub-standard washing and housing facilities available to Aboriginal families were ignored. Many Aboriginal parents saw education in the western system as important, and moved to towns to further their children's education. Some families even moved over the border from New South Wales to Victoria in order to acquire access to quality public education. It was not until after 1949 that Aboriginal children were allowed greater access to New South Wales state schools, but they were still ostracised by the colour bar affecting swimming pools and picture theatres. Western education was a potential tool of equality, but it also eroded Aboriginal language and beliefs, instilled a sense of cultural inferiority and narrowed gender role options. Not surprisingly, Aboriginal children were frequently apprehended by state truancy inspectors, who sent them away to juvenile institutions.

On the missions, little attention was paid to sex education and girls were not taught about menstruation, conception or even childbirth. Teenage pregnancy became increasingly common; some reports indicate that this was especially so where girls were sent out to service in non-Aboriginal homes.

Throughout the twentieth century, government policies on sex and marriage between Europeans and Aborigines reflected continuing insecurity regarding the ability to maintain white domination. Moral and sexual panic combined to entrench fears of 'contamination'. Reserve superintendents, missionaries, and other agents of the state prevented Aborigines from freely choosing a partner or marrying. This was done on the basis of skin colour and eugenic theories, or according to definitions of respectability. In Western Australia after 1905, and after 1911 in the Northern Territory, the written permission of the Chief Protector was required before any marriage of an Aborigine could take place. The Commissioner of Native Affairs was entitled to refuse permission on the grounds of 'gross disparity in the ages of the parties', an ordinance intended to break up the traditional marriage system whereby a young woman might be betrothed to a much older man. Missionaries and employers also discouraged traditional marriages.

Miscegenation, or sexual relations between the races, was viewed as a crime against one's race, and against the ideal of White Australia. Intermarriage therefore became subject to state approval. If a lighter-skinned Aboriginal girl married a white man, this could be approved because it would lead to the 'breeding out of colour'. A black girl marrying a white man was considered undesirable. During the 1920s and 1930s, Northern Territory women of full Aboriginal descent found that permission to marry a white man was invariably refused. In Western Australia a half-caste man who cohabited with or married an Aboriginal woman was deemed an Aborigine, whereas if he married a non-Aborigine, he was given more autonomy and could not be transferred to another district. If an Aboriginal woman married a white man, he was not permitted onto a reserve, and could be prosecuted.

Various states prohibited sexual intercourse between an Aboriginal woman and non-Aboriginal man, with penalties of 50 pounds or six months imprisonment. In Western Australia Aboriginal women had been prevented from making money out of prostitution by the Girls Enticement Act of 1844, and after 1905 they were also prohibited from the vicinity of pearlers or 'other sea boats'. There was no need to legally ban the association of Aboriginal men and white women as they were already effectively prohibited by contemporary social mores and inequalities of power.

Curiously evasive legislation revealed public shame at the frequency of black female–white male relations, as exemplified by the 1911 ordinance in the Northern Territory that prohibited Aboriginal women from wearing 'male' clothing while in the company of a non-Aboriginal man. A 1918 amendment made 'habitual' consorting an offence, but not casual consorting. In 1933 it became illegal to procure a woman for carnal knowledge, and a 100 pound fine or three months imprisonment, or both, could follow. Soliciting prostitution by an Aboriginal or part-Aboriginal woman also became an offence. South Australian legislation followed the Northern Territory lead, while in Western Australia, men convicted of cohabitation could face up to two years imprisonment. Yet despite all the legislation demanding 'respectable behaviour', very few men were actually charged; police themselves participated in the illegal activity, and the men convicted were invariably poor whites rather than the more powerful station managers or owners. Outside the public gaze, casual associations were condoned, but men who acknowledged black women as mistresses or cared for offspring were considered more threatening to the status quo.

The movements and associates of Aboriginal girls and women were closely scrutinised. In the Northern Territory during World War II, authorities attempted to segregate Aborigines and half-caste girls from the soldiers in case the men contracted venereal disease. In 1941, despite the dominance of assimilationist ideals, the Territory's legislation became much more rigid and curfews were enforced. If an Aboriginal woman married a white man without permission, she could be guilty of an offence; if she failed to marry but lived with him, she was guilty of a criminal offence. If she married legally, she could be made exempt from Aboriginal legislation, but prevented from associating with Aborigines. In order to enjoy civil rights, some Aborigines applied for exemption from the Aboriginal legislation, but exempted men could be penalised for having an Aboriginal girlfriend.

The restrictive legislation was a major factor in the break-up of families. Ella Simon's elderly father was forced to move out of her home near the Aboriginal reserve at Purfleet in New South Wales because he was white. His white relations never spoke to her and refused to invite her to his funeral. Until the lifting of restrictions on alcohol consumption, an Aboriginal wife could not have a drink with her white husband nor in some cases a son with his father. Children like the Verburgs of Adelaide River were not allowed to live or even spend time with their mother because she was Aboriginal. Their German father and Aboriginal mother agreed to separate to prevent the children being taken to a half-caste home. Legislation aimed to control Aboriginal women's sexuality branded them as 'damned whores', and their colour meant they were viewed as unfit mothers.

Because Aboriginal marriage was not recognised, and because they were black in a white Australia, all Aboriginal children were in a sense considered illegitimate. The state rather than their families had ultimate control over them. A network of legislation enabled the respective states and the Northern Territory to exert great authority over Aboriginal children. In many cases, the Protector or Director of Aborigines was their legal guardian despite the fact that the biological parents were alive. While most white fathers did not acknowledge their half-caste offspring, as depopulation threatened community continuity, elders decided to 'keep' such children. In Aboriginal communities children were seldom considered orphans because of the network of adults who had obligations towards their wellbeing. Western Australian and Queensland governments made token attempts to gain support from white fathers, but the mother's word regarding paternity was often discounted therefore proof was lacking. Aboriginal mothers were usually considered promiscuous, liars, or both.

Government policies of the 1920s and 1930s had targeted children as the group who could be most successfully 'uplifted'. A 1926 report of the New South Wales Aborigines' Protection Board stated that 'the continuation of this policy of dissociating the children from camp life must eventually solve the Aboriginal problem'. The 'problem' was defined as Aboriginality itself: that is, Aborigines' colour and different culture. Linking sexuality and Aboriginality, Commissioner Neville of Western Australia argued, 'You cannot change a native after he has reached the age of puberty, but before that it is possible to mould him'. 'In Western Australia', he boasted, 'we have power under the act to take any child from its mother at any stage of its life, no matter whether the mother is legally married or not'. The 1937 federal conference on Aboriginal welfare targeted children as the group to be changed and civilised. They had to be removed from the 'degrading influences' of the camps, which meant removal from their parents, Aboriginal relations and cultural training.

Racial ideology assumed that 'half-caste' children especially should be brought up as Europeans. For 128 years, therefore, in South Australia such children were subject to closer regulation and treated 'as if they had no parents, and their parents as if they had no children'. It was a harshly effective strategy that succeeded in breaking up many families and communities and causing them to lose traditional knowledge.

In Queensland and New South Wales after 1915, children could be classed as neglected and institutionalised merely because of their Aboriginality. White authorities had control over the 'care and custody' of children, and on reserves in Queensland and Western Australia they were segregated in dormitory systems for 'training and discipline'. This was supposed to inculcate western thinking and habits, but by confirming the official position that Aboriginal parents were considered unsuitable child rearers, it gravely damaged self-esteem. Fred Clay, whose family was removed to Palm Island in the 1930s, was shocked when his mother and sisters were put into the women's dormitory and he into the boys'; after that time he had to apply for the superintendent's permission to see his mother.

There are countless poignant stories of mothers who attempted all sorts of strategies to hide their children from white authorities. In the Northern Territory, where police seized all lighter-skinned children once they were three or four years old, mothers rubbed children's skins with fat and charred corkwood to disguise their colour; families camped in the bush, out of sight, moving frequently, and always keeping a lookout. They had to disguise the smoke of their fires and surreptitiously collect water after sunset – all to hold on to their own children. Others living in Darwin had the chance to talk to the children at the compound fence, telling them about their skin names, relations and dreamings. Annie Phillips remembered the women's corroborees held for the stolen children; the women only stopped their dancing, which was prohibited by the superintendent, after he fired several shots at them. In New South Wales, mothers swam across the Murray and went into hiding in order to keep and rear their own children.

Aboriginal mothers and fathers were well aware that the taking of Aboriginal children had a long history. Aboriginal children were simply taken by or 'given' to respectable childless couples in the white community. The Aboriginal Protection Board scheme of New South Wales formally operated from around 1910 until the 1960s. Authorities justified the removal of children on the grounds of 'training' for social, moral or material improvement. At the same time government authorities used cheap labour to satisfy demand and lessen the state's upkeep bill. With domestic service becoming increasingly unpopular as an option for white girls in Australia's 'egalitarian' society, Aboriginal children became a sort of child proletariat. In New South Wales alone from 1912 to 1938, 1500 children, mainly girls, were taken under the Aboriginal Protection Board scheme, and many more under the state's Children's Relief scheme. Between 1883 and 1969, approximately 5625 children were taken from their families and controlled by the state in New South Wales alone. After 1936 the status of 'ward' was applied to

Aborigines; this supposed attempt to avoid racist terminology enabled even greater control over children's custody, employment and wages.

Such children had little choice over their employment, and were usually indentured as so-called 'apprentices'; girls were invariably trained as domestics, and boys as farmhands. The protection of apprenticeship legislation was denied them. To avoid losing a mother's labour, employers would adopt out or send Aboriginal children away. Coral Edwards's and Peter Read's *The Lost Children* movingly portrays the heartbreak and personal identity crises that followed such dislocation of families. Women like Margaret Tucker, Monica Clare and Glenyse Ward have written poignant stories about their degrading and cruel work experiences as young domestics. While many suffered from not being given adequate food or were subjected to sexual exploitation, a girl absconding from employment was subject to greater discipline in a home or institution.

In theory, the assimilation policy, at its height in the 1950s, promised opportunities for the whole of Aboriginal society. In contrast earlier policies had often focussed on children on the basis that adults were beyond hope of 'civilisation'. Yet despite new psychological theories stressing the importance of the mother–child bond, during the 1950s, the number of separations did not decrease. Peter Read blamed the assimilation policy:

A baby placed with white parents would obviously be more quickly assimilated than one placed with black parents. So ran official thinking, but more importantly, so also ran the feelings of the majority of honest and conscientious white citizens. The popular image of Aboriginality was a run-down camp, devoid of truly Aboriginal culture, overrun with children and dogs. Drunks, broken windows, dirt, disease.

While this stereotype can now be seen as racist or ethnocentric, white Australians' often unquestioning acceptance of the link between material comfort and happiness during this era meant that the ideal 'comfortable, suburban home' was considered far preferable to the generally poorer living conditions of Aborigines.

Although the assimilation policy was agreed to by the heads of state and territory Aboriginal affairs authorities in 1937, its ideals were not immediately introduced in all states. Rights such as child endowment and the aged pension became available to 'non-nomadic' Aborigines in the 1940s, but in the following years, war matters generally preoccupied governments. The war itself sped up the process of Aboriginal incorporation into the wider society and by 1951 all Australian governments claimed they had adopted a policy of 'assimilating' Aborigines. In 1961 a common definition was adopted:

> The policy of assimilation means that all Aborigines and part-Aborigines are expected eventually to attain the same manner of living as other Australians and to live as members of a single Australian community enjoying the same rights and privileges, accepting the same responsibilities, observing the same customs and influenced by the same beliefs, as other Australians.

This statement implied the eventual disappearance of Aborigines, but it also promised equality.

The policy assumed a monolithic and homogeneous Australia and the possibility of enforcing social change. At a time when the nation had received a huge influx of various European nationals after World War II, the assimilation policy created a nationalistic fiction. By setting up an imagined model of Australia as a community of shared interests and beliefs, it again reinforced Aborigines in their place as 'the other', a people excluded. The assimilation policy offered a chance for Aborigines to 'fit in': the price was that they stop being culturally distinctive, that they learn to conform. White Australians would not have to change at all in their attitudes to Aborigines.

Like earlier policies, assimilation portrayed Aboriginality as a thing of the past, but the thrust had shifted from biology to lifestyle, from skin colour to what was inside people's heads. Oblivious to the cultural bias inherent in the new disciplines of psychology and other social sciences, their proponents promised methods of cultural indoctrination via behaviour modification. The Aboriginal child was classed as 'deprived' of important stages in early development.

On the more positive side, better educational opportunities created the beginnings of an articulate middle class, with talented spokespersons like Charles Perkins. Assimilation policies also sought to improve hygiene and material conditions for Aborigines, and some progress was made towards better health and housing.

More money was indeed spent on Aboriginal affairs but while their bodies became healthier and their population increased, their culture was being attacked. The states made it increasingly difficult for Aborigines to stay in reserve or mission communities, forcing them to obtain special permits to do so. Dispersal of residents endangered both the coherence of Aboriginal communities and their hold over reserve lands. When the Tasmanian islander peoples were offered housing in Launceston during the 1950s, they had to relinquish their previous communities. Despite being starved of funds and suffering a poor muttonbird season, many refused to leave, even for short periods, because they wanted to 'hold on' to the land. In New South Wales, housing and relocation policies were equally disruptive and once housed, Aborigines became subject to restrictions on who could stay and visit. Finding that their white Australian neighbours were reluctant to accept them as equals and because they had to stick by their own people, most defied the rules.

Aborigines who had moved to towns came under increased scrutiny. Aboriginal parents were constantly assessed according to ideal middle-class standards of housekeeping. The fact that most welfare inspectors were male did not help; they usually had mothers or wives who performed the shopping, cleaning, cooking and general housework, and lacked personal experience of the everyday ordeal of cleaning and recleaning after young children, or the stresses of pregnancy and caring for small babies. Yet these inspectors snooped into washbaskets, kitchen and food cupboards, and ticked off on their forms whether children's noses were clean.

Aboriginal women were expected to behave like the idealised images of women portrayed in the advertisements of magazines such as the *Women's Weekly*. White women were scrutinised mainly by people they knew: their husbands, their mothers and neighbours, while Aboriginal women's mothers, relations or neighbours did not necessarily endorse such housekeeping ideals, nor did they always value the 'privacy' offered by the nuclear family model. In addition they often lacked basic material comforts and domestic labour-saving devices.

Assimilation thus made new demands on mothers. Along with the frustrations and isolation of the housewife's role, there was increased pressure to supervise children's schooling, purchase clothing and consumer items, and pay bills. But the state did not regard Aboriginal women as having full rights or freedoms as mothers, and subjected them to special regulations and strict sexual codes of conduct. If parents failed in the eyes of the state, they lost the right to see their children at all. This severed their relationship with their offspring and had traumatic effects on their ability to bond with subsequent children. Aboriginal mothers were blamed for the dislocation; indeed they were blamed for being Aboriginal. Anxiety, depression, confusion and most of all, anger and despair resulted. Yet amidst the many outside intrusions, Aboriginal families struggled to live in their own social worlds, with their own kin support.

The state took on a collective responsibility for Aboriginal children and a more intrusive fathering role if children had 'European blood'. But the state was a callous and authoritarian father. Institutionalisation or a servile status alienated rather than civilised. Children were subject to strict discipline, with homes emphasising rigid controls, confinement, timetables, containment, curbing of the usual childhood freedoms. While this environment would have been stressful to all children, it was particularly so for Aboriginal children due to their different cultural education.

More needs to be known about how Aborigines coped with these impositions. The Aboriginal population rose dramatically from the 1950s; maternal fertility increased so that it was not uncommon for women to have six children. Dietary factors, earlier menstruation and teenage pregnancies resulted in longer childbearing spans. The community's desire to build up their lost numbers, including those who disappeared into state control, must also be taken into account. Aboriginal women often had a series of male partners throughout their adult life, and they considered it socially acceptable to have children by more than one father. Women not uncommonly had children by white men who were casual partners. Poverty and poor health affected the lot of Aboriginal families, and urban people were often under greater pressure to conform than rural Aborigines, especially than those in remote areas, who had a greater chance of holding onto their land, language and cultural knowledge. While Aboriginal men took on the main breadwinning role when work was available, many women worked for wages as well as rearing large families. By the 1950s, as Aboriginal families increasingly moved into urban areas, alcohol consumption by men became more and more common, as did higher rates of imprisonment in state gaols.

Usurpation of their land and poor economic opportunities had a great impact on Aborigines, but it was the Aboriginal family that bore the brunt of the tragedy. The law had 'denied and denuded the basic unit of society ... [and] replaced it with artificial surrogates'. Each member was also humiliated and stripped of human dignity, and this was largely beyond the comprehension of whites. No matter what power struggles occurred between Aboriginal men and women, these paled in comparison with the impact of outside forces on their family and private lives. For Aboriginal people were continually singled out on the basis of their colour. In urban areas they survived through a strong sense of community, but those removed from support structures by institutionalisation – in juvenile centres, police cells or gaols – became vulnerable individuals indeed. By the 1950s some Aborigines, such as Rosalie Kunoth-Monks, co-star of Chauvel's film *Jedda*, had achieved celebrity status. Kunoth-Monks survived to become a conservative politician and to lead Alice Springs protests against alcohol abuse in 1990. Other famous Aborigines like artist Albert Namatjira and actor Robert Tudawali met tragically early deaths, related at least partially to their sufferings due to lack of civil rights and subsequent clashes with the law over alcohol. Tudawali also suffered marital and clan conflicts because of his exposure to the world of film. Aboriginal people who were lent tenuous spaces in white Australian history have much more to teach us about how their marriages and family relationships were affected by their struggles with a pervasive and persistent colonialism.

13 Affirmations of Difference

In August 1963 the Yirrkala people of northern Australia presented a bark petition, written in their language, to the House of Representatives. They wished to make known their opposition to plans by the mining company Nabalco to take over sections of their traditional lands on the Gove Peninsula. A select committee of inquiry was followed by a hearing in the Northern Territory Supreme Court, where, eight years after the original petition had been served, Judge Blackburn found that although the clans had proven a spiritual relationship with the land, this was not compensatable as a property right under Australian law. In August 1966 the Gurindji people walked off Wave Hill pastoral station, leased by the British company Vestey's, in protest at their inadequate pay and conditions of work. In the following year they addressed a petition to the governor-general asking for title to about 1300 square kilometres of their land and occupied part of the station at Daguragu (Wattie Creek), in an attempt to force the government to recognise their land rights.

The unprecedented prosperity of Australian society in the two decades after the war rested on the exploitation of the land. To the wealth deriving from wool, wheat, beef, fruit and dairy exports in the 1950s was added the new income provided by discoveries of oil, iron ore, bauxite and uranium in the 1960s. Following the location of large deposits of iron ore in the Pilbara region of Western Australia, Hammersley Iron negotiated significant contracts to supply Japanese steel mills. Australia continued its tradition of supplying raw materials to other countries that would then export the manufactured commodities back to Australia. The only change was that in these years Japan gradually replaced the United States and Britain as Australia's major trading partner. Increasingly, as mining companies scoured northern Australia for untapped mineral resources, they encroached on traditional but thriving Aboriginal communities.

The land was at the heart of the conflict between Aborigines and Europeans in Australia; for the latter, primary industries were crucial to their colonial role as suppliers of raw materials within the imperial division of labour. But the land was more important to Aboriginal communities. It was not just that they were the prior owners; the land was necessary to the continuation of their culture. As Aboriginal priest Pat Dodson explained to a Catholic conference:

Land is the generation point of existence; it's the spirit from which Aboriginal existence comes. It's a place, a living thing made up of sky, of clouds, of rivers, of trees, of the wind, of the sand, and of the Spirit that has created all those things; the Spirit that has planted my own spirit there, my own country ... It belongs to me; I belong to the land; I rest in it; I come from there.

No longer a priest, Pat Dodson is now the Chairman of the Council for Aboriginal Reconciliation.

These differing attitudes to the land and differing demands made upon it had significant consequences for the country itself. Whereas Aboriginal communities were committed to nurturing and sustaining the earth and the diversity of life on it, British settlers were intent on exploitation and despoliation, forcing it to yield up its riches, absorb their fertilisers and bring forth commercial crops. Animals and plants deemed of no economic use were ruthlessly swept aside. Feminist writers have pointed to the ways that the bush has been represented by white writers as a feminine 'other', imagined as the body of a woman that must be possessed and ravished, as a cruel vengeful mother or an unyielding mistress against which man has to prove himself. They have suggested a connection between the misogyny evident in much Australian culture and the rape of the land. The progressive degradation of the soils, the pollution of rivers and sea and the erosion of wilderness have, however, become major concerns of the environmental movement, comprising women and men, that has burgeoned in all Australian states since the 1960s. Green activists have often drawn inspiration from the Aboriginal relationship with the land, but there have also been tensions around issues such as mining, residence and hunting. The environmentalist emphasis on preservation is often at odds with Aboriginal desires to use the land in old and new ways.

White authorities initially replied to Aboriginal claims for the return of their land by insisting that Aborigines individually buy parcels of it. Some groups and individuals have become fully integrated into the capitalist economy. Others have adopted different approaches. Assimilationist aims to introduce European modes of living were seen as an attack on Aboriginal culture, with its distinctive relationship to country and community. The land was their communal heritage. Assimilation moreover had proven a mockery: Aboriginal people were conspicuous in their poverty, unemployment, ill health, substandard housing and excessively high mortality levels. Many concluded that it was time they began to rebuild their culture in their own way, on their own terms.

Thus Faith Bandler, when vice-president of the Federal Council for the Advancement of Aborigines and Torres Strait Islanders in the late 1960s, questioned the use of the term 'advancement'. 'I am rather sorry', she said, 'that it has been used in various committees established to assist the Aboriginal people. I am not convinced that it is advancement for the indigenous Australians to become like the European Australians'.

Aboriginal actions and arguments began to have political effect. In 1967 a referendum to include Aboriginal people in the census and give the commonwealth government power to legislate on their behalf was overwhelmingly endorsed by the Australian people. For the first time since their dispossession Aboriginal people were recognised as part of the Australian nation. The first Minister for Aboriginal Affairs was appointed: a new start seemed possible.

The retirement of Sir Robert Menzies as prime minister in 1966, the departure of the 'patriarch', was symbolic. 'Old-fashioned' Menzies and wife Dame Pattie were replaced by the 'with-it swinger' Harold Holt and effervescent Zara. The following year Arthur Calwell, characterised by Donald Horne in *The Lucky Country* as 'antediluvian – some relic of early man', was replaced as leader of the ALP by the up-to-date Gough Whitlam. Convention and security had become suffocating; youth demanded its day.

Ironically, Menzies's commitment to education had produced a large population of university students, often schooled in the critique of the new social sciences and whose affluence and idealism made them ready and eager to overthrow the old order associated with Menzies and Calwell. Across the country the old concern to preserve the status quo, to conserve uniformity, to safeguard the Australian way of life and the family home from subversion was giving way to demands for change. Freedom took on a new meaning and acquired a new look: short skirts, long hair, unisex, kaftans and beads, demonstrations and marches.

Opposition to Australia's engagement in the Vietnam War in the late 1960s provided a focus for people's radical political engagement. American attempts to defeat the Vietnamese national liberation movement, and the Australian Government's involvement with the system of conscription by lottery – the whole 'industrial-military' complex – were attacked at demonstrations, sit-ins and teach-ins. Sons were joined by their mothers in campaigns against conscription and the war. Those evading the call-up went into hiding. Some were gaoled. Hundreds of thousands of people marched in the streets seeking a moratorium, an end to Australia's involvement in the 'unjust' war. One of the most authoritative leaders to emerge in the anti-war movement was Jim Cairns, the future deputy leader of the Labor Party and a long-standing advocate of more constructive relations with Asian countries.

Armed with a university education and the pill, many young women determined to escape from the orbit of their mothers and follow in the steps of their brothers. With their fellow students, in organisations such as Students for a Democratic Society, they fashioned their identity around their youth. Domesticity and the family were identified as oppressive and stifling. Young women expected to enjoy sexual, economic and political freedoms – just like men. The 'permissive sixties' saw women separate sex from reproduction in the same way men did. Women campaigned for and won reforms in abortion law. The experience of sexual freedom was one condition for the emergence of women's liberation. Heterosexual women were outraged by the realisation that in sexual relations with men they were invariably positioned as 'sex objects' – that in magazines, pornography, films, advertising and, significantly, beauty contests – women were scrutinised by the male gaze. It was in sexual relations with men that many young women first felt their inequality and powerlessness. On the other hand the emphasis on freedom of sexual expression and identity in the 1950s and 1960s ultimately enabled lesbian women to define an alternative female identity, independent of relations with men. The critique of sex roles and the family that was characteristic of the early phases of women's liberation owed much to lesbian women, who saw clearly the relationship between women's oppression and heterosexuality, with its definitions of femininity and masculinity as dichotomous and complementary 'roles'.

Women's liberation, at one level, was a generational rebellion, a rejection of mothers and maternity. At another level it was an effect of women's new economic position and aspirations. When students looked beyond the privileged world of the university they began to identify with broader political struggles – especially the campaign for equal pay – being waged by women in the trade unions. The participation of women, especially married women, in the paid workforce increased rapidly as the economy diversified and office and service work expanded during the 1960s; barriers to women's employment, such as the bar on married women's employment in the Commonwealth Public Service, were dismantled as employers and politicians wooed women into paid work. Between 1966 and 1986 the proportion of women in the paid workforce increased from 40.9 to 47.6 per cent and would climb to over 50 per cent by the next decade. In 1967 a women's bureau was created within the federal Department of Labour and National Service.

As paid work became an ever more normal and permanent aspect of life for women, so their inferior pay rates seemed increasingly intolerable. Campaigns were waged by groups as diverse as teachers, clerical workers and meat industry workers. Women's organisations such as the Union of Australian Women, the Federation of University Women and the Federation of Women Voters presented submissions to the arbitration court. Trade union activist Zelda D'Aprano drew attention both to women's unequal pay and the long tradition of feminist protest by chaining herself to the Commonwealth Building in Melbourne in October 1969. The bright young men then making their careers in the Labor Party argued that the male family wage was an anachronism; women were breadwinners too. On behalf of the meat workers, R. J. Hawke submitted that the difference in men's and women's wages was a relic of assumptions and conceptions that existed at the beginning of this century. Appearing for the Federated Clerks' Union in New South Wales a few years later, Neville Wran QC, future premier, stated: 'No longer is the social and industrial climate one in which it can be said that women's place is in the home, our society is now geared to a participation of women at all levels'. Responding to women's needs as paid workers, the Liberal government, now led by John Gorton, announced in 1970 that the commonwealth government would henceforth subsidise child care centres. Spurred on by interventions from the medical profession, a spirited public debate ensued around the issue of 'maternal deprivation' and the proper place of mothers and children. Women in paid work became politically active in campaigns for child care, the first demonstration in Melbourne taking place in February 1972. The Liberal government proceeded with a Child Care Act in that year, but the conservatives were generally in retreat.

Maternal deprivation had a different meaning for Aboriginal people. Subject to the systematic removal of children from their mothers by the state throughout the century, many Aboriginal families were only just beginning to reunite. Their experience generated different political priorities, policies addressed to the recovery of their families and communities, and the re-establishment of their bonds with each other and with the land. Following the persistent refusal by the conservative government to treat land rights seriously and suggestions that it was all a Communist plot, Aboriginal people established a tent embassy on the lawns in front of Parliament House in 1972 to signify their status as a dispossessed and unrepresented nation within a nation. Attempts to remove their camp by force attracted embarrassing publicity for the federal Liberal government. The leader of the Labor opposition, Gough Whitlam, visited the embassy and made known his party's sympathy with Aboriginal claims, guaranteeing land rights and recognition of sacred sites. The Labor Party pledged to restore self-determination to the Aboriginal people.

Everywhere people were calling for change. In the 1969 election Labor came close to winning government. Unsettled by near defeat and internal dissension, the Liberal Party replaced the unconventional John Gorton with the uninspiring William McMahon. The

Labor Party looked confidently to the next election and prepared to persuade the electorate that at last it was time. On a wide range of issues Labor promised a decisive break with the past. Following the visits to China by, first, Whitlam and then United States President Nixon, the ALP argued for official diplomatic recognition of China, a major customer for Australian wheat. Labor also promised to end conscription and Australian involvement in the Vietnam War, and offered new deals to cities, schools, universities, women, migrants and Aborigines. In the weeks preceding the election the newly formed Women's Electoral Lobby conducted a survey of candidates' attitudes to issues of importance to women in Australia: equal pay, equal opportunity in employment and education, free contraception, abortion on demand and free 24-hour child care. A number of Labor candidates, notably Gough Whitlam himself, scored highest; some Liberal, Country Party and DLP respondents distinguished themselves as the most reactionary.

As Labor was becoming more responsive to feminist demands on issues such as child care, women's right to work and equal pay, so women, especially young educated 'working' women, were beginning to swing their support to the party. Beneficiaries of the economic boom of the 1960s, women filling jobs in the professions, in offices and universities acquired a new public identity and a new sense of themselves, a shift in subjectivity with significant long-term political consequences. Women's flight from domesticity was a key factor in the election of Labor. As with women, so with students. Research conducted for the conservative government in 1972 confirmed the 'isolation of the Liberal Party from the universities and other groups in the community at the cutting edge of social change and development'. In numerous ways the conservative government of the 1960s produced the conditions of its own downfall.

The election of the Whitlam Labor government was followed by further political and social change. Conscription and Australian participation in the Vietnam War came to an abrupt end. Gaoled draft resisters were freed and prosecutions against others were dropped. The 'luxury' tax on contraceptives was lifted. The government successfully intervened to have the equal pay case before the arbitration court re-opened and put a case supporting the outcome of equal pay for work of equal value. Negotiations paved the way for the appointment of academic Stephen FitzGerald as Australia's first ambassador to Beijing. The granting of mining leases on Aboriginal reserves was immediately suspended. A Department of Aboriginal Affairs was created and a National Aboriginal Consultative Committee appointed. Government expenditure on Aboriginal affairs increased substantially, but so did tensions over Aboriginal self-determination. Increasingly Aborigines resisted white control over their lives. With the advent of Labor, the White Australia Policy was officially ended and racially selected sports teams were banned from entering Australia.

Spending on welfare, education, child care and the arts increased dramatically. In addition, the improved pay and conditions of public servants – a 35-hour week, equal pay, paid maternity leave – made them pacesetters for other groups of workers. In 1973 legislation provided state income for sole supporting parents. The Australian Pre-Schools Committee was established to administer the 5 million dollar allocation to child care. In 1975 a Family Law Act was passed that removed the concept of fault from divorce proceedings and instituted more equitable arrangements for the settlement of custody and the distribution of property and maintenance. As was their custom, Australian feminists looked to the state to improve women's status and conditions. Government appointments created a group of 'femocrats', feminists enticed into the bureaucracy by the prospect of effecting major social change. Elizabeth Reid was appointed in 1973 as the first Adviser on Women's Affairs to the prime minister, succeeded by Anne Summers and Sara Dowse. Government largesse financed projects as diverse as women's refuges, rape crisis centres, a research project on women's history and in 1975 International Women's Year. In the states, women's demands for equal access to jobs and income led to the passage of anti-discrimination legislation and later the adoption of equal opportunity and affirmative action policies. In 1975 South Australia passed the Sex Discrimination Act and New South Wales and Victoria followed in 1977.

New gains generated fresh insights. As middle-class educated women consolidated their position in the workforce, they began to recognise that paid work, like other areas of public life, was organised on men's terms. The assumptions of national political economy worked against women. The worker was assumed to be male:

independent, autonomous, free from domestic responsibilities. Women began to realise that the ideal of independence rested on men's unspoken dependence on mothers, wives and secretaries. Women juggling paid work with the need to care for children began to demand that the organisation of work take account of the realities of human interdependence. In 1979 the ACTU, activated by the demands of women workers, established the right of all women in the workforce to maternity leave, a right yet to be enjoyed in practice by the vast majority of women.

Labor's campaign to win office had led to the identification, indeed the constitution, of key constituencies: the 'women's vote', the 'Aboriginal vote' and the 'migrant vote'. The 1972 election and its aftermath encouraged the translation of a personal identity into a political mobilisation. 'Disadvantage' was transformed into 'difference'. Migrant welfare groups, established in the 1960s, were drawn into the political process. The new Labor Minister for Immigration, Al Grassby, became famous for his celebrations of ethnic difference as well as his colourful clothes. In 1973 in a speech entitled 'A multi-cultural society for the future' he explicitly rejected the policy of assimilation. Within a few years 'ethnic groups' had transformed into 'communities' and multiculturalism was adopted as official policy enjoying bipartisan political support. But the meaning of multiculturalism, its possibilities and limitations, would be a matter of continuing argument. In these political processes many migrant women felt silenced by the predominantly male leadership of ethnic organisations, as well as by the Anglo-Celtic domination of the women's movement. This sense of exclusion spurred many non-English-speaking women to form separate organisations and provide separate services to women from non-English-speaking backgrounds. The Australian Migrant Women's Association and the Women's Group of the Federazione Italiana Lavoratori Emigrati e Famiglie (FILEF) provided networks of support and distributed multilingual material on issues such as childcare, outwork, trade unions and sexual harassment. Second generation women from ethnic minority backgrounds have in turn become key figures in the debate about a multicultural identity for Australia in the 1980s and 1990s.

The pace of change in the 1970s was exhilarating to some, threatening to others. Radical economic reforms – such as the plan to establish a national health scheme, Medibank – provoked, as ever, the vested interest of the medical profession to mobilise resistance and sow the seeds of fear and anxiety. In federal parliament the conservative opposition, floundering under the ineffectual leadership of Billy Snedden, resolved in 1974 to block supply. A double dissolution followed and the Whitlam Labor government was again returned to office – but their real power was effectively limited by their lack of a majority in the Senate. Economic conditions worsened as Australia settled into the long recession that followed the long boom. The remedial strategy of tariff cuts only added to unemployment. The Whitlam government seemed prone to crisis. Swelling government deficits led to cost-cutting budgets. A series of ministerial embarrassments culminated in the media construction of the 'loans affair' and the Labor government fell into disarray. The efforts of the Minister for Energy and Resources, Rex Connor, to raise loans in the oil-rich Middle East to finance his vision of Australian-owned resources and industry provoked a frenzy of condemnation that focussed on the foreign figure of Tirath Khemlani. The alien 'Arab' became a symbol of the illegitimacy of the Labor government. Deputy Prime Minister Jim Cairns's association with Junie Morosi, an attractive woman of Asian descent, was another. The impression of Labor's unfitness to govern was confirmed by the dismissal, the governor-general's extraordinary decision to sack the prime minister in November 1975.

Although the conservative Fraser government elected following the Dismissal sought in many ways to dismantle the reformist economic and social structures set in place by the Labor government, it encouraged the proliferation of ethnic, cultural and racial diversity. A variety of multicultural programs was promoted, the Australian Institute of Multicultural Affairs was established in 1980 and the government presided over the advent of large-scale immigration from Southeast Asia. Thousands of Cambodian and Vietnamese refugees took their place in the industrial workforce and the unemployment statistics.

During the 1970s Aborigines became more forthright in their demands for recognition of their rights as the original inhabitants of Australia, for recognition of their sovereignty. Activists such as Pat O'Shane, Gary Foley, Cheryl Buchanan and Roberta Sykes organised land rights campaigns. The most comprehensive land rights, which included sea and mineral rights, were introduced in the Northern Territory in 1976 – following the passage of commonwealth legislation, first introduced by the Whitlam government – and were able to be claimed on the basis of 'traditional ownership'. Here at last was some recognition of Aborigines' prior ownership of the land. Land Councils were set up as representative organisations, but being initiated by white male bureaucrats, they institutionalised the idea that this was men's business. In New South Wales, South Australia and Victoria, women played more crucial roles in land rights negotiations, often dominating the work at the grassroots level. Because of the masculine structures of white government and bureaucracy, most projects involving Aboriginal people have entrenched men's power at women's expense. Yet Aboriginal women know their own strength and power and work separately and with their men to overcome the effects of colonisation and ongoing racism. Their initiative has been evident in the numerous health, welfare and legal services set up by and for Aboriginal communities. In New South Wales, for example, Shirley Smith was a leading organiser of the Aboriginal Health Service. In Alice Springs, Freda Glynn has been a central figure in establishing the local media network. Women's authority has enabled them to take a leading role in the movement against alcohol in the Aboriginal community. Aboriginal women's confidence in the power of women and their organisational independence have in turn inspired white women interested in attaining autonomy.

Aboriginal women have also insisted that white women recognise their different priorities. As Pat O'Shane argued in the late 1970s, the aims of white women are not necessarily those of black women. She suggested that 'whereas for the majority of women involved in the women's movement, sexism is what the great fight is all about, for Aboriginal women – when they look at all the medical, housing, education, employment and legal statistics – it becomes very clear that our major fight is against racism'. In 1981, when the national unemployment rate was 5.9 per cent, the rate for Aborigines and Torres Strait Islanders was 24.6 per cent.

During the 1980s, Australians witnessed the self-aggrandisement of a wealthy few and the growing poverty of the many. New class divisions also opened up between women, as educated middle-class professionals and those aspiring to middle management took advantage of the favourable climate established by affirmative action legislation, while the majority of women workers remained segregated in low paid, insecure jobs in factories, offices and homes. The latter often worked at providing personal services for the former – and for men. By 1988 women comprised 58 per cent of the workforce in recreation, personnel and other services, 65 per cent in community services and 50 per cent of finance, property and business services. Aboriginal and some migrant women, as well as sole parents who were also sole breadwinners, were especially disadvantaged. A movement for the liberation of all women seemed to be securing the individual advancement of a few. Women still performed the bulk of domestic work and caring, the labour of love. The very success of the liberal feminist measures enshrined in equal opportunity and affirmative action legislation highlighted their limitations in dealing with the entrenched sexual division of labour on which the organisation of paid work is premised. Nor could such programs remedy class, ethnic and racial inequalities.

The new Labor government, led by Prime Minister Bob Hawke, who came to office in 1983, attempted to pursue a commitment to social reform while inaugurating an era of financial deregulation. Special attention was paid to the increasingly powerful 'green vote' and to the demands of feminists, who were becoming more vociferous within the Labor Party. Before the 1970s most successful women parliamentary candidates had represented the conservative parties. By the 1980s, Labor Party women had made substantial new gains. In 1989 there were 53 Labor Party women MPs in Australian parliaments compared with 21 Liberal and nine National Party women representatives. Many of the Labor women, including Susan Ryan, who was appointed Minister for Education and Minister assisting the Prime Minister on the Status of Women, and Senator Margaret Reynolds, who succeeded her in the latter portfolio, had been active members of the Women's Electoral Lobby. By the early 1990s, two Labor women had been elected premiers of their states, Carmen Lawrence in Western Australia and Joan Kirner in Victoria. But although women politicians had become suddenly prominent, their numbers were still disproportionately low – only 11.7 per cent of the members of all Australian parliaments in 1989.

Women's citizenship was circumscribed – no longer seeking or awarded the status of citizen mothers, Australian women still found the achievement of citizenship on the same basis as men elusive. Denied equal participation in political representation and in the defence forces (though integrated in the air force, army and navy, women are still excluded from specified combat duties), they occupied a different and subordinate position in relationship to the nation state. Majority rule has yet to be achieved. Women are still considered to be represented and protected by men, their capacities for self-government and self-defence unrealised as they wage daily battles with male violence and a legal system that institutionalises male interests.

In 1984 the Hawke government initiated reforms to address women's continuing inequality, passing the Sex Discrimination Act, which prohibited direct and indirect discrimination on the grounds of sex, marital status or pregnancy in employment, education and the provision of services. It also made sexual harassment unlawful in employment and education.

In 1986, affirmative action legislation was passed by the government, requiring companies and tertiary education institutions to remove the barriers to women's equal participation in the workforce. But worship of the market – that fickle, anxious, nervous god – gradually eclipsed visions of a fair society and dominated public discourse about the 'national interest'. A promise to legislate for Aboriginal land rights on a national basis was discarded by Prime Minister Hawke in response to pressure from Western Australian Labor interests and mining companies.

The logic of the old imperial division of labour in which Australia was nurtured took its course in the 1980s. As in the 1920s, overseas debts spiralled; export income lagged. Dependence on primary products for all our export income appeared to be somewhat foolhardy. The treasurer, Paul Keating, attempted to jolt Australians into recognition of our condition by warning that unless we changed our economic orientation, we would soon be a 'banana republic'. Reliance on wool rather than bananas for our export income did not make us inherently superior or economically secure. Cast as the suppliers of raw materials in our colonial relationship with Britain, then the United States, then Japan, Australians had been discouraged from developing local manufacturing as an export industry. High tariffs applied indiscriminately in the past had not only allowed a drift into costly inefficiency, but led ultimately to the foreign ownership of manufacturing as overseas companies, searching for new markets, sought to escape the barrier of tariffs by setting up business inside Australia. We now have the highest levels of overseas ownership of all developed countries with the exception of Canada. When the recession proved that it was no longer advantageous to remain here, companies under orders from abroad closed down factories, such as the GMH plant at Pagewood in New South Wales in 1980, and the Nissan plant in Victoria in 1992, throwing thousands out of work.

During the last twenty-five years Japan has been Australia's major trading partner. Australia has become increasingly oriented to Asia in other ways as well. An increasing proportion of migrants, refugees and tourists come from Asian countries and some families have adopted children from countries such as Korea. Australians are adjusting with some difficulty to a sense of themselves as part of the Asia–Pacific region, coming to terms with unfamiliar cultures, values and languages.

The cure for Australia's malaise favoured by economic ideologues of the 1980s, lured by the peculiarly mesmerising and arid image of the 'level playing field', was financial and industrial deregulation, the complete abolition of tariff protection and the 'freeing up' of labour. The treatment exacerbated the illness. Factories closed or moved offshore, pursuing, like the growing band of white male 'sex tourists' in Southeast Asia, the dream of cheaper and more docile labour than that available in Australia. The workforce in the textiles, clothing and footwear industries – important employers of migrant women – were slashed. Between 1973 and 1980, 46 000 jobs were lost in clothing and textiles, while imports of these goods increased rapidly. The car industry has also 'shed' thousands of workers. The decline of car manufacturing in Australia has particular implications for male workers, who make up 73 per cent of the industry's workforce. While trade unions promoted the restructuring of awards and work to provide more rewarding careers for employees, employers were restructuring work in other ways, contracting tasks overseas, maximising outwork at home, increasing part-time and casual work. Their profit-making motive coincides with the interests of significant groups in the workforce – mothers and tertiary students, for example – who often want to work fewer or irregular hours, a shorter week or a shorter year.

The restructuring of the labour market has been accompanied by a restructuring of domestic relationships. The old nuclear family of breadwinning father, stay-at-home mother and two children has become a small minority. More families depend on the combined earnings of both parents – and older children, when jobs are available. More likely to be cared for by women other than their mothers when young than twenty years ago, children nevertheless remain at least partly dependent on their parents for longer periods as they prolong their education. Many families struggle to survive on a lone mother's income. Women are more able to live apart from men, but they are more likely than men to live in poverty. As the high incidence of divorce makes marriage less permanent, more people are opting for cohabitation instead of marriage. Ex-nuptial births have increased so that by 1988 they constituted almost 20 per cent of all Australian births. Households fragment, re-form, blend and diversify. Lesbian and homosexual households have become more popular. While many women eschew motherhood as a too costly option, the desperate maternal desire of others leads to IVF procedures and surrogacy. The production of babies is now more than ever the business of medical scientists as well as of women. Men's appropriation of birth, once metaphorical, becomes ever more actual.

In 1988 women comprised 78.8 per cent of the part-time workforce and part-time jobs were increasing in number faster than full-time ones. Having ignored women's responsibility for domestic work and the care of families for too long, the trade union movement now seeks to recognise and incorporate women's experience and concerns into strategies aimed at improving the conditions of part-time work and curbing the rapid decline in trade union membership. Feminists in the labour movement seek ways to achieve a balance in all working people's lives – enabling men and women to share the unpaid work of caring for families as well as the paid work of shop or office. In 1990 the ACTU resolved to recommend a year's unpaid paternity leave as a right for all male workers: women's successful integration into the workforce required men's integration into child care. Neither maternity nor paternity leave, however, has been enshrined in legislation.

A redistribution of work is also one answer to the ever widening discrepancy between the lives of the unemployed and the employed, who in many sectors are working longer hours, not fewer. Social commentators have again begun to advocate a more equitable sharing of the available work as a basis of a fairer society. Australia, once a leader in fashioning a welfare state – however limited – now lags behind most European countries. Unlike Australia, many of these countries have made paid parental leave and sick child care leave mandatory, while Italian feminists seek to establish the 'right to care' as a national right.

In 1988, two centuries after the British arrival in New South Wales, Australians were invited to participate in the 'celebration of a nation'. There were eager participants and a host of beneficiaries, but many expressed doubts about the meaning of this public event. Depressed by the economic outlook, anxious about the future, cynical about political pomp and pretence, guilty about the national history of white supremacy and the dispossession of the Aboriginal people, many declined to join in the festivities or did so with ambivalence. One event that was marked by conviction, joy and solidarity, however, was the Australia Day march of Aborigines and their supporters, led by Galarrwuy Yunupingu, head of the Northern Land Council, from Redfern Oval to Hyde Park, which became a celebration of their people's survival. 'We hope to establish a future for Australia, and that future is very simple and clear', said Yunupingu, 'white Australia together with Aboriginal, and then we are all Australians'. It was also an occasion to formulate future goals. Since the 1970s Aboriginal and non-Aboriginal Australians have been campaigning for a treaty that recognises that a negotiated peace must occur between Aborigines and the representatives of those who invaded their lands. In 1988 at the Barunga festival in the Northern Territory, Yunupingu presented Prime Minister Hawke with the Barunga Statement, a declaration of Aboriginal claims. The prime minister, in turn, pledged that a treaty would be signed by 1990, a promise that remains unfulfilled. To promote Aboriginal self-determination, the Labor government gave the administration of their affairs to a new body, the Aboriginal and Torres Strait Islander Commission (ATSIC), established in 1989 and chaired by Lois O'Donoghue. There is considerable disagreement over the extent to which it simply serves the white system, but many Aborigines are intent on using it as a vehicle for the ultimate achievement of self-government.

As Australians take on the challenge of reshaping our nation state in the decade leading up to the centennial of our commonwealth, we can learn much from the first Australians in their respect for life and the land, their restraint and generosity and their insistence on equality in difference and cohesion in diversity. We must also learn to come to terms with our shared past. The investigations of the Royal Commission into Aboriginal Deaths in Custody, whose report was published in 1991, gave much publicity to the history of racist oppression that was the background to the series of black deaths in prisons, police stations and other places of detention. The reports emphasised that the solution to the continuing oppression lay in the hearts and minds of all Australians. The recent Mabo case, in which the High Court overturned the concept of Australia as *terra nullius* by recognising 'native title' to Australian lands, opens the way for compensation claims by dispossessed Aboriginal Australians and thus some limited resolution to the problem of a nation built on theft.

During the 1980s, the per capita income of Australians declined in comparative terms. Furthermore, the gap between the few rich and the many poor widened, with a growing proportion of people slipping into poverty. The entry of mothers and wives into paid work, once fought for as a right, became for most families an economic necessity. While one effect of the long recession has been to exacerbate class differences between women and between men, another has been to render some people endlessly idle, while others suffer from overwork. Studies show that, contrary to myth, employed Australians work longer hours than most of their European counterparts and women in particular, who combine paid work with unpaid domestic labour and go without leisure, are stretched and stressed. Forty per cent of men and women in the workforce have young children to care for. However, while Australian average income has declined relative to that in comparable countries, the distribution of income between men and women seems to be changing for the better. Australian women in full-time jobs now earn 85 cents for every male dollar, still a way short of equal pay, but a much higher proportion than women earn in the United States – around 65 cents – for example. The different patterns suggest the importance of a centralised award system for women and the dangers in the moves towards the 'freeing up' of the labour market.

The severity of the current recession, combined with a postmodern loss of faith in grand political projects, has stifled movements for reform. Feminist calls to employers to restructure the working day and provide family leave in recognition of the human needs of their workers, socialist plans for the restructuring of the work process, Aboriginal campaigns for land rights and self-determination and environmentalist efforts to protect the natural world from further despoliation are all deemed unaffordable in hard times. When hundreds of thousands are out of work, the restructuring of work is cast as a luxury. Yet it is possible that a redistribution of work, a sharing of paid and unpaid work, together with a more equitable distribution of national income would not only reduce unemployment, but also lead to more balanced relationships between women and men, Aborigines, Asians and Europeans, the land and the people. In the reconstruction of the nation that will proceed in the last years of this century, it is to be hoped that political movements can be rekindled to challenge the prevailing narrow economic paradigm of the national interest and allow for the renewal of Australia as a just, fair and heterogeneous society. The other major challenge of the years leading up to 2001 is to reconcile the imperative towards uniformity inherent in the fashioning of a republican nation state with a recognition of the diversity and even incommensurability of the claims emanating from people of different gender, and ethnic, racial, sexual and regional backgrounds. The challenge is to find ways of making the self-government promised by a republic a reality for groups such as Aborigines, women and ethnic minorities, whose lives until now have been largely ruled by white men of British descent. Those who comprise the nation should share equally in its government.

Endnotes

1 BIRTHPLACES

8 Collins's quote comes from D. Collins (ed. B. H. Fletcher), *An Account of the English Colony in New South Wales*, 2 vols, London, 1798, 1802 (Royal Australian Historical Society & Reed Books, Sydney, 1975), p. 464.

10 Hunter's statement comes from J. Hunter, *A Historical Journal of Transactions at Port Jackson and Norfolk Island*, Angus & Robertson, London, 1968 (1793), p. 360.

Tench's comment is in W. Tench, 'A narrative of the expedition to Botany Bay', 1789, in W. Tench, *Sydney's First Four Years*, Angus & Robertson, Sydney, 1961, p. 184.

Quote regarding Barangaroo's intentions and Phillip's reaction is from Hunter, *A Historical Journal*, p. 360.

13 Kate Langloh Parker's explanation is cited in A. Montagu, *Coming into Being Among the Australian Aborigines*, Routledge & Kegan Paul, London, 1974, pp. 219–21.

14 The painting referred to is reproduced as Plate 20, Watling 48, in R. Lampert, 'Aboriginal life around Port Jackson, 1788–92', in B. Smith & A. Wheeler (eds), *The Art of the First Fleet*, Oxford University Press, Melbourne, 1988.

The Aboriginal words come from Collins, *An Account of the English Colony*, Appendix, p. 509.

16–17 The comment on the boys' ceremonies is from Collins, p. 477.

19 The description of family life is from Collins, p. 493.

22 The reference to the Aboriginal women's behaviour in the presence of the British comes from Collins, p. 464.

The Bradley quotes are from W. Bradley, *A Voyage to New South Wales*, Trustees of Public Library of NSW & Ure Smith, Sydney, 1969, p. 59; also cited in G. Williams & A. Frost, 'New South Wales: expectations and reality', in G. Williams

& A. Frost (eds), *Terra Australis to Australia*, Oxford University Press, Melbourne, 1988, p. 180.

23 Southwell's comments are from D. Southwell to Mrs J. Southwell, Southwell Papers, *Historical Records of New South Wales (HRNSW)*, 2, p. 691.

For the reference to the meat shortage, see D. Southwell to Rev. Butler, 14 April 1790, Southwell Papers, *HRNSW*, 2, p. 707.

2 CONCEIVING A COLONY

27 Matra's proposal has been published in the *Historical Records of New South Wales (HRNSW)*, 1, 2, and in G. Martin, *The Founding of Australia*, Hale & Iremonger, Sydney, 1978.

29 For the *Mercury* mutiny see the biography of Charles Peat in J. Cobley, *The Crimes of the First Fleet Convicts*, Angus & Robertson, Sydney, 1970.

30 The government document reporting these decisions is published in *HRNSW*, 1, 2, and in Martin, *The Founding of Australia*.

30–1 'R.H.''s letter is in the Brabourne Papers, 3, Mitchell Library.

31 Phillip's 'Blueprint' for his colony, dated February 1787, is published in J. King, *In the Beginning: The Story of the Creation of Australia from the Original Documents*, Macmillan, Melbourne, 1985. His hopes for the island women are included in 'Comments upon his Instructions', published in O. Rutter, *The First Fleet*, Golden Cockerel Press, London, 1937.

Phillip's Commissions and Instructions are published in *Historical Records of Australia (HRA)*, 1.

31–2 M. Roe, *Quest for Authority in Eastern Australia 1835–1851*, Melbourne University Press, Melbourne, 1965, p. 6, condemns the 'brute force', and A. Summers, *Damned Whores and God's Police*, Penguin Books, Ringwood, 1975, p. 270, the 'imperial whoremaster'.

32 The diary of Lieutenant Ralph Clark (Mitchell Library, C 219) describes the embarkation of the convicts in irons.

32–3 The story of Holmes and Kable is told in 'Narrative relating to a convict ordered to be transported to Botany Bay', published in *Scots Magazine*, 48, November 1786, republished in *The Push from the Bush*, 17 April 1984.

33 Clark's diary 18 May 1787 describes the 'abandoned women'.

34 The voyage of the *Lady Penrhyn* is described in P. J. Fidlon & R. J. Ryan (eds), *The Journal of Arthur Bowes Smyth*, Australian Documents Library, Sydney, 1979.

35 Bowes's journal, 6–7 February 1788, describes the landing of the women.

Endnotes

C. M. H. Clark, *A History of Australia*, 1, Melbourne University Press, Melbourne, 1977, p. 88, proposes the orgy, and R. Hughes, *The Fatal Shore*, Collins, London, 1987, pp. 88–9, celebrates it as 'the first bush party in Australia'.

36–45 My description of the day to day life of the colony is reconstructed from the accounts in J. Cobley, *Sydney Cove 1788, 1789–1790, 1791–1792* and *1793–1795*, Angus & Robertson, Sydney, 1980, 1980, 1983 and 1985.

36–7 Phillip's dispatch to the home government, 15 May 1788, is published in *HRA*, 1, 2.

37 Biographical details of these convicts' lives are taken from Cobley, *The Crimes of the First Fleet Convicts*.

37–8 The trial of Rope and Price, 2 June 1788, is at 5/1147, Archives Office of New South Wales, Minutes of the Proceedings of the Court of Criminal Jurisdiction.

38 The invaders wrote extensively about the Aborigines in their diaries and journals. This evidence is gathered from Cobley, *Sydney Cove 1788*, and from K. Willey, *When the Sky Fell Down*, Collins, Sydney, 1979.

39 N. G. Butlin, *Our Original Aggression*, Allen & Unwin, Sydney, 1983, gives the most recent discussion of the course and the effects of the smallpox epidemics.

Phillip describes Bloodsworth's emancipation in a dispatch of 5 October 1791, *HRNSW*, 1, 2.

40 For these various escape routes see W. Tench, *A Complete Account of the Settlement at Port Jackson*, Library of Australian History, Sydney, 1979 (London, 1793), pp. 243–7, and D. Collins, *An Account of the English Colony in New South Wales*, 2 vols, London, 1798, 1802 (Royal Australian Historical Society, Sydney, 1975), pp. 186–7.

Ruse told Tench his story in November 1790: Tench, *A Complete Account*, p. 197.

40–1 The land grants are described in J. F. Campbell, 'The dawn of rural settlement in Australia', *Journal of the Royal Australian Historical Society (RAHS)*, 11, 2, 1925. Tench visited the settlers in December 1790, Richard Atkins in May 1792.

41 Phillip commented on the settlers in his dispatch on 19 March 1792, *HRNSW*, 1, 2.

42 William Nicol, quoted in Cobley, *1789–1790*, p. 250, was among those who marvelled at the old convict mother.

43–4 H. King, *Elizabeth Macarthur and her World*, Sydney University Press, Sydney, 1980, p. 8, describes these early ventures.

44 See S. Macarthur Onslow, *Some Early Records of the Macarthurs of Camden*, Angus & Robertson, Sydney, 1914 (Rigby, Adelaide 1973), and H. Heney (ed.), *Dear*

Fanny: Women's Letters to and from New South Wales 1788–1857, Australian University Press, Canberra, 1985, for Elizabeth Macarthur's letters.

44–5 For details of the settlers' successes and failures, see B. Fletcher, 'The development of small scale farming in New South Wales under Governor Hunter', *RAHS*, 50, 1 June 1964.

45 Marsden's complaint is in Cobley, *Sydney Cove 1793–1795*, January 1793; Burn's petition in Cobley, *1791–1792*, November 1792.

46 Collins was the official who judged the Burns: Collins, *An Account of the English Colony*, pp. 392–3.

Mrs Paterson's letter is published in Heney (ed.), *Dear Fanny*, pp. 17–18.

For primary accounts of the Castle Hill revolt see the *Sydney Gazette*, 11 March 1804, and King to Hobart, 12 March 1804, *Historical Records of Australia (HRA)*, 1, 4.

47 A. G. L. Shaw, 'Labour', in G. J. Abbott & N. B. Nairn, *Economic Growth of Australia 1788–1821*, Melbourne University Press, Melbourne, 1969, pp. 109–11, gives numbers employed and wage levels.

48 For the careers of Kable, Underwood and Lord see the *Australian Dictionary of Biography*, 1, 2, Melbourne University Press, Melbourne, 1966, 1977, and D. R. Hainsworth, *The Sydney Traders*, Cassell Australia, Melbourne, (1972).

49 *HRNSW*, 5, 14 August 1804, King to Banks.

49–50 King's comments are in *HRNSW*, 6, 12 August 1806.

50 Catchpole's letters are in Heney (ed.), *Dear Fanny*: see especially pp. 14, 24, 48.

Bird's biography and letter are in Heney, pp. 16–17.

51 G. M. Dow, *Samuel Terry: The Botany Bay Rothschild*, Sydney University Press, Sydney, 1974, p. 47.

Marsden's Female Register is discussed in P. Robinson, *The Hatch and Brood of Time*, Oxford University Press, Melbourne, 1985; see also Marsden to Cook, 21 November 1807, *HRNSW*, 6, p. 380ff.

51–2 King's dispatch of 12 August 1806 commenting on Marsden's categories is in *HRNSW*, 6, pp. 150–1, 162.

52 The instructions to Bligh are in *HRA*, 1, 6, Castlereagh to Bligh, dispatch no. 1, 31 December 1807.

For Bligh on the settlers see Bligh to Windham, CO/201/44, p. 263ff, Australian Joint Copying Project (AJCP) reel 22.

53 The addresses are to be found as enclosures from Bligh to Castlereagh, 29 January 1807, CO/210/46, p. 200ff, AJCP reel 23.

ENDNOTES

See B. Fletcher, 'The Hawkesbury settlers and the Rum Rebellion', *RHAS*, 54, 3 September 1968, for the old emancipist's reminiscences.

3 TRANSPLANTING PATRIARCHY

55 H. Heney (ed.), *Dear Fanny: Women's Letters to and from New South Wales 1788–1857*, Australian National University Press, Canberra, 1985, p. 42, publishes Marshall's letter, and tells her story.

See *Historical Records of New South Wales (HRNSW)*, 7, p. 292 for Macquarie's proclamation.

55–6 J. Ritchie, *Lachlan Macquarie: A Biography*, Melbourne University Press, Melbourne, 1986, is the latest biography; the quotations are from p. 123.

56 M. Saclier, 'Sam Marsden's colony: notes on a manuscript in the Mitchell Library, Sydney', *Journal of the Royal Australian Historical Society*, 52, 2, June 1966, pp. 101–2, discusses Marsden's contribution.

The tale of Clorinda is cited in C. M. H. Clark, *A History of Australia*, 1, Melbourne University Press, Melbourne, 1977, p. 257.

57 The list of convicts, a 'Return of Persons in the Employ of Government at Sydney and Parramatta, who are married or living with Women unmarried, and their numbers of Children ... December 1819', is among the evidence of the Bigge Report in the correspondence of the Secretary of State, CO/201/118/A–3, pp. 66–9; reel 106 of the Australian Joint Copying Project. Additional information on the lives of the artisans and their dependants has been gathered from the convict indents, registers of baptism, death and marriage, the 1828 census, and the returns of 'Superintendents, Clerks, and Overseers of the Crown, with the Salaries and the Number of Government Men allowed them as Remuneration for their Services', 1819 and 1820, CO/201/118/A31, pp. 147–58; Beverley Earnshaw did this research.

The evidence of the Chief Engineer of the Colonial Establishment was given to Bigge on 27 October 1819; it is reprinted in J. Ritchie (ed.), *The Evidence to the Bigge Reports*, 1, Heinemann, Melbourne, 1971, p. 3.

59 B. Smith, *A Cargo of Women: Susannah Watson and the Convicts of the Princess Royal*, New South Wales University Press, Sydney, 1988, p. 60.

59–60 Messling's interview with Bigge is published in M. Aveling & J. Damousi (eds), *Stepping out of History*, Allen & Unwin, Sydney, 1991, pp. 15–16.

60 Marsden tells his story in J. Ritchie (ed.), *The Evidence to the Bigge Reports*, 2, Heinemann, Melbourne, 1971, pp. 109–10.

Smith, *A Cargo of Women*, p. 68, cites the colonial secretary's reply to the inquiring clergyman.

CREATING A NATION

60–1 The account of the white advance is drawn from R. Broome, *Aboriginal Australians*, Allen & Unwin, Sydney, 1982, and H. Reynolds, *The Other Side of the Frontier*, Penguin, Ringwood, 1982.

61 Macquarie's Aboriginal 'experiments' are described in Macquarie to Bathurst, 8 October 1814, *Historical Records of Australia (HRA)*, 1, 7, p. 369, republished in J. Woolmington, *Aborigines in Colonial Australia 1788–1850*, Cassell, Melbourne, 1973, p. 22.

Macquarie's 1816 proclamation to the Aborigines is to be found in *HRA*, 1, 9, pp. 141–5.

61–2 Ann McGrath brought together details given here of the conduct of Macquarie's 'Congress'. See also J. Brook & J. L. Kohen, *The Parramatta Native Institution and the Black Town: A History*, University of New South Wales Press, Kensington, 1991.

62 For the failure of Macquarie's efforts see Woolmington, *Aborigines in Colonial Australia*, pp. 24–5.

Major Druitt reported the shape of his male workforce in his evidence to Commissioner Bigge, published in Ritchie (ed.), *The Evidence to the Bigge Reports*, 1, pp. 4–7.

63 A. G. L. Shaw, *Convicts and the Colonies*, Faber & Faber, London, 1966, gives the classic statement of the 'disreputable lot' school of thought, and S. Nicholas (ed.), *Convict Workers: Reinterpreting Australia's Past*, Cambridge University Press, Sydney, 1988, gives the revision.

63–4 Shaw, *Convicts and Colonies*, discusses Macquarie's motives; the quote comes from p. 81. For life in the barracks see M. Sullivan, 'The Hyde Park Barracks', in A. Atkinson & M. Aveling (eds), *Australians 1838*, Fairfax Syme & Weldon, Sydney, 1987, pp. 285–9.

64 Macquarie's self-defence to the Commission of Inquiry is published in Ritchie (ed.), *The Evidence to the Bigge Reports*, 1; the quote here is from p. 227.

64–5 The Macquaries' relations with the emancipists are discussed in Ritchie, *Lachlan Macquarie*, ch. 6.

65 B. H. Fletcher, *Landed Enterprise and Penal Society*, Sydney University Press, Sydney, 1976, p. 129, cites Macquarie's hope for the emancipists.

65–6 The convicts' protests are cited in A. Atkinson, 'Four patterns of convict protest', *Labour History*, 37, November 1979.

66 The New South Wales landowner was James Atkinson; his *Account of the State of Agriculture and Grazing in New South Wales* is cited in Shaw, *Convicts and the Colonies*, p. 220.

Endnotes

Neale is cited in T. Rayner, 'Master and servant in the New Norfolk Magistrates Court 1838', *The Push from the Bush*, 6, May 1980, p. 36.

67 The stories of Ann Walker and Caroline Thomas are told in Smith, *Cargo of Women*, p. 48.

Smith in *Cargo of Women* cites Marsden's account of the riot on p. 55.

68 Macarthur's evidence to Bigge is published in Ritchie (ed.), *The Evidence to the Bigge Reports*, 2, pp. 73–4.

The unsympathetic observers found their platform in the Report of the Select Committee on Transportation, 1838, first published in the House of Commons Papers for 1837–38, 22, 669; republished in M. Clark (ed.), *Sources of Australian History*, Oxford University Press, London, 1957, p. 217.

69 The quote is from a poem published in *The Colonist*, 2 January 1839, and republished and discussed in E. Webby, 'Reactions to the Myall Creek Massacre' *The Push from the Bush*, 8, December 1980, p. 13.

Bigge's comments are cited in B. Earnshaw, *Fanned into Flame: The Spread of the Sunday School in Australia*, Board of Education, Diocese of Sydney, Sydney, 1980, pp. 14–15.

70 For percentages signing the register, see J. F. Cleverley, *The First Generation*, Sydney University Press, Sydney, 1971, p. 134.

Thomas Galvin's letter to the Reverend Thomas Hassall, May 1822, in Hassall Family Papers, Mitchell Library, Sydney. See also A. Atkinson, *Camden*, Oxford University Press, Melbourne, 1988, especially p. 15.

Mrs Elizabeth Paterson reported the aims of the Female Orphan School in October 1800; her letter is published in Heney (ed.), *Dear Fanny*, pp. 17–19.

71 E. Windschuttle, 'Discipline, domestic training and social control: the Female School of Industry, Sydney, 1826–1847', *Labour History*, 39, November 1980, p. 13, cites Eliza Darling's intentions.

72 For Margaret Gold's poem, see Windschuttle, 'Discipline, domestic training and social control', p. 9.

72–3 William Rope's memorial is cited in P. Robinson, *The Hatch and Brood of Time*, Oxford University Press, Melbourne, 1985, p. 118. Robinson demonstrates the marriage patterns of the native born.

73 B. H. Fletcher, *Ralph Darling: A Governor Maligned*, Oxford University Press, Melbourne, 1984, p. 152, describes Darling's instructions.

73–4 Wentworth's call for a farm for every currency lad is cited in Fletcher, *Ralph*

Darling, p. 151; his picture of the brooding native born in Robinson, *The Hatch and Brood of Time*, p. 121.

74 *Sydney Gazette*, 30 October 1823; cited in C. M. H. Clark, *A History of Australia*, 2, Melbourne University Press, Melbourne, 1968, pp. 157–8.

Kable's boast is cited in Clark, *History of Australia*, 2, p. 157.

75 Some of the Kables' continuing troubles with the law are detailed in the court records, Archives Office of New South Wales (AONSW) 4/8471, February 1825, Windsor no. 26; AONSW 4/8475, May 1826, Windsor no. 14; and AONSW 4/8486, November 1832, Windsor no. 5.

The depositions against Rope are to be found at AONSW 4/8475, Windsor no. 39.

Hall's comment is cited in the introduction to E. Perkins (ed.), *Charles Harpur: Stalwart the Bushranger*, Currency Press, Sydney, 1987, p. xxxii.

76 Donohoe's 'slave of passion' speech is in Act II, iv, of *The Tragedy of Donohoe*, p. 95, in Perkins (ed.), *Charles Harpur*; the 'bondman of a tyrant' reference is in Act II, ii, p. 94.

77 Report of the Select Committee on Transportation, 1838, cited in Clark (ed.), *Sources of Australian History*, pp. 222–3.

See Shaw, *Convicts and Colonies*, p. 206, for Bishop Polding's denunciation of the penal settlements.

The Report of the Select Committee on Transportation, 1838, in Clark (ed.), *Sources of Australian History*, pp. 196–7, condemned the 'ferocious' convict women.

The landowner quoted here is James Macarthur; see A. Atkinson, 'Master and servant in Camden Park, 1838, from the estate papers', *The Push from the Bush*, 6, May 1980, p. 56.

78 J. B. Hirst, *Convict Society and Its Enemies*, Allen & Unwin, Sydney, 1983, p. 207, cites a radical settler on the status of the convicts.

The resolutions of the New South Wales Legislative Council are published in C. M. H. Clark, *Select Documents in Australian History*, Angus & Robertson, Sydney, 1950, p. 154.

4 MAKING MALE AND FEMALE WORLDS

79 The immigration figures for New South Wales and Van Diemen's Land are compiled from R. B. Madgwick, *Immigration into Eastern Australia*, Sydney University Press, Sydney, 1969, pp. 223–5; the South Australian figures are from D. Pike, *Paradise of Dissent*, Melbourne University Press, Melbourne, 1957, p. 517.

79–80 Mrs King's letters to her husband have been published in D. Walsh (ed.), *The*

Endnotes

Admiral's Wife: Mrs. Phillip Parker King, Hawthorn Press, Melbourne, 1967. Miss Waring's story is told in P. Clarke, *Pen Portraits: Women Writers and Journalists in Nineteenth Century Australia*, Allen & Unwin, Sydney, 1988, pp. 20–3.

80 R. Wighton (ed.), *A Mother's Offering to Her Children, by a Lady Long Resident in New South Wales*, Jacaranda Press, Queensland, 1979 (1841), p. 214.

M. Aveling (ed.), *Westralian Voices: Documents in Westralian Social History*, University of Western Australia Press, Nedlands, 1979, document 6.15, pp. 302–3, tells Emma Mould's story.

80–1 A sample indenture is printed in Aveling (ed.), *Westralian Voices*, document 2.16, pp. 86–7.

81 The gentlewoman's fate is described in A. Burton (ed.), *Wollaston's Picton Journal 1841–1844*, University of Western Australia Press, Nedlands, 1975, pp. 30–1.

82 Wollaston in Burton (ed.), *Wollaston's Picton Journal*, p. 129.

Mrs Bussell's letter is cited in E. Shann, *Cattle Chosen*, University of Western Australia Press, Nedlands, 1978, pp. 49–50.

83 J. Duxbury, *Colonial Servitude: Indentured and Assigned Servants of the Van Diemen's Land Company 1825–41*, Monash Publications in History, 4, Melbourne, 1989, pp. 18–19, cites the management's complaints.

83–4 Wakefield's prophecies are cited in Pike, *Paradise of Dissent*, pp. 74, 79.

84 Molesworth's comparison was made to the House of Commons in the debate of the Waste Lands of the Colonies; it is cited in M. Clark (ed.), *Sources of Australian History*, Oxford University Press, London, 1957, pp. 145–6.

For the promises of the colonists to the Colonial Office see the 'First Annual Report of the Colonization Commissioners of South Australia, 1836', in the *House of Commons Papers, 1837*, cited in A. Atkinson & M. Aveling (eds), *Australians 1838*, Fairfax Syme Weldon Associates, Sydney, 1987, p. 291. The Acting Governor urged compensation in dispatch no. 16, 5 October 1838, South Australian Archives, GRG/2/6/1, and a committee of leading colonists talked of 'moral rights' – see GRG/35/211/11, pp. 242–3. The *Southern Australian*, 27 October 1838, denied them exclusive land rights.

85 The absconders' petition is cited in J. Cashen, 'Masters and servants in early South Australia', *The Push from the Bush*, 6, May 1980, p. 29; see also South Australian Archives GRG/24/1, 1837/470a.

87 Gipps's joke is published and explained in A. G. L. Shaw (ed.), *Gipps–Latrobe Correspondence 1839–1846*, Miegunyah, Melbourne, 1989, pp. 119–21.

87–8 Chisholm tells this story in *Female Immigration, Considered, in a Brief Account of the Sydney Immigrants' Home*, James Tegg, Sydney, 1842, p. 45; cited in M. Hoban, *Fifty-one Pieces of Wedding Cake: A Biography of Caroline Chisholm*, Lowden Publishing Co., Kilmore, Victoria, 1973, pp. 85–6.

88 Chisholm's vow and her view of women's wages are cited in M. Kiddle, *Caroline Chisholm*, Melbourne University Press, Melbourne, 1950, pp. 15, 58.

89 The prospective husband's promises are cited in Hoban, *Fifty-one Pieces of Wedding Cake*, p. 85.

For Sarah Crouch, see E. Windschuttle, 'Women, class and temperance: moral reform in eastern Australia 1832–1857', *The Push from the Bush*, 3, 1979, and A. Atkinson & M. Aveling (eds), *Australians 1838*, p. 252.

The Powers' story is told in 'Document: the tale of an errant wife', *The Push from the Bush*, 16, 1983, p. 71.

90 Louisa Clifford's diary is published in L. Frost (ed.), *No Place for a Nervous Lady: Voices from the Australian Bush*, McPhee Gribble, Melbourne, 1984, p. 51.

91 The quotations from Spark's diary about his wife's pregnancies are in A. Abbott & G. Little (eds), *The Respectable Sydney Merchant: A. B. Spark of Tempe*, Sydney University Press, Sydney, 1976, pp. 122, 123, 162.

91–2 Spark's diaries, pp. 133, 183, describe Maria Spark's childbirths.

92 Sophie Dumaresq's letter of 20 February 1830 is published in H. Heney (ed.), *Dear Fanny: Women's Letters to and from New South Wales 1788–1857*, Australian National University Press, Canberra, 1985, pp. 97–8.

93–4 Annie Baxter's journal is published in L. Frost (ed.), *No Place for a Nervous Lady*; the quotations cited are from pp. 100, 109.

94 Chisholm's words are cited in A. Summers, *Damned Whores and God's Police*, Penguin, Ringwood, 1975, p. 291.

94–5 See Paine's *Rights of Man* (1791–2), ed. H. Collins, Penguin, London, 1969, pp. 86, 89, 201.

95 B. H. Solonon & P. S. Berggren (eds), *A Mary Wollstonecraft Reader*, Mentor, New York, 1983, p. 344.

96 M. Sullivan, *Men and Women of Port Phillip*, Hale & Iremonger, Sydney, 1985, pp. 218–21, describes the Melbourne bread riots.

97 The Sydney riot is described in R. Knight, *Illiberal Liberal: Robert Lowe in New South Wales 1842–1850*, Melbourne University Press, Melbourne, 1966, pp. 44–5.

97–8 Parkes's participation in the election is described in A. W. Martin, *Henry Parkes: A Biography*, Melbourne University Press, Melbourne, 1980, pp. 49–50.

98 Parkes's verse, his rhetoric and the motto of the *People's Advocate* are all cited in Martin, *Henry Parkes*, p. 51.

Harpur's 'The Tree Of Liberty' (1853) is republished in I. Turner (ed.), *The Australian Dream*, Sun Books, Melbourne, 1968, pp. 50–1.

99 The *Sydney Morning Herald*'s account of the protest meeting is reprinted in Clark (ed.), *Sources of Australian History*, pp. 243–53.

100 The digger's doggerel is cited in G. Serle, *The Golden Age: A History of the Colony of Victoria, 1851–1861*, Melbourne University Press, Melbourne, 1963, p. 164.

The early protest meetings are described in B. Kent, 'Agitations on the Victorian gold fields, 1851–4: an interpretation', *Historical Studies*, 6, 23, November 1954.

101 The account of the diggers' move to arms is drawn from Serle, *The Golden Age*, pp. 166–7.

102 Macarthur is cited in A. Atkinson, 'Demanding the vote for women, 1857–58', *The Push from the Bush*, 25, October 1987, pp. 52–3.

The mechanics' debate is reproduced in Aveling (ed.), *Westralian Voices*, pp. 284–7.

103 The letters are republished in Atkinson, 'Demanding the vote for women'. They were originally published in the *Sydney Morning Herald*, 13 August 1857, 2 July 1858, 7 July 1858.

The intelligent young woman was Jane Ryrie. Her letter is published in Heney (ed.), *Dear Fanny*, pp. 133–5.

Menie's letters are published in A. W. Martin, *Letters from Menie: Henry Parkes and His Daughter*, Melbourne University Press, Melbourne, 1983, pp. 6, 15.

104 Lucy Hart's letter is published in M. Aveling & J. Damousi (eds), *Stepping Out of History*, Allen & Unwin, Sydney, 1991, document 3.6, pp. 43, 44.

The observer was William Kelly. His *Life in Victoria*, London, 1859, is cited in C. Harris, The respectable working class family and the labour movement in nineteenth century Victoria, MA thesis, Monash University, 1987, p. 167.

The *Argus* reported the complaints of the Eight-Hour Day agitators on 27 November 1855, and an *Argus* editorial commended an ideal artisan on 21 April 1856; both are cited in Harris, The respectable working class family, pp. 299, 213.

105 H. Golder, *Divorce in Nineteenth Century New South Wales*, New South Wales University Press, Kensington, 1985.

The artisans are reported in Aveling (ed.), *Westralian Voices*, p. 287.

5 MAN'S SPACE, WOMAN'S PLACE

107–8 Caroline Chisholm's lecture is cited in M. Hoban, *Fifty-one Pieces of Wedding*

Cake: A Biography of Caroline Chisholm, Lowden Publishing Co., Kilmore, Victoria, 1973, pp. 392–3.

109–10 The radical's vision of rural Australia and the wage-earner's letter to the *Argus* are cited in C. Harris, The respectable working class family and the labour movement in nineteenth century Victoria, MA thesis, Monash University, 1987.

115–16 The story of the Durack family is told in Mary Durack, *Kings in Grass Castles*, Corgi, London, 1976 (1959). Patrick Durack's comment on white women and the outback is on p. 285.

118 The bishop's delineation of gender was published in the Church of England *Messenger*, 6 October 1881, p. 22.

119 Christiana Blomfield's letter is in P. Clarke & D. Spender (eds), *Lifelines: Australian Women's Letters and Diaries 1788–1840*, Allen & Unwin, Sydney, 1992, pp. 99–100.

The Elliotts' experiences are described in Joseph Elliott, *Our Home in Australia: A Description of Cottage Life in 1860*, Flannel Flower Press, Sydney, 1984.

120 Matilda Murray-Prior's fears are recorded in Rosa Praed, *My Australian Girlhood*, T. Fisher Unwin, London, 1904, p. 51.

In Richard Twopeny, *Town Life in Australia*, Penguin, Ringwood, Victoria, 1976 (1883), pp. 82–3.

121–2 For Rosa Praed's experiences of her neighbours in the Queensland outback, see Praed, *My Australian Girlhood*.

123 The story of Ellen Kelly and her family is told by M. Lake, 'The Trials of Ellen Kelly', in M. Lake & F. Kelly (eds), *Double Time: Women in Victoria – 150 Years*, Penguin, Ringwood, Victoria, 1985, pp. 86–96.

124 The Curries' family life is described in more detail in P. Grimshaw, 'Marriages and families', in G. Davison, J. McCarty & A. McLeary (eds), *Australians 1888*, Fairfax Syme Weldon Associates, Sydney, 1988, pp. 297–322.

125 Mary Gilmore writes of rural life in *Old Days: Old Ways*, Angus & Robertson, Sydney, 1936 (1934), p. 18.

125–7 Ada Cambridge describes her neighbours and her family life in her autobiography, *Thirty Years in Australia*, Methuen, London, 1903.

127–8 The Johnses family life is described in more detail in Grimshaw, 'Marriages and families', in Davison, McCarty & McLeary (eds), *Australians 1888*, pp. 297–322.

128 Ada Cambridge's comment on clergymen's wives is in her *Thirty Years in Australia*, pp. 87–8.

ENDNOTES

128–9 The examples of poor working-class wives are cited in Grimshaw, 'Marriages and families', in Davison, McCarty & McLeary (eds), *Australians 1888*, pp. 319–20.

6 SEX, VIOLENCE AND THEFT: 1830–1910

132–3 Amy Laurie's story is from A. Laurie & A. McGrath, 'I Was a Drover Once Myself: Amy Laurie of Kununurra' in I. White, D. Barwick & B. Meehan (eds), *Fighters and Singers*, Allen & Unwin, Sydney, 1985, p. 81.

134 Banggaiyerri's explanation appears in J. Sullivan & B. Shaw, *Banggaiyerri*, Australian Institute of Aboriginal Studies, Canberra, 1983, pp. 65, 67, 68.

135 Pepper's explanation is contained in P. Pepper, *You Are What You Make Yourself to Be*, Hyland House, Melbourne, 1980, p. 15.

139 The quote about the 'awful and alarming extent' of prostitution is from *British Parliamentary Papers*, Papers relevant to the Aborigines, Australian Colonies, 8, p. 178.

The assertion regarding the declining births by 1841 is in *British Parliamentary Papers*, 8, p. 176.

140 The Wesleyan report is from *British Parliamentary Papers*, 8, p. 176.

143 Jimmie Barker's reference to Christmas comes from J. Matthews, *The Two Worlds of Jimmie Barker*, Australian Institute of Aboriginal Studies, Canberra, 1977, p. 3.

144 Evidence of Annie Baxter's resolve may be found in her journals, cited in L. Frost (ed.), *No Place for a Nervous Lady*, McPhee Gribble, Melbourne, 1984, p. 100.

145 Emmalin's comment on guns is from P. Sharp, A study of the relationships between colonial women and black Australians, MA thesis, Deakin University, 1991, pp. 47–8.

The quote about Mrs Lister comes from J. F. Stevens, Histories of pioneers in the Clarence, Hunter and Richmond River districts and south-east Qld, Mitchell Library MSS 1120, cited in Sharp, Relationships between colonial women and black Australians, pp. 57, 61.

147 The story about 'educated men' is from *British Parliamentary Papers*, 8, pp. 262, 274, 275, 280.

148 The assertion about hanging and the 'terror of the law' is cited in C. Harris, 'The terror of the law', *Hecate*, 8, 1982, p. 28.

149 The quote about thinking Campbell 'a blackfellow' is from M. Prentis, 'The life and death of Johnny Campbell', *Aboriginal History*, 15, 1990.

150 Cooper's use of the expression 'blood from a stone' was cited in A. Markus (ed.), *Blood From a Stone*, Monash University, Clayton, 1986.

7 CONTESTED DOMAINS

153 Quotation from the first edition of the *Dawn*, May 1888, republished in O. Lawson (ed.), *The First Voice of Australian Feminism: Excerpts from Louisa Lawson's The Dawn 1888–1895*, Simon & Schuster, Sydney, 1990, p. 23.

154 Bessie Harrison Lee's comment is in her memoir, *One of Australia's Daughters*, Richard J. James, London, 1926 (1906), p. 151, published under the name 'Cowie'.

158 The story of the driver is told in the *Boomerang*, 26 November 1887, p. 8.

160 The account of Frances Perry's activities at the Lying-in Hospital is in the manuscript diary of Curtis Candler held in the State Library of Victoria (SLV).

162 The letter between the Bussell sisters is in E. Shann, *Cattle Chosen*, University of Western Australia Press, Nedlands, 1978 (1926), p. 47.

The reminiscences of Jane Caverhill (Reminiscences of her childhood, 1840's–1850's) are held in the manuscript collection of the SLV.

163 The letter of Charles Bernnell is cited in P. Grimshaw, C. Fahey, S. Janson & T. Griffiths, 'Families and selection in colonial Harsham', in P. Grimshaw, C. McConville & E. McEwen (eds), *Families in Colonial Australia*, Allen & Unwin, Sydney, 1988, p. 121.

164–5 Fuller details on the South Melbourne material can be found in J. Beer, C. Fahey, P. Grimshaw & M. Raymond (eds), *Colonial Frontiers and Family Fortunes*, Melbourne University Press, University Monograph Series, Melbourne, 1987, Chapter 6, 'Raising a family'.

165–6 William Lane's column on Chicago's young working women is in the *Boomerang*, 3 December 1887, p. 11.

166 The report of working women's silence before factory inspectors is in the *Chief Inspector of Factories Report 1889*, Government Printer, Melbourne, 1889, p. 8.

170 For fuller detail on Harriet Dugdale and her *A Few Hours in a Far-off Age* see H. Radi (ed.), *200 Australian Women: A Redress Anthology*, Women's Redress Press, Sydney, 1988, p. 25.

172 The terrible sufferings of Emma Clark are described by M. James in 'Not bread but a stone: women and divorce in colonial Victoria', in Grimshaw, McConville & McEwen (eds), *Families in Colonial Australia*, pp. 42–8.

172–3 Louisa Lawson wrote of the divorce extension bill in New South Wales in the first edition of the *Dawn*, May 1888.

ENDNOTES

175 Bert Facey wrote of his childhood experiences in Kalgoorlie in *A Fortunate Life*, Penguin, Ringwood, Victoria, 1983 (1981), pp. 11–12.

8 GENDERED SETTLEMENTS

177–8 The quotation of C. H. Pearson is from his *National Life and Character*, Macmillan, London, 1893, p. 16.

182 The poem is from the *White Ribbon Signal*, November 1907, p. 259. I owe this reference to Lindy Coverdale.

183 The quotations from Bessie Harrison Lee (Cowie) are from *Mrs Pumpkin Goes to Town*, J. J. Howard, Melbourne, n.d. [c. 1890], pp. 3, 14, 34, 37.

184 The Windeyer judgment is cited in P. Grimshaw, 'Marriages and families', in G. Davison, J. McCarty & A. McLeary (eds), *Australians 1888*, Fairfax Syme Weldon Associates, Sydney, 1988, p. 311.

Brettena Smyth's statement is in her *Limitation of Offspring*, Rae Bros., Melbourne, 1893, p. 11.

184–5 Louisa Lawson's comments on motherhood are from the *Dawn*, August 1889 and July 1892, cited in O. Lawson (ed.), *The First Voice of Australian Feminism: Excerpts from Louisa Lawson's* The Dawn *1888–1895*, Simon & Schuster, Sydney, 1990, pp. 120, 172.

185–6 Rose Scott's comment is from the *Australian Woman's Sphere*, December 1903, p. 379.

The comment on 'the hand that rocked the cradle' is from the *Australian Woman's Sphere*, January 1902, p. 135.

187 The *Bulletin* excerpts are dated 20 October and 3 November 1888, cited in M. Lake, 'The politics of respectability: identifying the masculinist context', *Historical Studies*, 22, 86, April 1986, p. 129.

The Victorian politician's opinions are recorded in the *Australian Woman's Sphere*, 1, 1, 1900, p. 11. I owe this reference to Patrick Seal.

188 The excerpt from William Lane's *The Workingman's Paradise* is cited in L. Dale, *The Rural Context of Masculinity and the 'Woman Question'*, Monash Publications in History, 8, Melbourne, 1991, p. 21.

188–91 For the quotations from the *Tocsin* and further details, see P. Grimshaw, 'The "equals and comrades of men"? Labour and "the woman question" in Melbourne', in S. Magarey, S. Rowley & S. Sheridan (eds), *Debutante Nation: Feminism Contesting the 1890s*, Allen & Unwin, Sydney, 1993, pp. 100–14.

191 The quotation from William Lane's *The Workingman's Paradise* is on page 9 (Sydney University Press, Sydney, 1980 [1892]).

192 Alfred Deakin's statement is cited in C. Waldby, The political regulation of motherhood in Australia, 1880–1914, BA Honours thesis, University of Sydney, 1983, p. 26.

192–3 The two politicians' definitions of Australian character are from *Victorian Parliamentary Debates (VDP)*, 1891, 66, Legislative Assembly, p. 379; and *VDP*, 1899–1900, 91, Legislative Council, p. 516.

193–4 The clerical comment on the 'population problem' is in the Church of England *Messenger*, 11 February 1901.

194 The excerpt from the New South Wales Royal Commission is cited in N. Hicks, *'This Sin and Scandal': Australia's Population Debate 1891–1911*, Australian National University Press, Canberra, 1978, pp. 22–3.

195–6 The Lawson excerpt is from the *Dawn*, August 1901, p. 7.

200–1 Mr Justice Higgins's findings are cited in E. Ryan & A. Conlon, *Gentle Invaders: Australian Women at Work 1788–1974*, Penguin, Ringwood, 1989, pp. 91–2.

202 The excerpt on the Mother's Union is from the Church of England *Messenger*, 1 February 1896.

203 Sister Esther's speech is from the *Report of the Fourth Australian Church Congress. Held at Ballarat 21st November–25th November 1898*, n.p., Melbourne, 1898, p. 103.

Archbishop Clarke's comment is from the *Messenger*, 28 October 1910.

9 GIVING BIRTH TO THE NEW NATION

205–6 For reports of the WOC resolution, the deputation's arguments and the prime minister's explanation concerning the maternity allowance, see the *Argus*, 5 September 1912; *Age*, 5, 6 September 1912; and *Commonwealth Parliamentary Debates (CPD)*, House of Representatives, 21, 24 September 1912, p. 3322.

206 The non-party feminist protest is made by the *Woman Voter* (the monthly letter of the Women's Political Association), 9 October 1912.

207 The male defence of the law of marriage can be found in the *Argus*, 29 August 1912, and *Age*, 5 September 1912.

208 *Australian Medical Gazette*, 2 March 1912.

209 The warning about the consequences of equal pay is to be found in the minutes

ENDNOTES

of the Women's Industrial Convention 23–5 September 1913, p. 7, University of Melbourne Archives.

210 Justice Piddington's observation on work is quoted by Michael Roe in *Nine Australian Progressives: Vitalism in Bourgeois Social Thought 1890–1960*, Queensland University Press, St Lucia, 1984, pp. 222, 230.

The heralding of women's release from specialisation is to be found in Ada Holman's article 'Primitive woman' in *Lone Hand*, 1 June 1915.

210–11 Minutes of the Women's Industrial Convention, pp. 17–18.

212 The Brisbane woman's recruiting advice is cited in C. Shute, 'Sexual mythology 1914–1918', *Hecate*, 1, 1, 1975, p. 9.

213 Vida Goldstein's question is in Shute, 'Sexual mythology', p. 11.

213–14 The account of the racial fears invoked in the conscription debate is to be found in M. Lake, *A Divided Society: Tasmania During World War I*, Melbourne University Press, Melbourne, 1975, pp. 73, 74.

214 The conscriptionist meeting is discussed in J. Smart, 'The right to speak and the right to be heard: the popular disruption of conscriptionist meetings in Melbourne 1916', *Australian Historical Studies*, 92, April 1989, p. 209.

214–15 The prime minister's 'Call to the Women of Australia' is in M. Jennings, *Australia in the Great War*, Appendix D, Hill of Content, Melbourne, 1969, pp. 87–92.

216 The New South Wales housewives' petition is cited in M. Foley, The women's movement in New South Wales and Victoria 1918–38', PhD thesis, History department, University of Sydney, 1985, p. 109.

217 The *Woman's Voice* is cited in Foley, The women's movement, p. 16.

On banking as a woman's occupation see Judgment of the Full Bench delivered by J. Piddington, Bank Officers Case 1928, File A2/37/10, Australian National University Archives of Business and Labour, Canberra, cited in C. Fox & M. Lake, *Australians at Work: Commentaries and Sources*, McPhee Gribble, Melbourne, 1990, pp. 157–8.

218 For the national significance attributed to the 'Landing at Gallipoli' see, for example, speeches and editorials in the Brisbane *Courier*, 26 April 1916; *Argus*, 25 April 1917, 26 April 1920.

Age, 5 June 1919.

218–19 *Lone Hand*, 1 March 1919, quoted in Shute, 'Sexual mythology', p. 19.

219–20 *World*, 18 June 1919, quoted in Lake, *A Divided Society*, p. 188.

220 Hughes in *CPD*, 89, p. 12169, cited in Stuart Macintyre, *The Oxford History of Australia 1901–1942*, 4, Oxford University Press, 1986, p. 178.

Representations of the Bolshevik as rapacious male in conservative women's propaganda are cited in Foley, The women's movement, pp. 47–52, 381–3.

221 Piddington's comments are to be found in the Report of the Royal Commission into the Basic Wage, *Commonwealth Parliamentary Papers (CPP)*, 1920–21, 4, p. 28.

223 Ethel Osborne, *Report of an Inquiry into the Conditions of Employment as Regards the Health of Female Workers in the Printing and Allied Trades*, Sydney, c. 1925.

224 Factory workforce figures cited in E. Ryan & A. Conlon, *Gentle Invaders: Australian Women At Work 1788–1974*, Penguin, Ringwood, 1989, pp. 112–13.

E. J. Brady, *Australia Unlimited*, Melbourne, 1918, p. 14.

225 Senator Stewart in *CDP*, Senate, 79, 22 May 1916, pp. 8194–5.

Anxieties about the future of the race cited in M. Lake, *The Limits of Hope: Soldier Settlement in Victoria 1915–38*, Oxford University Press, Melbourne, 1987, p. 21.

H. Rider Haggard and Prime Minister Hughes cited in Lake, *Limits of Hope*, pp. 31–2.

226 Bruce at the Imperial Conference, *Age*, 15 August 1923.

227 Royal Commission on Health, Minutes of Evidence and Report, *CPP* 1926–28, 4, p. 32.

228 Truby King reported in the *Argus*, 17 January 1923.

228–9 Rewards due to maternal citizenship, see *Australian National Review*, 24 January 1922, and Royal Commission on Child Endowment or Family Allowances, Minutes of Evidence, *Australian Parliamentary Papers*, 1929, p. 1116.

10 DEPRESSION DREAMING

231 Vera Scantlebury Brown's diary quoted in K. Reiger, 'Vera Scantlebury Brown: professional mother', in M. Lake & F. Kelly (eds), *Double Time: Women in Victoria – 150 Years*, Penguin, Ringwood, Victoria, 1985, p. 294.

232 The recollection of the fight against dirt in the country is in W. Lowenstein, *Weevils in the Flour: An Oral Record of the 1930s Depression in Australia*, Hyland House, Melbourne, 1978, p. 53.

233 M. Tucker, *If Everyone Cared*, Grosvenor Books, Melbourne, 1987 (reprint), p. 111.

Lilian Locke-Burns quoted in *Labor Call*, 26 June 1919.

233–4 Rural women's comments cited in M. Lake, *The Limits of Hope: Soldier Settlement in Victoria 1915–38*, Oxford University Press, Melbourne, 1987, p. 36.

ENDNOTES

234 Nettie Palmer's essay cited in D. Jordan, 'Nettie Palmer: the writer as nationalist' in Lake & Kelly (eds), *Double Time*, p. 235.

Marjorie Barnard's tribute is quoted in D. Modjeska, *Exiles at Home: Australian Women Writers 1925–1945*, Angus & Robertson, Sydney, 1981, p. 83.

235 Eleanor Dark's remarks cited in D. Modjeska, 'Rooms of their own: the domestic situation of Australian women writers between the wars', in E. Windschuttle (ed.), *Women, Class and History: Feminist Perspectives on Australia 1788–1978*, Fontana, Sydney, 1980, p. 340.

Muriel Heagney's observation recorded in the Royal Commission on Child Endowment or Family Allowances, Minutes of Evidence, *Australian Parliamentary Papers*, 1929, 11, p. 1116.

235–6 Dame Janet Campbell, 'Report on Maternal and Child Welfare in Australia', *Commonwealth Parliamentary Papers (CPP)*, 1929–30–31, 11, pp. 4, 6.

236 Jean Daley's evidence in Royal Commission on Child Endowment or Family Allowances, Minutes of Evidence, pp. 1195–6.

Muriel Heagney's evidence in Royal Commission on Child Endowment or Family Allowances, Minutes of Evidence, p. 1136.

236–7 Royal Commission on National Insurance for Unemployment, Second Progress Report, *CPP*, 1926–27–28, 4, p. 16.

Royal Commission on Child Endowment, Minority Report, p. 1392.

Royal Commission on National Insurance, p. 11.

237–9 Understandings of soldier settlers and the comment by a settler's wife are to be found in Lake, *The Limits of Hope*, pp. 173, 174, 198.

239 The description of the masculine New Woman is from *Table Talk*, 14 May 1925, quoted in B. Cameron, 'The flappers and the feminists' in M. Bevege et al. (eds), *Worth Her Salt: Women at Work in Australia*, Hale & Iremonger, Sydney, 1982, p. 267.

240 Jean Daley's reflections on spinsterhood in *Woman's Clarion*, vol. 6, no. 70, August 1927.

241 The bushworker's comment on the 1920s depression is quoted in Lowenstein, *Weevils in the Flour*, p. 47.

242 Men's inferiority complex is referred to in a letter to the prime minister and Minister for Home Affairs, from 'Parkes Barracks' for the Unemployed, 6 October 1931; Series A1, Item 1932/114, Australian Archives, Canberra.

244 Arbitration court judgment quoted in L. J. Louis & I. Turner, *The Depression of the 1930s*, Cassell, Melbourne, 1968, p. 86.

Daisy McWilliams's recollections are included in L. Fox (ed.), *Depression Down Under*, Hale & Iremonger, Sydney, 1989, pp. 18–19.

245 Women's letters about the effects of childbirth in the Wallace Collection, University of Melbourne Archives and National Health and Medical Research Council, Eighteenth Session, 22–24 November 1944; Report on the Decline of the Birth Rate; Analysis of Letters Received.

On withdrawal at Brunswick and backyard abortions see R. Wilson (ed.), *Good Talk: The Extraordinary Lives of Ten Ordinary Women*, McPhee Gribble, Melbourne, 1985, pp. 152, 20.

Daisy McWilliams in Fox (ed.), *Depression Down Under*, p. 19.

245–6 On fear of pregnancy and marital discord see letters in the Wallace Collection, University of Melbourne Archives.

246–7 Discussion of Amy Johnson's significance in J. Thomas, 'Amy Johnson's triumph, Australia 1930', *Australian Historical Studies*, 90, April 1988, p. 75.

247 *Australian Women's Weekly*, 4 April 1933.

247–8 On women's determination to avoid childbearing see letters in National Health and Medical Research Council, Report on the Decline of the Birth Rate, pp. 77–8, and Wallace Collection, University of Melbourne Archives.

248 Protest against southern Europeans contained in Resolution, Australian Workers' Union, Westralian Branch, Unemployment and Southern Europeans, 1928, AA CRS A458 745/1/306, Prime Minister's Correspondence Files, Australian Archives, Canberra.

248–9 National Council of Women address reported in the *Argus*, 31 March 1931.

Ruby Duncan's election campaign reported in M. Foley, The women's movement in New South Wales and Victoria 1918–38, PhD thesis, History department, University of Sydney, 1988, p. 359.

250 Mary Bennett to Bessie Rischbieth, 16 November 1934, in Rischbieth Papers 2004/12/–, National Library of Australia.

251 *Sydney Morning Herald*, 11 August 1934.

251–2 W. Denning, 'The economic woman', *Australian National Review*, 1 July 1938. Muriel Heagney, *Are Women Taking Men's Jobs?*, Melbourne, 1935, p. 12.

252 John Hughes cited in P. Johnson, 'Gender, class and work: the Council of Action on Equal Pay campaign in Australia during World War II', *Labour History*, 50, May 1986, p. 132.

253 Women's confessions of selfishness in letters in Wallace Collection, University of

Endnotes

Melbourne Archives and the National Health and Medical Research Council, Report on the Decline of the Birth Rate, p. 75.

J. J. Dedman introducing the White Paper on Full Employment, House of Representatives, *Commonwealth Parliamentary Debates*, 182, 30 May 1945, pp. 2238–40.

11 Freedom, Fear and the Family

255 Betty Hayles reported in the *Sydney Morning Herald*, 22 October 1940, quoted in C. Shute, 'From balaclavas to bayonets', in E. Windschuttle (ed.), *Women, Class and History: Feminist Perspectives on Australia 1788–1978*, Fontana, Sydney, 1980, p. 366.

256 Women's defence of their uniforms in Shute, 'From balaclavas to bayonets', pp. 374–5.

256–7 Norman Makin reported in *Commonwealth Parliamentary Debates (CPD)*, House of Representatives, 166, p. 149.

Harold Holt reported in *CPD*, House of Representatives, 27 March 1941, 166, pp. 338–40.

257 A. P. Elkin, *Our Opinions and the National Effort*, War Pamphlets, 202, Sydney, August 1941, p. 13.

Joint Committee on Social Security, First Report, 24 September 1941, *Commonwealth Parliamentary Papers*, 1940–43, 2, p. 759.

258 News of war, *Sydney Morning Herald*, 9 December 1941.

Curtin's undertaking from *Digest of Decisions and Announcements*, 11, p. 13, quoted in S. J. Butlin & C. B. Schedvin, *War Economy 1942–45*, Australian War Memorial, Canberra, 1977, pp. 31–2.

258–9 Curtin's appeal to the United States in the *Herald*, 27 December 1941.

262 Diary quoted in M. Lake, 'Female desires: the meaning of World War II', *Australian Historical Studies*, 24, 95, October 1990, p. 267.

264 *Going Jeep*, a collection of verse by Tom Ugly on the theme of the relations between Australian women and American servicemen (Pinnacle Press, Sydney, 1944).

265 Reports of divorce in the *Sydney Morning Herald*, 12, 26 March, 2 April, 7 October 1950; *Age*, 4, 24 January, 15 September 1950.

267 R. G. Menzies, *The Forgotten People*, quoted and discussed in J. Brett, 'Menzies' forgotten people', *Meanjin*, 2, 1984, p. 263.

268 Advertisement in the *Australian Women's Weekly*, 10 February 1950, p. 35.

The Communist as a snake and liberalism's credo quoted in S. Alomes et al., 'The social context of postwar conservatism', in A. Curthoys & J. Merritt (eds), *Australia's First Cold War 1945-1953: Society, Communism and Culture*, 1, Allen & Unwin, Sydney, 1984, pp. 10, 27.

G. L. Wood, 'Conception of freedom', quoted in S. Rees & J. Senyard, *The 1950s: How Australia Became a Modern Society and Everyone Got a Job, a House and a Car*, Hyland House, Melbourne, 1987, p. 38.

269 The 'Call to Australia' reported in the *Age*, 11 November 1951.

270 *Examiner* quoted in P. Ranald, 'Women's organisations and the issue of Communism', in A. Curthoys & J. Merritt (eds), *Better Dead than Red: Australia's First Cold War 1945-1959*, 2, Allen & Unwin, Sydney, 1986, p. 52.

The divorce in the *Sydney Morning Herald*, 26 March 1950.

David Mace in the *Sydney Morning Herald*, 25 June 1950.

271 On lesbianism in 1950s Melbourne see R. Ford, Deviance and desires: meanings of lesbianism in post-war Australia, 1946-1960, BA Honours thesis, History/Women's Studies, La Trobe University, 1992.

271-2 On the necessity of population see *Australia and the Migrant 1953* quoted in Rees & Senyard, *The 1950s*, p. 107.

273 Request to Gwen Meredith quoted in Rees & Senyard, *The 1950s*, p. 109.

275 J. D. Pringle, *Australian Accent*, Chatto & Windus, London, 1958, p. 39.

276 Feminist Club's resolution reported in the *Sydney Morning Herald*, 16 December 1950.

12 THE STATE AS FATHER: 1910-60

279 The quotation referring to Bett-Bett is from A. Gunn, *The Little Black Princess*, Robertson & Mullens, Melbourne, 1924 (1905), p. 4.

286 The quote about Cohen's joining the army is from B. Cohen, *To My Delight*, Aboriginal Studies Press, Canberra, 1987, p. 105.

Noonuccal's statement comes from an interview cited in R. A. Hall, *The Black Diggers*, Allen & Unwin, Sydney, 1989, pp. 68-9.

288 The Girls Enticement Act of 1844 is cited in J. McCorquodale, Aborigines: a history of law and injustice, 1829-1985, PhD thesis, University of New England, 1985, pp. 127-9.

290 The 1926 Report is cited in P. Read, *The Stolen Generations*, New South Wales Ministry of Aboriginal Affairs, Occasional Paper 1, Sydney, n.d., p. 2.

Neville's statements were made at the 1937 Conference of Commonwealth and

ENDNOTES

State Aboriginal Authorities, cited in B. Gammage & A. Markus (eds), *All That Dirt*, History Project Incorporated, Canberra, 1982, pp. 1–3.

Comment about South Australian half-caste children's treatment was made by McCorquodale, Aborigines: a history of law and injustice, p. 110.

291 Annie Phillips's story is told in B. Cummings, *Take this Child*, Aboriginal Studies Press, Canberra, 1990, p. 78.

292 P. Read's discussion of assimilation is contained in C. Edwards & P. Read (eds), *The Lost Children*, Doubleday, Sydney, 1989, pp. xv–xvi.

293 The definition of assimilation is contained in the Native Welfare Conference, Commonwealth and State Authorities: Proceedings and Decisions, January 1961.

296 The statement about the law and artificial surrogates comes from McCorquodale, Aborigines, p. 131.

13 AFFIRMATIONS OF DIFFERENCE

298 Pat Dodson addressing a Catholic conference quoted by L. Lippmann, *Generations of Resistance: The Aboriginal Struggle for Justice*, Longman Cheshire, Melbourne, 1981, p. 47.

299 Speech made by Faith Bandler at the Annual General Meeting of the Aboriginal Children's Advancement Society, 21 February 1969, cited in *Kirinari*, 1, 4, 1969, p. 23.

302 Neville Wran addressing the New South Wales branch of the Municipal Employees' Union quoted in E. Ryan & A. Conlon, *Gentle Invaders: Australian Women at Work*, Penguin, Ringwood, 1989, p. 164.

303 Liberal Party research cited in H. McQueen, *Gone Tomorrow: Australia in the 80s*, Angus & Robertson, Sydney, 1982, p. 183.

307 P. O'Shane, 'Is there any relevance in the women's movement for Aboriginal women?', *Refractory Girl*, 12 September 1976, p. 33.

312 Yunupingu quoted in K. Anderson (ed.), *Australians 1988*, Fairfax Syme Weldon Associates, Sydney, 1989, p. 14.

Bibliography

Abbott, A. & Little, G. (eds), *The Respectable Sydney Merchant: A. B. Spark of Tempe*, Sydney University Press, Sydney, 1976.

Allen, J. *Sex and Secrets*, Oxford University Press, Melbourne, 1990.

Alomes, S. et al., 'The social context of postwar conservatism', in A. Curthoys & J. Merritt (eds), *Australia's First Cold War 1945–1953: Society, Communism and Culture*, 1, Allen & Unwin, Sydney, 1984.

Anderson, K. (ed.), *Australians 1988*, Fairfax Syme Weldon Associates, Sydney, 1989.

Atkinson, A., 'Four patterns of convict protest', *Labour History*, 37, November 1979.

—— 'Master and servant in Camden Park, 1838, from the estate papers', *The Push from the Bush*, 6, May 1980.

—— 'Demanding the vote for women, 1857–58', *The Push from the Bush*, 25, October 1987.

Atkinson, A. & Aveling, M. (eds), *Australians 1838*, Fairfax Syme Weldon Associates, Sydney, 1987.

Attwood, B., *The Making of the Aborigines*, Allen & Unwin, Sydney, 1989.

Aveling, M. (ed.), *Westralian Voices: Documents in Westralian Social History*, University of Western Australia Press, Nedlands, 1979.

Aveling, M. & Damousi, J, (eds), *Stepping Out of History*, Allen & Unwin, Sydney, 1991.

Beer, J., Fahey, C., Grimshaw, P. & Raymond, M., *Colonial Frontiers and Family Fortunes*, Melbourne University Press, University Monograph Series, Melbourne, 1987.

Brett, J., 'Menzies' forgotten people', *Meanjin*, 2, 1984.

Brook, J. & Kohen, J. L., *The Parramatta Native Institution and the Black Town*, University of New South Wales Press, Kensington, 1991.

Broome, R., *Aboriginal Australians*, Allen & Unwin, Sydney, 1982.

Burgmann, V. & Lee, J., *A People's History of Australia since 1788*, 4 vols, McPhee Gribble, Melbourne, 1988.

Burton, A. (ed.), *Wollaston's Picton Journal 1841–1844*, University of Western Australia Press, Nedlands, 1975.

Butlin, N. G., *Our Original Aggression*, Allen & Unwin, Sydney, 1983.

Butlin, S. J. & Schedvin, C. B., *War Economy 1942–45*, Australian War Memorial, Canberra, 1977.

Cameron, B., 'The flappers and the feminists', in M. Bevege et al., *Worth Her Salt: Women at Work in Australia*, Hale & Iremonger, Sydney, 1982.

Carter, B. et al, 'Borning', *Australian Aboriginal Studies*, 1, 1987.

Cashen, J., 'Masters and servants in early South Australia', *The Push from the Bush*, 6, May 1980.

Clark, C. M. H., *Select Documents in Australian History*, Angus & Robertson, Sydney, 1950.

—— *A History of Australia*, 1, Melbourne University Press, Melbourne, 1962.

—— *A History of Australia*, 2, Melbourne University Press, Melbourne, 1968.

Clark, M. (ed.), *Sources of Australian History*, Oxford University Press, London, 1957.

Clarke, P. & Spender, D. (eds), *Lifelines: Australian Women's Letters and Diaries 1788–1840*, Allen & Unwin, Sydney, 1992.

Cobley, J., *The Crimes of the First Fleet Convicts*, Angus & Robertson, Sydney, 1970.

—— *Sydney Cove 1788, 1789–90, 1791–92 & 1793–95*, Angus & Robertson, Sydney, 1980, 1980, 1983 and 1985.

Cohen, B., *To My Delight*, Aboriginal Studies Press, Canberra, 1987.

Collins, D. (ed. B. Fletcher), *An Account of the English Colony in New South Wales*, Reed Books, Sydney, 1975.

Cummings, B., *Take This Child*, Aboriginal Studies Press, Canberra, 1990.

Dale, L., *The Rural Context of Masculinity and the 'Woman Question'*, Monash Publications in History, 8, Melbourne, 1991.

Davison, G., *The Rise and Fall of Marvellous Melbourne*, Melbourne University Press, Melbourne, 1978.

Dixson, M., *The Real Matilda*, Penguin, Ringwood, 1976.

Dow, G. M., *Samuel Terry: The Botany Bay Rothschild*, Sydney University Press, Sydney, 1974.

Durack, M., *Kings in Grass Castles*, Corgi, London, 1976 (1959).

Duxbury, J., *Colonial Servitude: Indentured and Assigned Servants of the Van Diemen's Land Company 1825–41*, Monash Publications in History, 4, Melbourne, 1989.

Earnshaw, B., *Fanned into Flame: The Spread of the Sunday School in Australia*, Board of Education, Diocese of Sydney, Sydney, 1980.

Edwards, C. & Read, P. (eds), *The Lost Children*, Doubleday, Sydney, 1989.

Elliot, Joseph, *Our Home in Australia: A Description of Cottage Life in 1860*, Flannel Flower Press, Sydney, 1984.

BIBLIOGRAPHY

Evans, R. & Saunders, K. (eds), *Gender Relations in Australia*, Harcourt Brace Jovanovich, Sydney, 1991.

Facey, B., *A Fortunate Life*, Penguin, Ringwood, 1983 (1981).

Fidlon, P. J. & Ryan, R. J. (eds), *The Journal of Arthur Bowes Smyth*, Australian Documents Library, Sydney, 1979.

Fitzgerald, S., *Rising Damp: Sydney 1870–90*, Oxford University Press, Melbourne, 1987.

Fletcher, B., 'The development of small scale farming in New South Wales under Governor Hunter', *Journal of the Royal Australian Historical Society*, 50, 1 June 1964.

—— 'The Hawkesbury settlers and the Rum Rebellion', *Journal of the Royal Australian Historical Society*, 54, 3 September 1968.

Fletcher, B. H., *Landed Enterprise and Penal Society*, Sydney, Sydney University Press, 1976.

—— *Ralph Darling: A Governor Maligned*, Oxford University Press, Melbourne, 1984.

Foley, M., The women's movement in New South Wales and Victoria 1918–38, PhD thesis, History Department, University of Sydney, 1985.

Ford, R., Deviance and desires: meanings of lesbianism in post-war Australia, 1946–1960, BA Honours thesis, History/Women's Studies, La Trobe University, 1992.

Fox, C. & Lake, M., *Australians at Work: Commentaries and Sources*, McPhee Gribble, Melbourne, 1990.

Fox, L. (ed.), *Depression Down Under*, Hale & Iremonger, Sydney, 1989.

Frost, L. (ed.), *No Place for a Nervous Lady*, McPhee Gribble, Melbourne, 1984.

Gammage, B. & Markus, A. (eds), *All That Dirt*, History Project Incorporated, Canberra, 1982.

Gilmour, M., *Old Days: Old Ways*, Angus & Robertson, Sydney, 1936 (1934).

Golder, H., *Divorce in Nineteenth Century New South Wales*, University of New South Wales Press, Kensington, 1985.

Grimshaw, P., 'Bessie Harrison Lee and the Fight for Voluntary Motherhood', in M. Lake & F. Kelly (eds), *Double Time: Women in Victoria – 150 Years*, Penguin, Ringwood, 1985.

—— ' "Man's Own Country": women in colonial Australian history', in N. Grieve & A. Burns (eds), *Australian Women: New Feminist Perspectives*, Oxford University Press, Melbourne, 1986.

—— 'Marriages and families', in G. Davison, J. McCarty & A. McLeary (eds), *Australians 1888*, Fairfax Syme & Weldon, Sydney, 1988.

—— 'The "equals and comrades of men"? Labour and "the woman question" in Melbourne', in S. Magarey, S. Rowley & S. Sheridan (eds), *Debutante Nation: Feminism Contests the 1890s*, Allen & Unwin, Sydney, 1993.

—— 'In Pursuit of True Anglican Womanhood in Nineteenth Century Victoria, 1880–1914', *Women's History Review*, 2, 3, 1993.

Grimshaw, P., Fahey, C., Janson, S. & Griffiths, T., 'Families and selection in colonial Horsham', in P. Grimshaw, C. McConville & E. McEwen (eds), *Families in Colonial Australia*, Allen & Unwin, Sydney, 1988.

Hall, R. A., *The Black Diggers*, Allen & Unwin, Sydney, 1989.

Harris, C., 'The terror of the law', *Hecate*, 8, 1982.

—— The respectable working class family and the labour movement in nineteenth century Victoria, MA thesis, Monash University, 1987.

Heney, H. (ed.), *Dear Fanny: Women's Letters to and from New South Wales, 1788–1857*, Australian National University Press, Canberra, 1985.

Hicks, N., *'This Sin and Scandal': Australia's Population Debate 1891–1911*, Australian National University Press, Canberra, 1978.

Hirst, J. B., *Convict Society and Its Enemies*, Allen & Unwin, Sydney, 1983.

Hoban, M., *Fifty-one Pieces of Wedding Cake: A Biography of Caroline Chisholm*, Lowden Publishing Co., Kilmore, 1973.

Hughes, R., *The Fatal Shore*, Collins, London, 1987.

James, M., 'Not bread but a stone: women and divorce in colonial Victoria', in P. Grimshaw, C. McConville & M. McEwen (eds), *Families in Colonial Australia*, Allen & Unwin, Sydney, 1988.

Jennings, M., *Australia in the Great War*, Appendix D, Hill of Content, Melbourne, 1969.

Johnson, P., 'Gender, class and work: the Council of Action on Equal Pay campaign in Australia during World War II', *Labour History*, 50, May 1986.

Jones, H., *In Her Own Name: Women in South Australian History*, Wakefield Press, Netley, South Australia, 1986.

Kelly, F., 'Feminism and the family: Brettena Smyth', in E. Fry (ed.), *Rebels and Radicals*, Allen & Unwin, Sydney, 1983.

Kennedy, R. (ed.), *Australian Welfare History: Critical Essays*, Macmillan, Melbourne, 1982.

Kent, B., 'Agitations on the Victorian gold fields, 1851–4: an interpretation', *Historical Studies*, 6, 23, November 1954.

Kiddle, M., *Caroline Chisholm*, Melbourne University Press, Melbourne, 1950.

King, H., *Elizabeth Macarthur and her World*, Sydney University Press, Sydney, 1980.

King, J., *In The Beginning: The Story of the Creation of Australia from the Original Documents*, Macmillan, Melbourne, 1985.

Kingston, B., *My Wife, My Daughter and Poor Mary Ann*, Nelson, Melbourne, 1975.

—— *The Oxford History of Australia 1860–1900*, 3, Oxford University Press, Melbourne, 1988.

Bibliography

Knight, R., *Illiberal Liberal: Robert Lowe in New South Wales 1842–1850*, Melbourne University Press, Melbourne, 1966.

Kohen, J. & Lampert, R., 'Hunters and fishers in the Sydney region', in D. Mulvaney & J. P. White (eds), *Australians 1788*, Fairfax Syme Weldon Associates, Sydney, 1989.

Lake, M., *A Divided Society: Tasmania During World War I*, Melbourne University Press, Melbourne, 1975.

—— 'The politics of respectability: identifying the masculinist context', *Historical Studies*, 22, 86, April 1986.

—— *The Limits of Hope: Soldier Settlement in Victoria 1915–38*, Oxford University Press, Melbourne, 1987.

—— 'Female desires: the meaning of World War II', *Australian Historical Studies*, 24, 95, October 1990.

Lake, M. & Kelly, F. (eds), *Double Time: Women in Victoria – 150 Years*, Penguin, Ringwood, 1985.

Lampert, R., 'Aboriginal life around Port Jackson, 1788–92', in B. Smith & A. Wheeler (eds), *The Art of the First Fleet*, Oxford University Press, Melbourne, 1988.

Langford, R., *Don't Take Your Love to Town*, Penguin, Ringwood, 1988.

Langton, M. & Horner, J., 'The day of mourning', in B. Gammage & P. Spearritt (eds), *Australians 1938*, Fairfax Syme Weldon Associates, Sydney, 1987.

Laurie, A. & McGrath, A., 'I was a drover once myself: Amy Laurie of Kununurra', in I. White, D. Barwick & B. Meehan (eds), *Fighters and Singers*, Allen & Unwin, Sydney, 1985.

Lawson, O. (ed.), *The First Voice of Australian Feminism: Excerpts from Louisa Lawson's The Dawn 1888–1895*, Simon & Schuster, Sydney, 1990.

Lippmann, L., *Generations of Resistance: The Aboriginal Struggle for Justice*, Longman Cheshire, Melbourne, 1981.

Louis, L. J. & Turner, I., *The Depression of the 1930s*, Cassell, Melbourne, 1968.

Lowenstein, W., *Weevils in the Flour: An Oral Record of the 1930s Depression in Australia*, Hyland House, Melbourne, 1978.

McCorquodale, J., Aborigines: a history of law and injustice, 1829–1985, PhD thesis, University of New England, 1985.

McDonald, P., *Marriage in Australia*, Department of Demography, Research School of Social Sciences, Australian National University, Canberra, 1975.

McGrath, A., *Born in the Cattle: Aborigines in Cattle Country*, Allen & Unwin, Sydney, 1987.

—— 'Aboriginal and Australian culture', in N. Meaney (ed.), *Under New Heavens*, Heinemann Educational, Melbourne, 1989.

―― 'Travels to a distant past: mythologies of the outback', *Australian Cultural History*, 10, 1991.

―― 'Citizenship, rights and Aboriginal women', *Journal of Australian Studies*, June 1993.

―― 'Colonialism, crime and civilisation', *Australian Cultural History*, 12, 1993.

McIntosh, M. & Rothwell, E., 'Maddie', *Aboriginal History*, 3, 1979.

Macintyre, S., *Winners and Losers*, Allen & Unwin, Sydney, 1985.

―― *The Oxford History of Australia 1901–1942*, 4, Oxford University Press, Melbourne, 1986.

―― *A Colonial Liberalism*, Oxford University Press, Melbourne, 1991.

McQueen, H., *Gone Tomorrow: Australia in the 80s*, Angus & Robertson, Sydney, 1982.

Magarey, S., *Unbridling the Tongues of Women: A Biography of Catherine Helen Spence*, Hale & Iremonger, Sydney, 1985.

Markey, R., *The Making of the Labor Party in New South Wales 1880–1900*, New South Wales University Press, Sydney, 1988.

Markus, A. (ed.), *Blood From a Stone*, Monash University, Clayton, 1986.

Martin, A. W., *Henry Parkes: A Biography*, Melbourne University Press, Melbourne, 1980.

―― *Letters from Menie: Henry Parkes and His Daughter*, Melbourne University Press, Melbourne, 1983.

Martin, G., *The Founding of Australia*, Hale & Iremonger, Sydney, 1978.

Matthews, J., *The Two Worlds of Jimmie Barker*, Australian Institute of Aboriginal Studies, Canberra, 1977.

―― *Good and Mad Women*, Allen & Unwin, Sydney, 1984.

Modjeska, D., 'Rooms of their own: the domestic situation of Australian women writers between the wars', in E. Windschuttle (ed.), *Women, Class and History: Feminist Perspectives on Australia 1788–1978*, Fontana, Sydney, 1980.

―― *Exiles at Home: Australian Women Writers 1925–1945*, Angus & Robertson, Sydney, 1981.

Montagu, A., *Coming into Being Among the Australian Aborigines*, Routledge & Kegan Paul, London, 1974.

Ngabidj, G., *My Country of the Pelican Dreaming*, Aboriginal Studies Press, Canberra, 1981.

Oldfield, A., *Woman Suffrage in Australia: A Gift or a Struggle?*, Cambridge University Press, Sydney, 1992.

Onslow, S. Macarthur, *Some Early Records of the Macarthurs of Camden*, Angus & Robertson, Sydney, 1914 (Adelaide, 1973).

O'Shane, P., 'Is there any relevance in the women's movement for Aboriginal women?',

Bibliography

Pepper, P., *You Are What You Make Yourself to Be*, Hyland House, Melbourne, 1990.

Perkins, E. (ed.), *Charles Harpur: Stalwart the Bushranger*, Currency Press, Sydney, 1987.

Pike, D., *Paradise of Dissent: South Australia 1829–1857*, Melbourne University Press, Melbourne, 1957.

Praed, Rosa, *My Australian Girlhood*, T. Fisher Unwin, London, 1904.

Prentis, M., 'The life and death of Johnny Campbell', *Aboriginal History*, 15, 1990.

Pringle, J. D., *Australian Accent*, Chatto & Windus, London, 1958.

Quiggin, P., *No Rising Generation*, Department of Demography, Research School of Social Sciences, Australian National University, Canberra, 1988.

Radi, H. (ed.), *200 Australian Women: A Redress Anthology*, Women's Redress Press, Sydney, 1988.

Ranald, P., 'Women's organisations and the issue of Communism', in A. Curthoys & J. Merritt (eds), *Better Dead Than Red: Australia's First Cold War 1945–1959*, 2, Allen & Unwin, Sydney, 1986.

Rayner, T., 'Master and servant in the New Norfolk Magistrates Court 1838', *The Push from the Bush*, 6, May 1980.

Read, P., *The Stolen Generations*, New South Wales Ministry of Aboriginal Affairs, Occasional Paper 1, Sydney, n.d.

Rees, S. & Senyard, J., *The 1950s: How Australia Became a Modern Society and Everyone Got a Job, a House and a Car*, Hyland House, Melbourne, 1987.

Reiger, K., *The Disenchantment of the Home*, Oxford University Press, Melbourne, 1985.

Reynolds, H., *The Other Side of the Frontier*, Penguin, Ringwood, 1982.

—— *Frontier*, Allen & Unwin, Sydney, 1987.

—— *With the White People*, Penguin, Ringwood, 1990.

Ritchie, J. (ed.), *The Evidence to the Bigge Reports*, 1, Heinemann, Melbourne, 1971.

—— (ed.), *The Evidence to the Bigge Reports*, 2, Heinemann, Melbourne, 1971.

—— *Lachlan Macquarie: A Biography*, Melbourne University Press, Melbourne, 1988.

Robinson, P., *The Hatch and Brood of Time*, Oxford University Press, Melbourne, 1985.

Roe, M., *Quest for Authority in Eastern Australia 1835–1851*, Melbourne University Press, Melbourne, 1965.

—— *Nine Australian Progressives: Vitalism in Bourgeois Social Thought 1890–1960*, Queensland University Press, St Lucia, 1984.

Rosser, B., *Dreamtime Nightmares*, Australian Institute of Aboriginal Studies Press, Canberra, 1985.

Rowley, C. D., *Outcasts in White Australia*, Penguin, Ringwood, 1970.

Ryan, E. & Conlon, A., *Gentle Invaders: Australian Women at Work 1788–1974*, Penguin, Ringwood, 1989.

Ryan, L., *The Aboriginal Tasmanians*, University of Queensland, Brisbane, 1989.

Saclier, M., 'Sam Marsden's colony: notes on a manuscript in the Mitchell Library Sydney', *Journal of the Royal Australian Historical Society*, 52, 2, June 1966.

Sawer, M. & Simms, M., *A Woman's Place*, Allen & Unwin, Sydney, 1993.

Schaffer, Kay, *Women and the Bush*, Cambridge University Press, Sydney, 1988.

Serle, G., *The Golden Age: A History of the Colony of Victoria, 1851–1861*, Melbourne University Press, Melbourne, 1963.

Shann, E., *Cattle Chosen*, University of Western Australia Press, Nedlands, 1978.

Sharpe, P., A study of the relationships between colonial women and black Australians, MA thesis, Deakin University, 1991.

Shaw, A. G. L., *Convicts and the Colonies*, Melbourne University Press, Melbourne, 1966.

—— 'Labour', in G. J. Abbott & N. B. Nairn, *Economic Growth of Australia 1788–1821*, Melbourne University Press, Melbourne, 1969.

—— (ed.), *Gipps–Latrobe Correspondence 1839–1846*, Miegunyah, Melbourne, 1989.

Shute, C., 'Sexual mythology 1914–1918', *Hecate*, 1, 1, 1975.

—— 'From balaclavas to bayonets', in E. Windschuttle (ed.), *Women, Class and History: Feminist Perspectives on Australia 1788–1978*, Fontana, Sydney, 1980.

Simon, E., *Through My Eyes*, Collins Dove, Melbourne, 1987.

Smart, J., 'Feminists, food and the fair price: the cost of living demonstrations in Melbourne, August–September 1917', *Labour History*, 50, May 1986.

—— 'The right to speak and the right to be heard: the popular disruption of conscriptionist meetings in Melbourne 1916', *Australian Historical Studies*, 92, April, 1989.

Smith, B., *A Cargo of Women: Susannah Watson and the Convicts of the Princess Royal*, University of New South Wales Press, Sydney, 1988.

Stanner, W. E. H., 'The history of indifference thus begins', *Aboriginal History*, 1, 1, 1977.

Sullivan, J. & Shaw, B., *Banggaiyerri*, Australian Institute of Aboriginal Studies, Canberra, 1983.

Sullivan, M., *Men and Women of Port Phillip*, Hale & Iremonger, Sydney, 1985.

Summers, A., *Damned Whores and God's Police*, Penguin, Ringwood, 1975.

Tench, W., 'A narrative of the expedition to Botany Bay 1789', in L. F. Fitzhardinge (ed.), *Sydney's First Four Years*, Angus & Robertson, Sydney, 1961.

Thomas, J., 'Amy Johnson's triumph, Australia 1930', *Australian Historical Studies*, 90, April, 1988.

Tucker, M., *If Everyone Cared*, Grosvenor Books, Melbourne, 1987.

Bibliography

Turner, I. (ed.), *The Australian Dream*, Sun Books, Melbourne, 1968.

Waldby, C., The political regulation of motherhood in Australia, 1880–1914, BA Honours thesis, University of Sydney, 1983.

Waldren, I., Aboriginal women as domestic servants in NSW 1850–1969, BA Honours thesis, University of New South Wales, 1991.

Walsh, D. (ed.), *The Admiral's Wife: Mrs. Phillip Parker King: A Selection of Letters 1817–56*, Hawthorn Press, Melbourne, 1967.

Webby, E., 'Reactions to the Myall Creek Massacre', *The Push from the Bush*, 8, December 1980.

Willey, K., *When the Sky Fell Down*, Collins, Sydney, 1979.

Williams, G. & Frost, A., 'New South Wales: expectations and reality', in G. Williams & A. Frost (eds), *Terra Australis to Australia*, Oxford University Press, Melbourne, 1988.

Willmot, E., *Pemulwuy: The Rainbow Warrior*, Weldon, Sydney, 1987.

Wilson, R. (ed.), *Good Talk: The Extraordinary Lives of Ten Ordinary Women*, McPhee Gribble, Melbourne, 1985.

Windschuttle, E., 'Women, class and temperance: moral reform in eastern Australia 1832–1857', *The Push from the Bush*, 3, 1979.

—— 'Discipline, domestic training and social control: the Female School of Industry, Sydney, 1826–1847', *Labour History*, 39, November 1980.

Woolmington, J., *Aborigines in Colonial Australia 1788–1850*, Cassell, Melbourne, 1973.

Index

A
Aboriginal and Torres Strait Islander Commission, 312
Aboriginal Health Service, 307
Aboriginal Protection Board, 291
Aborigines
  alcohol, 142–3
  Armed services, 285–6
  attempts to 'civilise', 141
  birthplace, significance of, 10–12
  birth practices, 7–12
  ceremonies, 16–18
  childbirth beliefs, 13–14
  children *see* children, Aboriginal
  citizenship granted, 299
  clothing and ornamentation, 21–2
  deaths in custody, 313
  deracination, 25–6
  dispossession, 131–50
  education, 61–2, 286–7
  employment, 282–5
  expected to disappear, 146–7
  family life, 19
  kinship system, 15–6
  land compensation in 1830s SA, 84–5
  land rights, 297–9, 302, 306–7
  Macquarie's 'civilising' attempt, 60–2
  marriage, 287–8, 289
  men *see* men, Aboriginal
  murder of, 135, 147
  place in 1880s social reform agenda, 154
  population, 138
  protest groups, 281–2
  reaction to European land devastation, 22–3
  reserves, 147, 280–1
  rise of common consciousness, 150
  self-determination, 312
  sexual interaction with Europeans, 25–6
  smallpox, 39, 137–8
  state control, 280–1, 287–94, 295–6
  treatment by farm helpers, 69
  white attitudes, 279–81, 294
  women *see* women, Aboriginal
Aborigines Protection and Restriction of the Sale of Opium Act of 1897, 147

Aborigines' Protection Board, 290
abortion, 228, 235–6, 245
  law reform, 300
Abrahams, Esther, 57
ACTU (Australian Council of Trade Unions), 205, 244, 311
'address to the governor' (1807), 53–4
Adult Migrant Education Scheme, 273
affirmative action legislation, 309
agricultural settlements, 175
Air Force, 256
airlines, 266
alcohol, 89, 153–4, 173–4
  see also temperance movement
  effect on Aborigines, 142–3
Allen, Margaret, 59
Allen, Professor Marshall, 235
All For Australia League, 248
ALP *see* Australian Labor Party
Amalgamated Miners' Association, 151
Amalgamated Shearers' Union, 151
Americans in Australia during World War II, 261–4
America *see* United States
Anderson, Francis, 37
Angill, William, 85
anthropologists, 146
anti-Americanism, 276
anti-sweating movement, 170
Anzac Day, 218
ANZUS treaty, 277
arbitration system, 200, 241
Archibald, J. F., 186
aristocracy, Australian, 79–80
Arndell, Thomas, 56
Arthur, Governor George, 83
assignment of convicts, 65–9
assimilation policy, 273, 277–8, 292–4, 299
assisted immigration, 79–81, 86–7, 226, 266
ASU (Amalgamated Shearers' Union), 151
Atkinson, James, 80
ATSIC (Aboriginal and Torres Strait Islander Commission), 312
Austin, Mrs James, 162
Australasian Bank, 217

349

Australian (newspaper), 73
Australian Aborigines' League, 282
Australian Aborigines' Progressive Association, 281–2
Australian Association of Woman Pilots, 276
Australian Council of Trade Unions (ACTU), 205, 244, 311
Australian Institute of Multicultural Affairs, 306
Australian Labor Party (ALP)
  fall in 1931, 250
  formation, 181
  motherhood endowment, 222
  Whitlam promises support to Aborigines, 302–6
  women in, 197, 308
Australian Migrant Women's Association, 205
Australian National University, 266
Australian Pre-Schools Committee, 304
Australian Shearers' Union, 188
Australian Women's Army Service, 257
Australian Women's Guild of Empire, 249
Australian Women's National League (AWNL), 197, 220, 266
Australian Workers' Union, 188, 248

B
babies, 120
'bachelor girls', 247
Baines, Jennie, 216
Ballarat gold field, 101
Ballarat Reform League, 101
Bandler, Faith, 299
Barak, William, 150
Barangaroo, 9–12, 26
Barber, Elizabeth, 34, 37
Barker, Jimmie, 143–4, 281, 282
Barsby, Samuel, 36
Barton, George Bruce, 80
Barunga Statement, 312
basic wage, 221–3
Bates, Daisy, 146
Batman, John, 134
Baxter, Annie, 144, 145
Bear-Crawford, Annette, 170, 171
Bellamy, Edward, 167
benevolent societies, 160
Bennelong, 9–10, 15, 19, 26
Bennett, Mary Montgomery, 250
Bentham, Jeremy, 76–77
Bernell, Charles, 162–3
Better Farming Train, 228
Bibulman people, 146
Bicentennial, 312
Bigge, Commissioner J. T., 57, 65, 69
Bird, Sara, 50
Birgin, Margaret, 58
birth
  Aboriginal, 7–12
  hospitalisation, 236
  men's attitude to, 91–2

birth (continued)
  pioneers, 120
birth control *see* contraception
birthplace in Aboriginal society, 10–12
birthrate
  after World War II, 271–2
  decline, 191, 193–4, 235
  need for increase, 207
Blackburn, Judge, 297
Blake, Harriet, 58
Bleakley, J. W., 280
Bligh, Governor William, 52–4
Blomfield, Christiana, 119
Bloodsworth, James, 39
Bolshevism, 220
Boomerang (paper), 158
Borrie, W. D., 270
Bowes, Lieutenant, 34–5
Bradley, Lieutenant William, 22
Brady, E. J., *Australia Unlimited*, 224
Brand, Mary, 37
'bride ships', 272
Brigg, James, 139
Brigg, Mary Ann, 139
Brisbane, Governor, 58
Brisbane Trades and Labour Council, 152
Bromham, Ada, 227
Brown, Edward, 231
Brown, Thomas, 37
Bruce, Prime Minister Stanley Melbourne, 226–7, 241
Bryant, William, 37
Buchanan, Cheryl, 306
Bulletin (magazine), 186–8
Burn, Simon, 37, 40–1, 45–6
Burns, Frances, 45–6
bushrangers, 75–6
Bussell, Bessie, 162
Bussell, Fanny, 80–2

C
Cadigal people, 10
Caiger, George, *The Australian Way of Life*, 270
Cairns, Jim, 300, 306
Calwell, Arthur, 266, 299
Cambell, Dame Janet, 235
Cambridge, Ada, 125–6
Cameron, Donald, 142
Campbell, Johnny, 149
capitalism introduced, 83–4
capital offences, 28
Cascades Factory, Hobart, 67
Castle Hill uprising, 47
Castles, Sarah, 145
Catchpole, Margaret, 50, 51
Catholicism
  Irish convicts, 45–6
  'Movement', 269
Caught, Helen, 256
Caverhill, Jane, 162

INDEX

charities, 160–1
Charker, Mary Ann, 92
Charter Conferences (1943), 263
Charter Movement, 269
Chartist Movement, 95, 101–2
chastity, convicts, 33–4
Chifley, Prime Minister Ben, 266–7
childbearing *see* motherhood
childbirth *see* birth
child care
  Aboriginal society, 15
  centres established, 302
  government subsidy, 304
Child Care Act (1972), 302
child endowment, 222–3, 257, 268
childhood endowment, 237
children, Aboriginal
  interaction with whites, 140–1
  mixed descent, 139
  naming, 12–13
  pre-European lifestyle, 14–15
  rearing, 140
  seizure by the state, 289–92
children, white
  after World War II, 271
  babies, 120
  convicts, 42–3
  rural life, 124
  urban life, 125–7
children's book, first, 80
China, 303, 304
Chinese in Australia, 177
Chisholm, Caroline, 87–9, 90, 107–8
Christian socialists, 156
church
  see also Catholicism
  social assistance, 159–60
  women in, 202–3
cities, growth, 163–4
Clark, Emma, 172
Clark, James, 172
Clarke, Henry Lowther, 203
class
  see also working class
  1980s, 307–8
  antagonism, 151
Clay, Fred, 291
Clayton, George, 37
cleanliness, 232–3
Clifton, Louisa, 90, 94
clothing, Aboriginal, 21–2
Cock, Robert, 84
cohabitation
  Aborigines and whites, 142, 288
  convicts and emancipists, 51–2, 55–60, 57
  modern times, 311
Cold War, 268, 270
Collins, Lieutenant David, 7, 11–12, 19
Commonwealth Bank, 266
Communism, 249, 266–70, 277

Communist Party, 220
  banned, 277
Connor, Rex, 306
conscription
  Vietnam War, 300, 303
  World War I, 213–15
  World War II, 261
consumerism, 239
contraception, 93–4, 184, 191, 194–5, 245–6, 248, 271
convicts
  assignment, 65–9
  children, 42–3
  escape attempts, 40
  farm workers, 68
  in Sydney Cove, 35–8
  labour, 36, 39–40
  land grants, 40–1
  Macquarie's reforms, 62–4
  marriage, 37–8, 49–50, 52, 57–9
  punishment, 67
  transportation *see* transportation
  women, 49–52, 66–7
Cook, Joseph, 211
Coonardoo (novel), 251
Cooper, William, 150, 282
Copland, Professor D. B., 243
Coral Sea, Battle of, 261
cost of living commission (1919), 221
Council of Action for Equal Pay, 257
country life, 121–5
country towns, 125–6
Country Women's Association, 228
Cowan, Edith, 227
craft unionism, 151
Crouch, Sarah, 89
crown land, sale of, 86
currency lasses and lads *see* native born
Currie, Ann, 124–5
Curtin, John, 237, 258–9

D
Daley, Jane (Jean), 205, 236, 240
Dalton, Elizabeth, 56
D'Aprano, Zelda, 301
Dark, Eleanor, 234–5
Darling, Eliza, 71
Darling, Governor, 58–9, 73–4
Daruk people, 21, 23
Darwinism, social, 177, 179–80
Dawn (journal), 153
Dawn Club, 171
Deakin, Alfred, 192
Dedman, J. J., 253
Defenders (Irish Catholics), 46
democracy
  debate over, 102–3
  rise of, 94–6
  sex-specific, 104–5
Democratic Labor Party, 277

351

Denning, Warren, 251
depression
  1840s, 88, 95–6
  1890s, 174, 180
  1930s, 241–52
Devanny, Jean, 234
Dismissal (1975 constitutional crisis), 306
divorce law, 265, 270, 304, 311
  reform, 105, 172–3
Dodson, Pat, 298
domestic labour *see* servants
domestic science courses, 228
domestic violence, 172–3
Donohoe, John, 75–6
Dowse, Sara, 304
dress reform, 171
Druitt, Major George, 62
Dudgens, Elizabeth, 37
Dugdale, Harriet, 170–1
Dumaresq, Sophie, 92
Duncan, Ruby, 249
Duntroon Military College, 209
Durack, Patrick, 115–16
Dyson, Ted, 187

E
education, 61–2
  Aborigines, 286–7
  for girls, 171
  native born, 68–72
egalitarianism on the goldfields, 100
eight-hour working day, 104
Eldershaw, M. Barnard, 234
elections, 1840s, 96–8
elitism, 179–80
Elkin, Professor A. P., *Marriage and the Family in Australia*, 257, 270
Elliott, Joseph, 119
Elliott, Rebecca, 119
emancipists, 47–9
  Macquarie's reforms, 64–5
emigration to Australia *see* immigration
Empire Air Defence Scheme, 256
employer–employee relations, 79–86
environmentalism, 299
Eora people, 14
equal pay, 208, 210–11, 252–4, 276, 301–2
  armed forces, 257
  World War II, 259
Equal Status Committee, 252
eugenics, 246
Eureka Stockade, 101
Evatt, H. V., 277
ex-convicts *see* emancipists
ex-nuptial births, 205, 275, 311
  laws, 194

F
Fabianism, 180
Facey, Bert, 175

factories, 166, 209
  see also manufacturing
  women in, 223–4
Fadden, Arthur, 258
Falleni, Eugenia, 240
families
  after World War II, 270–1
  early NSW, 52–4
  reliance on, 161–2
  restructuring, 311
  size, 184
Family Law Act (1975), 304
family planning clinics, 246
'family wage', 201
farming
  Aborigines, 141
  after World War I, 224–6
  convict workers, 68
  early Sydney, 44–5
  rural life, 121–5
  smallholdings, 107, 109, 123–4, 162–3
Federation, 181, 192–3
Female Factory (Parramatta), 49
'Female Register', 51–2
Female School of Industry, 71–2
feminism
  see also women's movement
  ALP, 303–4
  labour movement, 311
  opposition to Communism, 249
  sexual morality, 250
  work with Aboriginal women, 250
  World War II, 263–4
'femocrats', 304
Few Hours in a Far-Off Age, A, 171
finger transformation, Aboriginal, 16
fire, Aboriginal use, 25
First Fleet, 32–5
Fisher, Prime Minister Andrew, 201, 205–6, 211

fishing, Aborigines, 20–1
FitzGerald, Stephen, 304
'flappers', 239
Flinders Island, 138
floggings, 66–7
Flower, Bessy, 142
Foley, Gary, 306
food production in Aboriginal society, 19–21
food shortages
  1788, 23
  during World War I, 216
Forgotten People, The, 267
franchise *see* suffrage
Franklin, Miles, 122, 169, 234
Fraser family, 148
freedmen *see* emancipists
free market, 83
freethinkers, 171
Friendship (ship), 33–4
full employment, 253

INDEX

G
Gallipoli, 212, 218
Galvin, Thomas, 57, 70
games, Aboriginal, 15
gaol *see* imprisonment
Gellibrand, Joseph Tice, 83
gender roles
  1830s, 88–9
  1850s, 102–5
  1860s, 117–18
  Aboriginal society, 19–21
  views after World War I, 228–9
George, Henry, 167
Gilmore, Mary, 125
Gipps, Governor, 87, 88
girls, education, 71
Girls Enticement Act (1844), 288
Glynn, Freda, 307
Gold, Margaret, 71–2
gold licences, 100–2
gold rushes, 99–101, 109, 112, 135
Goldstein, Vida, 169, 196–7, 212–13
Good Neighbour Council, 273
Gooroobarrooboollo, 19
Gorton, John, 302
Gove Peninsula, 297
government role
  in development, 113
  in social assistance, 159
Governor brothers, 149
Grassby, Al, 205
Green, Hannah, 37
Groupers, 277
Gsell, Bishop, 142
guardianship law reform, 172
Gunn, Jeannie, 145
  We of the Never Never, 279
Gurindji people, 297

H
Hagenauer (missionary), 135, 142
Hagggard, Sir H. Rider, 225
'half-caste' children, 290
Hammersley Iron, 297
Harford, Lesbia, 240
Harpur, Charles, 76, 98
Hart, John, 104
Hart, Lucy, 103–4
Harvester Case judgment, 200
Hassall, Reverend Thomas, 70
Hawke, Prime Minister R. J. (Bob), 301–2, 308
Hayles, Betty, 255
Haynes, William, 37
head shaving, 67
Heagney, Muriel, 221, 229, 235, 236, 252
Henning, Rachel, 162
Higgins, Justice, 200, 208
Hindmarsh, Governor, 85
Holloway, E. J., 241
Holmes, Susannah, 32–3, 37

Holt, Harold, 257, 299
home ownership, 274
homosexuality, 77, 270–1, 311
Hope, Stanton, 274
hospitals for women, 207
Hotham, Governor, 100–1
hours of work, 104
housewives' associations (World War I), 216
Howse, Mrs John, 256
Hughes, Prime Minister, 213, 219–20, 221, 225
hulks, 28–9
Hunter, Lieutenant (later Governor), 10, 45
Hyde, Mary, 51, 57

I
immigration
  1830–50, 79–86
  1920s, 226
  after World War II, 272–3
  assisted *see* assisted immigration
  marriage, 103–5
  protests against, 248
  women, 205
  workers, 272
imprisonment
  18th century England, 28–9
  absconding servants, 85
  penitentiaries, 77
income tax
  Commonwealth responsibility, 266
  first ALP administration, 201
indentured labour, 80–5
individualism, 155–6
industrial disputes *see* strikes
Industrial Workers of the World, 219
industry
  see also manufacturing; primary industries
  growth in the 1880s, 113
  women in, 208–9, 223–4, 251–2
  World War II, 260
infanticide, 140
infant mortality rate, 235
infant welfare centres, 207, 227
infant welfare movement, 232
influenza
  decimates Abrigines (1840s), 139
  pandemic (1919), 220
initiation ceremonies, Aboriginal, 16–17
Innes, George, 66
Innett, Ann, 52
interventionism, 181
Irish convicts, 45–6
IVF procedures, 311

J
Japan
  trading partner, 310
  World War II, 258–9, 261
John, Cecilia, 213
John, Reynell, 127–8

Johns, Alice, 127–8
Johnson, Amy, 246
Johnston, Lieutenant George, 46, 56, 58
Joint Committee on Social Security, 257

K
Kable, Edgar, 75
Kable, Henry, 37, 48
Kable, Jack, 74–5
Kalkadoon people, 136
Kanakas, 178–9
Keating, Paul, 309
Kelly, Ellen, 123
Kelly, Ned, 123
Khemlani, Tirath, 306
King, Governor, 49–50, 51–2
King, Harriet, 79–80
King, Truby, 228
kinship system, Aboriginal, 15–16
Kirner, Joan, 308
Knights of Labor, 152
Kunoth-Monks, Rosalie, 296

L
Labor Party *see* Australian Labor Party
labour market
  see also waged work
  legislation, 85
labour movement *see* Australian Labor Party; union movement
Lady Penrhyn (ship), 33, 34–5
land
  Aboriginal ownership, 281–2
  basis of class, 81
  European devastation, Aboriginal reaction to, 22–5
  grants to convicts, 40–1
  reform, 108–10
  rights, Aboriginal, 297–9, 302, 306–7
  rights of native born, 73
Land Acts, 111
Land Army, 257
Land Councils, 307
Lane, William, 151–2, 158, 165, 167–8, 188, 191
Lang, J. T., 244
Langloh Parker, Kate, 13
Langord, Ruby, 282
Lawler, Ray, *Summer of the Seventeenth Doll*, 275
Lawrence, Carmen, 308
Lawson, Henry, 187
Lawson, Louisa, 151, 153, 157, 169, 171, 172, 184, 195–6
Lawson, Peter, 153
Lee, Bessie Harrison, 151, 153–4, 157, 169, 173, 182–4, 187
Lee, Harrison, 154
Leonski, Edward, 264
lesbianism, 239–40, 270–1, 301, 311
Lesley, George, 144–5

Lewis, Essington, 260
Lewis, Sarah, 210
Liberal Christianity, 180
liberalism, 155–6
Liberal Party, 266–8, 302
Limitation of Offspring, 184
literacy, 70
living wage, 221–3
'loans affair', 306
Locke-Burns, Lilian, 170, 233
Lord, Simeon, 48, 51, 57
Lowe, Robert, 97–8
Loyal Associations, 46
Lying-in Hospital (Melbourne), 160–1
Lyons, Enid, 263, 267
Lyons, Joseph, 250

M
Mabo case, 313
MacArthur, General Douglas, 261
Macarthur, Elizabeth, 43–4
Macarthur, Emmalin, 144–5
Macarthur, James, 102
Macarthur, John, 43–4, 53, 65
MacCormack, Mary, 37
Mace, Dr David, 270
McEwen, John, 277
Macguire, Anne, 152
Macintyre River, 135
MacKeller, Justice Charles, 194
Mackenzie, Keith, 251
Mclaughlin, James, 66
McMahon, William, 302
Macquarie, Elizabeth, 65
Macquarie, Governor Lachlan, 54–8, 60–4, 73
McWilliams, Daisy, 244, 245
Makin, Norman, 256
malgin, 16
manhood suffrage, 102
Mannix, Archbishop Daniel, 215
manufacturing
  see also factories
  mid-war expansion, 223–4
  post-war, 274
  protection, 209
marriage
  see also cohabitation
  Aborigines, 142–3, 287–8, 289
  after World War II, 265
  Bulletin's views, 187–8
  convicts, 37–8, 49–50, 52, 57–9
  men's role, 91–5
  native-born, 72–3
  necessity, 103–4
  official attitude to, 51–2, 55–7
  pioneers, 116–17
  relations between partners, 89–90
  women's attitudes, 90–5
Marriage and Heredity, 184
Marsden, Reverend Samuel, 45, 51–2, 60, 65, 67

INDEX

Marsh, Rosetta, 56
Marshall, Mary, 38, 55
Marxists, 156
  see also Communism
massacres of Aborigines, 135
maternal mortality rate in the 1920s, 235–6
maternity allowance, 206
  see also motherhood endowment
maternity leave, 205
Matra, James, 27, 29–30
Maynard, Fred, 281
Medibank, 306
men, Aboriginal
  attitude to women, 18–19
  ceremonies, 16–17
  child-care, 15
  employment, 282–3
  food production roles, 19–21
  loss of womenfolk, 142
men, white
  1950s, 274–5
  abduction of Aboriginal women, 139
  attitude to childbirth, 91–2
  attitude to marriage, 104
  basic wage, 221–2
  benefits of marriage, 58
  chastity, 33–4
  convict labour, 36
  democracy, 94–6, 98
  depression of the 1930s, 244
  employment reform in the 1880s, 154–9
  Federation, 192–3
  imagined role in new colony, 27
  land use, 108–12
  medical establishment, 227–8
  pioneers, 115–16
  role in economic development, 113–14
  role in marriage, 91–5
  roles see gender roles
  suffrage, 99, 102
  supporters of women's rights, 171
  transportation, 32–3
  views of women's movement, 187–9
  waged work, 158, 168, 210
  wages, 200–1, 209
  working-class, 158–9
  World War I, 211–13, 216, 218
  World War II, 256–7, 264
Menzies, Prime Minister Sir Robert G., 255, 258, 266–8, 276–7, 299–30
Mercury (ship), 29, 32
Meredith, Gwen, 273
Messenger, 202
Messling, Thomas, 59–60
metal trades during World War II, 260
Michener, James, 274
midwives, 120
migrants see immigration
Miklouho-Maclay, Baron Nikolai, 149
Mildren, Lizzie, 145

military training, compulsory, 209–10
Mill, John Stuart, 156–7, 170
Miners' Federation, 267
'miner's right', 102
mining, 112
  Aboriginal objections to, 297–8
miscegenation, 139–40, 143–4, 287–8
missionaries, 135, 141–2
Molesworth, William, 84
Montagu, Ashley, 13–14
Moorhouse, James, 117–18
Morosi, Junie, 306
motherhood
  1890s, 118–21
  1920s, 232–7
  debate, 181–6, 193
  depression of the 1930s, 245
  labour movement views, 191
  scientific, 228
  upon Federation, 207–8
motherhood endowment, 222, 229, 237
  see also maternity allowance
'mothers' schools', 227
Mothers' Union, 202
Mould, Emma, 80–2
'Movement, The', 269
multiculturalism, 205, 306
munitions industry, 260
murder of Aborigines, 135, 147
Murray-Prior, Matilda, 120, 121
Muscio, Mildred, 237
mutinies
  against Bligh, 53
  Castle Hill, 47
  convicts, 29, 30
  Parramatta Factory, 67
Mutual Protection Society, 96
Myall Creed massacre, 135

N
Nabalco, 297
Namatjira, Albert, 296
names, Aboriginal, 12–13
national character, 177, 181
National Council of Women (NCW), 197, 217, 248
National Life and Character, 177–8
native born
  attitudes of, 74–6
  education, 68–72
  employment, 73
  marriage, 72–3
Native Institution, 61
native police, 136
'native title', 313
NCW (National Council of Women), 197, 217, 248
Neale, Catherine, 66
Neville, Commissioner, 290
New Australia (Paraguay), 152

New South Wales Corps, 43
'new unionism', 157, 167
Ngabidj, Grant, 134
Ngarrindjeri people, 141
Nicholson, William, 111
Niemeyer, Sir Otto, 243
novels, Australian, 234

O
O'Donoghue, Lois, 312
Ogilvie, Mary, 145
Orphan Schools, 70–2
Osborne, Dr Ethel, 223–4
O'Shane, Pat, 206–7

P
Paine, Thomas, 94–5
Palmer, Nettie, 234
Palmer, Vance, *The Legend of the Nineties*, 275
Palm Island, 280
Pankhurst, Adela, 213, 216, 249
Parker, Kate Langloh, 146
Parkes, Henry, 97, 98
Parkes, Menie, 103
parliaments
    established, 96
    women in, 263, 308
Parr, William, 37, 40–1
Parramatta Factory, 49, 67
paternity leave, 311
Paterson, 'Banjo', 187
Paterson, Elizabeth, 46
patriarchy defended, 104–5
Pearson, C. H., 171, 177
penitentiaries, 77
pensions, 201
    see also maternity allowance
Pepper, Phillip, 135
Perkins, Charles, 294
Perry, Elizabeth, 40
Perry, Frances, 160
Petrov, Vladimir, 277
Phillip, Governor Arthur, 9–11, 30–2, 31, 35–7
Phillips, A. A., *Australian Tradition*, 275
Phillips, Annie, 291
Piddington, Justice A. B., 210, 221–2
Pike, Justice, 238–9
police crush Aboriginal resistance, 136
Political Labor Council, 205
polygamy, 142
Poonindie (South Australia), 141
population
    see also birthrate
    1792, 42
    1805, 47
    1828, 69
    1830–50, 79
    1891, 116
    1912, 208
    1950s, 274

population (continued)
    Aboriginal, 138, 150
Port Phillip District
    immigration, 87
    suffrage, 99
    Tasmanian blacks sent to, 137
poverty, Aboriginal, 144
Power, Elizabeth, 89
Power, William, 85
Praed, Rosa, 121–2
premiers, women, 308
Presbyterian Ladies' College (Melbourne), 171
prices during World War I, 216
Prichard, Katharine Susannah, 234, 251
primary industry
    see also farming; mining
    after World War I, 224–6
    women in, 208
Pringle, J. D., 275
Prior, Catherine, 36
prisons *see* imprisonment
profiteering during World War I, 216
progressivism, 180
promiscuity among convicts, 33
property law reform, 172
prostitution
    Aborigines, 284, 288
    Aborigines forced into by whites, 139–40
    early immigrants, 87
protectionism, 209
Protector (of Aborigines), 84
protest movements, 1880s and 1890s, 155
puerperal fever, 120
Pulley, Elizabeth *see* Rope, Elizabeth

Q
Qantas, 266
Queensland Aborigines, 280
Quinn, Martin, 58, 59

R
race
    Aborigines' fight against racism, 307
    eugenics, 246
    maternity allowance, 206
    motive for Federation, 191–3
    social Darwinism, 177–9
Racial Hygiene Clinics, 246
Rafferty, Chips, 275
rape, 147–8
rationing after World War II, 266
Read, Peter, 292
rebellion *see* mutinies
recession, 1980s and 1990s, 309–10, 313–14
Red Cross, 215
reform, social, 151–8
refugees, 272, 306
Reghan, David, 59
Reiby, Mary, 50
Reid, Elizabeth, 304

INDEX

reserves, Aboriginal, 147, 280–1
respectability, 82
'returned soldiers', 217–18, 219
Returned Soldiers' and Sailors' Imperial League of Australia, 217–18
Reynolds, Senator Margaret, 308
Richardson, Henry Handel (Ethel), 128, 234
Rights of Man, 94
Rischbieth, Bessie, 250, 269–70
Robertson, John, 108, 111
Robinson, George Augustus, 134, 137, 149
Rogers, Elizabeth, 129
Rope, Anthony, 37–8, 39, 41, 45, 75
Rope, Elizabeth (nee Pulley), 32–5, 37, 41, 45
Rope, Mary, 72
Rope, William, 73, 75
Roth, W. E., 280
Rottnest Island, 137
Royal Australian Air Force, 256
Royal Commission into Aboriginal Deaths in Custody, 313
Royal Commission on Child Endowment or Family Allowances (1927–1928), 236–7
Royal Commission on National Insurance (1926–1927), 236–7
RSL (Returned Soldiers' and Sailors' Imperial League of Australia), 217–18
rum trade, 43, 52–3
rural life, 121–5
Rural Workers' Case of 1912, 208
Ruse, James, 40–1
Ryan, John, 72
Ryan, Susan, 308

S
Santamaria, B. A., 269
Saunders, Reg, 286
Savage, Ann Jane, 151
Scantlebury Brown, Dr Vera, 231–2
Scott, Rose, 169, 171, 185, 196
Scullin, Prime Minister James Henry, 241, 243, 244
seasonal work
  Aborigines, 283
  effect on family, 236
secondary industry *see* manufacturing
second fleet, 44
servants, 66, 166–7
  relations with employees, 80–2
Sex Discrimination Acts, 304, 309
sex education, Aboriginal, 287
sexual interaction between blacks and whites, 139–40, 143–4
  prohibited, 287–9
sexual pleasure as every woman's right, 262
Shipley, Mary, 51, 56
Sideway, Robert, 38, 55
Simon, Ella, 282, 289
Simpson, John, 32–3
smallholdings, 107, 109, 123–4, 162–3

smallpox epidemic, 11, 39, 137–8
Smith, Shirley, 307
Smyth, Brettena, 184
Snedden, Billy, 306
Social Darwinism, 177, 179–80
socialism, 151–2, 156, 219
socialist-feminists, 190
social mobility, 272
'social purity', 194
'social question', 155, 157
social reform, 151–8
social security, 253
soldier settlement after World War I, 225–6, 237–9
South Australia
  indentured labour, 84–6
  manhood suffrage, 102
Spark, Alexander Brodie, 91
Spence, Catherine, 169–70
Spence, William Guthrie, 151–2, 167
Spencer, Herbert, 147
sport, 74–5
squatters, 108, 110–12, 123
Stanley, Millicent Preston, 235, 249
status
  Aboriginal society, 16, 18
  early European society, 24
Stead, Christina, 234
Stewart, Senator, 225
Street, Jessie, 263, 269–70
strikes
  1890, 175–6
  1919, 267
Subjection of Women, The, 156–7
suffrage
  initial, 99–100
  men, 102
  women, 171, 176, 185–6, 192–3
Sullivan, Jack, 134
Summers, Anne, 304
surrogacy (childbirth), 311
Swan River Colony, 80–1, 90
Sweetman, Thomas, 82
Sydney, Lord, 27, 33
Sydney Gazette, 74
Sykes, Roberta, 306

T
Tahitian women as brides for convicts, 30–1
Tangey, Dorothy, 263
Tasmania
  Aborigines, 134, 137, 138, 281
  indentured labour, 83
tax *see* income tax
temperance movement, 89, 153–4, 173–4
Tench, Captain Watkin, 10
tent embassy, 302
terra nullius, 133–4
Terry, Sam, 51, 56
theatre

theatre (continued)
  Australian, 275
  early, 75-6
Thomas, Caroline, 67
Thunderbolt (bushranger), 139
Tobruk, Siege of, 261
Tocsin (journal), 188-91
tooth removal ceremony, 17
Torres Strait Islanders, 281
trades unions *see* union movement
Trans-Australian Airlines, 266
transportation, 27-35
  criticised, 77-8
  renewal, 98-9
treaties between whites and Aborigines, 134
tree felling, Aboriginal reaction to, 23
Trucaninni, 149
Tucker, Margaret, 233
Tudawali, Robert, 296
Turner, H. G., 225
Twopenny, Richard, 120

U
underemployment, 237
Unemployed Workers' Movement, 242
unemployment
  1920s and 1930s, 241-2
  abolition central to democracy, 258
  Aboriginal, 307
  benefit payments, 253
  insurance, 237
uniforms, women's (World War II), 256
union movement
  1850s, 104
  1880s and 1890s, 151-2, 157-9, 167-8, 175-6, 181
  Aborigines, 285
  Communists in, 267
  women during World War II, 259
  women in, 200, 210
  women's issues, 186-8, 311
Union of Australian Women, 276
United Australia Party, 250
United Council for Women's Suffrage, 170
United Nations, 269-70
United States
  reliance on, 277
  revolution, 27-8
  sentiments against, 276
  Warld War II, 261-2
universities, women's rights to enter, 171
University of Adelaide, 171
unmarried mothers, maternity allowance for, 205-7
urbanisation, 209
urban life, 125-30
utopian socialists, 156

V
Van Diemen's Land Company, 82

venereal diseases, 25, 140, 262
Victoria
  see also Port Phillip District
  manhood suffrage, 102
Victorian Trades Hall Council, 210
Vietnam War, 300, 303
voting *see* suffrage

W
waged work
  men, 158, 168, 210
  women, 157, 165-7, 170, 189-90, 210-11, 273-4, 304-5
wages
  1920s, 241
  1930s, 243
  Aborigines, 283-4
  armed forces, 257
  basic, 221-3
  emancipists, 47
  Harvester Case judgment, 200-1
  indentured servants, 85-6
  men, 209, 221-2
  women, 130, 208-9, 223
  World War II, 260
wages boards, 199
Wakefield, Edward Gibbon, 83-4
Wakehurst, Lady, 256
Walker, Ann, 67
Wallace, Dr A. V., 246
Wangaratta, 125
Ward, Fred, 139
Ward, Russel, *The Australian Legend*, 275
warfare against Aborigines, 134-6, 149
  women's role, 145
Waring, Charlotte, 79-80
Warreweer, 7, 19
War Service Homes, 218
Watson, James, 92
WCTU *see* Woman's Christian Temperance Union
WEB (Women's Employment Board), 260
welfare reform, 198-9
welfare state, 201-2
Wentworth, William Charles, 73-4
Westlock, Samuel, 85
White Australia Policy, 219, 266, 304
Whitlam, Gough, 299, 302-3
widows, 165
  pensions, 258
wife-beating, 89
Willard, Frances, 173
Wilson, Mrs, 129
Windeyer, Justice, 184
Windeyer, Lady Margaret, 171
Wiradjuri people, 136
Withen, Mrs, 210
wives, search for, 87-9
WOC (Women's Organising Committee), 205
Wollaston, John, 82

INDEX

Wollstonecraft, Mary, 95
Womanhood Suffrage League, 171
'woman question', 155–7
Woman's Christian Temperance Union (WCTU), 153, 157, 173–4, 186–7, 207
Woman's Suffrage Society, 171
Woman's Voice, 217
women, Aboriginal
  ceremonies, 16
  childbirth, 7–12
  excluded from maternity allowance, 206
  food production roles, 19–21
  independence, 12, 18–19
  land rights struggle, 307
  marriage with whites, 143
  pressures of white lifestyle, 232–4, 294–6
  rape by white men, 147
  relations with white women, 144–6
  role and power, 17–19
  sexual relations with white men, 139–40, 287–9
  stereotyped as prostitutes, 284
  welfare after World War I, 228
  white women's concern during the depression, 250
  women's movement, 307
women, white
  see also motherhood; women's movement
  1950s, 275–6
  after the depression, 253
  after World War II, 265
  ALP, 303, 308
  attitude to marriage, 90–5
  basic wage, 223
  church work, 202–3
  citizenship, 309
  class divisions open, 307–8
  cleaning work, 232–3
  convicts, 49–52, 66–7
  depression of the 1930s, 242–6
  during the depression, 251
  elected to Parliament, 263
  families' reliance on, 161–2
  Federation, 192–3, 196
  'flappers', 239
  immigrants, 79–81, 87–8, 103–4
  independence, 80, 82
  in industry, 208, 223–4, 251–2
  lesbians, 239–40
  less rational and more spiritual, 91
  Liberal Party, 266–8
  liberal reform in the 1880s, 155–7, 168–73
  liberation movement, 300–1
  male democracy, 94–6
  marriage, 103–4
  marriage laws, 172–3
  migrants, 205, 273
  novelists, 234
  oppose Bolshevism, 220
  pioneers, 115–16

women, white (continued)
  political influence, 196–8
  post-war workforce, 273–4
  rape by black men, 148
  relations with Aborigines, 144–6
  results of marriage, 58
  rights, 104–5
  role in economic development, 114–15
  roles *see* gender roles
  rural industry, 208
  rural life, 121–5
  suffrage, 99, 102–3, 171, 176, 185–6, 192–3
  transportation, 32–4
  unfitted for politics, 105
  union movement, 200
  urban life, 125–9
  waged work, 157, 165–7, 170, 189–90, 210–11, 304–5
  wages, 130, 201, 208–9
  welfare after World War I, 227–8
  working class, 199–202
  World War I, 211–18
  World War II, 255–64
Women for Canberra movement, 263
Women's Australian Auxiliary Air Force, 256
Women's Australian National Services, 256
Women's Charter for Equality, 269
Women's Electoral Lobby, 303
Women's Emergency Signalling Corps, 256
Women's Employment Board, 260
Women's Flying Club, 256
Women's Hospital (Melbourne), 205
Women's Industrial Convention (Melbourne, 1913), 210
women's movement
  see also feminism
  motherhood debate, 182–5, 195–6
  post-suffrage activism, 196–200
  rise of, 153–4, 170–3
  women's suffrage, 185
Women's Organising Committee, 205
Women's Peace Army, 213
Women's Reform League, 220
Women's Royal Australian Navy Service, 257
Women's Transport Corps, 256
Women's Voluntary National Register, 256
Women Workers of New South Wales, 233
Wood, Sarah, 56, 57
Woodcock, Joseph, 59
Woodward, Mrs F. J., 256
work ethic, 141
workforce *see* waged work
working class
  see also union movement
  1860–90, 164–7
  struggle, 154–9
  women, 190–1, 199–202
Workingman's Paradise, The (novel), 152, 188, 191
World War I
  Aborigines, 285

World War I (continued)
  aftermath, 219–20
  conscription, 213–15
  men during, 211–12, 216, 218
  women during, 211–18
World War II, 253–4, 255–65
  Aborigines, 285
  aftermath, 265–6

World War II (continued)
  sexual activity during, 262–4
Wran, Neville, 302

Y
Yirrkala people, 297
Young Women's Christian Association, 197
Yunupingu, Galarrwuy, 312